SOUTH AFRICA'S WEAPONS
OF MASS DESTRUCTION

SOUTH AFRICA'S WEAPONS OF MASS DESTRUCTION

HELEN E. PURKITT
AND
STEPHEN F. BURGESS

INDIANA UNIVERSITY PRESS
Bloomington & Indianapolis

This book is a publication of
Indiana University Press
601 North Morton Street
Bloomington, IN 47404-3797 USA

http://iupress.indiana.edu

Telephone orders   800-842-6796
Fax orders   812-855-7931
Orders by e-mail   iuporder@indiana.edu

© 2005 by Helen E. Purkitt and Stephen F. Burgess

The paper used in this publication meets the minimum requirements of American National Standard for Information Sciences—Permanence of Paper for Printed Library Materials, ANSI Z39.48-1984.

Manufactured in the United States of America

Library of Congress Cataloging-in-Publication Data

Purkitt, Helen E., date
South Africa's weapons of mass destruction / Helen E. Purkitt and Stephen F. Burgess.
p. cm.
Includes bibliographical references and index.
ISBN 0-253-34506-5 (cloth : alk. paper) — ISBN 0-253-21730-X (pbk. : alk. paper)
1. Weapons of mass destruction—South Africa. I. Burgess, Stephen Franklin. II. Title.
UA856.P87 2005
358'.3'0968—dc22
2004021137

1 2 3 4 5 10 09 08 07 06 05

CONTENTS

Acknowledgments

Many individuals and institutions on both sides of the Atlantic have provided invaluable help in completing this book. We gratefully acknowledge the time and cooperation of all who made this book possible. We also gratefully acknowledge the financial support necessary to make this book possible from the Institute of National Security Studies (INSS), U.S. Air Force Academy and its director, James Smith; the U.S. Air Force's Counterproliferation Center and its director, Barry Schneider; and the Department of Political Science and the Naval Academy Research Council at the United States Naval Academy. For assisting with the research and writing of the book, we would like to thank our spouses, Janet C. Beilstein and James W. Dyson. For making publication possible we acknowledge the efforts of Dee Mortensen and the editorial staff of Indiana University Press. We would also like to thank the many interviewees in South Africa and the United States. In particular, we are especially grateful to Jakkie Cilliers and his colleagues at the Institute of Security Studies, Pretoria; Helmoed Romer-Heitman, *Jane's Defence Weekly* Southern Africa correspondent; Dr. Renfrew Christie, University of the Western Cape; and Mr. Nick Badenhorst, private defense analyst, for providing their expertise.

By its very nature this type of book is bound to spark some controversy. We would like our readers to know that we followed standard professional guidelines in deciding when to report allegations and disputed facts. Thus, we required at least two independent sources of corroboration to consider any claim worthy of reporting.

When a source wished to remain anonymous, we maintained our guarantee of anonymity, but we also required verification by other sources. For example, while several analysts have been critical of some of the information reported in *Plague Wars,* we have only reported information from *Plague Wars* that we corroborated through other sources. We also did our own research confirming information about right-wing supremacist activities during the post-1994 era. Several of these activities, discussed in earlier publications such as *Plague Wars,* are amplified in this book.

The views expressed in this book are those of the authors and do not reflect the official policy or position of the U.S. government, the Department of Defense, the U.S. Naval Academy, or Air University.

SOUTH AFRICA'S WEAPONS
OF MASS DESTRUCTION

ONE

Introduction: The Ongoing Problem of South Africa's Unconventional Weapons

In the 1970s and 1980s, apartheid South Africa secretly developed nuclear, biological, and chemical weapons of mass destruction (and several launch vehicles to deliver them).[1] South Africa's covert programs fit the pattern of states, mainly in the Middle East and Asia, which secretly developed weapons of mass destruction during a period of heightened international tensions and in defiance of the 1970 Nuclear Nonproliferation Treaty, the 1972 Bacteriological and Toxin Weapons Convention, and an emerging sanctions regime. Yet in the 1990s, South Africa became the first known state to dismantle its nuclear, biological, and chemical weapons.

Experts continue to disagree about which factors best account for the decision of the former South African regime to dismantle some of its covert weapons programs, but there is general agreement that the decisions were a response to changes in the international, regional, and domestic environment. Most analysts also agree that sustained pressures by Western countries, especially the United States, played a key role in the decision to close down the secret biological and chemical weapons program called Project Coast and may have played a behind-the-scenes role in pressuring the de Klerk government to close down the nuclear-bomb program as well. Western pressures, the need to free up resources for domestic reforms, limited consumer demand for commercial satellite-launch vehicles, and an expected political transition all influenced the de Klerk government's decision to close down a sophisticated space-launch-vehicle program. A ceremony to celebrate the dismantling of this sophisticated launch vehicle (which could easily have been modified to function as a multistage missile) was held only weeks after the Mandela government came to power in 1994. Since the 1994 elections, the South African government has been a disarmament trendsetter, leading the way in international negotiations to extend the Nuclear Non-Proliferation Treaty indefinitely and create an African Nuclear-Weapon-Free Zone of unprecedented scope.

Disarmament proponents hope that South Africa has established a map for rolling back weapons of mass destruction that other states will follow. It is logical that if states in the Middle East, Asia, and elsewhere experience similar changes and feel the kind of pressures that caused South Africa to disarm, they might emulate the same pattern. To date, the record has been mixed. Since the early 1990s, several countries have undertaken or made progress in covert weapons of mass destruction programs and research and development programs to develop missiles. However, a few countries have chosen the same path as South Africa by closing down secret nuclear, biological, and chemical weapons or space-launch-vehicle research programs.

A large number of variables from different research perspectives and levels of analysis are also required to identify the conditions which led South Africa and a few other states to roll back their weapons programs. Our research suggests that several theoretical concepts and empirical insights derived from neorealist theory of international relations,[2] organizational and bureaucratic politics research,[3] comparative foreign policy, and political psychological perspectives are needed to fully explain why states develop weapons of mass destruction.[4] For example, recent research using different methodologies confirms the importance of understanding how groups of political decision makers reach agreement about the nature of the problem that requires immediate action. Agreement within a small group about the nature of the problem, or the shared problem representation, is important because the options that will be taken by political decision makers are derived from the groups' shared understanding of the problem. Throughout our study of political decision making by senior politicians in South Africa about covert weapons of mass destruction policies, we attempted to determine who were the critical political leaders, how they reached agreement on the nature of the immediate problem at hand, how they reached decisions about these problems, and how changes in the composition of the group members and changes in their environment influenced these shared problem representations over time.[5] The South African case illustrates how the relative importance of different variables changes and interacts through different event sequences over time.

Chapter 2 discusses some of the more important insights that emerge across cases where nation-states have pursued covert weapons of mass destruction programs. Chapters 3 through 7 describe and analyze the factors that explain the evolution of South Africa's policies toward covert weapons of mass destruction programs and then their rollback. Chapter 8 describes important political trends in post-apartheid South Africa that are important for understanding residual proliferation concerns and identifies important unanswered questions about South Africa's past weapons of mass destruction programs. Chapter 9 discusses the relevance of different theoretical approaches for understanding similarities and differences between South Africa's nuclear-weapons program and Project Coast and for comparing similarities and differences across cases where countries have or have not dismantled secret weapons of mass destruction programs. Some policy lessons based on South Africa's past experiences with nuclear, biological, and chemical programs that may be relevant to understanding future nuclear, biological, chemical, and missile proliferation cases are presented and discusssed in the Appendix. We also identify topics that we believe require more attention in public discussions of the proliferation of current and future nuclear, biological, and chemical weapons and missiles.

RECENT PROLIFERATION CONCERNS AND UNANSWERED QUESTIONS

The South African experience with dismantling secret weapons programs is proving to be a seminal case for understanding just how difficult it can be to achieve complete rollback of nuclear, biological, and chemical weapons programs. In 1993, President F. W. de Klerk made a surprise announcement that South Africa had secretly built and then unilaterally dismantled a covert nuclear-weapons program. In subsequent years, some evidence and many unsubstantiated allegations have surfaced suggesting that the official account of South Africa's dismantling of its covert weapons of mass destruction programs is incomplete. There are doubts today about whether the full scope of the nuclear-weapons program was disclosed in the early 1990s. Rumors circulating in recent years claim that certain weapons systems capable of launching nuclear, biological, and chemical shells were spirited out of the country by rogue elements of the former defense and security establishment prior to the 1994 elections.[6] Such rumors persist in part because of the lack of official documentation about covert policymaking during the apartheid era. The rumors seemed more plausible during the 2000s after incidents of political violence by right-wing white supremacists resurfaced, including a plot to overthrow the government of President Thabo Mbeki.[7]

Even more doubts exist today about the effectiveness of the dismantlement of South Africa's secret chemical and biological warfare programs managed collectively under the auspices of Project Coast. Concerns about proliferation threats grew after Dr. Wouter Basson, director of Project Coast, was arrested in 1997. Police investigators discovered that Basson had saved several trunkfuls of Project Coast documents that were supposed to have been destroyed in 1993. The public heard for the first time about the products that Project Coast scientists developed at special hearings held during the closing days of the Truth and Reconciliation Commission hearings in the late 1990s. However, many questions were not explored in the few days allowed for the commission's Project Coast hearings. Many anticipated that unanswered questions would be addressed during Dr. Basson's criminal trial, which lasted thirty-two months. Instead, Basson's trial, the most expensive in South Africa's history, ended in

April 2002 with a full acquittal by a judge appointed during the apartheid era.[8] The state prosecutors and many members of the public who wanted to learn more about what acts transpired under the auspices of Project Coast were frustrated by the inability of the judicial system to obtain more answers or a criminal conviction against the former head of the biowarfare program. While the state appealed the ruling in the Basson trial, few analysts today believe that Wouter Basson will be convicted of criminal charges in the future.

In a twist of fate no one foresaw, several events in the United States have sustained interest in America about South Africa's biowarfare program long after its termination. One episode occurred in Irvine, California, in 2000. A brilliant but eccentric medical doctor and microbiologist, Dr. Larry Ford, killed himself while police were en route to arrest him for allegedly organizing a contract murder on his business partner, who co-owned a biotech firm called Biofem with him. After Ford's death, local police discovered that he had been recruited as a summer intern to work on a U.S. biowarfare program while still in high school. The police also uncovered documents and obtained sworn testimony from close acquaintances of Ford that confirmed that he had a long-standing personal and professional relationship with Dr. Wouter Basson. Additional public disclosures in the case stopped after police discovered that Dr. Ford kept biowarfare agents and high-powered weapons buried at his Irvine home. These discoveries led the police to call in the FBI, which immediately declared the case to be a weapons of mass destruction investigation and imposed national-security restrictions on further public disclosures.

National interest in the Ford case and the South African biowarfare program was renewed after anthrax-letter attacks in October 2001 killed five and infected at least eighteen individuals in the United States. The anthrax-letter attacks were classic terrorist acts that succeeded in instilling panic and terror in millions of Americans. In addition to triggering widespread fear among the American public, the attacks caused a major disruption in U.S. mail service and served as a major impetus for new national initiatives designed to counter or cope with future biological attacks on the homeland.[9] Ford's claims to have worked as a biowarfare scientist for the U.S. government, his links to South African scientists, and his boasts to friends that he manufactured anthrax in order to protect hidden stashes of biowarfare agents and guns led several reporters to question whether one or more of his associates might have been involved in the anthrax attacks.[10]

Since 2001, there have been a number of high-profile media investigations, including a coordinated investigation sponsored by the *New York Times* and the American television program *60 Minutes*. This investigation generated a few new details about the nature of the relationship between Ford and Basson and raised new questions about the extent of official or unofficial cooperation in biowarfare research and development activities by South African and American scientists during the apartheid era.[11]

Concerns about the possible proliferation of biological weapons originating from South Africa escalated with the publication of a series of articles in the *Washington Post* in April 2003. The articles revealed that a former Project Coast scientist, Dr. Daan Goosen, had offered an entire collection of pathogens, including genetically modified pathogens, to the FBI in exchange for US$5 million and immigration permits for nineteen of his associates and their families in early 2002. While personal financial motives were the primary impetus of these scientists, their spokesperson, Dr. Goosen, claimed that the former Project Coast scientists had decided to approach the FBI after receiving overtures by several foreigners who were interested in purchasing biological pathogens. These foreigners included "a German treasure-hunter and a man claiming to be an Arab sheik's agent."[12]

The worst fears of many analysts and policymakers were confirmed by this incident. These former biowarfare scientists, who were having trouble making a living in South Africa, had retained specimens and documents that were supposed to have been destroyed over a decade before and were hinting that they would sell their biowarfare expertise and stash of genetically modified biological agents to the highest bidder if guaranteed employment was not forthcoming. Even more questions were raised a few months after the *Washington Post* interview when Dr. Goosen claimed that his group of former Project Coast scientists had informed South African officials that they had retained proscribed biological agents in their homes. Goosen claims that South African government officials took DNA fingerprints but allowed the scientists to keep the biological agents.[13]

The recent revelations in the South African case reconfirm warnings made by proliferation and terrorist experts that arms control and other approaches designed to limit the spread of nuclear, biological, and chemical weapons of mass destruction have failed to address newer proliferation threats.[14] The South African case also underscores the fact that there are several complicated longer-term proliferation concerns associated with nuclear, biological, and chemical rollback. Recent efforts by a variety of actors to acquire biological agents in South Africa and the still largely unexplained links of American microbiologists to Project Coast illustrate why we must now be concerned about the use of weapons of mass destruction by individuals, small groups, or networks of groups long after the official program of a nation-state is eliminated.

While a discussion of how to cope with changing and increasingly complicated threats of the proliferation of weapons of mass destruction is beyond the scope of the book, we believe that a more thorough understanding of the complexities that should be expected in future dismantlement efforts can be gleaned from understanding the problems encountered in the South African case. Throughout our narrative of how and why South Africa built and then dismantled a host of nuclear, biological, and chemical programs, we highlight areas of factual disagreements, differences in interpretation, and important unanswered questions.

South Africa in a World
of Proliferating Weapons

The unleashed power of the atom has changed
everything save our modes of thinking, and thus
we drift toward unparalleled catastrophes.
—Ralph E. Lapp[1]

The world has lived with weapons of mass destruction for more than half a century. They remain a grave concern for humanity. Five states openly developed nuclear weapons in the 1940s and 1950s, and at least four more, including South Africa, developed them covertly in the 1960s, 1970s, and 1980s.[2] More than a dozen states, including South Africa, covertly developed biological-weapons programs, and more than a dozen, including South Africa, developed chemical weapons programs.

Nuclear weapons were used twice in August 1945 against the Japanese cities of Hiroshima and Nagasaki and were never used again, presumably because of their devastating impact.[3] Battlefield nuclear weapons were developed but have never been used, due to morality issues and the danger of escalation into full-scale nuclear war.[4] Biological and chemical weapons have been used more frequently than nuclear weapons because they can be employed on a smaller scale on the battlefield, for assassinations, and to neutralize terrorists who hold large numbers of civilian hostages. Chemical weapons have been used to poison enemy soldiers as well as civilian noncombatants. Iraq used chemical weapons in the 1980s to kill and wound thousands of Iranian troops and thousands of Iraqi Kurdish villagers. At the end of 2002, Russian Special Forces used an incapacitating gas to neutralize Chechen rebels holding 700 civilian hostages in a Moscow theater before storming the theater; however, 115 hostages were killed in the rescue attempt.[5]

Alleged incidents of the use of biological weapons are difficult to document. Only Japan's experiments with biowarfare in the 1940s to infect hundreds of Chinese noncombatants are well documented. Other experiments using cholera and other agents as part of counterinsurgency warfare against demands for independence throughout Africa and Asia starting in the 1960s have proved more difficult to document.[6] Until recently, it was widely believed that there had never been a successful attempt to use biological agents as weapons against political opponents in the United States.[7] However, the anthrax-letter attacks of October 2001 in Florida, Washington, D.C., and New York changed the conventional wisdom and brought to national prominence an awareness that there have been other attempts in the United States to use biological agents in recent years. Today, most Americans are aware that there may be future biowarfare attacks in their local communities.

When the focus shifts from the use of biological agents by nonstate actors to why political leaders of nation-states decide to develop weapons of mass destruction, neorealist theory offers the most comprehensive explanation for why states have developed weapons of mass destruction from 1914 onward. This theory assumes that states behave as rational actors who pursue their self-interest, including the vital interests of survival and maximizing national power.[8] Neorealists such as Kenneth Waltz and John Mearsheimer, like classical realists, emphasize that countries seek to maximize their national interests using a variety of means.[9] Neorealist theory contends that states first develop nuclear, biological, and chemical weapons in order to maximize power and win wars but later use them for deterrence and defense. Neorealists theorize that as rivals developed weapons of mass destruction and less powerful states, such as Iraq, Iran, and North Korea, rose to challenge the United States, weapons of mass destruction were desired by Iran, Iraq, North Korea, and other challengers of the United States in order to provide the means to deter stronger adversaries and ensure regime survival.

The modern history of the use of weapons of mass destruction begins in World War I, when chemical weapons were first developed and used by Germany, the United Kingdom, France, and other states to disrupt large troop formations and gain advantage and achieve eventual victory on the battlefield.[10] While more than 100,000 soldiers were killed and a million injured by mustard gas and other chemical weapons, ultimately they did not prove decisive or reliable.[11]

The horrors created by chemical weapons in World War I led to the 1925 Geneva Protocol for the Prohibition of the Use in War of Asphyxiating, Poisonous or Other Gases, and of Bacteriological Methods of Warfare, which forbids the use of chemical and biological weapons in warfare. In spite of the protocol, a number of states, including South Africa, developed and stockpiled chemical weapons and many experimented with biological weapons to try to gain strategic advantage, especially with the approach of World War II.[12]

During World War II, most states did not wage chemical or biological warfare but continued to develop, produce, and stockpile such weapons in case their adversaries violated the Geneva Protocol. Only Japan and the Soviet Union chose to use biological and chemical weapons, while most states that could have used such weapons did not. In recent years, evidence has emerged that the Soviet Union used biological and chemical weapons as part of their defensive efforts to survive the brutal Nazi German invasion from 1941 to 1943.[13] Japan used them against China, a much larger but less-advanced adversary that did not have the means to retaliate. In the 1930s, Japan was a challenger to the international status quo and was attacking a much larger adversary, and its leaders felt that they needed the advantage against China that biological and chemical weapons provided.[14]

In the 1940s, Hitler's Nazi German regime used chemical agents to kill millions of Jewish and other civilians in the death camps. However, Nazi Germany did not use chemical and biological warfare on the battlefield for a number of reasons: Hitler had been gassed in 1918, and he and other Nazi German military leaders had learned that chemical weapons did not provide a decisive battlefield advantage.[15]

Scientific advances at the start of World War II made the development of nuclear weapons a real possibility, and the United States proceeded to develop them. The ability of American and expatriate scientists to master atomic fission led to the first nuclear-weapons state, and the United States used atomic bombs to end World War II. From 1945 to 1949, the United States enjoyed enormous strategic advantage over its new rival, the Soviet Union. In the meantime, the Soviet Union covertly collected U.S. atomic secrets and developed nuclear weapons as part of its challenge to postwar U.S. dominance, particularly after the onset of the Cold War in 1947.

From the late 1940s through the mid-1950s, the United Kingdom and France followed the precedent of the two global superpowers and began to develop nuclear weapons. Ostensibly, the two West European nations wanted to protect themselves against the Soviet Union because U.S. security guarantees were losing credibility, especially after the United States opposed the United Kingdom and France in the Suez crisis of 1956. However, by the late 1950s, as nuclear devices were assembled and tested, it appeared that they were being developed to maintain prestige, especially as the status of the United Kingdom and France as imperial powers continued to wane.[16]

As the 1950s progressed, nuclear deterrence developed between the two superpowers as intercontinental ballistic missiles and thermonuclear warheads were developed and became capable of inflicting millions of casualties. After the 1962 Cuban Missile Crisis led the world to the brink of nuclear war, deterrence was solidified and became enshrined in the concept of mutual assured destruction. At the same time, the two superpowers continued to explore ways to use nuclear weapons, including tactical and intermediate-range weapons, to avoid retaliation and escalation. The two superpowers also shifted from a quest for offensive advantage to the defensive and to maintaining stability through deterrence.[17]

In the 1940s and 1950s, the United States and the Soviet Union developed large stockpiles of biological weapons for strategic offensive purposes.[18] Biological weapons were widely perceived to be weapons of mass destruction that could be used to cause widespread illness and incapacitation without the extraordinary loss of life inflicted by nuclear weapons. During the same period, the two superpowers and a few other states continued to produce and stockpile arsenals of chemical weapons for battlefield use. During the postwar period, a larger number of states, including South Africa, continued to prepare to defend against chemical and biological warfare.

Enthusiastic support for the promised benefits of nuclear power led the Eisenhower administration to sponsor the Atoms for Peace program in 1953.[19] In the 1960s, the United States, France, and other states also began to export nuclear hardware and material and promote the development of nuclear energy and "peaceful nuclear explosions" programs for constructing mines and canals, which opened the door for secret nuclear-weapons research in later years. South Africa, Israel, India, Brazil, Argentina, and other states took advantage of nuclear technology–sharing by the United States, France, and other states to develop nuclear energy. In several cases, nuclear-energy research and peaceful nuclear explosion programs provided an important basis for building nuclear weapons. U.S. nuclear-energy research programs, particularly peaceful nuclear explosions, helped create the foundation necessary to conduct secret nuclear-weapons research activities in South Africa. In fact, virtually all of the other nation-states who participated in U.S.-sponsored Atoms for Peace and peaceful nuclear explosion programs, that were also involved in intense and ongoing conflicts and arms races with neighbors and regional allies, opted to use their access to fissile material to initiate covert weapons research within a decade of obtaining the requisite nuclear-energy materials. Although Brazil and Argentina later closed down their nascent covert nuclear-weapons programs in response to intense outside pressures, India, Israel, and probably Iran continued to pursue such programs, despite calls from abroad to quit.[20]

WEAPONS OF MASS DESTRUCTION
AND ARMS CONTROL

Nonproliferation efforts began in the early 1960s, after the United States, the Soviet Union, and the United Kingdom realized that they were unlikely to use nuclear and biological weapons. As this realization spread among the major powers, they collectively reached the conclusion that it was in their interest to prevent other states from developing and ultimately using them. Neorealist theory offers a good explanation of the promotion of non-proliferation norms and incentives by the United States, the Soviet Union, and the United Kingdom: they wanted to limit the number of potential challengers.[21]

The United States, the Soviet Union, and the United Kingdom led the international movement to establish norms and create incentives that influenced many states to forsake the development of weapons of mass destruction. Security guarantees, especially for European states, and the threat of sanctions outweighed many states' security interests in developing weapons of mass destruction programs for defensive and deterrence purposes.[22]

China's 1964 nuclear test and Chairman Mao's declaration that he was prepared to wage nuclear war alarmed both the United States and the Soviet Union. The prospect that more states could acquire nuclear weapons pushed the two superpowers and other states to promote negotiations for the Nuclear Non-Proliferation Treaty from 1964 to 1968 and for the International Atomic Energy Agency (IAEA) to monitor compliance with that treaty. In 1968, the United States, the Soviet Union, the United Kingdom, and fifty-nine states without nuclear weapons signed and later ratified the Nuclear Non-Proliferation Treaty. South Africa, France, China, India, and Pakistan chose not to sign the treaty, although the significance of this fact did not become clear for a number of years.[23]

The Nuclear Non-Proliferation Treaty recognized five nuclear-weapons states—the United States, the Soviet Union, the United Kingdom, France, and China—and allowed them to keep their arsenals while forbidding other states from developing them. Many states that could have developed nuclear weapons accepted the nonproliferation arguments and incentives presented by the two superpowers and other supporters of the treaty. The two principal positive incentives to sign the treaty were security guarantees and assistance from the United States and other states for the peaceful development of nuclear power. As the treaty came into effect in 1970, it became illegal for all but the five nuclear-weapons powers to develop nuclear arsenals. In the 1970s and 1980s, more than 100 states ratified the Nuclear Non-Proliferation Treaty, and more than 180 eventually joined the nuclear nonproliferation regime. Only four years after the treaty came into effect, the influence of the new nonproliferation regime was evidenced by adverse international reaction when India conducted a "peaceful nuclear explosion" test in May 1974.

While there was widespread diplomatic condemnation of India after the 1974 test, several countries, including South African officials, focused on the fact that the costs to those who violated the Nuclear Non-Proliferation Treaty would be limited to diplomatic protests. Some former South African officials claimed in retrospective interviews that they were surprised by the intense behind-the-scenes pressure from both the United States and the Soviet Union to stop their intended first test of a nuclear weapon in 1977.[24]

Over time, the prohibitions embodied in the Nuclear Non-Proliferation Treaty; concerns about continuing proliferation of nuclear, biological, and chemical weapons; and changes in the international system led additional states to support the treaty. From the 1960s until 1992, France and China rejected the treaty on the grounds that it reflected the hegemonic interests of the two superpowers. France also wanted no restrictions on its ability to market a wide range of nuclear-energy facilities. However, with the collapse of the Soviet Union and the end of the Cold War, both France and China decided to accede to the Nuclear Non-Proliferation Treaty. In 1992, both states also committed themselves to halting the sale of technology that could be used to build nuclear weapons.[25]

Biological weapons came under attack in the 1960s because of media campaigns that exposed the horrors caused by such weapons. The negative consequences of biological weapons for large numbers of people were documented in medical research. Strategic studies also tended to converge on the finding that the weapons had limited utility on the battlefield. In 1969, the United States abandoned its biological-weapons program. Afterward, the United States enlisted the support of the Soviet Union and other states to negotiate the Bacteriological and Toxin Weapons Convention of 1972, which was signed and ratified by 141 states. Unlike its decision to abstain from the Nuclear Non-Proliferation Treaty regime, South Africa decided to join the Bacteriological and Toxin Weapons Convention, which came into effect in 1975.

The reasons why South Africa and many other nation-states had few qualms about joining the Bacteriological and Toxin Weapons Convention became apparent over time. Throughout the late 1970s, many states resisted U.S. efforts to establish a regime to monitor the convention, and the convention came into existence with weak monitoring arrangements and incentives. Subsequently, the Soviet Union, South Africa, Iraq, and other states were able to violate the convention without detection or punishment.[26] Even if an international monitoring organization existed, monitoring biowarfare proliferation would be especially difficult because biological-weapons facilities can have dual uses and are easily concealed. The weaknesses of the Bacteriological and Toxin Weapons Convention allowed the Soviet Union to illegally develop and maintain massive stockpiles of biological weapons for more than two decades and to cover up a major release of anthrax in 1979 that killed scores of civilians.[27]

In the 1970s, the United States and other countries worked to establish norms, institutions, and legislation to prevent proliferation through a mixture of carrots and sticks. However, as more countries undertook nuclear and biological research, the United States and its allies began to threaten and punish states that would not adhere to the Nuclear Non-Proliferation Treaty and the Bacteriological and Toxin Weapons Convention and that developed weapons of mass destruction.[28] In 1978, the Carter administration used the newly enacted Nuclear Nonproliferation Act, the Arms Export Control Act, and the Foreign Assistance Act to apply sanctions against Pakistan and to threaten to do so against South Africa. The United States also threatened action against states suspected of developing biological weapons.[29]

However, detente between the United States and the Soviet Union and their cooperation in confronting South Africa were seriously eroded with the communist takeover of Ethiopia and massive Soviet assistance to that country, and the shift in U.S. support for the dictatorship in Somalia in 1978. After the Soviet occupation of Afghanistan in late 1979, successive U.S. presidents waived sanctions on foreign assistance to Pakistan.

DEVELOPING WEAPONS IN DEFIANCE
OF NORMS AND SANCTIONS

A number of states, including South Africa, developed weapons of mass destruction programs in the 1970s and 1980s in defiance of the Nuclear Non-Proliferation Treaty, the Bacteriological and Toxin Weapons Convention, and threats of sanctions. States that refused to accept the Nuclear Non-Proliferation Treaty regime of weapons inequality and that went on to develop nuclear weapons included India, Pakistan, South Africa, and Israel. Several others, including Brazil, Argentina, and a number of Middle East states, have tried to develop them. Since nuclear aspirants had come under the scrutiny of the United States and other Nuclear Non-Proliferation Treaty states, they proceeded to try to develop nuclear-weapons programs secretly. Covert development became the norm after the 1974 Indian peaceful nuclear explosion test met with widespread condemnation from Nuclear Non-Proliferation Treaty states and the media.

In the late 1970s, biological weapons joined chemical weapons as the poor man's nuclear weapons. A number of states in the Middle East, including Iraq, Iran, Egypt, North Korea, China, and Taiwan, covertly developed biological-weapons programs.[30] States that defied the Bacteriological and Toxin Weapons Convention and U.S.-led pressure from the West concealed their biological-weapons programs and claimed that the facilities were being used for peaceful and defensive purposes; these states included South Africa.[31]

A few states with scientifically and industrially advanced sectors, including China, South Africa, and possibly Israel, India, and Pakistan, developed both nuclear-weapons and biological-weapons programs. Iraq, Iran, and North Korea developed biological-weapons programs while they attempted to build the capacity and acquire the resources to develop nuclear-weapons programs. States that lacked the scientific and industrial capacity and resources, including Libya and Syria, first acquired chemical-weapons programs and then sought to develop or acquire biological agents, which were more difficult to weaponize.

Throughout the 1960s, as biological-weapons programs earned a negative reputation, the United States reviewed its position on biological warfare. In 1969, it announced that it was dismantling its biological-weapons program. During the 1970s, in the wake of the Nuclear Non-Proliferation Treaty, nuclear-weapons programs lost their aura of legitimacy. The change was exemplified by the backlash against the 1974 Indian test and the warnings by the United States and its allies in subsequent years that they would act strongly against any nuclear testing. Given repeated threats of condemnation and sanctions, a major question that needs to be answered is why South Africa and a number of other states, particularly in the Middle East and Asia, continued to covertly develop weapons of mass destruction programs in the 1970s and 1980s.

EXPLANATIONS FOR DEFIANCE OF NONPROLIFERATION PROTOCOLS

Neorealist theory partly explains why states defied nonproliferation standards and punishments and developed weapons of mass destruction. Most of the states in the Middle East and Asia faced possible threats from hostile states and had few if any security guarantees. South African leaders in the 1970s and 1980s also believed that they faced possible threats. Political leaders in these states sought to gain offensive advantage or defensive deterrence capabilities through weapons of mass destruction in spite of the threat of sanctions, preventive action, and preemptive attack.

From its founding in the late 1940s, Israel faced possible threats to its survival; from the 1950s onward, it began developing nuclear and chemical weapons and perhaps also biological weapons.[32] However, Israel did not declare its possession of weapons of mass destruction or its programs to develop them. Instead, it continued to maintain a stance of "nuclear ambiguity"; disclosure might have triggered a nuclear arms race in the Middle East. Such an arms race might have provoked the Soviet Union and possibly even alienated the United States. The Israeli threat prompted a number of Middle East states, including Egypt, Libya, Syria, Iraq, and Iran, to seek to develop chemical and biological weapons. Iraq and Iran also sought to develop nuclear weapons. Egypt used chemical weapons in Yemen from 1963 to 1967 and continued to develop a biological-weapons program even while making peace with Israel in the late 1970s.[33]

The political leadership in North Korea has demonstrated a similar pattern of defiance in recent years. Faced with perceived threats from the United States and South Korea, North Korea built chemical and biological-weapons stockpiles and violated the Nuclear Non-Proliferation Treaty in the 1990s after agreeing to the terms of that treaty in 1985. In addition, Iraq and Iran faced threats from each other and from Israel and the United States, and developed weapons of mass destruction. These "second-generation" weapons of mass destruction states and proliferators all had relatively low levels of industrial and scientific development and faced international barriers to acquiring nuclear-weapons materials. These conditions may explain why the so-called axis of evil states developed chemical weapons first, then biological weapons, and finally nuclear weapons.[34]

Neorealist theory does not completely explain why some nation-states developed weapons of mass destruction in the face of norms and sanctions while others did not. For example, the theory does not explain the cases of Morocco, Jordan, and other states that faced threats to survival and had no security guarantees but did not develop weapons of mass destruction.[35] Neorealist theory does not entirely account for the South African nuclear-weapons program, which originated well before potential threats escalated to major proportions and before the establishment of the nonproliferation regime. While Israel and India faced possible threats, other factors, such as the influence of nuclear scientists and the development of nuclear-energy and peaceful nuclear explosion programs from the 1950s onward, help explain the development of their nuclear-weapons programs in the face of growing outside pressures.[36]

In the case of South Africa, neorealist theory ignores the importance of ideology and emotions, including a growing fear of abandonment by the West and a collective sense that the nation had been betrayed. These beliefs and feelings played a central role in the commitment P. W. Botha and other apartheid leaders made to develop nuclear weapons and sophisticated long-range missiles. Senior South African politicians, members of the ruling Afrikaner elite, and scientists, engineers, and military officers involved in defense research and development shared a sense that they had been abandoned by the United States after it intervened in Angola in the mid-1970s. The sense of betrayal and abandonment was fueled further by escalating violent opposition at home, increased pressures from international anti-apartheid opponents, and a recognition by leaders of government, the political Afrikaner elite, and the wider defense-establishment elite that time was not on their side.[37] As both a strategic rationale and a rationalization, former apartheid leaders viewed weapons of mass destruction as a form of insurance and political leverage to guarantee Western involvement in the event that the apartheid regime found itself "up against the wall facing an overwhelming communist threat" at home and in the region.[38] For senior members of the South African military and its armament and procurement community, nuclear weapons served as a valuable force multiplier and technological engine that provided the rationale for ever-more-sophisticated research and development on warheads and launch vehicles.[39]

Neorealist theory also cannot explain why it was so difficult for the Russians to end their biological-weapons program well after any possible threat had diminished following the end of the Cold War in 1991. Until recently, neorealist theorists ignored or downgraded dangers associated with the unanticipated consequences of sharing secrets about nuclear, chemical, or biological weapons and passing the technologies along to friends and allies. However, the case of South Africa, along with the cases of Israel, Argentina, Iran, and several other countries, illustrates that the early transfer of nuclear technology and attempts by the United States, the United Kingdom, and France to build nuclear power plants in countries perceived to be allies during the Cold War played a crucial but unanticipated role. Several states used these technologies in their efforts to develop fissile materials for covert nuclear-bombs programs. While Israel was instrumental in helping South Africa build sophisticated nuclear capabilities and launch vehicles, our study indicates that the United States also played a key, albeit unintended, role by supplying fuel and expertise for nuclear research for peaceful purposes.

In a similar manner, the lax security surrounding biological- and chemical-weapons research in the United States and Western countries through the 1980s helped Iraq and several other countries, including possibly South Africa, acquire the agents necessary to pursue sophisticated biochemical research.[40] The "blowback" cost of lax research and monitoring procedures became apparent to most Americans only after the October 2001 anthrax-letter murders in the United States. After its initial investigation, the FBI acknowledged that the highly refined anthrax spores used in the attacks were derived from a strain developed at a secret U.S. biowarfare lab.[41]

Neorealist theory has failed to anticipate many of these issues because the approach views the state as a rational unitary actor behaving according to its own interests. In contrast, domestic-oriented explanations work to understand how organizational and bureaucratic politics, political and economic pressures, or more fundamental political-psychological processes influence the political decision-making process. A comparative perspective helps determine the relative importance of different variables across nation-states and cultures. Each of these perspectives is used throughout the book to complement neorealist theory in explaining why South Africa developed weapons of mass destruction in the face of an emerging nonproliferation regime during the 1970s and 1980s.[42]

Past organizational politics research has documented the central role played by standard operating procedures and the pervasiveness of "satisficing" in complex organizations.[43] These two concepts may explain why national agencies within the United States and other Western states continued to use lax security procedures when supplying researchers in other countries with deadly viruses and pathogens through the 1980s. This perspective may also help explain why a number of countries decided to keep previously established weapons programs secret after the nonproliferation regime was established.

In several cases, atomic scientists and powerful bureaucratic supporters played instrumental roles in making the transition from 1960s nuclear-energy and peaceful nuclear explosion programs to nuclear-weapons programs in the 1970s. In the 1950s and 1960s, a number of countries, including South Africa, Israel, and India, developed peaceful nuclear-energy programs. In several countries, a corps of scientists and high-level political proponents of nuclear-weapons programs considered peaceful nuclear-energy programs to be legitimate scientific enterprises. India, Israel, and South Africa benefited from three factors: the 1950s Atoms for Peace program of the United States, the relative availability of nuclear technology, and technical assistance from France. In both Israel and India, scientists and political leaders worked together to develop nuclear-weapons programs; Israel's leaders included David Ben-Gurion and Shimon Peres and India's included Jawarahal Nehru and Indira Gandhi.[44] When sanctions related to the Nuclear Non-Proliferation Treaty were threatened, scientists, bureaucrats, and hawkish political leaders in these countries continued to push for funding for increasingly expensive nuclear-energy programs that could be used to produce weapons. Government leaders, backed by scientists and other supporters, wanted to ensure that the nuclear-weapons option remained open as a "national asset."[45]

Militarization and the capacity to maintain secrecy help explain why a number of countries decided to keep or develop weapons programs after the onset of the nonproliferation regime. In the 1970s, the leaders of India, Israel, South Africa, and other countries reacted to U.S.-led nonproliferation efforts by converting parts of their nuclear programs to secret nuclear-weapons programs. South Africa militarized its program in the late 1970s, which paralleled the trend in Iraq, Pakistan, North Korea, and other states that concealed their nuclear-weapons programs by placing them under secret military control.[46]

Military secrecy also characterized most weapons of mass destruction programs, especially in the wake of the Nuclear Non-Proliferation Treaty and the Bacteriological and Toxin Weapons Convention. The need to protect one's own country from destruction, avoid preemptive strikes and sanctions, and prevail in warfare drove a number of weapons of mass destruction states to establish programs that were managed by a cadre of top military men and were highly compartmentalized. Scientists working on one aspect of a weapons of mass destruction program often did not have a complete picture of what the final product would be. The South African chemical and biological warfare program followed this pattern of military secrecy.

The need for secrecy may explain why so many of the second-generation covert biowarfare programs were managed by a single individual, and only a handful of top political leaders had full knowledge about the scope and activities of a highly compartmentalized research and development program. Both Colonel Dr. Wouter Basson, who managed the South African chemical and biological warfare program, and Lieutenant General Ishii Shiro, the head of Japan's World War II biological warfare program, exercised total control of their programs. Both individuals shared certain characteristics, including a willingness to supervise experiments using deadly agents on human subjects.

To understand the culture of secrecy and militarization that develops in weapons of mass destruction programs and nuclear, biological, and chemical weapons programs, one needs to examine the political psychology of the individuals and groups involved in making the policy decisions to initiate or dismantle weapons of mass destruction. One approach is to identify the core beliefs of groups of decision makers and the wider cultural elite. Once these factors are identified, analysts can track when and how changes in these shared beliefs and collective emotional responses affected changes in political policies.[47] This body of research builds on earlier work about the importance of understanding a group's shared scripts and stories about past political events and history.[48]

In all of the known past cases where political leaders of a country opted to develop covert nuclear weapons, there is evidence that political leaders and key members of the wider political elite changed their beliefs about the need to move from research to implementation of weapons of mass destruction programs. This finding suggests that changes in shared beliefs about the usefulness of weapons of mass destruction and other beliefs associated with the concept of "political will" are the keys to understanding when and why political leaders embark on secret nuclear, biological, and chemical weapons programs. While this statement sounds similar to what traditional realists have said for decades, the core analytical tasks revolve around understanding who the influential political actors are and their core beliefs, their perceptions about threats, their emotional responses to those threats, and their beliefs about how best to promote national-security interests. For example, perceptions of senior South Africa politicians and elite evolved from their viewing the country as part of the Western alliance to seeing themselves and their country as treated increasingly like a political pariah by Western countries by the mid-1970s.

Until the mid-1970s, politicians, senior military officers, and scientists working on secret programs that built weapons of mass destruction and/ or nuclear, chemical, and biological weapons shared a common goal of containing communism worldwide. The shared beliefs help explain the high level of commitment and dedication among scientists and researchers working for secret nuclear and biochemical programs in South Africa and other countries. As apartheid came under attack, senior South African political and military leaders increasingly relied on long-standing covert links with another increasingly isolated state, Israel, to develop a network of sanctions-busting chemical and biological agents. They also used several other unconventional means to obtain needed materials and expertise to continue South Africa's covert chemical and biological warfare programs.

To understand South Africa's commitment to building covert nuclear weapons and tactical and long-range missile systems in conjunction with

Israel, one must also appreciate the key role played by a shared under-standing of history among Afrikaners whose loyalty to the National Party rested to a great extent on a shared anti-British ideology, a collective me-mory of the harsh treatment Afrikaners received after their defeat in the Anglo-Boer War, and a messianic nationalist view that the Afrikaners were "God's chosen people" who were destined to rule South Africa. The iconoclastic character of the Afrikaner nationalists developed through 300 years of settler history, a Calvinist belief in predestination, and a series of wars with African kingdoms and the British Empire. The beliefs about predestination and the role of Afrikaners as God's chosen people were ev-ident in the racist apartheid system that elevated Afrikaners at the expense of other groups. This ideology was accompanied by fear that was mani-fested in apprehension about growing threats from communists, Blacks, and the Soviet Union. However, as South Africa faced growing isolation from former Western friends, political leaders increasingly found com-mon cause with another embattled but chosen people, the Israelis. In both countries, a collective mind-set, described as the laager complex in South Africa and the Masada complex in Israel, deepened and served as an im-portant tie that bound the leaders of the two countries.[49]

Since core political beliefs are difficult to change even in the face of overwhelming information that indicates a need for change, a major theo-retical issue in South Africa and other cases where countries decided to close down weapons of mass destruction programs and/or nuclear, bio-logical, and chemical weapons programs relates to the general question of what key factors caused senior political officials to change their core be-liefs.[50] There are also many unanswered questions about the decision-making process during this period.

In 1994, the first election in South Africa to include all races brought to power a new set of political and military leaders who ruled jointly in a "coalition of enemies." This unusual coalition, led by Nelson Mandela and the African National Congress (ANC), agreed not to resurrect the dis-mantled space-launch-vehicle program that masked a multistage covert program to develop missiles. The Mandela-led government went on to be-come a nuclear nonproliferation trendsetter and a strong advocate of in-ternational efforts to strengthen regimes that supported nonproliferation of weapons of mass destruction and nuclear, biological, and chemical weapons. In our research, we found that political and economic domestic constraints, substantial external pressure, and limited international de-mand for additional civilian space-launch facilities during the mid-1990s were the most important factors influencing the ANC-led government to dismantle a high-tech but costly satellite program. In hindsight, it appears that the sustained pressure by the United States and other key Western members of the Missile Technology Control Regime (MTCR) to disman-tle the program before organized opposition within the ANC-led govern-ment or wider society could develop was the decisive factor in understanding why a government that was committed to developing a high-tech civilian industrial sector agreed to dismantle the nascent satellite-launch sector so quickly.

Many questions about the dismantlement process in South Africa remain unanswered. In sorting out what is known and what remains to be explained in the South African disarmament story, we rely on prior theory and research about how people use socially constructed scripts and stories to accept major changes in foreign policy, even those aspects of policy that aren't explained to the public. Because deception is an intricate part of politics and because much of the archival data needed for definitive interpretations of South Africa's dismantlement process remain sealed or were destroyed, we take care to identify unanswered questions and plausible rival descriptions of the dismantlement process. As more evidence has surfaced over the past decade that suggests that South Africa's nuclear, biological, and chemical weapons dismantlement process was incomplete, more individuals are accepting one of the alternative scripts about the recent past in South Africa.

Comparative foreign policy offers useful insights into why individual political leaders working in regimes and political systems that share important similarities chose to take the lead in developing weapons of mass destruction in defiance of sanctions. These insights are useful complements to neorealist explanations. Moreover, variables related to domestic and political psychology provide more complete explanations of why some foreign-policy decision makers are risk-takers while others are risk aversive when it comes to developing covert weapons of mass destruction and missile programs.

There are several explanations for risk-taking behaviors. First, government leaders may be sociopathic, paranoid, and mistrustful of status-quo powers such as the United States, which can lead to emotional decision making and the secret development of weapons of mass destruction. Second, leaders and regime supporters may believe in an extreme form of nationalism, which produces isolationism and aggressive foreign-policy behavior.[51] High levels of nationalistic pride and a deep fear of adversaries can explain why leaders of certain states resist the Nuclear Non-Proliferation Treaty and develop nuclear weapons.[52] Other leaders may define or frame the vital national-security problems facing their country in such a way that they believe they have no other option but to develop weapons of mass destruction and missiles. Mao's decision to start a nuclear-weapons program that was too primitive to be used against either the United States or the Soviet Union and his declaration that China was prepared to fight nuclear war epitomize extreme nationalism.[53] Regimes in Libya, Syria, Iraq, and Iran came to power through revolution and exhibited extreme nationalist (or even religious) hatred toward Israel and the United States and perpetuated hatred and revolutionary fervor. These regimes developed weapons of mass destruction programs which they could use to proclaim their ability to attack or even destroy Israel and other adversaries. The sociopathology of leaders (which might include paranoia, isolationism, and aggressiveness) helps to explain the pursuit of weapons of mass destruction by Saddam Hussein's Iraq and Kim Jong Il's North Korea, but it does not explain other cases.

In all of the modern cases of countries that have decided to undertake covert nuclear, biological, and chemical weapons programs, whether the leaders appear to be sociopathic or normal, one cannot help but be struck by the important role emotions play that reinforce perceptions and core beliefs about one's enemies and the fear of encirclement by adversaries and/or abandonment by allies and friends. In the case of countries that decided to "go nuclear" or pursue secret nuclear, biological, and chemical weapons research, the leaders' shared beliefs that enemies threatened the very survival of the regime or political system are a common element.

Jonathan Tucker finds that political factors explain biological-weapons development. He argues that an important factor is the existence of an autocratic/dictatorial regime which maintains "restricted press and speech" and "extreme military secrecy."[54] These factors are present in the cases of Egypt, Iran, Iraq, Libya, and Syria today, and they were present in China, North Korea, and Taiwan in the 1970s and 1980s.

In South Africa, the push to build increasingly sophisticated long-range missile launchers and engage in cutting-edge biological warfare research occurred after the government had become extremely repressive and was being run by a small group of "securocrats."[55] These sophisticated programs also benefited from key inputs and support from outside actors and covert relationships formed during the Cold War. When combined with political, bureaucratic, and psychological factors, these variables constitute a pattern that favors the development of biological weapons and heightens risk-taking behavior and the possibility that biological weapons might be used.

According to Tucker, Jordan and Morocco chose not to develop biological-weapons programs in spite of possible threats from Israel and other states. They have not evidenced extreme military secrecy or severely restricted the press and free speech. Therefore, even though a government may be authoritarian and feel threatened by neighbors who possess weapons of mass destruction, it appears that it will not develop a biological-weapons program unless there is also extreme military secrecy and restricted freedom of press and speech.

South Africa's weapons of mass destruction programs were developed under similar conditions as those in the Middle East and Asia. The South African government, which was led by P. W. Botha in the late 1970s and 1980s, perceived a threat, had influential scientists, was autocratic and dictatorial (especially toward the black and Coloured population), restricted press and speech, and exercised great military secrecy (especially in developing its chemical and biological warfare program). However, South

Table 1. Predisposing Domestic Factors for Biological Weapons Proliferation (at time program began)

Factors	Egypt	Iraq	Iran	Israel	Libya	Jordan/Morocco	Syria	South Africa
Autocratic/dictatorial regime	Yes	Yes	Yes	No	Yes	Yes	Yes	Yes
Isolation or pariah status	No	No	No	Yes	Yes	No	No	Yes
Aggressive foreign policy	No	Yes	No	Yes	No	No	No	Yes
Extreme military secrecy	Yes	Yes	Yes	No	Yes	No	Yes	Yes
Sociopathic national leader	No	Yes	No	No	No	No	No	No
Restricted press and speech	Yes	Yes	Yes	Yes	Yes	No	Yes	Yes
Biological weapons capability	Yes	Yes	Yes	Latent	Yes	No	Yes	Yes

Source: Jonathan Tucker, "Motivations for and against Proliferation: The Case of the Middle East," in *Biological Warfare: Modern Offense and Defense*, ed. Raymond A. Zilinskas (Boulder, Colo.: Lynne Rienner, 2000), 49. We have added South Africa to the table and have altered Tucker's analysis of Israel, asserting it had an "aggressive foreign policy" and "restricted press and speech." Iraq's biological weapons program was started in the 1980s when Iraq was not isolated or had not acquired pariah status. In fact, the United States and other Western countries were leaning toward Iraq in the war against Iran.

Africa diverges from the pattern evident in most autocratic states in that it maintained a form of "controlled democracy" for whites. The apartheid regime did not suppress the liberal English-language press as long as whites as individuals, members of the press, and opposition groups did not challenge the fundamental premises of the apartheid status quo. Thus, the English-language and Afrikaans press was able to report on some aspects of the apartheid regime and the security state, although military secrets relating to weapons of mass destruction were off-limits.

In South Africa, support for the ANC by some members of the white political elite and overwhelming support from the majority public, who were willing to engage in sustained and varied forms of political protest, pressured apartheid leaders and their supporting elite into decisions to dismantle the weapons of mass destruction programs and negotiate a peaceful transition to a new political status quo. However, this process was long and tortuous. Many individuals were banned, jailed, or killed as a result of their efforts to pressure the government. The government's realization that it had to change occurred only after a protracted period of rolling mass demonstrations that brought the country to the brink of civil war.

The ability of the liberation struggle to expose the existence of a secret nuclear-weapons program was an important aspect of the overall struggle. Several members of the multiracial anti-apartheid elite sacrificed their personal security to expose details about the secret nuclear-weapons program. These opponents included a few white anti-apartheid activists who had access to classified materials during the apartheid era.[56] Since many anti-apartheid activists were also ardently opposed to nuclear power, members of the Green Party felt that monitoring South Africa's nuclear-energy industry closely for signs of renewed covert activities was important, even after the secret nuclear-weapons program had been terminated. Organized groups in South Africa who remain opposed to nuclear power and hold stances that are similar to other Green Party issues continue to closely monitor the activities of the South African government and private-sector actors in the fields of nuclear power and biotechnology.[57]

EXPLANATIONS FOR NUCLEAR, BIOLOGICAL, AND CHEMICAL WEAPONS ROLLBACK

Our survey of recent proliferation trends and the academic explanations for these trends suggest that the emphasis by neorealists on the importance of the end of the Cold War and the collapse of the Soviet Union provides only a partial explanation for weapons of mass destruction disarmament by South Africa, Ukraine, Belarus, Kazakhstan, and other states. When Ukraine, Belarus, and Kazakhstan became new independent states with nuclear weapons in December 1991, they faced a security threat from Russia and domestic pressures to keep the weapons. Nonetheless, by 1996, all three had disarmed and joined the Nuclear Non-Proliferation Treaty because the United States and NATO allies buttressed their sovereignty, used economic incentives, and appealed to their desire for international prestige. These new states in transition from authoritarianism could not resist the power of the Nuclear Non-Proliferation Treaty regime.[58]

A similar disarmament process was evident in South Africa in the period leading up to the transfer of power from the white minority to the black majority. A major push by the government and outside powers led to an accelerated dismantlement process.[59] The realization that power would be passed to the black majority, represented by the ANC, led the regime, under great pressure by the United States, to strive to prevent the transfer and proliferation of its nuclear, biological, and chemical weapons programs. The regime and the United States feared proliferation, but there was an additional psychological motivation. The enmity and fear of Afrikaner leaders, including de Klerk, toward the ANC led them to reject the concept of weapons of mass destruction in the hands of an ANC regime.

These cases also demonstrate that several types of factors must be taken into account in order to understand when disarmament of weapons of mass destruction will occur. These include the role of outside actors, the economic and psychological costs of long-term comprehensive international sanctions, the decline of regional security threats, changes in domestic politics, and anti-proliferation pressures on vulnerable states undergoing change.[60] A common factor in each case was a significant change in the perceptions of political leaders because of changes in one or more core beliefs or changes in the composition of the political leadership. In each of these cases, key political leaders changed their beliefs either before or after new leaders joined the deliberations. New voices contributed different representations of the nature of the immediate problems facing the national government and the relative importance of policy priorities, the importance of weapons of mass destruction, perceptions of threats, and foreign policy. In contrast, leaders in older nuclear states, such as India and Pakistan, who maintained remarkably stable beliefs and continued to see each other as the enemy, continued to defy the Nuclear Non-Proliferation Treaty. India reemerged from the "nuclear closet" with a nuclear test in May 1998, in part because of domestic pressures, and Pakistan reciprocated.

The determinants of nuclear, biological, and chemical weapons disarmament reviewed here suggest that if the weapons of mass destruction disarmament pattern of South Africa, Ukraine, Belarus, and Kazakhstan is to be followed by states in the Middle East and Asia, volatile regional situations will have to become much more peaceful, substantial democratization will have to take place, and political leaders will have to change some core shared beliefs or new leaders will have to come to power. Given the impasses in disagreements between Arabs and Israelis, India and Pakistan, China and Taiwan, and North Korea and the United States, disarmament of weapons of mass destruction is unlikely to occur in these countries any time soon. In those regions, conflict resolution and complete democratization may occur in the long term. New political leaders will also have to come to the forefront. Until that time, nonproliferation and counterproliferation pressures must be maintained and intensified. In the short and medium term, South Africa, Ukraine, Belarus, and Kazakhstan are more likely to remain outliers than disarmament trendsetters.

THREE

Origins and Evolution
of Nuclear-Weapons
Research and Development

Nuclear weapons provide stability. The most influential factors influencing a country's decision
to undertake a covert nuclear weapons program
are the views of a country's leaders.
—Kenneth Waltz[1]

South Africa is the only African country to have produced nuclear weapons. To understand why and how South Africa covertly pursued the development of nuclear, and later chemical and biological, covert weapons programs, one needs to appreciate three characteristics usually associated
with crime: motive, opportunity, and means. The historical record clearly
indicates that the motives and perceptions of threats of South Africa decision makers under apartheid were important factors fueling support for
sophisticated nuclear warheads and launch vehicles.

Under the apartheid system, political leaders increasingly adopted a
siege mentality as the country became isolated from former allies in the
West and more-severe international economic sanctions were implemented. Most Afrikaans-speaking South Africans held beliefs which grew out
of their shared cultural experiences of being dominated by English-speaking South Africans in the political and economic realms from the time of
the defeat of the Boers in the Anglo-Boer War until 1948 when the Afrikaner National Party regained political power.[2] During the postwar period, the majority of English-speaking white South Africans, while unhappy with the greater privileges Afrikaners enjoyed in politics, also shared
the overarching apartheid goal of preserving white advantage in South
African society. Only a relatively small but committed number of English-
speaking whites, along with an even smaller number of Afrikaners, opted
out of the status quo or joined the liberation struggle for a new political
order.

The Afrikaans- and English-speaking scientists who worked on the covert nuclear, biological, and chemical programs also shared a strong sense of patriotism. The Afrikaans- and English-speaking scientists who worked on the covert nuclear, biological and chemical programs were united by a strong commitment to make sure the programs were successful. This group of well-trained and creative scientists and engineers formed the human capital needed to design and build sophisticated weapons systems in an increasingly isolated scientific environment.

A third important cluster of variables relates to the large deposits of strategic natural resources, particularly uranium, available in South Africa at the beginning of the nuclear age. The desire to exploit large reserves of uranium in order to maintain industrial development served as the initial catalyst for exploring the feasibility of exploiting the new nuclear power technology. After the National Party regained political power in 1948, South African political leaders continued nuclear research for both peaceful and military purposes.

Timing also played a role in South Africa's decisions to develop secret nuclear weapons. South African scientists demonstrated the feasibility of uranium enrichment at the same time that the country began to experience increased threats from enemies in the region and throughout the world. Thus, a confluence of events over time figured into the decision-making calculus of key senior political, military, and nuclear power officials. As the country developed the capability to produce sophisticated nuclear weapons and an increasingly sophisticated defense industry, South Africa's political leaders faced growing threats to political stability from domestic opponents and newly independent nation-states in the region. Faced with growing threats and the capability to build weapons of mass destruction, South Africa's political leaders opted to build six nuclear weapons.

Over time, the combination of technical abilities and increased perceptions of threat fueled support for even-more-sophisticated nuclear warheads and a variety of launch vehicles capable of carrying strategic and tactical nuclear warheads. Smaller nuclear warheads and longer-range missiles came to be viewed as important force multipliers for a military that was having trouble obtaining parts and new technologies from abroad for their air force. Throughout the 1970s, South Africa's senior politicians became increasingly committed to the belief that secret weapons of mass destruction and launch vehicles were useful tools of diplomacy.[3]

South African politicians were adept at exploiting opportunities to develop nuclear weapons in a changing domestic, regional, and international environment. Early technical exchanges with Western states helped South Africa obtain the necessary training and knowledge needed to launch a covert nuclear program. As South Africa increasingly became viewed as a "pariah state," it forged new covert relationships with Israel and other states around the world. The country's leaders opted to develop increasingly sophisticated tactical and strategic weapons and launch vehicles once the six nuclear bombs were built. The concept of "encirclement," or perceptions of heightened threats from all quarters—at home, in the region, and abroad (the laager complex)—figured prominently in the minds of senior South African political and military officials. This concept increasingly became both the motive and the rationale for undertaking sophisticated new weapons research and development.

Additional indirect evidence of the dynamic interaction between perceptions of threats and South Africa's nuclear capability was confirmed recently in a declassified top-secret national-security memo from March 1975. The memo, entitled "The Jericho Weapons Missile System," noted that the South African government was considering buying ballistic missiles tipped with nuclear weapons that had a 500-kilometer range. This range would reach several African capitals (Lusaka, Zambia, for example) if the missile was forward deployed at or beyond South Africa's borders. The memo quoted the director of strategic studies, who felt that "a direct and/or indirect nuclear threat against the RSA [Republic of South Africa] had developed to the point of being a real danger" that required a reappraisal of strategic policy. The memo stressed both "the deterrent effect and additional flexibility which [nuclear warheads] offer . . . as well as the reduction in losses of vital aircraft."[4]

The commitment to acquire and build nuclear warheads covertly required the formulation of a strategy for threatening to use nuclear weapons. The new commitment also required a consensus among those who knew about the covert weapons programs concerning what parts of the "nuclear story" would and would not be disclosed to the outside world. Although the complete archival record necessary to understand the full range of nuclear programs supported by the apartheid regime has not yet been disclosed, much of what South Africa developed under the rubric of the nuclear-bomb program is now known. The complete story will not be written for decades, but enough of the story has been published or leaked to glean useful insights into contemporary nuclear proliferation trends.

This chapter describes the roots and evolution of South Africa's policies as its leaders approved a series of research and development activities related to the development of nuclear weapons during the 1970s. The roots of the nuclear program can be traced back to South Africa's membership in the Western alliance and participation in the Western campaign during the Cold War. As an ally of the United Kingdom in the 1940s and 1950s, South African political leaders had access to nuclear resources and knowledge associated with programs designed to develop nuclear energy. They were interested in exploiting the new technology for both peaceful and military purposes from the outset. The desire to exploit the country's extensive uranium deposits stimulated the development of the industrial and human infrastructure necessary to build nuclear weapons. The ability of South African scientists and engineers to keep current with the latest technological advances in nuclear power was facilitated by South Africa's participation in peaceful nuclear-energy programs sponsored by the United States and Western counties. During the 1970s, South African leaders cultivated new covert collaboration with Israel in order to secure nuclear-tipped warheads and other systems that senior South African politicians viewed as vital for national security during the mid-1970s.

The decision of Prime Minister John Vorster to approve the construction of new facilities in the 1970s signaled an important shift from research to implementation in the priorities of the nuclear program. Within a short time period in the mid-1970s, Prime Minister Vorster approved the construction of the Koeberg nuclear power station in the Western Cape and the continued development of an indigenous highly enriched uranium program. Secretly, Vorster also approved the construction of nuclear bombs and a test site that was to be built in the Kalahari Desert. He also established diplomatic relations with Israel and traveled there to approve a series of covert agreements, although the number and exact nature of these covert arrangements remain a matter of some dispute.

As the first country to voluntarily dismantle an active nuclear-weapons program, South Africa offers a wealth of case-specific insights that can improve our understanding of the critical factors that influence political leaders in nuclear threshold states as they decide to develop or forego the option of gaining nuclear technology. We found it necessary to combine factors from neorealist theory, organizational politics theory, and political psychology theory and other important political and economic variables to understand and explain why and how South Africa's changing national-security perspective led to the initiation and development of covert weapons of mass destruction programs. Our account also illustrates how the relative importance of independent variables changed over time and how the interpretation of different streams of interacting events led senior political leaders to change their policies and priorities over time.[5]

AFRIKANER NATIONALISM AND THE ORIGINS OF SOUTH AFRICA'S NUCLEAR RESEARCH PROGRAM

Before South Africa earned a reputation as one of the world's premier "pariah states," it was a highly respected actor in international relations. Much of the credit for South Africa's positive image goes to Afrikaner intellectuals and politicians who projected positive and romantic images about Afrikaner history and culture to the world. In America, the Anglo-Boer War came to be seen as a heroic struggle by the Boers for their freedom against British imperialism. This image earned Afrikaners sympathy and admiration in the United States, Europe, and Russia through the 1950s.[6]

Other distinctive aspects of Afrikaner nationalism, such as a collective sense of humiliation and a commitment to never again experience the extensive loss of lives, livelihoods, and political influence that followed the Anglo-Boer War, figured less prominently in romantic stereotypes of the Afrikaners. Most Western descriptions of Afrikaner nationalism also omit the key role played by a secret self-help organization called the Afrikaner Broederbond (Afrikaner Brotherhood, or "AB," as it was known) in helping the Afrikaner National Party regain power in 1948. The Broederbond was originally formed in 1918 to promote Afrikaner nationalism and harness the political, social, and economic forces in South Africa to establish and perpetuate Afrikaner domination. By the late 1970s, the AB had organized a network of over 800 cells throughout the country. Broederbond members were active in government, commerce, and other organizations at every level of society. The extensive influence of the organization is suggested by the fact that nearly all senior Afrikaner politicians in the national government prior to 1994 were Broederbond members, including Prime Ministers D. F. Malan, J. G. Strijdom, Hendrik F. Verwoerd, John Vorster, and P. W. Botha and Presidents P. W. Botha and F. W. de Klerk.[7]

FACTORS THAT FACILITATED INITIAL DUAL-USE NUCLEAR RESEARCH

From the creation of the Union of South Africa in 1910 until the Afrikaner National Party regained political power in 1948, the country's national-security strategy was determined by its status as a self-governing dominion of the British Empire. The United Kingdom provided security guarantees during the two world wars, and South Africa reciprocated by dispatching military forces in Africa, Europe, and Asia. South African experiences with chemical warfare in World War I led to defensive preparations against chemical and biological warfare and to the stockpiling of mustard gas in World War II. As a consequence of its experiences, South Africa developed a modest amount of scientific, technological, and industrial experience, capacity, and resources that would later be used to develop weapons of mass destruction. Even more important, South African scientists developed scientific and technical connections with the United Kingdom and other Western states that would prove invaluable in future years.

The country's international status and prestige throughout the interwar years was also enhanced by the actions of such high-profile leaders as Generals J. C. Smuts and J. B. M. Hertzog.[8] General Smuts went on to earn an international reputation as a Commonwealth statesman by serving as a member of the British War Cabinet during World War I and playing a lead role in shaping the League of Nations. Prime Minister J. C. Smuts, who led South Africa from 1918 to 1924 and again from 1939 to 1948, also developed nuclear ties with Western powers. During the war years, as a close confidant of Churchill, Smuts met with many of the nuclear scientists involved in the Manhattan Project and was a tireless advocate of South Africa's ability to play a role in Western efforts to exploit the atom.[9]

Smuts facilitated requests to investigate reported deposits of radium and pitchblende in South Africa and South West Africa (Namibia) and encouraged large-scale sampling of South Africa's potential uranium base by geological advisors to the Manhattan Project.[10] Smuts asked the South African Chamber of Mines in 1945 to assess the amount of low-grade uranium in gold deposits. The mining-industry studies found that uranium coexisted with gold in nearly all gold mines and boreholes found in South Africa.[11] This finding assured South Africa a role in Western efforts to develop nuclear power and weapons even after Afrikaner nationalists regained political control of the government in 1948.

1948: AFRIKANER NATIONALISTS GAIN EXCLUSIVE CONTROL IN SOUTH AFRICA

The triumph of the National Party in 1948 marked the beginning of the era when the South African government established a comprehensive system of de jure racial segregation known as apartheid.[12] The British had instituted discriminatory policies against Blacks and Coloureds even before South Africa became a protectorate. However, the National Party elevated the idea of apartheid, or separation of the races, to the central principle guiding government policies for over four decades. In many areas of law and public policy, implementing apartheid required the government to roll back or change the limited legal and political rights of Blacks and Coloureds in order to construct an elaborate system of enforced apartheid.

After 1948, South Africa shifted its diplomatic efforts by moving closer to the United States, Germany, France, and Israel while downgrading a close working relationship with the United Kingdom. The search for new relationships stemmed from the desire of Afrikaner leaders to reduce the country's dependence on the United Kingdom. The ideology of the National Party was anti-British because of the Anglo-Boer War. The iconoclastic character of the Afrikaner nationalists developed through 300 years of settler history, a Calvinist belief in predestination, and a series of wars with African kingdoms and the British Empire. The belief in predestination as God's chosen people was evident in the racist apartheid system that elevated Afrikaners at the expense of other groups. This ideology was accompanied by a psychology of fear that manifested itself in apprehension about growing threats from communists, Blacks, and the Soviet Union.[13] These core beliefs shared by most Afrikaners during the 1950s fueled a shift in South Africa's security strategy toward an alliance with anticommunist forces led by the United States. This shift is partly explained by South African displeasure at British policy, which supported majority rule in its African possessions and opposed white minority rule. By 1960, a number of independent African states had been admitted to the British Commonwealth and were demanding the removal of South Africa. After the Sharpeville Massacre of March 1960, Great Britain abstained from a UN Security Council resolution condemning the massacre and calling for UN sanctions. These and other factors led South Africa to withdraw from the Commonwealth and to declare itself a republic on May 31, 1961.

Throughout the 1950s, there was a widespread desire among Afrikaans- and English-speaking members of the government, military, and business sectors to develop an independent nuclear industry. Several groups in South Africa stood to benefit from the exploitation of the country's natural resources and the development of a modern defense industry. Government support for these sectors was widely viewed as a way for the country to overcome its status as a "technological colony" of the West.[14]

The economic and technical arguments for developing modern nuclear-energy and defense sectors were bolstered by the increasingly hostile reaction the new regime faced internationally in response to the new policy of apartheid. By the early 1960s, African states constituted the largest voting bloc of countries in the United Nations. This reality led Western countries to pay attention to the commitment of African states to independence in Portuguese Africa, British-ruled Rhodesia, and South African–occupied South West Africa and the elimination of apartheid in South Africa. The diplomatic positions of the United States, the United Kingdom, and other European countries, particularly in the context of the multilateral diplomacy of the UN, became increasingly critical of South Africa's internal and regional policies while continuing to maintain cordial bilateral relations with the new apartheid regime of South Africa.

In the area of nuclear-energy research, the newly elected government moved quickly to shift the development of uranium production from the control of the prime minister and a few trusted advisors to a permanent organized body. One of the first major acts passed by the National Party government was the Atomic Energy Act that established an Atomic Energy Board (AEB), later renamed the Atomic Energy Corporation (AEC), to oversee nuclear activities in South Africa. The AEB was only one of many institutions established as a result of Smuts's interest and initiatives that ultimately also provided the institutional base for a nuclear research program.[15] The 1948 Atomic Energy Act extended the state's wartime power to proscribe materials and declared secret virtually all information about strategic minerals (mainly uranium and thorium). The act also authorized secret trials for persons who violated secrecy laws related to nuclear materials and prohibited all forms of speech related to nuclear topics.[16] This act was indicative of the increasingly authoritarian political order that was assembled in order to establish the new "apartheid" social and political order in postwar South Africa.

From the outset there was a close working relationship between the Chamber of Mines and the AEB. The mining industry quickly moved to erect uranium plants in cooperation with the AEB. Starting in 1950, the South African mining industry concluded a number of contracts with the uranium-purchasing organization set up by the United States and British governments known as the Combined Development Agency. Technical assistance from the United States and the U.K. helped establish the first uranium plant at the West Rand Consolidated Mine in October 1951.[17] The first uranium plant opened in 1952, and by 1955 sixteen mines were authorized to produce uranium.[18]

Throughout the 1950s, uranium exports grew, becoming a lucrative source of export earnings. By the end of the 1950s, the profits from uranium export earnings for the mining houses were proportionately higher than the profits from gold.[19] By 1978, South Africa's known uranium reserves were among the largest in the world.[20] South Africa's abundant uranium reserve and early role as a uranium exporter are often cited as critical factors that contributed to its early involvement in nuclear research.[21] Revenues from uranium and gold sales also provided a significant share of the resources necessary to fund South Africa's early nuclear research programs. Strong support by top political leaders and Western powers for the continued exploitation of uranium reserves ensured that South Africa would remain an important actor in the global effort to exploit this new energy source.

SOUTH AFRICA'S ROLE AS AN APPENDAGE OF THE WEST

South Africa's importance as a source of uranium reinforced its status as a major military ally of Great Britain and a loyal member of the Western political camp for the first decades of the Cold War. Primarily due to South Africa's security relationship with Great Britain and growing military cooperation with the United States, the country was viewed in most Western capitals as a loose appendage of the North Atlantic Treaty Organization (NATO). During the Truman administration, the United States considered South Africa a friendly but remote country in a region seen to be under European tutelage. The region suffered a similar benign neglect under President Eisenhower.[22] The United States saw South Africa as an important country, and thought U.S. interests faced no serious threats.[23] Like the United States, Great Britain was unwilling to provide security guarantees for South Africa. The 1955 Simonstown security agreement between South Africa and the United Kingdom was less than Pretoria had hoped for because there were no explicit security guarantees. South Africa interpreted the agreement as a general security commitment, while the United Kingdom and its ally, the United States, interpreted the accord as providing Allied navies access to Simonstown and other facilities along the South African coast.[24]

Throughout the 1950s, South Africa's security strategy contributed to an alliance of anticommunist forces led by the United States. Although the South African military was scaled down to minimal levels after the war, South Africa contributed a small contingent to the Korean War and sent representatives to several allied training programs. South Africa may have also participated in monitoring Operation Argus, secret nuclear tests the United States conducted in the area known as the South Atlantic Anomaly in 1958.[25] Throughout the first several decades after World War II, South Africa's apartheid system was not a liability in dealings with Western leaders. In the aftermath of World War II, racial segregation and a belief in the superior status of whites were widely viewed as the natural order of things in many parts of the West.[26]

SOUTH AFRICA'S PEACEFUL NUCLEAR-ENERGY PROGRAMS AND WESTERN NUCLEAR DIPLOMACY

The unbridled sense of optimism in the 1950s and 1960s about the potential benefits of nuclear power stimulated the establishment of programs to exploit nuclear energy for peaceful purposes in several countries around the world. South Africa was one of a few countries outside the West that emerged from World War II as an independent state with a modern economic base and the educational, scientific, and technical infrastructure necessary to develop an indigenous nuclear-energy sector. A great deal of evidence indicates that South Africa's political leaders were able to exploit the nation's participation in nuclear-energy programs to develop covert programs that explored the military implications of nuclear power throughout the 1950s.[27]

In 1958, the South African Cabinet expanded the mission of the Atomic Energy Board to include research and development. Establishing a program to build a core group of nuclear scientists and engineers was one of the top priorities of the director of research at the AEB, Dr. A. J. A. Roux. He sent several scientists and engineers overseas to receive advanced education in their scientific disciplines.[28]

South Africa took advantage of several educational opportunities designed to promote the peaceful use of nuclear energy in both the United Kingdom and the United States. In many cases, these exchanges built on relationships established by scientists and engineers during the war, including spending time with scientists who had worked on the Manhattan Project. Other South African scientists went to universities in the United Kingdom, the United States, and Europe for advanced degrees in the nuclear sciences. These exchanges created close personal relationships that facilitated technical, economic, and political cooperation among South

Africa, the United States, Great Britain, Germany, and France. Ambassador Donald Sole, a former senior South African diplomat who worked on nuclear affairs throughout the postwar era, has described how these exchanges were formalized in a 1957 cooperation agreement that covered the peaceful uses of atomic energy. Sole estimates that eighty-eight South Africans were trained in various aspects of nuclear engineering in the United States.[29]

Relationships among South African and British nuclear scientists and diplomats were especially close. Despite the anti-British rhetoric of the National Party government in 1948 and South Africa's exit from the Commonwealth in 1961, Great Britain considered South Africa to be one of its most dependable allies at international nuclear conferences and at International Atomic Energy Agency meetings throughout the 1950s and 1960s. The United Kingdom provided South African professionals with training facilities and information on health matters and safety in nuclear plants. South Africa's Atomic Energy Board and the United Kingdom's Atomic Energy Authority established a collaborative agreement in 1957. Great Britain also played a key role by helping to finance the development of South Africa's uranium potential; it purchased thousands of tons of South African uranium and processed uranium oxide (U-308).

South Africa also cultivated close scientific ties with Germany that proved useful in its efforts to develop an indigenous nuclear enrichment process. German and South African diplomats maintained frequent contacts on nuclear issues after the First International Conference on the Peaceful Uses of Atomic Energy, held in Geneva in August 1955. The links between scientists in the two countries continued to grow close as both countries developed indigenous nuclear-energy programs. South African nuclear scientists made frequent visits to German nuclear centers at Julich and Karlsruhe throughout the 1950s. Dr. A. J. A. (Ampie) Roux, who became known as the "father" of the South African bomb, visited Germany on a regular basis as head of the South African AEB. Dr. Waldo Stumpf, the AEB's chief executive officer in the 1990s, studied in Germany for two years. The inventor of Germany's jet-nozzle enrichment process, Professor Becker of Karlsruhe, visited the South African AEB headquarters at Pelindaba, as did several other German nuclear scientists.[30]

South Africa's early relations with France were not as warm or friendly as the ones it cultivated with the United Kingdom and Germany. However, relations between the two countries grew as France balked at the safety restrictions Canada and other Western sources imposed on the purchase of uranium. France's claim to the right to purchase uranium free of safeguards may have given South Africa a psychological advantage in the French market. As France developed its nuclear-weapons and nuclear-energy programs in the 1960s, it became an important market for South Africa's uranium and a potential supplier of South Africa's first nuclear power station.[31]

South Africa's most valuable diplomatic and technical relationships in the nuclear-energy field were with the United States, which provided extensive political and technical assistance until the 1960s. These programs facilitated South Africa's efforts to develop several reactors and helped it explore the potential of nuclear power for weapons research. For example, South Africa parlayed its participation in the Atoms for Peace program into political influence at international forums dealing with nuclear issues. Under the program, South Africa was one of only six other Western countries invited by the United States to participate in the exploratory discussions that ultimately led to the establishment of the International Atomic Energy Agency (IAEA) in Vienna in 1957. As one of the drafters of the IAEA Statute and a founding member of the agency, South Africa took a permanent seat on the Board of Governors reserved for the most nuclear advanced African state. South Africa became a major beneficiary of global efforts to share nuclear knowledge and expertise. It was also active in other international bodies that addressed nuclear matters and played an important role in the work of the London-based Nuclear Suppliers Group.[32]

South Africa obtained necessary equipment at discounted prices for its indigenous peaceful nuclear programs through close links with the U.S. Atoms for Peace program and other peaceful nuclear-energy programs available during the Eisenhower administration.[33] Under the Atoms for Peace program, the United States provided subsidies that enabled foreign countries to purchase experimental reactors from the United States. It offered South Africa a $350,000 subsidy to purchase a weapons-grade experimental reactor in 1957.[34] A bilateral agreement between the United States and South Africa allowed South Africa to purchase a 6.66-megawatt Oak Ridge–type research reactor that had the potential to be upgraded to 30 megawatts. The United States also agreed to train South African personnel and supply highly enriched uranium for the reactor.[35]

Other scientists and engineers involved in weapons research worked at one of the several scientific research institutes established and supported by the South African government after World War II. One of the most important research bodies involved in early nuclear-related research and the development of chemical weapons was the state-owned Council for Scientific and Industrial Research. The Applied Radioactivity Division of the council started researching radioisotopes in the late 1940s. By the mid-1950s, the division had developed an indigenous cyclotron.[36] In subsequent years, council researchers and other researchers made significant contributions to the development of the nuclear bomb and several launch-vehicle programs. However, since the Council for Scientific and Industrial Research was chartered to conduct basic and industrial research, only a few council scientists were involved full-time in the earliest research to explore the potential of nuclear and chemical weapons.[37] A great deal of basic research conducted by scientists in Afrikaans-speaking universities and researchers who worked for state parastatals made important contributions to lines of research that fed into the country's covert weapons-research programs.

South African policymakers and scientists, like their counterparts in the West, were aware of the close marriage between nuclear research for peaceful purposes and weapons research. A. J. A. Roux noted the links between peaceful and military applications in a comprehensive nuclear development plan written in 1958.[38] In a document often described as a guide to South Africa's early nuclear research, Roux stressed that South Africa's nuclear cooperation with the West opened doors to important secret developments in the field of nuclear power.[39] That same year, Roux outlined a set of proposals for an ambitious nuclear research and development program to the AEB and the minister of mines. His proposals included support for basic research on the development of nuclear energy; specific proposals for mining, extracting, and processing uranium and thorium; research on the development of applications of radioisotopes and radiation; and data about the exploration of the viability of producing nuclear energy using an indigenous heavy-water reactor. Despite some dissent, the Cabinet accepted these proposals in 1959 with only minor changes.[40] That same year, Parliament passed the authorizing legislation, the Atomic Energy Act, to establish peaceful nuclear research and development programs.

PRECURSORS TO NUCLEAR WEAPONS: DEVELOPING SOUTH AFRICA'S HIGHLY ENRICHED URANIUM AND HUMAN AND PHYSICAL INFRASTRUCTURE

South Africa's early commitment to exploit nuclear power led its government to adopt an ambitious research and development program. A Nuclear Power Committee was formed to study the possibility of using nuclear power reactors in the South African electricity network. This committee recommended a line of research that led to the introduction of two nuclear power reactors into the national electricity grid at Koeberg outside Cape Town in the 1980s. The government also channeled large amounts of financial support into nuclear power, nuclear engineering physics, medicine, and management in order to build a modern nuclear-energy sector. These public resources attracted many talented scientists and engineers into fields related to nuclear energy and defense for several decades. Many engineers and scientists who had been trained abroad in the 1960s went to work at the AEB or on related defense projects when they returned to South Africa.[41]

In the early 1960s, the AEB built new headquarters outside Pretoria at a site called Pelindaba. The new center, an easy commute from Pretoria, sponsored several programs related to uranium enrichment and reactor development. The center's name was taken from a 1920 plan to establish a township on the site and is derived from the Zulu word *pelile* (meaning "finished") and *indaba* (meaning "council or discussion").[42] Several classified and unclassified projects were sponsored under the auspices of the AEB. One project, which remained secret for a decade, tried to develop a unique process for enriching uranium. Other projects related to building a nuclear reactor were unclassified. AEB officials expanded the nuclear-energy facilities at Pelindaba in order to generate enough nuclear energy for peaceful and weapons research. All the projects were driven in part by a desire to exploit a local natural resource, uranium, since most power and research reactors used enriched uranium.[43]

The AEB's capacity to produce highly enriched uranium was greatly enhanced with an experimental nuclear reactor, the Safari-1, which had been supplied by the United States under the Atoms for Peace program. The United States also supplied highly enriched uranium for over a decade, until pressures against the apartheid regime caused it to unilaterally suspend shipments of highly enriched uranium fuel to South Africa.[44] The United States had supplied nuclear aid because the reactor was a research reactor designed to produce radioisotopes for medical and industrial uses.[45] The reactor provided other scientists ample opportunities to use the facility. The government earned large profits from the reactor, and it is still producing large amounts of isotopes. By 1978, the economic value of uranium oxide produced by industry was estimated to be about 500 million rand.[46]

The indigenous uranium-enrichment program, which started in 1961, originally explored several different approaches. Scientists there rejected the gaseous diffusion and gas centrifuge processes for enriching uranium on the grounds that it was too expensive and technically demanding. In 1969, the decision was made to abandon work on a nuclear power reactor because financing both it and the indigenous vortex-tube enrichment initiative would be too expensive. By the end of 1967, the vortex-tube uranium-enrichment process had made steady progress and was able to produce highly enriched uranium on a laboratory scale.[47]

South Africa's uranium-enrichment process was an indigenous isotope separation technology similar to a stationary wall centrifuge. Several critics of the apartheid regime claimed that this process was a modified version of the Becker jet-nozzle process developed at Karlsruhe, Germany. Investigations by outside technical personnel concluded that the process, while similar to the Becker process, was unique enough to be considered a truly indigenous design.[48] As more people became aware of the project, the government publicized its existence and in 1970 created a separate state corporation, the Uranium Enrichment Corporation (UCOR), to run the enrichment program. UCOR and the AEB merged in 1982 to form the Atomic Energy Corporation (AEC).[49]

The success with indigenous enrichment led to the construction, in early 1969, of a pilot enrichment plant next to the Pelindaba Research Center called the Y-Plant, or Valindaba; it was part of UCOR.[50] In Zulu, Pelindaba means "we don't talk about this anymore"; while Valindaba means "we don't talk about this at all."[51] While it remains uncertain exactly when South Africa's secret nuclear-weapons program commenced, several analysts speculate that the commitment to build Valindaba signaled that any internal debates about the wisdom of nuclear-weapons research ended during the 1960s. What is clear is that once the capability was demonstrated, the country's political leaders quickly opted to exploit the new technology for military purposes. In July 1970, Prime Minister Vorster announced the development of the new uranium-enrichment process and invited collaboration by noncommunist countries in developing the process.[52]

A few analysts have claimed that South Africa may have acquired a nuclear bomb from Israel in the 1960s, a full decade before the country acknowledges developing nuclear weapons. The two countries had allegedly collaborated in the area of nuclear energy throughout the 1960s.[53] However, these claims have never been substantiated by official government sources, although the country had the requisite skills and resources to undertake secret weapons research by the mid-1960s. The Safari-1 reactor went critical (that is, it reached a stage where it was producing self-supporting nuclear chain reactions) in 1965 under strict safeguards in an agreement signed by the United States, South Africa, and the IAEA. A report in *Newsweek* in 1967 noted that France was prepared to supply highly enriched uranium for the Safari-1 reactor and hinted that it might also supply highly enriched uranium for military purposes.[54]

The Atomic Energy Board that was established in 1949 was renamed the Atomic Energy Corporation in the early 1970s. Secretly, the AEB was also charged with developing an indigenous source of weapons-grade nuclear fuel and a prototype nuclear bomb. The AEB has long acknowledged that it sponsored work on a heavy water–moderated and sodium-cooled power reactor for several years. The reactor, which used a U.S. supply of 2 percent enriched uranium and 5.4 metric tons of heavy water, went critical in 1967.[55] Officially, the nuclear power reactor project was terminated in 1969.[56] However, the AEB sponsored work on the heavy water–moderated and sodium-cooled power reactor technology "and on the reactor-physics of the concept . . . for a few more years" after the program was terminated.[57] All the officials involved in this reactor program insist that the original project was abandoned because it couldn't compete with light-water reactors and threatened to drain resources from the more promising uranium-enrichment program. However, uncertainty has increased over time about the amount and purpose of nuclear fuel produced by the AEB and AEC. As the United States imposed additional export controls and the high costs of a planned uranium-enrichment plant increased, the South

African government expanded the pilot Y-Plant to a small production facility, called the Z-Plant, in order to produce enough low-enriched uranium (uranium consisting of less than 20 percent U-235) for the Koeberg nuclear power plant near Cape Town. The new Z-Plant was built adjacent to the Y-Plant.[58] The Z-Plant was part of the AEB, which had been secretly charged with developing an indigenous source of weapons-grade nuclear fuel and a prototype nuclear bomb in the 1940s. Throughout the 1960s, several senior South African officials had difficulties making subtle distinctions between peaceful and military applications of highly enriched uranium programs in public statements. For example, in his public announcement about the enrichment process program in 1970, Prime Minister Vorster emphasized the peaceful aims of the program but went on to warn that South Africa would not be limited to the promotion of peaceful applications of nuclear energy.

In the same speech in which he announced that a pilot plant was under construction, Vorster also noted that South Africa would not agree to IAEA safeguard inspections for the plant. Foreshadowing similar debates that would occur decades later between the IAEA and other countries suspected of developing nuclear weapons, South African officials claimed that such inspections might endanger commercial secrets related to the unique South African process of enriching uranium. These facts underscore a trend seen all too often in recent years; once enriched uranium is produced locally for peaceful purposes, it is also exploited for military applications in covert weapons-research programs.

PRECURSORS TO NUCLEAR WEAPONS: NUCLEAR MINING RESEARCH AS A COVER FOR THE DEVELOPMENT AND TESTING OF A NUCLEAR DEVICE

In the 1960s, the South African government sponsored research that explored the feasibility of using nuclear technology for mining because it provided work for the experimental reactor physicists who had worked on the defunct reactor.[59] Also, Western programs encouraged peaceful nuclear explosive research. Considerable amounts of nuclear data and technology were transferred to South Africa under the auspices of the U.S. Swords into Plowshares program and other programs.[60] American technology again unwittingly contributed to South African nuclear weapons. Warnings by nuclear industry experts that peaceful nuclear-energy research would give South Africa access to technology that could be used to develop propellants and ignite a gun-type uranium bomb were ignored.[61]

In 1969, the AEB established an internal committee to investigate the economic and technical aspects of using peaceful nuclear explosions in mining.[62] In 1970, the AEB released a report that identified a wide range of applications for nuclear explosives.[63] That same year, the AEB recommended the development of gun-type, implosion, boosted fission, and thermonuclear designs for peaceful nuclear explosions.[64] After an internal study reported that civil applications using nuclear explosions were feasible, the AEB undertook a limited program that was housed in its Reactor Development Division and assigned personnel to work on the research for these designs.[65] Nine working groups were set up; even researchers assigned to the Health Physics groups at the AEB were involved in the research and development on various research problems related to peaceful nuclear explosions.[66] Within a few years, research and development was also under way on lithium isotope separation.[67] In 1971, Minister of Mines Carl de Wet reportedly gave the AEB permission to begin secret research and development work on nuclear explosive devices. Within a few years, AEB scientists were estimating the seismic damage of peaceful nuclear explosions in South Africa for yields ranging from 1 to 1,000 kilotons.[68] The AEB was in charge of the secret project until the prototype device was tested in the late 1970s. AEB personnel worked closely with personnel at Kentron South, an ARMSCOR (Armament and Procurement Agency) facility, and with personnel at several other facilities throughout the 1970s to develop and test the prototype gun-type device. One account claims that a dummy fissile component was tested at Kentron South in 1974.[69]

1974: TECHNICAL SUCCESS CREATES POLITICAL SUPPORT FOR THE BOMB

The year 1974 was a banner one for South Africa's nuclear program. A small AEB team, working under tight security at the AEB's Somchem propulsion lab in the Cape Province, succeeded in testing a scale model for a gun-type device in May 1974. This test demonstrated the feasibility of building a homegrown bomb. Several participants, including Waldo Stumpf, the head of the AEC during the 1990s, stressed the significance of these tests in convincing AEB officials that a nuclear explosive device was feasible.[70]

Technical successes and the availability of homegrown technical expertise were important factors that influenced Prime Minister Vorster's decision to expand nuclear-weapons research. After consulting with the relevant cabinet heads, the chief of the defense force, and the chief of the atomic energy program, Vorster ratified the decision to develop nuclear weapons in 1974.[71] Vorster and his key advisors also approved a number of ongoing and new initiatives related to the nuclear-weapons program, including the construction of a new test site that included two test shafts that were more than 200 meters deep, drilled at a site at Vastrap in the Kalahari Desert.[72] Vorster also gave the final go-ahead to build the Koeberg nuclear power plant. After the Y-Plant was completed, the United

States and South Africa approved an agreement under which the United States would provide enriched fuel for South Africa's two large nuclear reactors.

Thus, by 1974, plans were in place for all the essential components for indigenous uranium enrichment in South Africa. By combining decisions related to nuclear power and nuclear weapons, Vorster redefined the thrust of ongoing nuclear-weapons research.[73] The decision was taken at a time when South Africa was increasingly cut off from Western suppliers and facing increased threats in the region by forces backed by the Soviet Union and other communist states.[74] The enthusiasm of the scientists as they worked toward the completion of the nuclear cycle may have helped to persuade Vorster to authorize the funding required to develop South Africa's uranium-enrichment process. In fact, some analysts have claimed that the persuasiveness of the arguments put forward by nuclear scientists was a major component of the agreement by senior officials to approve the nuclear buildup. The next step was to construct a nuclear weapon.[75]

TESTING REQUIRES MILITARY INVOLVEMENT AND INTERNATIONAL EXPOSURE POSTPONES NUCLEAR TESTING

One cannot understand the development of South Africa's nuclear-weapons program without understanding the role of a parastatal called ARMSCOR in the nation's military-industrial complex. The South African armaments industry emerged from World War II as a small but respected producer of ammunition and armaments, especially rifles and cannons. As ARMSCOR's procurement and production of weapons for the South African Defence Force (SADF) grew, state procurement functions were assigned to a state-owned national armament board. In 1968, the state established ARMSCOR to serve as the chief supplier and purchaser of arms for the South African government. Defence Minister P. W. Botha was one of the strongest backers of the new organization. According to several accounts, he helped ensure that adequate funds would be available for defense research and development. Some analysts also credit Botha and the head of ARMSCOR, Commandant Piet Marais, with enlisting the support of the private sector to ensure that ARMSCOR would be successful. In 1976, the government merged its armament and manufacturing facilities with the state procurement agency, the Armaments Board, to form a consolidated parastatal. Over time, ARMSCOR grew into a conglomerate of modern state-run companies that were involved in a variety of defense industries, from ammunitions to state-of-the-art explosive devices, as the country became increasingly isolated.[76]

ARMSCOR grew on the heels of a large modern national-armament-industry state. In this process, ARMSCOR assumed many of the functions that formed integral parts of the army, navy, and air force in other defense establishments. In some instances, ARMSCOR acted as the principal when acquiring materials. ARMSCOR also served throughout the 1980s as a critical catalyst for sophisticated secret research and development programs.

Many observers and insiders claim that the passage of UN Security Council Resolution 418 in 1977, which called for a mandatory arms embargo against South Africa, was another major factor in stimulating the growth of ARMSCOR. According to one recent account, November 4, 1977, the day UN Resolution 418 was passed, was celebrated within the South African industrial system as the onset of the growth in the South African military-industrial complex.[77]

Until the late 1970s, South Africa's Atomic Energy Board was the lead agency responsible for developing a prototype nuclear bomb and enriched fuel. In 1977, the AEB built its first nuclear device at the Pelindaba facility. This is the same year the Y-Plant reached full operation but, since the Y-Plant had not yet produced enough highly enriched uranium, Pelindaba used low-enriched uranium.[78] The AEB had already started constructing three test shafts at the Vastrap Testing Range at the Waterkloof Air Force Base in the Northern Cape.[79] This site was chosen for a fully instrumented nuclear test in 1973 because it was large and isolated and had deep underground rock formations that would keep ground-level radioactive releases to a minimum. The military was brought into the program at this point to develop the test site as a military installation to maintain a more plausible cover story and to provide adequate security. If asked, the South African military said they were building an underground munitions-storage facility.[80]

In order to determine the limits of the radioactive release of their nuclear explosive device, the Atomic Energy Board needed a fully instrumented nuclear test. A large test site was selected in the northern portion of the Cape Province. In the early 1970s, the Defence Forces bought the site and developed it as a military test site. They drilled bore holes and prepared for the first oversize instrumented test devices. By August 1977, preparations for a simulation of all activities for a test explosion—for example, a dummy run—had been completed. The National Institute for Defence Research (NIDR) planned to test a truck-mounted multiple-rocket launcher called the "Stalin Organ" at the same time. However, the cold test by the AEB was aborted after an unmarked plane flew over the site and the South African government was informed by representatives of foreign governments that the site had been detected. Sensitive equipment was quickly removed from the site and the boreholes were filled with sand. The site remained unused for several years.[81]

According to a recently published insider's account, the timing of the first actual test explosion was determined by two factors: the availability of enough enriched uranium and when a trigger mechanism would be ready. The South African researchers set the date for a test explosion for the latter half of 1977, because this was when they estimated that enough enriched uranium would be available and when the trigger mechanism, fashioned from a shortened naval gun, would be ready. Even this modest test of the triggering mechanism required a great deal of cooperation among scientists and engineers from several different institutes and the construction of makeshift facilities. Since Kentron South lacked the expertise or facilities to work with propellants, a temporary facility was built at the National Institute for Defence Research at Somerset West.[82] Personnel from NIDR helped select a propellant, and AEB members had to be trained on how to conduct the test. The three insiders report that by mid-1977, "a gun type triggered device was completed and two greatly oversized 'cold' instrumental devices were satisfactorily tested."[83] Another account notes that the South Africans seemed to be in a hurry to complete a fully instrumented "cold test" using a depleted-uranium fissile component.[84]

In an effort to further disguise the reasons for the new equipment and trailers placed on the site, the NIDR simultaneously tested a truck-mounted multiple-rocket launcher, their version of the Soviet "Stalin Organ." The day after the rocket tests, an unmarked light aircraft flew over the borehole sites. The South Africans never learned the origin of the unmarked aircraft. That same week, a Soviet satellite discovered the site. After this discovery, Western nations and the Soviet Union pressured the South African government not to test a nuclear explosive and demanded an international inspection.[85]

As a result of the international pressure, Prime Minister Vorster told Defence Minister P. W. Botha to order ARMSCOR officials to quickly abandon the test.[86] NIDR and AEB staff dismantled any equipment that could have a military purpose. According to insiders involved in the test, several important lessons were learned from the international disclosure. There was a general recognition that it was not possible to conduct secret nuclear tests. This recognition led to research to "reduce the size and yield of the devices such that it could be shipped to the site and detonated in a very short period of time." The first fast-deployment test was ready within six months.[87]

After the Vastrap test was canceled, the AEB continued to work at Pelindaba on nuclear devices to make them smaller and more effective than the first nuclear device (nicknamed "the monster" because it reportedly weighed more than three metric tons).[88] A second, smaller device, co-denamed "Melba," was produced at Pelindaba's Building 5000 complex. A criticality test (a test to see whether or not the device is producing the necessary chain reactions) was carried out during late 1979 at Building 5000 after sufficient fissile material had been produced.[89]

Years later, ARMSCOR officials would claim that the Vastrap site was constructed to bolster the credibility of a nuclear bluff.[90] However, several analysts argue that the test was merely postponed and moved to an alternate site. A still-unexplained double flash in the South Atlantic, picked up on September 22, 1979, by a U.S. Vela satellite, has been cited to bolster the plausibility of this theory and as evidence that South Africa was able to proceed swiftly in efforts to develop smaller nuclear devices. Many Western analysts have concluded informally that the 1979 incident was an Israeli–South African nuclear test of either a low-yield tactical nuclear warhead, an enhanced-radiation weapon (that is, a neutron bomb), or a fission primary for a thermonuclear device in the approximate range of 2 kilotons.[91] Some analysts have claimed that Taiwanese officials were present at the 1979 test.[92] A commission established by the Carter administration found that the evidence was too inconclusive to prove that the flash was a nuclear explosion.[93]

A recently declassified top-secret memo from 1975 adds further credence to the idea that the double flash observed in 1979 was a test of a more-sophisticated nuclear warhead than the "museum pieces" declared by F. W. de Klerk in the early 1990s. According to the memo, South Africa could place a warhead on a missile or a South African Air Force plane. The author of the memo urged the government to buy or build a nuclear warhead and suggested alternative launch vehicles such as television-guided bombs or surface-to-surface missiles. South Africa did not yet have these weapon systems in its arsenal in the mid-1970s, and the purpose of the memo was to urge the country to buy or build them quickly.[94] Although the details of the test remain shrouded in mystery, Defence Minister P. W. Botha was happy with the results. At a Cape Province National Party Congress just three days after the "flash," an upbeat Botha warned that potential enemies of South Africa had better think twice, as they "might find out that we have military weapons they do not know about."[95]

DOMESTIC AND INTERNATIONAL UNREST FUELS AUTHORITARIANISM AND COVERT NUCLEAR RESEARCH AND DEVELOPMENT

South Africa's ability to conduct secret nuclear-energy and -weapons research was facilitated by changes in the political system toward authoritarian rule designed to protect and maintain apartheid. Although de facto and de jure segregation had existed in South Africa before 1948, the apartheid laws passed by leaders of the Nationalist Party imposed a new social and political order that attempted to guarantee increased power and privilege for a growing Afrikaner elite. To meet the objectives envisioned by the apartheid vision, it became necessary to regulate virtually all aspects of political, economic, and social life on the basis of race laws backed by a growing security force. The imposition of apartheid and the growing authoritarian nature of the state were supported by wide margins in the 1958 general elections, the first in which Blacks were completely excluded.

African nationalist movements, notably the African National Congress, organized a number of wide-scale mass actions throughout the 1950s, including strikes, boycotts, and civil disobedience, that disrupted governmental activities. A cycle of political opposition, vicious government crackdowns against dissidents, increasingly restrictive security measures, and international protests ensued. South Africa's role in the world gradually changed from an appendage of the West to a world pariah. The protest movement entered a more intense phase after the government-inflicted Sharpeville massacre of March 21, 1960. In a Pan-Africanist Congress campaign of massive civil disobedience, black Africans turned themselves in to South African police stations without mandatory passbooks. In Sharpeville Township, South African Air Force jets and South African Police armored cars failed to intimidate the more than 5,000 Blacks who had assembled in front of the police station. A nervous police force of 300 fired into the crowd after people allegedly began to push through the gates of the police station.[96] More than 100 protesters were wounded and 69 were killed.

Widespread repression by the government following Sharpeville broke the back of the Pan-Africanist Congress and banned the ANC but failed to stem the rising tide of militancy among black activists. In 1961, the ANC and the South African Communist Party jointly formed a military wing called Umkhonto we Sizwe (MK, or Spear of the Nation). After the MK bombed infrastructure targets, the entire leadership of the ANC, including Nelson Mandela, was arrested in 1962. Although Mandela had gained international prominence for his rhetorical skills at political trials in 1962 and 1964, he and other members of the ANC leadership were imprisoned for life. These incidents marked the start of a more intense cycle of political protests, government repression, and counterviolence that continued to grow in intensity until the lifting of the ban on the ANC and the release of Mandela in February 1990.

Widespread international condemnation and a growing political and diplomatic campaign to isolate South Africa grew in the aftermath of the Sharpeville massacre. In 1962, the United Kingdom imposed restrictions on the sale of arms to South Africa. The United States announced in 1963 that it too would no longer sell arms to South Africa. The same year, the UN Security Council imposed a voluntary arms embargo on South Africa.[97] The leaders of newly independent countries in Africa, led by the countries bordering South Africa, took the lead in campaigns to isolate South Africa in the United Nations and other international forums.[98]

One of South Africa's responses was to pull away from the United Kingdom; in 1961, South Africa withdrew from the British Commonwealth. During the 1960s, the ruling Afrikaner elite, led by Prime Ministers H. F. Verwoerd and John Vorster, distanced South Africa from the international community and developed a laager (or "circle the wagons") complex.[99] Afrikaner nationalists came to see themselves as a besieged minority who had been betrayed by the West and who felt threatened by black nationalists and communists backed by the Soviet bloc.[100] The combination of extreme nationalist pride and a heightened fear of adversaries created a quintessential example of oppositional nationalism and may have been a factor in South Africa's refusal to sign the Nuclear Nonproliferation Treaty in 1968. From 1961 to 1972, the number of international organizations South Africa participated in decreased from forty to two.[101] Growing international condemnation was the context within which South African government officials agreed to initiate covert nuclear-weapons research.

RISE OF NEW THREATS IN THE 1960S IN RHODESIA AND SOUTH WEST AFRICA

South Africa's Afrikaner nationalist leaders and many of the government's white supporters felt heightened perceptions of external threats throughout the 1960s as the United Kingdom granted independence to several African colonies in the region. In 1965, it signaled its intention not to support white settlers in Rhodesia in their Unilateral Declaration of Independence and led a campaign to impose UN sanctions on the regime. And it did not oppose a growing campaign by two guerrilla movements, the Zimbabwe African National Union (ZANU) and Zimbabwe African Peoples Union (ZAPU). Perceptions of external threats increased in 1966 after an abortive effort by guerrillas of the South West African Peoples Organization (SWAPO) to infiltrate South African–occupied South West Africa (Namibia). For the first time, the South African government faced attempted guerrilla incursions into what it felt was its territory.[102]

Growing diplomatic condemnation by Western countries, the beginnings of an international sanctions movement, and SWAPO's initial efforts to penetrate into South West Africa all contributed to a heightened sense of threat among South African politicians and whites living throughout the region. While the South African Defence Force[103] quickly crushed SWAPO's border incursion, fears of encirclement among South African leaders continued to be bolstered by a largely symbolic international diplomatic offensive to bring pressure against South Africa's rule in South West Africa. Led by the newly independent African states in the UN General Assembly, the UN submitted the issue of South Africa's occupation of South West Africa to the International Court of Justice.

South Africa's National Party government repeatedly cited growing domestic unrest, the increased possibility of sabotage by guerrillas in neighboring countries, and the threat orchestrated from Moscow to justify a sixfold increase in defense expenditures from 1961 to 1968. In 1968, the position of secretary of the defense shifted from a civilian to a military position. This shift led to a deterioration of civilian oversight over the military, a change that would have devastating implications in years to come.

A weak Parliament dominated by the National Party became even weaker when the opposition was reduced to only one member, Helen Suzman. The loss of nominal parliamentary oversight, the growing role of the military in government structures, the passage of increasingly authoritarian detention and censorship laws, and the erosion of civil rights protection ensured widespread erosion of norms of public accountability. The Afrikaner leadership was free to pursue research and development related to weapons of mass destruction behind a cloak of secrecy.[104]

The continuing militarization of society in the 1970s led to substantially higher levels of public funds for defense. These increased resources funded several off-line projects designed to develop an indigenous arms production and procurement system and a modern nuclear industry. As democratic institutions and legal checks were eliminated from the system, Afrikaner nationalist leaders and scientists were more free to pursue research and development behind a cloak of secrecy. Although the exact date that the government decided to go nuclear remains in dispute, some insiders have claimed that the South African government made the decision to build nuclear weapons during the tumultuous 1960s.[105]

The steady growth of funds throughout the 1970s also transformed the nuclear-energy sector into an attractive career path for promising Afrikaans scientists and engineers, who were lured by offers of subsidized advanced education at home and abroad, abundant research money, and promises of guaranteed employment.[106] As the domestic nuclear-weapons, public arms-production, and arms-procurement sectors in South Africa grew under the auspices of the parastatal ARMSCOR, the distinction between programs designed to develop peaceful and military applications in nuclear research blurred further.

Throughout the duration of the covert programs there was a close working relationship among personnel working at the AEB, ARMSCOR, and the Defence Forces facilities. However, in the late 1970s, after the AEB tested a prototype device, Prime Minister P. W. Botha shifted responsibility for producing nuclear weapons from the AEB to ARMSCOR. On October 31, 1978, Botha approved the formation of a cabinet-level committee to supervise the military aspects of the nuclear devices. From 1979, when the new committee got under way, until the dismantlement of the bomb program, members of this triparty committee included representatives of the AEB, ARMSCOR, and the Defence Forces. While ARMSCOR was in charge of building military weapons, a great deal of effort went into avoiding duplication by constructing multipurpose facilities that could be used by ARMSCOR and the Defence Forces. For example, Kentron South, a state-owned lab operated by ARMSCOR until the 1990s, worked closely with the National Institute for Defence Research facilities of the Council for Scientific and Industrial Research at Somerset West for rocket tests. Other tests were conducted at Defence Force bases and facilities. The South African government also used personnel and facilities at other state-run facilities as well as engineers, scientists, and laboratory facilities at private corporations to work on aspects of the highly compartmentalized covert projects.[107]

SOUTH AFRICA SHIFTS SOURCES OF HIGHLY ENRICHED URANIUM AFTER THE U.S. EMBARGO OF 1978

South Africa's difficulties in obtaining highly enriched uranium mirrors a pattern repeated often in recent years as more nation-states and nonstate actors have attempted to obtain the materials necessary to build nuclear weapons. One of the most important constraints on nation-states and other actors from going nuclear is the difficulty of securing adequate supplies of highly enriched uranium or weapons-grade plutonium. In the case of South Africa, an interruption in highly enriched uranium supplies from the United States caused only a temporary problem; there was a surplus of highly enriched uranium for sale because most member nations of the IAEA had scaled back their plans to build nuclear power plants.

Until the U.S. Congress blocked the sale of fuel elements in 1975, the South Africans had planned to buy fuel for its two reactors at the Koeberg power plant from the United States. From the South African perspective, the U.S. congressional action voided a 1974 contract under which the United States would provide enrichment services to Koeberg for its fuel. Instead, the two Koeberg reactors were built by the French Framatome-Framateg consortium based on a U.S. Westinghouse design.[108]

Under the 1974 enrichment agreement, South Africa's Electricity Supply Commission (ESCOM) shipped normal uranium to the U.S. Department of Energy for enrichment. However, in 1978, the U.S. Congress ruled that U.S.-enriched uranium could not be supplied to countries that did not allow international inspections.[109] Since South Africa would not agree to IAEA inspections, the United States unilaterally interrupted the highly enriched uranium contract with South Africa.

The decision forced South Africa to look elsewhere for suppliers. South Africa was able to obtain highly enriched uranium from other Western sources but was careful to keep specific details about the sources of highly enriched uranium secret. By 1981, South Africa had purchased supplies of highly enriched uranium worth $250 million from France after receiving tacit approval from U.S. officials.[110] The French government and Framatome denied the reports but acknowledged that Framatome supplied rods of enriched uranium to South Africa under a contract signed in 1976.[111] ESCOM's energy manager also confirmed that South Africa acquired highly enriched uranium from Switzerland and Belgium after clearing these purchases through the IAEA.[112]

Among many seasoned South African politicians, diplomats, and professional military officers, the U.S. decision to unilaterally break the enrichment contract remained a vivid event loaded with negative affect for many years. For many South Africans involved in nuclear research and development, the U.S. action was an unforgivable insult. Many Afrikaners felt that the United States betrayed them again when the U.S. Congress passed the Clark amendment banning U.S. aid to any faction in the Angolan war.[113] These two events became linked in the minds of most Afrikaners working for the South African national-security establishment, since in both situations, South African officials felt they had been "abandoned" by the Americans. This selective reading of the American position on sanctions tends to ignore the fact that U.S. sanctions were first levied unilaterally in 1970 after South Africa refused to sign the Nuclear Non-Proliferation Treaty. Thus, for most outside observers, U.S. sanctions in the late 1970s that ended exports to South Africa were merely a continuation of ongoing U.S. sanctions policies.[114]

U.S. sanctions failed to stop the development of South Africa's nuclear-weapons capabilities.[115] Instead, they may have inadvertently encouraged development of an indigenous nuclear fuel capability. And international sanctions failed to stop covert cooperation between South Africa and Israel.

NUCLEAR COLLABORATION BETWEEN SOUTH AFRICA AND ISRAEL BUILDS ON PERSONAL RELATIONSHIPS AND CONVERGING NATIONAL INTERESTS

South Africa's nuclear collaboration with Israel was the natural outgrowth of interpersonal links and close working relations between the two governments. Despite the wartime positions of National Party officials (who had pro-Nazi sympathies and who banned Jews from National Party membership during World War II), there was widespread support in South Africa for the Jewish effort to establish a national homeland after the war. In 1948, Prime Minister Malan's government relaxed restrictions on flows of foreign currency to Israel, thereby permitting large sums of money to flow into the fledgling state. These interpersonal financial flows between white South Africans and Israelis continued through subsequent decades and were stimulated by new professional relationships. In 1972, South African Jews sent more than $30 million to Israelis. Remittances from South Africans to Israelis were the second-largest source of foreign capital flowing into Israel during the 1990s. People-to-people linkages continued through subsequent decades, stimulated by interpersonal and new professional relationships.

Official military and intelligence cooperation can be traced back to the establishment of the state of Israel. A South African founded the Israeli Air

Force.[116] Close working relationships between Israeli and South African military personnel led to a cross-fertilization of ideas. The structure of the SADF was modeled along the lines of the citizen-based Israeli Defense Force. Both countries relied heavily on rapid mobilization of citizen-soldiers and trained personnel for preemptive strikes in an effort to maintain force readiness against a numerically superior "enemy." The SADF adopted counterinsurgency tactics that were heavily influenced by the lessons the Israeli Defense Force learned in fighting the Palestine Liberation Organization in the mid-1960s.[117]

By the 1970s, South Africa and Israel were routinely conducting joint military training and exchange programs. Israeli military advisors were involved in planning South Africa's invasion into Angola. After the Yom Kippur War of 1973, the Israelis sought spare parts for Mirage jets from South Africa. In return, Israeli defense experts assisted the South African Air Force in constructing a network of modern air bases.[118]

Israel and South Africa may have discussed cooperation in the field of nuclear-weapons research as early as 1955.[119] In 1963, South Africa began regular shipments of uranium to Israel. In exchange, Israel may have sold South Africa a nuclear explosive device as part of a quid pro quo in order to obtain funds to complete its nuclear facility at Dimona.[120] Throughout the 1970s, as the laager complex deepened among South African political decision makers, a similar sense of isolation, the Masada complex, was developing in Israel.[121]

During the 1970s, South Africa and Israel entered into a series of covert defense agreements that led to broader nuclear cooperation.[122] In 1973, Brigadier General J. Blaauw played a key role in strengthening military cooperation between the two states by arranging military exchanges and by establishing a close relationship with Israel's Council for Scientific Liaison, which was involved in making clandestine military and nuclear purchases for Israel. In 1976, Brigadier Blaauw, who was retired by then, was reportedly approached by an Israeli inquiring about the purchase of yellow cake (uranium ore concentrate). Israel bought 50 metric tons of yellow cake for use in their secret plutonium reactor at Dimona. There are reports that South Africa received 30 grams of tritium from Israel in return as part of a cover exchange that was codenamed "Teeblare" (or Tea Leaves).[123] These claims received more credibility in the late 1990s when a U.S. military analyst reported that the tritium was used "to support AEC work on boosted fission weapons."[124]

In the mid-1970s, as Prime Minister John Vorster approved construction of nuclear bombs, an indigenous highly enriched uranium program, and a test site in the Kalahari Desert, he also traveled to Israel to establish diplomatic relations and approve a series of covert agreements. The two countries engaged in a long-term secret relationship to test nuclear weapons and develop multistage missiles. Several details about when and where these collaborative activities took place are still subject to some dispute.

Some evidence indicates that the two countries conducted secret tests in the 1970s. In addition to the "dual flash" in 1979, a few analysts have claimed that three "tremors" reported in northern Cape Province and the Namib Desert throughout the mid-1970s were actually small underground tests.[125] These tremors may have been natural, they may have been underground tests conducted for Israel in South Africa, or they may have been a still-undisclosed South African covert program; the truth must remain a matter of speculation until more details are made public about when South Africa started to build battlefield weapons that were capable of carrying older or state-of-the-art (that is, neutron) nuclear shells.[126] Recent disclosures suggest that there were underground tests in the mid-1970s. According to one recent account by a senior former official, an underground nuclear test and demonstration facility constructed beneath a military test range in the Kalahari Desert was built in the same place where years earlier the AEC had attempted to conduct a secret underground test and demonstration.[127]

The two countries concluded a series of covert military agreements at a secret meeting between Prime Minister John Vorster, Defence Minister P. W. Botha, and Defense Minster Shimon Peres in Geneva in 1975. Vorster ratified the covert nuclear agreements during a visit to Israel in 1976. The agreements covered a number of areas involving the exchange of materials and agreements to coordinate testing and the development of advanced weapons systems, including access to Israeli missile technology.[128] Over an eighteen-month period after Vorster's visit, Israelis exchanged 30 grams of tritium for advanced research for 50 tons of South African uranium.[129] South Africa later sent additional shipments of uranium north for Israel's use and safekeeping.[130]

MOTIVES FOR BUILDING COVERT
NUCLEAR WEAPONS IN THE 1970s

Most official South African accounts of why South Africa developed nuclear weapons emphasize a growing insecurity among political leaders related to the rise of security threats in the region and South Africa's alleged status as an international pariah.[131] The rhetoric describing perceptions of threats during this era frames references to a perceived need to develop a nuclear deterrence in terms of a rather fuzzy threat—a "total onslaught" by communist adversaries. Public statements tied security to the ascension of Marxist regimes in Angola and Mozambique and an increase in the Soviet Union's and Cuba's backing of the Popular Movement for the Liberation of Angola government. In private, South African officials also worried about growing instability at home.[132]

A great deal of care needs to be exercised in considering the perceptions of threats of South African decision makers as a rationale for devel-

oping nuclear weapons. The public and private rationales of senior officials for developing weapons of mass destruction tend to blur the timing
of important occurrences. For instance, the revolutions in Angola and
Mozambique were still embryonic in 1974, when South Africa conducted
its first nuclear test. The involvement of outside actors, including the October 1975 intervention of South African troops in Angola and the dramatic air bridge to bring thousands of Cuban troops to Angola in November 1975, had not yet occurred.

However, South African leaders had been concerned about the growing threat of communism since the beginning of the Cold War. South
Africa started to feel surrounded and under siege as independent African
states began to accept aid and advisors from either the Soviet Union or
China. Many apartheid leaders were also alarmed by claims that the Soviets had allegedly fitted Egyptian Scud missiles with nuclear warheads after
Israel started to prepare to use nuclear weapons if the country was overrun
during the Yom Kippur War of 1973.[133]

Prime Minister Vorster's decision to go nuclear is best viewed as an adjustment strategy of South African leaders, who realized that they faced an
increasingly hostile environment at home as well as abroad and as the capability to produce nuclear weapons and launch vehicles came on line.[134]

What was new about the threats facing the apartheid regime in the latter half of the 1970s was that South Africa for the first time faced the possibility of border incursions by ANC and SWAPO forces residing in bases
located in hostile neighboring countries. The country felt increasingly isolated from former military allies and political friends. The United Kingdom had formalized the new status quo by terminating the Simonstown
Agreement in 1975. South African leaders felt a heightened sense of immediate threats after the country lost an important regional security buffer
zone with the fall of the Portuguese empire in the mid-1970s, the breakdown of order in Angola, and the first incursions by SWAPO guerrillas
from neighboring Angola into South African–administered South West
Africa. These were defining events that sharpened perceptions of threats
among Afrikaners throughout the latter 1970s.

As perceptions of threats increased, members of the Afrikaner elite
viewed changes in U.S. foreign policy as acts of betrayal and abandonment. According to senior apartheid South African leaders, the United
States encouraged the SADF to enter Angola in October 1975 and then
abandoned it to face tens of thousands of Cuban forces alone.[135] South
Africa's military intervention in Angola in October 1975, much like the
U.S. involvement in Vietnam, proved to be an increasingly costly counterinsurgency campaign over the next thirteen years.[136]

A sense of outrage and abandonment among apartheid leaders and
most members of the Afrikaner elite grew exponentially the following
year when the U.S. Congress passed the Clark amendment in January

1976. As the U.S. government distanced itself from South Africa's military intervention in Angola, South African leaders felt they were surrounded by communist forces and unscrupulous enemies.[137] These events intensified the laager complex among senior Afrikaner officials. In February 1976, Defence Minister P. W. Botha addressed Parliament and warned of a "total onslaught" against South Africa and the "buildup of more sophisticated arms in neighboring states" and called for a "deterrent to be able to resist a fairly heavy conventional attack on South Africa."[138]

Growing domestic unrest also played a role in increasing the laager mentality of apartheid leaders and fueling support for secret weapons of mass destruction within the Cabinet. In June 1976, uprisings began in the huge Soweto Township bordering Johannesburg, which brought a new wave of unrest to South Africa after more than a decade of relative calm. Vivid pictures of police shooting black schoolchildren who were protesting new apartheid legislation that required Afrikaans to be used as the language of instruction in township schools flashed around the world and fueled outside protests against the apartheid regime. International calls for sanctions grew during the subsequent protests, which lasted for months.[139]

The Soweto uprisings marked the beginning of an era in which black youths boldly entered the political world. The wave of rebellion continued into 1977, and anti-regime activities would persist until 1984, when an even greater uprising commenced and lasted until 1986. Fears of a total onslaught were fueled by reports that hundreds of young black South Africans were volunteering for guerrilla training at liberation movement camps in the region. The government responded by banning nearly all organizations opposed to apartheid.[140] The 1976–1977 uprisings led the apartheid regime to search for ways to control or incapacitate large groups of people, including the use of chemical and biological weapons. By the end of the 1970s, realities on the ground were catching up with the perception of "encirclement."

The regime's brutal suppression of young people led to renewed calls for new measures to isolate South Africa. After Soweto, international isolation of the apartheid regime became more intense and comprehensive. The United States blocked the sale of two more nuclear power plants to South Africa and terminated shipments of enriched uranium. Further political and diplomatic isolation occurred in 1977, when the IAEA revoked South Africa's permanent seat on the agency's Board of Governors because of the apartheid regime's secret nuclear policies and its spurning of the Nuclear Non-Proliferation Treaty.

In 1977, the UN Security Council imposed a mandatory arms embargo against South Africa.[141] Without access to military aid, South Africa's military modernity decreased drastically. A huge amount of money was redirected to rebuild ARMSCOR into a truly indigenous arms-manufacturing agency. In the 1980s, ARMSCOR became the lead agency in weaponizing the nuclear research and development program in South Africa. Some political insiders familiar with the inner workings of the apartheid government of Prime Minister John Vorster emphasize the factional infighting among political leaders within the inner circle. These analysts stress that the "siege mentality" of Vorster and his closest advisors derived from political fears of losing political power to a faction within the National Party led by Defence Minister P. W. Botha. These fears became a reality in 1978 when a scandal coined "Muldergate" forced Vorster to resign. P. W. Botha succeeded Vorster as prime minister. To this day, the role Botha played in exposing a corruption scandal that tainted Vorster so that he was forced to resign from office quickly has never been fully explained.[142] The following year, South Africa, one of the first countries to sign the IAEA Treaty in 1957, was denied participation in the General Conference of the IAEA held in India in 1979.

While analysts disagree on the relative importance of neorealist strategic concerns about South Africa's survival, the perceptions of senior politicians of increased threats, and political factionalism and cutthroat politics within the inner circle, what is clear from this tumultuous period of South African politics is that apartheid leaders all viewed their country as facing hostile forces. They adopted the imagery of the garrison state fighting for its very survival in an implacable, hostile world.[143] The shared perceptions of increased, albeit blurred, security threats were reinforced by costly demands for higher levels of domestic security. By the late 1970s, national service call-ups had doubled.

A number of aspects of South Africa's early experience with nuclear-weapons development are relevant for understanding the factors that influence whether the leaders of a country decide to "go nuclear." They include the following:

1. Top political leaders play a critical role in setting the priorities and direction of nuclear programs.
2. Western programs designed to promote the development of peaceful uses of nuclear energy play an important role in spreading the knowledge necessary to build a secret nuclear-weapons research and development program.
3. Access to a minimum supply of highly enriched uranium is a major hurdle in developing a secret nuclear-weapons program.
4. Several developed economic sectors are necessary in order to develop an indigenous nuclear-energy program and a covert nuclear-weapons program. Substantial economic resources and covert relations are necessary to purchase the technology and expertise through secret means.
5. A core group of scientists and engineers who have the technical expertise and political commitment necessary to develop a covert nuclear-weapons program and keep the details secret is crucial.
6. Access to state-of-the-art foreign technology and foreign training in order to build indigenous nuclear weapons is crucial.

7. Interpersonal relationships are an important factor in determining national policy interests, shaping interstate relationships, and establishing the covert collaborations necessary to develop state-of-the-art nuclear weapons and missiles.
8. Unilateral and international sanctions and other rules of the nuclear nonproliferation regime are unable to prevent a committed deviant state from obtaining the necessary materials, technology, and expertise to develop nuclear weapons.
9. Bilateral international sanctions and export controls have unintended effects, which in the South African case led to the decision to build an indigenous highly enriched uranium production line rather than rely on foreign sources of fuel for the Koeberg nuclear power reactor. Sanctions also led South Africa to engage in extensive covert cooperation with another regional deviant (Israel).
10. Authoritarian states are able to keep many details about an extensive covert nuclear-weapons program secret for decades.

South Africa's experience in developing the nuclear bomb underscores the fact that a series of political leaders understood the importance of maintaining access to state-of-the-art nuclear knowledge, equipment, and fuel supplies. Political leaders across several decades were able to maintain access to nuclear fuel, advanced nuclear research, and missile technologies. They did this through a variety of means that included participation as a friend or ally in peaceful nuclear energy and military programs, covert cooperation and linkages, and, when all else failed, illegal arms sales. The benefits South Africa obtained from its participation in peaceful nuclear-energy programs and as partners in a number of military-related exchange programs underscore the need to track nuclear developments in states perceived as friends. South Africa's early commitment to developing a nuclear program for peaceful purposes also highlights the problems inherent in distinguishing between peaceful and military nuclear research and development. As Albright and O'Neill, among others, have noted, virtually every country that has developed a covert nuclear-weapons program in recent years also developed an indigenous enrichment process, ostensibly for peaceful purposes.[144]

One of the few difficulties South Africa's early nuclear program encountered was the need to coordinate the production of supplies of highly enriched uranium with the demands of the bomb-construction program. Lingering doubts about the size and means used to dispose of South Africa's stockpile of highly enriched uranium further underscore the potential benefits of a fissile materials cutoff treaty. The case of South Africa may be cited by those who argue that existing safeguard agreements and monitoring procedures should be strengthened even though policies that deny countries access to enriched uranium at best may only slow down the speed of nuclear proliferation. Improved safeguards and monitoring procedures of existing uranium-enrichment plants and checks on stockpiles of highly enriched uranium fuel supplies stand out as special concerns.

The South African case also highlights the partial effectiveness of international sanctions and the unintended consequences that may result from even highly successful national embargoes, export license agreements, and other restrictive measures. Much like a criminal deviant, the story of the nuclear-weapons program in South Africa suggests how difficult it is to prevent a committed threshold nation that is willing to use illegal methods from obtaining desired nuclear materials or technologies.

FOUR

Warheads, Missiles, and Nuclear-Deterrence Strategy

> Although the open use of nuclear weapons against
> the RSA [Republic of South Africa] by those powers
> which possess such weapons and the potential to
> deliver them can be discarded for the foreseeable
> future, we must accept that there is a danger that an
> enemy assuming an African identity such as terrorist
> organization or a OAU "liberation army" could
> acquire and launch against us a tactical nuclear
> weapon. China appears to be the most likely nuclear
> power to associate herself with such an adventure.
> —South African memo (1975)[1]

This quotation from a top-secret memo written by the director of South Africa's Arms Control Agency in 1975 highlights the fact that President F. W. de Klerk failed to disclose several details about the covert nuclear-weapons program in his March 1993 speech to Parliament. Instead, the memo indicates that South Africa strategists and political leaders as early as the mid-1970s were concerned about potential threats posed by tactical nuclear weapons. This time frame corresponds to the period when South Africa's political leaders approved construction of the nuclear-weapons program. The memo also highlights the fact that South African politicians, strategists, and military leaders, much like their Western counterparts, were focused on the possible use of battlefield nuclear weapons and strategies and on tactics to counter them during the 1970s. The memo confirms the growing concern among South African leaders that nuclear weapons would become available to subnational groups such as terrorist organizations "within the next ten years" and that "a confrontation between the Free World and the Socialist Block has been replaced by consultation, thus lessening the danger of nuclear escalation." The author echoed the conventional wisdom among senior politicians and military strategists in South Africa and around the world when he noted that "[t]he bi-polar conformation in world conflict has broken up into a multi-polar order. Western solidarity has been shattered by recent events and divergent interests and political systems. The proliferation of nuclear weapons and the potential capability for their manufacture by smaller nations has rendered a super-power strategy irrelevant in new aspects of localised conflict."[2]

RESPONSE TO "TOTAL ONSLAUGHT" THREATS

By the mid-1970s, South African defense planners had concluded that the most rational approach to coping with an increasingly hostile environment was to acquire modern tactical nuclear warheads by buying or building them. In this chapter, we focus on the principal factors which led South Africa to develop sophisticated warheads and other types of launch vehicles, including "stand-off television-guided bombs or surface-to-surface missiles, to augment aircraft as vehicle delivery systems for nuclear warheads."[3]

The chapter also details the evolution of South Africa's nuclear strategy. After approving the development of nuclear weapons in the mid-1970s, South African political leaders turned their attention to the issue of how nuclear weapons could be used to enhance the credibility of their nuclear-deterrence strategy and as a potential tool to defend the homeland. The targeting maps that accompanied the recently declassified memo pinpointed rebel—that is, ANC—bases in neighboring countries as potential targets of tactical nuclear weapons.[4]

The recently declassified memo illustrates well how international, regional, and domestic threats had blurred in the thinking of white South African politicians and strategic planners. Blended perceptions of threats became both the impetus and rationale for undertaking expensive and highly sophisticated military research and development programs during the 1980s.

In the wake of the collapse of the Portuguese empire in 1974 and arrival of Soviet-backed Cuban troops in Angola in 1975, the Soweto uprisings in 1976, the passage of UN Security Council Resolution 418 calling for a mandatory arms embargo against South Africa in 1977, and the domestic scandal that came to be called Muldergate in 1977–1978, Prime Minister Vorster stepped down suddenly in September 1978 and was replaced by Defence Minister P. W. Botha. Shortly after assuming office, Botha initiated his vision of a "total strategy" to ensure the survival of the regime. P. W. Botha differed from his predecessor in the degree that he was oriented toward the military, particularly the special forces, during his many years of service as defense minister.

After becoming prime minister, P. W., as associates commonly called him, instituted a complex strategy that included a range of modest political reforms to provide the impression that apartheid was being softened, along with the use of widespread coercive force against enemies at home and throughout the region.

Throughout his government career, Botha believed that covert operations backed by the iron fist of the military gave the South African minority regime sufficient power to defend against adversaries at home and throughout the region. From 1978 to 1989, the South African Defence Force and the South African Police (SAP) initiated a series of internal and external military and paramilitary operations. These included assassinations, torture, and smuggling as well as forgery, propaganda, and subversion. All were defined as legitimate weapons against the "total onslaught" of communist and black nationalist forces. These practices were established at the top and legitimized deviant behavior throughout the military, the police, and intelligence services.[5] Botha also consolidated political power in the hands of a State Security Council that ran the SADF and SAP and controlled more and more aspects of public life in South Africa.

P. W. Botha gave unconditional support to the development of advanced weapons projects, including weapons of mass destruction. He played a central role in all decisions related to the nuclear and space-launch program from 1966, when he was appointed defense minister, until February 1989, when he was forced to resign as state president after experiencing a massive stroke. Weapons of mass destruction, including nuclear, chemical, and biological weapons and a range of launch vehicles, were important tools for implementing Botha's "total strategy." Covert nuclear warheads and an arsenal of different types of missile systems came to be viewed as essential force multipliers for a military stretched thinner and thinner by operational demands at home and along the border, which included South West Africa (Namibia) and Angola.[6]

Throughout the 1980s, in addition to overseeing the completion of six World War II–type nuclear bombs, P. W. Botha supported research and development activities on state-of-the-art nuclear technologies and missiles. He secured the funds needed for a multistage rocket system, which he envisioned as playing a dual role as the country's premier nuclear deterrent and as a civilian-satellite launch vehicle. P. W. Botha is credited with being the architect of South Africa's nuclear strategy.

In the latter half of the 1980s, the regime faced growing domestic unrest and protests at home, and opponents in Angola who were armed with sophisticated weapons. The historical record shows that South Africa's top political leaders took solace in the knowledge that they had a demonstrable nuclear capability which could be used as a form of political leverage to obtain Western aid, especially from the United States, in the event of a serious military threat or the worst case, what they perceived as "total onslaught."[7]

Weapons of mass destruction were also increasingly viewed as force multipliers as South Africa's defense force became stretched thin in efforts to meet regional security missions and bolster increasingly challenging police functions at home. Against this environment, the leadership approved the development of sophisticated nuclear warheads and tactical conventional launch vehicles so the country had a range of tools in its military toolkit to help defend the homeland in the worst-case scenario.[8]

Decisions taken during the latter half of the 1980s, even more than those taken during the early 1980s, illustrate how perceptions of increased levels of threat drove South African officials to search for technological advantages. As sophisticated weapons came on line, they were adopted to meet the need for cost-effective weapons that could expand the reach and power of the defense force. Several events within the military defense establishment, political and economic situations at home, and growing security concerns in the region converged and encouraged a series of "incremental adjustments" to South Africa's nuclear strategy and capabilities.[9]

Over time, the South African military establishment used the growing isolation of the country, the need for a credible deterrent, and the increasing need for long-range surveillance to develop ever-more-sophisticated warheads and launch vehicles. Leaders of the apartheid state were faced with the need to develop a strategy for using the new warheads and launch vehicles. Timing and a long-standing commitment to maintain sophisticated defense capabilities in the face of increasing international sanctions played decisive roles in ensuring that apartheid leaders could implement a sophisticated nuclear-deterrence strategy.

The space-launch vehicle, a thinly disguised cover for the development of a multistage long-range missile system, was approved for both political and economic reasons. The project was viewed as one of several important technological bridges that would help South Africa maintain its competitive advantage with countries in the developed world and engage in projected high-growth sectors such as the ability to launch commercial satellites. Over time, the commercial possibilities of the "dual-use" space-launch program came to be viewed as an important high-technology sector that might be able to generate hard currency in the future; it also served as a useful cover for advanced missile research. Launch vehicles had to be periodically tested and maintained to ensure the smooth functioning of complex systems, whether the intent of the missile was to launch a nuclear warhead or a commercial satellite.[10] Botha supported the project despite rising costs and complaints from the military about the expense of "PW's exotic toys."[11] The decision to terminate the space-launch program was made before the Government of National Unity took power in 1994.

THE INTEGRATED TEAM OF ARMSCOR, SADF, AND AEC PERSONNEL BUILDS THE BOMB . . . SLOWLY

After P. W. Botha became prime minister in 1978, he formed a top-level committee, called the Witvlei (White Savannah) Committee, to evaluate the country's nuclear policy and oversee military aspects of nuclear devices.[12] The committee, composed of representatives of the parastatal Armament and Procurement Agency (ARMSCOR), the South African Defence Force, and the Atomic Energy Board, was asked to prepare a program to initiate a top-secret nuclear-weapons research program. Working groups were formed to study various aspects of establishing a military program, including strategy, test sites, security, and how to integrate the staff of the different institutions, as well as safety, insurance, medical aspects of the program and possible delivery systems.[13] The committee recommended that seven deliverable nuclear weapons be built under the management of ARMSCOR. Botha quickly accepted the committee's recommendations and shifted responsibility for producing nuclear weapons from the AEB to ARMSCOR in 1979.[14]

Some analysts contend that the Witvlei Committee approved two additional secret research and development programs—one to build thermonuclear or boosted weapons and another to develop a neutron bomb.[15] Although no former South African officials have yet acknowledged the existence of these programs, the public record indicates that some research and development on more-sophisticated programs were under way by 1979. For example, the mandate given to ARMSCOR included "studies of implosion and thermonuclear technology."[16] During that same year, the AEB also formed a group of fusion experts to keep "abreast of the latest international developments."[17]

Once ARMSCOR assumed responsibility for production, the objective of the program shifted to construction of a deliverable weapon that could be quickly deployed.[18] As the arms-production and arms-procurement sectors of ARMSCOR grew, the distinction between programs designed to develop peaceful and military applications in nuclear research was blurred further.[19] As weaponization progressed, several programs were consolidated under an ARMSCOR management team. This centralization of control was designed to ensure professional and tight control over previous nuclear-related research and development activities that had been conducted at several different locations.

Shifting the nuclear-bomb program to ARMSCOR signaled a division of labor that was enforced by ARMSCOR managers throughout the life of the program. However, the program was not strictly an ARMSCOR project. Instead, the program management team used an integrated team approach. The team included an ARMSCOR program manager who was responsible for program plans, budgets, and program management; a project officer from the South African Defence Force who was responsible for the logistical requirements of the end user; and an AEB project manager who was responsible for the technical execution of the project. As work on a guide bomb and an SADF reconnaissance satellite began in the early 1980s, the integrated-team approach required the South African Air Force to adopt a much larger technical component to deal with weapons-integration issues, nuclear strategy, command and control, and logistical issues.[20]

The new integrated-management approach led to the construction of a new ARMSCOR facility on the Kentron Circle just outside Pretoria in 1980. The aerospace subsidiary of ARMSCOR, Kentron Ltd., opened for business the following year, after most of the equipment and know-how needed to build a nuclear device was transferred from the AEB to ARMSCOR. Kentron built the nuclear bombs. Other mechanical and design work related to nuclear weapons, including the development of alternative and reliable triggers and probably the construction of smaller nuclear bombs, was completed at the new facility. Some of the members of the theoretical physics group who worked on the thermonuclear device design at the AEB also moved to ARMSCOR during this period. The AEB continued to supply the project with covert highly enriched uranium from gaseous to metallic form and provided technical advice. However, all physical traces of the secret program were removed from the AEB site.[21]

According to the official account, the nuclear-bomb construction program moved forward at a remarkably slow pace throughout the 1980s.[22] The first ARMSCOR device was not completed until 1982. This device, like the AEB explosive, did not meet the requirements of a "qualified" nuclear weapon—one that was capable of both sustaining a chain reaction and delivering the device that will detonate after release of the bomb. A fully qualified bomb was not completed until 1987.[23] Official reasons for production delays at ARMSCOR were given as a temporary but extended closing of the Y-Plant, repeated design modifications over the decade of the 1980s, and the result of data obtained from diagnostic safety and reliability tests that interfered with and extended production schedules.[24]

There is no agreement on the reasons for the long delays in building the bombs. Waldo Stumpf, the chief executive officer of the AEC, stated that the Y-Plant, which was placed in operation in 1978, never met its design output.[25] In his 1994 study, David Albright emphasized the organizational culture of ARMSCOR; engineers there worked for the military instead of in the "civilian scientific milieu" and the emphasis was on building deliverable devices. This may have slowed the completion process.[26] ARMSCOR senior managers repeatedly emphasized that it took a lot of time to build a reliable and safe bomb, especially given the restrictions on testing prototype vehicles that were necessary for secrecy. One source, who refused to go on the record, claimed that there was a catastrophic gas reaction at the Y-Plant that shut down production at the facility for over a year. Another study, citing another anonymous informant, concluded that the plant functioned flawlessly from 1976 through 1989.[27]

At least some of the confusion and contradictory claims about what nuclear warheads were built and when and how much nuclear fuel was produced was part of a wider strategy of obfuscation. One of the participants in the program recently explained how South Africa was able to build and maintain a sophisticated defense capability under the effects of a UN arms embargo:

> One of the typical strategies that was utilized in cases where there was a large gap between the existing capability of the local industry and the level to which it had to be improved to deal with state of the art technology was referred to as the "wooden horse" strategy. This metaphor was used to indicate that the initial technology transfer step would be as far as possible in the right direction, but it would be recognized as an intermediate step relative to the ultimate needs of Defence. . . . [T]his wooden horse would be a real-life goal, in contrast to a "dummy objective," otherwise the development engineers and scientists would rapidly run up against too many questions with unrealistic answers.[28]

The "wooden horse" strategy appears to have been employed by participants who worked on both the nuclear-bomb and nuclear-fuel programs. The result is a great deal of residual uncertainty about what was produced. What is certain is that the Y-Plant reopened in 1981 and produced fuel again. According to some sources, Botha may have also approved a plan in the early 1980s to conduct conceptual work on plutonium and the use of a nuclear research center near Mossel Bay, Cape Province, to produce plutonium and tritium.[29] These discrepancies and unsubstantiated claims may never be entirely reconciled, since nearly 12,000 pages of documentation were destroyed before the arrival of the first IAEA inspection team in the early 1990s.

The first fully "qualified" gun-type device that ARMSCOR built could be delivered by a modified Buccaneer bomber equipped with a rotary bomb bay used in Australian drop tests of British nuclear weapons.[30] Subsequent nuclear warheads were built for use in air-to-surface weapons (that is, a TV-guided glide bomb). These warheads could be carried on either the Buccaneer bombers or on one of the Air Force's Mirage fighter-bombers. According to official accounts, ARMSCOR had built three more deliverable devices, and the highly enhanced uranium core and the components for South Africa's seventh device had been manufactured by the time the program was shut down at the end of 1989.[31] As nuclear warheads came on line, they were increasingly viewed as "a force concept multiplier . . . a special payload for conventional delivery systems." This shifting perspective prompted further work on developing a nuclear-tipped payload that could be used for the SADF surface-to-surface missile using the launch rocket of its reconnaissance satellite.[32]

NUCLEAR SUCCESS
STIMULATES ADVANCED RESEARCH

The official version of events is that by 1986 P. W. Botha had ratified the decision to produce just seven nuclear weapons. The rationale was that this number would be enough to successfully achieve the deterrence-policy goal of a nuclear demonstration force. Several unofficial analyses have suggested that the reason for limiting the number of nuclear bombs, which many analysts have called "museum pieces," may have been because the government had other smaller and more-sophisticated weapons in its arsenal.[33]

By the mid-1980s the Kentron Circle was an expanded, well-equipped manufacturing and storage facility capable of turning out one or two nuclear devices annually. There were facilities at the Circle for conducting sophisticated research on implosion weapons and other sophisticated designs. P. W. Botha authorized work on advanced nuclear concepts at the new facility. According to official accounts, these studies were limited and mainly theoretical; they examined advanced concepts such as implosion devices and the production of lithium-6.[34]

Other hardware manufactured at AEC facilities to support the nuclear program was transferred to Kentron Circle in the mid- to late 1980s. The move to centralize existing hardware was designed primarily to improve control and the reliability of the bombs. One anecdote suggests that such a move may have been necessary. According to two analysts, one of the original nuclear devices had been stored in an abandoned coal mine or former military ammunition depot after the 1979 criticality test. When it was transferred to Kentron Circle, the launch keys could not be found. The door had to be cut open to extract the bomb, which was named "Melba."[35]

Throughout the last half of the 1980s, ARMSCOR also oversaw the completion of the remaining nuclear bombs and qualified and certified the safety of the devices and procedures for storing the six nuclear devices. By all accounts, the top priorities of the nuclear-weapons program ARMSCOR managed were safety, security, and the reliability of systems at all levels. Completed bombs were disassembled and stored in high-security vaults. No single person had access to the devices. Release from the vaults and assembly of the devices required access codes from three high-ranking officials from the AEC, ARMSCOR, and the SADF, and President Botha was the only one who had the detonation code.[36]

Even after the chief of the SADF had a formal order for a nuclear operation from President Botha, half of the code to open a special safe containing the codes for a launch at the operational level had to be handed to him by the chairman of ARMSCOR, while the other half of the code had to be handed to him by the chairman of the AEC. Security was further maintained by the principle of "need to know," which included careful checks on the flow of paperwork, software, and equipment, especially when materials were moved from one site to another. The buildings that housed nuclear weapons were designed in five concentric circles to ensure that the most sensitive materials would be in the middle and that access was controlled electronically. Sensitive facilities were also camouflaged to protect against discovery by satellite or air reconnaissance and hardened against sabotage attacks or natural events such as earthquakes. Reliability and redundancy were built into every phase of production, and operational procedures employed a buddy system, checklists, training, and repetition.[37] A similar set of physical checks and balances was used for works in progress.[38] For example, a joint SAAF/ARMSCOR program office was established in Pretoria and housed in a separate high-security area.[39]

The same set of procedures was enforced at air force bases that were involved in secret nuclear projects. Detailed, careful plans were also worked out for the actual deployment of the nuclear force. The two subcritical components of the nuclear warhead were to be joined on the flight line before being placed on a missile or glide bomb. Final authentication would take place in an aircraft or control room for a launch. According to one insider's account, these procedures had not yet been practiced at the time the program was terminated.[40] Well-coordinated procedures may also have been necessary because the nuclear program had advanced well beyond the initial six "museum pieces" that were initially built. Several different organizations were involved in developing more-advanced weapon systems made possible by the skills acquired in the bomb project.

SOUTH AFRICA DEVELOPS A SOPHISTICATED MILITARY-INDUSTRIAL COMPLEX UNDER P. W. BOTHA

The nuclear program progressed through several stages during the late 1970s and the 1980s. To understand why South Africa expanded its range of secret nuclear weapons and built a space-launch vehicle during the 1980s, one needs to appreciate the shared commitment to the goal of defense independence in the face of increased sanctions and isolation from previously friendly states in the West. This drive for independence was a major impetus behind the pursuit of alternative sources of energy, the development of a modern arms industry, and research on state-of-the-art nuclear, chemical, and biological weapons. For example, P. W. Botha continued to support development of the coal-to-oil Sasol project. By the late 1980s, Sasol's 2 and 3 plants were highly profitable plants that employed over 10,000 people. After several delays, the two nuclear reactors at Koeberg went critical in 1984 and 1985. Botha continued to support the development of nuclear fuels for peaceful purposes.

Botha implemented an integrated-committee approach to guide the secret nuclear-bomb programs after taking office. Representatives from ARMSCOR, the AEC, and the SADF were always present at meetings of the planning group. The air force played an increasingly larger role in formulating secret nuclear strategy and capabilities and developing increasingly sophisticated tactical and strategic missiles as possible launch vehicles.

Along with the reorganization of the public sector, Botha oversaw the mobilization of leaders in the private sector and academia to help support the expansion of secret nuclear-weapons and launch-vehicle projects during the 1980s. Officials who headed ARMSCOR, the SADF, public science councils, and private defense industries that were established in the face of increased sanctions and isolation from the West made this mobilization possible primarily because of their continued shared commitment to the goal of defense independence.

The South African armaments industry emerged from World War II as a small but respected producer of ammunition and armaments, especially rifles and cannons. As public defense procurement grew, state procurement functions were assigned to a state-owned national armament board. In 1968, the state established ARMSCOR to serve as the chief supplier and purchaser of arms for the South African government. Defence Minister P. W. Botha was one of the strongest backers of the new organization. According to several accounts, he helped ensure that adequate funds would be available for defense research and development. Some analysts also credit Botha and the head of ARMSCOR, Commandant Piet Marais, with enlisting the support of the private sector to ensure that ARMSCOR would be successful. In 1976, the government merged its armament and manufacturing facilities with the state procurement agency, the Armaments Board, to form a consolidated parastatal, ARMSCOR. Over time, ARMSCOR grew into a conglomerate of modern state-run companies that were involved in a variety of defense industries, from ammunitions to state-of-the art explosive devices, as the country became increasingly isolated.[41]

ARMSCOR grew on the heels of a large, modern national armament-industry state. In this growth process, ARMSCOR assumed many of the functions that in other defense establishments formed integral parts of the army, navy, and air force. In some instances, ARMSCOR acted as the principle when acquiring materials. ARMSCOR also served throughout the 1980s as a critical catalyst for sophisticated secret research and development programs.

After the UN mandatory embargo of 1977 was passed, national self-sufficiency and reduction of dependence on external supplies became an even higher priority of the government through the activities of ARMSCOR. The UN arms embargo, following on the heels of a large number of bilateral economic sanctions, including U.S. sanctions instituted after South Africa refused to sign the 1970 Nuclear Non-Proliferation Treaty, gradually made it more difficult for the country to obtain needed materials and spare parts.[42] As the international arms sanctions took effect, ARMSCOR became adept at substituting domestically produced components and using part-time purchasing agents to secure needed parts and technology abroad by any means necessary.[43]

ARMSCOR was able to attract some of the best experts from private industry and universities to work on South Africa's nuclear warhead and missile programs.[44] The organization also drew upon scientists and engineers employed by two spin-offs from the Council for Scientific and Industrial Research: the National Institute for Defence Research and the Chemical Defence Unit. The main focus of the National Institute for Defence Research was rocket and missile research. A team of council engineers also participated in the development of the Cactus (or Crotale) surface-to-air missile in France.[45] The increased pressures of sanctions and a steady allocation of public subsidies resulted in the development of a massive hi-tech industry. The production capacity ARMSCOR developed had the capability to far exceed South Africa's requirements.[46]

This fast tempo of weapons development by South Africa's defense system over a decade resulted in an impressive number of new weapons systems. During the 1980s, ARMSCOR built one new aircraft model, maintained in service or upgraded at least five other types of aircraft, developed five types of missiles, expanded South Africa's shipbuilding facilities, built a large number of armored vehicles, and constructed ammunition, communications, and control systems. An estimated 15,000 people worked directly for ARMSCOR and another 15,000 jobs were created by ARMSCOR contracts in the private sector.[47]

The temper of the times was such that ARMSCOR managers were able to enlist some of the brightest minds from the private sector and universities to work on a wide range of conventional and more exotic weapons systems. By the early 1980s, the hard-driving military-industrial complex fueled by ARMSCOR had built a number of systems, including

a family of mid-life-updated jet fighters, an in-flight refueler, a standoff guided bomb, an air-to-air missile family, a remotely piloted reconnaissance aircraft, a 155mm self-propelled (and towed) gun, an updated battle tank, an anti-tank missile, a new artillery rocket system, a new infantry fighting vehicle, a family of mine resistant vehicles . . . an updated submarine, a new family of electronic warfare equipment . . . and a number of new weapons systems under development.[48]

South Africa's conventional-weapons development continued unabated until the end of the 1980s. Botha and the National Party were able to sustain support for increased amounts of funds for defense research and development by using the growing laager mentality to pursue the development of more-advanced conventional and nuclear capabilities. By the mid-1980s, the hostility of Afrikaner rhetoric had escalated to the point where Afrikaner politicians were complaining that the West was aiding the destruction of capitalism.[49]

The escalating rhetoric reflected the reality that South African politicians and military leaders faced increased domestic threats, escalating military threats in Angola, and an increasingly hostile international arena. A coordinated mass action campaign by the United Democratic Front and increased incidents of violence in 1984 led the government to declare a partial state of emergency. As new organizations were banned, others sprang up to take their place. Many of the new organizations were supported with funds from the United States and Europe. In the face of escalating violence, several countries recalled their ambassadors from South Africa and imposed new sanctions measures. Pressures by the international disinvestment campaign on South Africa also took a toll. South Africa needed to finance its growing international debt with short-term rather than long-term loans more and more often. At the same time, in Angola, SADF troops faced more than 30,000 well-armed Cuban troops. Leaders of the SADF were demanding more funds to meet these threats and to start the long-delayed modernization of conventional weapon systems for the army, navy, and air force. By the mid-1980s, research and development for increasingly sophisticated conventional and nuclear weapons was starting to place a serious strain on the competing demands on a limited defense budget.

ADVANCED MISSILES AND LAUNCHERS AS CONVENTIONAL FORCE MULTIPLIERS

The defense system changed significantly during the 1980s as competing demands for increasingly scarce public resources forced a reassessment of South Africa's defense policies. In the mid-1980s, President P. W. Botha ordered an extensive review of the nuclear program and related programs that led to a reorganization of nuclear- and missile-related priorities. The decision resulting from the review was a reconfirmation of the value of the nuclear program.

Botha approved the continuation of theoretical work on advanced concepts such as implosion devices and lithium-6 production but ordered work related to plutonium devices to be abandoned and efforts to produce plutonium and tritium at a secret facility on the Gouritz River halted.[50] At the same time, he approved funds for upgrades to buildings and for ten new buildings at the Kentron Circle. After 1988, the Kentron Circle was renamed Advena Central Laboratories.

In the late 1980s, the new facility at Advena Central Laboratories conducted research to develop an implosion device to replace the gun-type device and conventional military pyrotechnics and missile-control components. The layout of the facilities suggests that the laboratory was working on more-advanced nuclear-weapons systems and delivery vehicles. For example, Hamann describes underground storage facilities under Kentron's Gerotek vehicle-testing facility that were designed for nuclear devices that "had a mass of about one metric ton, and used tungsten as a neutron reflector."[51]

In 1986, the South African government announced that it had developed a gas-turbine engine that could be used in long-range cruise missiles.[52] Although ARMSCOR denied any foreign involvement in its pursuit of medium- and long-range missiles, several analysts have compiled evidence that indicates that the South African government received extensive covert material help by Israel and other countries throughout the 1980s. The next logical step for South Africa would have been to develop implosion devices to fit one of the missiles. However, ARMSCOR officials have only admitted that they studied nuclear warheads. They explained to several outsiders that given South Africa's goal of limited deterrence, there was no reason to pursue implosion weapons.[53]

In 1993, the IAEA completed an official investigation about the research and development of South Africa's nuclear program. It found that South Africa's declared nuclear-weapons program ran through the end of 1989. South Africa worked to develop and produce deliverable gun-type devices and studied implosion and thermonuclear technology that included "boosted" devices.[54] It also worked on designs to increase the explosive yield of a fission device, and on research and development for the production and recovery of plutonium and tritium.[55] There have also been unofficial reports that by the mid-1980s, work was being done on an implosion weapon that could have been miniaturized for a nuclear shell. The completed design was allegedly built and tested (with a tungsten core) at a site near Potchefstroom.[56]

An account by three former insiders recently disclosed even more details about the full range of facilities involved in producing fuel, nuclear weapons, and launch vehicles. The new information paints a picture of a much-more-ambitious weapons program than was declared in 1993.[57] One interesting feature of recent analyses is an acknowledgment that South Africa relied heavily on underground facilities to hide secret nuclear reactors, stored weapons, testing facilities, and command and control centers.[58]

Fewer details have emerged about the capabilities of South Africa's land vehicles to launch WMD warheads. However, several of the systems listed in insider accounts and snippets of information that have emerged in recent years suggest that South Africa was able to develop a wide range of conventional vehicles from short-range tactical missiles to extended-range G5 and G6 artillery systems that were capable of firing nuclear (and possibly also chemical or even biological) warheads. These systems, combined with the fact that South Africa was working on a multistage long-range missile that could be used to launch nuclear warheads or satellites (with minor modifications), suggest that South Africa had a very sophisticated nuclear-weapons program by the time the programs were terminated.

South African weapon designers discovered in the 1980s, as have other covert weapon engineers in recent years, that there are few differences between a solid rocket motor used to launch satellites and a surface-to-surface missile. As one insider notes, "In the case of the satellite payload, an apogee kick motor is added to the rocket to propel the satellite into low earth orbit at the top of the rocket (parabolic) trajectory."[59] Even though South Africa had limited financial resources to devote to these sophisticated new weapons, the country's leaders insisted on pursuing a multi-stage launch vehicle under the guise of the civilian-satellite launch-vehicle program.[60]

FINANCIAL CONSTRAINTS
ON SOPHISTICATED RESEARCH
AND DEVELOPMENT PROGRAMS

It is clear from even the earliest public accounts of South Africa's most so-phisticated weapon-systems research and development that the push to build ever-more-complex systems hit very real financial constraints in South Africa by the late 1980s. Capital as well as experienced scientists and engineers had become very scarce by the late 1980s.[61] The heads of all of the uniform services—the army, air force, and navy—were demanding more and more funds to pay for increased operational requirements and the modernization of conventional forces.[62]

At the same time, there were increased demands on scarce public funds to finance programs for Blacks and Coloureds, especially increased social services, that P. W. Botha had promised after the leadership of the Na-tional Party agreed that some reforms to apartheid were essential if it was to stay in power. There were also huge costs associated with new pro-grams designed to address the shortage of skilled laborers. Spending to ex-pand educational opportunities for Blacks and Coloureds grew substan-tially during the 1980s. From 1980 to 1988, there was a nearly 425-percent increase in the number of black students in technical colleges and tech-nikons and a 240-percent increase in the number of black students en-rolled in teacher-training institutions and in universities.[63]

These converging demands placed pressures on the managers of South Africa's arms-expansion program to search for new partnerships and strategic concepts that would enable the military to maintain higher oper-ational commitments in the face of overwhelming conventional forces in Angola, and to continue funds for the development of weapons of mass destruction and increasingly sophisticated launch vehicles. Increasingly, as one insider noted, "force multiplication became the name of the game . . . and the nuclear deterrent is the ultimate force multiplier, because it pro-vides alternative payload-to-weapon systems needed for conventional force."[64]

While leaders of the South African Air Force considered their existing stock of aircraft to be more than adequate for delivering nuclear bombs, the cost of developing a long-range missile was based on long-term strate-gic considerations and the need to develop better real-time surveillance ca-pabilities. A feasibility study led to the development of a multistage mis-sile.[65]

Military and political leaders agreed that the South African defense es-tablishment could not afford to build a large long-range aircraft. They argued that instead South Africa should construct a space-launch vehicle, pointing out that such vehicles were more cost-effective, South Africa needed better surveillance and intelligence, and there would be considerable "savings" from not having to support aircraft to protect a missile during its flight. They also argued that South Africa needed a highly accurate means to deliver a nuclear payload and the project would keep experienced scientists and engineers employed once the nuclear bombs were built.[66]

Only a few details have been disclosed about how the early rocket industry in South Africa evolved from work on a short-range missile (that could fly 500 kilometers) to long-range missiles capable of flying 3,000 kilometers or farther. However, some idea of the degree of sophistication of South Africa's missile programs is indicated by the fact that plans were well under way to build a five-story multistage long-range missile and develop high-resolution satellites for both commercial and possible military applications. These plans continued until political decisions taken throughout the early 1990s led to the termination of the more-sophisticated missile programs.[67]

Throughout the 1980s, the South African government's allocation of extensive resources to maintain the momentum that had been built up in the research and development process led to the deployment of a variety of missiles and other platforms. Some of these were designed to serve as vehicles to deliver weapons of mass destruction. According to reports supplied to *Nuclear Fuel* by ARMSCOR officials as well as reports from numerous U.S. experts and officials and a few anonymous South Africans, the country devoted enormous resources to the development of ballistic missiles after it had built gun-type devices.[68]

Some of the early rocket research was conducted by scientists and engineers affiliated with the Council for Scientific and Industrial Research. Much like the involvement of council researchers in secret biowarfare research, the work of some researchers affiliated with the council became controversial after the secret weapons program was disclosed, because the council's mandate was to conduct scientific and industrial, not weapons, research. Several council products were the subjects of international boycotts after it became public knowledge abroad that the Council for Scientific and Industrial Research was engaged in research that had military applications. As international criticism and sanctions increased, rocket research and missile development and testing became highly classified activities. Several projects related to missile development were completed at Kentron, and rocket motors for South Africa's long-range missile and battlefield armor were tested at Somchem.[69]

The growing cost constraints of the 1980s forced engineers and scientists to be highly innovative in their efforts to obtain hardware force multipliers.[70] Research and development of smaller nuclear and other more-efficient battlefield warheads and battlefield armored, tactical, and even long-range missiles capable of carrying nuclear warheads or serving with only modest adjustments as a space rocket were all justified and pursued on the basis that they promised force multipliers for conventional forces. The drive to find force multipliers helps to explain why South African weapons developers designed and may have manufactured or intended to manufacture nuclear warheads ranging from low-yield miniaturized devices for artillery pieces, to warheads for launch from air and sea platforms, to long-range ground-launched ballistic missiles intended to eventually carry multiple independently targeted reentry vehicles (MIRVs).[71]

The rationale of force multipliers was a pervasive concept. It was used to justify additional funds to develop a wide variety of multipurpose facilities.[72] The South African government had to take this approach, given its shortages of capital and skilled manpower. The approach had the added advantage of hiding the scope of covert weapons of mass destruction research and development and the total costs of the program across several different government organizations.

The South African Air Force and ARMSCOR shared an office in Pretoria for a joint program whose personnel were physically organized on a need-to-know basis. Air force bases dispersed throughout the country housed special logistics facilities to store, maintain, and support nuclear-weapons payloads. The military test range in the Kalahari used earlier by the AEC was used again. An underground nuclear test and demonstration facility was built on the same site and re-rigged in preparation for an instrumented underground test. Two facilities were built near Bredasdorp—the ARMSCOR Overberg Test Range and the SAAF's Test Flight and Development Centre used for the satellite launch. The parastatal Somchem at Somerset West in the Western Cape developed and manufactured the rocket motors used for the launch rocket and a solid-fuel apogee kick motor to launch the satellite into orbit. It also built a facility in nearby mountains to test the huge motors.[73]

ARMSCOR's subsidiary, Kentron, was the main facility for the development of missile and other guided systems. ARMSCOR's officials maintained a close working relationship with AEC personnel. A facility at Irene near Pretoria developed the inertial components and platforms to guide the launch and orientation of the satellite in space, while Advena had a well-established record of developing propellants and rocket systems. ARMSCOR's Eloptro facility produced electro-optical systems for the reconnaissance satellite at Kempton Park. This system had a resolution power of approximately one meter at ground level. ARMSCOR's vehicle and environmental test facilities at Centurion near Pretoria developed and manufactured a mobile launch-vehicle system that had the ability to travel widely throughout South Africa over the most rugged terrain. These vehicles were vital for maintaining the air force's capability to provide mobile launches. Somchem used the facilities at a military test range in the Kalahari, as did the Joint Air Reconnaissance and Interpretation Centre, an organization involved in satellite photography.[74] Somchem also built and used a rocket-motor test bench at Hangklip. These facilities and programs were regulated by a variety of interagency committees. Ultimate governance and oversight was conducted by the Committee of Cabinet Ministers, chaired by President Botha, and overseen by an "Executive Committee," whose members consisted of the chief of the SADF, the chairman of ARMSCOR, the chairman of the AEC, the head of the National Intelligence Agency (NIA), and the director general of the Department of Foreign Affairs.[75]

COSTS, COMPARTMENTALIZATION, AND SECRECY

The diverse and complex nature of the programs and systems undoubtedly accounts for the widely varying estimates of the cost of South Africa's covert nuclear program. Only a handful of people, outside members of the Committee of Cabinet Ministers and President Botha, knew the full scope and cost of the program. Estimates of the cost of the nuclear-bomb program have ranged from between 800 million and 8 billion rand (approximately US$800 million to US$8 billion) for the 1971–1989 period. The costs of the program were spread over the budgets of the AEB, ARMSCOR, and the Uranium Enrichment Corporation (which was the AEC from 1982 onward). Analysts who have focused on the cost of the nuclear-bomb program insist that the program was not as expensive as some have claimed.[76] More recent estimates have been substantially higher because they often include the costs of other weapons systems or facilities.[77] Horton estimates that the total costs were closer to 7 billion rand (approximately US$7 billion).[78] Whatever they were, the expense was clearly beginning to thwart SADF efforts to obtain funds to modernize conventional forces by the end of the 1980s. In interviews with former senior SADF generals, we repeatedly heard complaints about the high costs of "PW's toys" by the end of the 1980s.[79]

RESEARCH AND DEVELOPMENT PARTNERS AND COVERT NUCLEAR AND MISSILE TECHNOLOGY

From the mid-1980s through the early 1990s, South African defense planners and arms-industry managers coped with mounting pressures on shrinking public revenues by increasing their efforts to obtain funds for a number of covert projects from alternative sources. As ARMSCOR's work on advanced ballistic missile and delivery systems progressed, it needed more foreign knowledge, technology, materials, and funds and South Africa formed several new covert relationships with several foreign governments.

Although South Africa had several foreign partners, Israel was ARM-SCOR's principal partner throughout this period. Joint ventures typically involved pooling of technological, financial, and other resources to develop a range of new arms from conventional weapons (for example, new types of armor plate for Israeli Merkava and South African Olifant tanks) to weapons of mass destruction. The two countries are alleged to have concluded a series of covert military agreements during the 1970s. While many details of the covert military agreements negotiated between the two countries in the 1970s remain secret, one provision allegedly committed Israel to arm eight missiles with "special warheads." Another agreement to cooperate in building an ICBM may have been concluded at a meeting between the heads of state of Israel and South Africa in Geneva in the mid-1970s.[80]

By the 1980s, South Africa's covert partnership with Israel had shifted from technology transfer in exchange for access to test sites and minerals to joint research, co-production, and licensing agreements, often after some initial financing from South Africa.[81] South Africa also illegally obtained substantial foreign inputs by negotiating covert transactions and contracts with foreign corporations and states.

Some analysts tie the onset of production of the Israeli–South African space launcher, known within South Africa as the RSA-3, to the ICBM agreement.[82] As weapons topped with conventional or nuclear warheads became cheaper to build than manned bombers and as demand for missiles grew, South Africa built a homegrown version of Israel's Jericho-2 missile system with extensive Israeli help. This missile was the RSA-3, although the Central Intelligence Agency called it the Arniston. Some of the technologies and materials used in this joint South African/Israeli missile project were secured illegally from the West, most notably the United States.[83]

The mutual interest of the two states in building a strategic missile is plausible given the fact that senior politicians and military officials in both states embraced a nuclear-deterrence policy in the 1970s that emphasized the capability to threaten an attack on Russian cities. Covert cooperation between the two states on long-range missile development throughout the 1980s may have been designed to allow both nation-states to obtain the missile capabilities needed to make this deterrence strategy plausible.[84]

Both countries shared an interest in developing multiple types of launch-vehicle platforms. Beit-Hallahmi reported that the two nations cooperated to build a nuclear submarine.[85] Other projects involved joint missile development and launch-vehicle testing. From the South African perspective, the missile-launch program, at least in the early days, was a low-risk path to cutting-edge research on weapons of mass destruction.[86] There are reports that the two countries collaborated on guided missiles for corvettes, cruise missiles, and mobile missile launchers. They reportedly developed a nuclear-delivery system so advanced that it was rumored to place Lagos, Nigeria, within South Africa's firing range as early as 1983.[87]

One of the best-publicized exchanges between Israel and South Africa involved rocket technology and tests. South Africa granted Israel access to the De Hoop missile test site and supplies of uranium in exchange for help in building indigenous South African missiles with greater range. South African and Israeli cooperation on an intermediate-range (1,000–1,200 kilometers) missile resulted in a two-stage solid-fuel ballistic missile, which was ready for testing by 1989.[88]

A new South African missile believed to contain Israeli Jericho-1 (and probably Jericho-2) technology, as well as the more-advanced Israeli medium-range Jericho-2 missiles were tested at the Overberg site in 1989, 1990, and possibly again in 1991.[89] Collaboration with Israel appears to have been critical in helping South Africa acquire a range of platforms capable of carrying nuclear warheads, including the rocket technology needed to transform a satellite launcher into a nuclear-tipped ballistic missile. By 1989, seventy-five Israeli engineers were reported to be working in South Africa on missile programs in exchange for a steady flow of enriched uranium.[90]

From 1989 to 1992, more than 200 South Africans reportedly visited Israel to work secretly on the missile program. Some details about the nature of these covert projects emerged during the spring of 1994 when a group of sixteen nuclear and rocket scientists, who had lost their jobs at ARMSCOR's advanced weapons complex at Advena, threatened to disclose details about South African–Israeli contracts if they were not given additional compensation. According to public reports that surfaced in the mid-1990s, one missile project, the RSA-3, had been fired only in static tests. Two all-terrain mobile launchers were allegedly built and tested at Advena in 1988 and 1989 but never used. The spokesman for this group claimed that after the initial 18-kiloton "dirty" bombs were developed, the groups secretly worked on more-powerful nuclear weapons until late in 1989, when de Klerk ordered that the program be stopped.[91] In exchange, Israel is reported to have sold South Africa a system of explosives designed to stop a missile in midflight at a predetermined point, which would allow it to fall onto a target city with an accuracy of less than one kilometer.[92]

THE INCREASED ROLE OF PRIVATE INDIVIDUALS AND DEFENSE CONTRACTORS IN SECURING ILLEGAL COMPONENTS FROM THE WEST

According to press disclosures and U.S. court records, several individuals in the United States and Europe who worked for small defense-contracting firms that operated as state agents or who were interested in personal gain helped South Africa secure materials and technologies for its missile and space-launch program. Illegally obtained U.S. items included such high-tech items as photo-imaging equipment, telemetry tracking equipment, and gyroscopes used in inertial guidance systems. In 1988, South Africa bought from West Germany at least one multisensor platform used to track missiles and satellites. But news of the deal for three platforms broke and international pressure scrapped the delivery of the remaining two.

U.S. citizens were also involved in covert research and development exchanges. For example, Clyde Ivy, an American engineer who allegedly had close ties to the intelligence community, was at ARMSCOR and Kentron until the early 1980s.[93] Later, when U.S. policy shifted toward vigorous enforcement of international sanctions, Ivy was indicted on charges of violating sanctions. Legal action against Ivy and the International Signal and Control Corporation by the United States was one of several residual issues that prevented close cooperation on defense and security matters between the two states for a few years in the mid-1990s.

Further details of alleged efforts by South African agents to illegally obtain U.S. materials emerged after a scientist involved with the U.S. Star Wars program (the Strategic Defense Initiative), who was the owner of Plume Technologies, was arrested on June 1990 on charges of allegedly smuggling technology to South Africa via West Germany. The technology could have been used to identify potentially hostile missiles. Another U.S. firm, York Company, was alleged to have smuggled computerized guidance equipment used in large ballistic missiles to South Africa. Other firms were implicated in charges of smuggling encoders used in guided missile systems.[94]

The Striker missile program involved a plan to sell a South African missile containing extensive U.S. components and technology to China in the late 1980s. Details came to light when the U.S. government brought an indictment against ISC, a U.K. corporation with headquarters in Lancaster, Pennsylvania, and nineteen codefendants, including individuals who worked for Kentron. Both Americans and South Africans were accused of evading the UN arms embargo of South Africa, the U.S. Comprehensive Anti-Apartheid Act, and the Arms Export Control Act in the late 1980s by trying to illegally import U.S. missile components for testing and evaluating a joint ISC/ARMSCOR missile program in 1991.[95] ARMSCOR and Kentron were accused of having established a number of front corporations to conceal illegal efforts to procure U.S. components and technology for the $300–500 million Striker contract over more than a decade. The plan was to portray the sale publicly as a sale by ISC of a European-developed missile. But after the missile developed operational problems (flight irregularities caused the missile to crash when launched from the ground), China insisted that the system be corrected and that the missile be modified for launch from helicopters. To correct the missile's operational problems and to satisfy the demands of the Chinese, ISC made plans to test the missile in the United States and then exchange technical data with Kentron. The missile was never qualified for helicopter launch capability, but it was tested at the Calspan Wind Tunnel facility in Buffalo, New York, in August 1987. For undisclosed reasons, China did not purchase the Striker missile.[96]

The most famous case of an illegal arms exchange during this period involved illicit dealings between the South African government and Gerald Bull, the inventor of the Bull Super Cannon. Bull's gun was in high demand throughout the world because it was capable of firing a small tactical nuclear shell. The South Africans claimed that they made their own modifications and unique contributions to an extended design of the G5 and G6 artillery systems.[97]

South Africa's development of long-range artillery and shells capable of carrying conventional and possibly nuclear shells remained a concern of Western countries throughout the 1980s. Concerns about South Africa's procurement and sales practices were revived in the early 1990s, after a Bull cannon that was rumored to have been built by ARMSCOR with foreign assistance was found by U.S. forces in Iraq.[98]

AN UNEXPLAINED INCIDENT: THE *HELDERBERG* CRASH

Another suspected partner of the apartheid regime was Taiwan. One of the most tragic and still-unexplained incidents that may indicate that South Africa had covert dealings with Taiwan related to missiles was suggested in November 1987, when a South African Airways Boeing 747, the *Helderberg,* exploded in midair on a flight from Taiwan to South Africa. Reports have claimed that the explosion was linked to components of a bomb (possibly a nuclear bomb) or possibly ammonium perchlorate, an ingredient used in solid-propellant rocket fuel.[99] The original investigation into the causes of the crash was inconclusive.

For years, reports circulated throughout South Africa and the world about the existence of a mysterious substance called red mercury that was apparently a new type of nuclear fuel used in miniature nuclear weapons. Such reports were fueled further by a series of particularly grisly murders in the 1980s of individuals who were rumored to have been involved in illicit deals to smuggle red mercury into South Africa from a number of locations, including Russia. None of these murders was solved.[100] Once the red mercury story emerged, relatives of the victims of the *Helderberg* crash lobbied investigators during the Truth and Reconciliation hearings to reopen the case.[101]

The South African government sponsored an investigation into the air disaster in conjunction with the Truth and Reconciliation hearings. Investigators working for the commission had access to the unscrambled flight recording from the ill-fated aircraft, which indicated that when the captain told crew members after takeoff about the cargo contents, they said it was "madness" to carry that kind of freight on a passenger aircraft. Although the new data contradicted testimony at an earlier investigation, no new inquiry into the cause of the *Helderberg* crash was ordered.[102]

"P. W." FORMULATES A STRATEGY OF NUCLEAR BLACKMAIL

Afrikaner "hawks" in John Vorster's Cabinet and P. W. Botha's government were strong and unwavering supporters of the development of nuclear weapons for use as a political rather than a strategic resource.[103] P. W. Botha is widely credited as the architect of key elements of South Africa's nuclear-deterrence strategy while serving as defense minister in Vorster's government.[104] After becoming South African prime minister and later state president, Botha maintained an active interest in overseeing details related to production and deployment of these devices and was willing to intervene personally to fund or secure requested resources for the bomb project.

South Africa's nuclear deterrence strategy has frequently been described as a three-stage policy. Stage one involved a "strategy of uncertainty," during which South Africa would neither confirm nor deny the existence of nuclear weapons to the outside world. Instead, the country would practice a policy of "progressive disclosures," a gradual communication of the country's nuclear capabilities though a succession of leaks and outside revelations, in response to requests for explanations of certain unexplained occurrences. Stage two was designed to cover future situations in which South Africa might face an overwhelming security threat (for example, an invasion by Cuba). At this point, South Africa planned to make this nuclear capability known on a confidential basis to the United States and other Western powers in an effort to obtain their aid and involvement. Stage three would involve an underground test to demonstrate South Africa's capability to the world.[105] Stage three was envisioned as a last step to be used only if South Africa found itself with its back against the wall.[106]

Another source of inspiration for South Africa's concept of nuclear blackmail may have been the remarkable success Israel had when it threatened to use nuclear weapons as a form of leverage against the U.S.; the United States reportedly resupplied the Israeli military during the 1973 Arab-Israeli war after the Israelis threatened to use their nuclear weapons.[107] The success of this attempt at blackmail using nuclear weapons would not have been lost on the South Africans. According to official sources, government policymakers hoped that a demonstration test would either bring aid to South Africa or convince the threatening nation to back off. Officials claim these nuclear weapons were viewed as "quick-fix" tools of political influence. These weapons were never integrated into South

Africa's military doctrine and the leadership of the South African Air Force (SAAF) was never asked to develop a list of possible targets.[108]

NUCLEAR STRATEGY: FLEXIBLE RESPONSE?

In 1994, the public revelation that there was an underground bunker in a military building in Pretoria fueled speculation that leaders of this era may have also envisioned a stage four, the actual use of these weapons, if South Africans leaders found their backs against a wall. This bunker added credibility to lingering suspicions among many ANC leaders and supporters that the Afrikaner-dominated government might have planned to use nuclear weapons against black South Africans or ANC opponents in neighboring states.[109]

Our research did not uncover evidence that the apartheid government ever planned to use nuclear weapons against its own citizens. However, the recently declassified South African memo quoted at the beginning of the chapter confirmed that former South African nuclear planners had, in fact, targeted sites of suspected ANC military bases in neighboring countries.[110] At the time of the political transition in South Africa in the mid-1990s, many ANC members believed that white Afrikaner decision makers would be willing to use nuclear weapons at home or in the region. This shared belief was a source of distrust among parties at the start of the multiparty negotiations that led to a peaceful political transition in 1994. The belief was reinforced by a component of the siege mentality of most top decision makers during the Vorster and Botha eras, a shared belief about the superiority of white rule in South Africa as one of the last outposts of "civilized" Western culture in Africa. Although these beliefs were rarely stated explicitly in public political statements, they were important elements of a widely shared ideology among whites who supported the Botha government.[111]

The secret memo quoted at the beginning of this chapter and the range of missiles and other launch vehicles developed by the South Africans indicate that P. W. Botha, much like his counterparts in the United States, the United Kingdom, and France, sought to acquire a national arsenal of nuclear weapons ranging from long-range to intermediate-range to short-range tactical weapons for possible use for either defensive or offensive purpose.

ARMSCOR officials offered an alternative explanation to David Albright in 1994.[112] They took the position that credibility required deliverability. If South Africa wanted to show its nuclear devices to the Western powers as part of its nuclear strategy, the devices would have to be deliverable. If the devices were only test devices, the Western powers might not take South Africa's threat seriously enough to intervene on its behalf.

There is also some evidence that suggests that South African officials may have used the possession of nuclear weapons in the 1980s to gain political leverage over the West, especially the United States, in the context of ongoing negotiations designed to end the Angolan conflict. By 1987 advanced weaponry, especially Soviet MiGs and anti-aircraft missiles, were pouring into Angola. There was concern at the time that MiGs with modern technological systems might challenge South Africa's domination of the air, and the South African government worried about the possibility of having to call up thousands of reservists to continue the war on the ground.[113]

In 1987, ARMSCOR received an order from the top to reopen the nuclear test site in the Kalahari Desert.[114] A water tower was placed over one of the shafts to provide a plausible cover story as ARMSCOR employees pumped water out of the two shafts. However, the way the test site was opened allowed surveillance satellites from the most sophisticated nations to easily observe what was happening on the ground. It is possible that the government was implementing stage two or preparing for stage three, even though most government insiders staunchly claim that the nuclear program never got past stage one.[115]

In 1988, South Africa's worst nightmares came true. In June, Cubans fought off South African troops in a battle outside Calueque, Angola. Cuban air superiority played a major role in this battle. Although South African forces made adjustments on the ground to counter the loss of air superiority, the shifting balance in forces must have fueled fears of a potential nuclear test or worse among all of the major international powers.[116]

It is not known whether the reopening of the Vastrap test site, subtle threats to use weapons of mass destruction on the ground, or battlefield actions played a role in subsequent international diplomacy. In 1988, an international diplomatic initiative sponsored by the United States, the Soviet Union, Portugal, and other Western members of the contract group succeeded in brokering a cease-fire among South Africa, Cuba, and Angola. The Tripartite Agreement in 1988 led to the withdrawal of Cuban and South African forces from Angola, the independence of Namibia, and a temporary end to almost fourteen years of war in Angola. The end of the "bush war" eliminated the immediate regional threat to the South African government. The demise of this threat and the collapse of the Soviet Union in 1989 are widely cited by former South African officials as the principal reasons why "the South African Defence Establishment could stop short of bringing the nuclear option into play."[117]

Several aspects of South Africa's experience with nuclear-weapons development are relevant for understanding the factors that influence whether the leaders of a country decide to pursue high-tech nuclear warheads and launch vehicles. Our case study identified several common themes that are important for understanding why South Africa pursued state-of-the-art weapon systems and missiles after building nuclear bombs.

1. The senior political leadership plays a critical role in determining the shape and scope of covert nuclear and missile programs.

2. Only a small number of scientists and engineers are needed to develop a secret nuclear-bomb program. Once completed, there are ongoing pressures to keep the nuclear scientists and engineers employed, even after the bombs were built.

3. A large modern human and physical infrastructure is needed to successfully develop sophisticated tactical and strategic warheads and delivery systems.

4. The high demand for medium- and long-range missiles among middle-level states and the creative lengths to which middle-level states go to build or buy medium- and long-range missiles capable of carrying nuclear weapons suggest that this trend will continue well into the twenty-first century.

5. The cost of building advanced long-range delivery systems, in terms of both financial resources and opposition at home and abroad, is very high.

6. Isolated states exhibit a strong tendency to band together and engage in a wide range of covert cooperative arrangements in order to develop nuclear weapons and launch systems that can be used to deter aggression and defend the homeland.

7. Individuals from defense sectors in developed countries can play a major role in helping developing countries obtain restricted technology, materials, and expertise.

8. Any national system designed to launch commercial space satellites or satellites for space exploration has two uses; the same launch vehicle can easily be modified to carry long-range warheads capable of carrying nuclear, chemical, or biological warheads.

9. Only a modest aerospace industry is needed to build a crude air-delivery system. Any country with a national airline has a crude delivery platform for nuclear weapons.

10. Perceptions of threats and the desire of national political leaders to pursue sophisticated nuclear weapons and launch vehicles are closely related. Perceptions of high threat fuel a country's willingness to pay any financial or diplomatic costs involved in developing weapons of mass destruction, while reductions in perceived threats in the regional or global environment can quickly lead a country's leaders to decide to denuclearize.

South Africa's experience in developing sophisticated warheads and launch vehicles once the nuclear bombs were built underscores the critical role that political leaders play in determining the scope and shape of a secret nuclear-weapons program. P. W. Botha, as defense minister, prime minister, and state president, was truly the patron saint of the nuclear-weapons and missile programs. The proof of this is how quickly these programs were dismantled once new leaders came to power. While only a handful of people knew the full scope of the nuclear program, the huge interagency coordinated effort by a group of well-trained and highly committed white South Africans under siege from all corners suggests that it will not be easy to replicate such a broad and sophisticated program in other countries.

The South African case also suggests that rogue states are able to secure needed technology and expertise by working covertly with other isolated states, employing large numbers of part-time sanctions-busting arms procurement agents deployed in countries around the world, and by entering into covert partnerships with other states and individuals. While few nation-states in the future will have the resources or expertise to challenge the superiority of the major powers at the high end of nuclear-delivery systems, the South African case suggests that we will see many more countries building dual-use satellite-launch vehicles that can easily be converted to long-range missiles. This proliferation trend is likely to continue as long as there is a demand for more satellite-launch vehicles. Thus, the South Africa case should stand as a sobering reminder of how easy it can be to substitute a nuclear warhead for a civilian satellite once a country has a multistage rocket.

The case also underscores how porous national and international control strategies, underlying licensing agreements, patents, and international regimes can be. Lingering uncertainties about the extent and nature of past South African research and development activities related to nuclear weapons and launchers, including questions about foreign involvement, underscore the difficulties of relying exclusively upon the existing nuclear nonproliferation regime to ensure compliance. Additional and expanded bilateral and multilateral cooperation measures, such as the development of a shared database and monitoring procedures, may be required to effectively monitor future movements of materials, technologies, and expertise needed to build advanced weapons systems worldwide while also verifying continued compliance with existing international safeguards.

Finally, the evolution of South Africa's nuclear program underscores the correspondence between broader domestic and international political trends and the evolution of covert nuclear-weapons programs. Technical means of collecting intelligence using satellites, drones, and other devices cannot collect the information needed to understand the motivations of policymakers or monitor activities that occur underground. Few informed political analysts were surprised in 1993 when South Africa acknowledged the existence of a nuclear-weapons program. This program had long been suspected as only one of several secret projects started after South African society underwent a militarization of the political system in the 1960s and the political leadership made the commitment to develop an indigenous arms industry. However, many politicians in the West were surprised by the breadth and degree of sophistication of covert nuclear programs. Similarly, few political observers were surprised by the revelations regarding the extensive cooperation between South Africa and Israel, but many outsiders have been surprised by the sophistication of these covert nuclear exchanges and by the willingness of the former apartheid regime to contemplate using nuclear weapons as tools of political influence toward the end of the 1980s.

FIVE

Project Coast and Its Origins

Medicine is my profession, but war's my hobby.
—Dr. Wouter Basson

Every time I leave Africa a disease breaks out.
—Jerry Nilsson

Project Coast actually had three different
program objectives: 1) scientific research
and development, 2) defense, and 3) security,
including very close cooperation with
American and British intelligence agencies.
—Thomas Byron[1]

South Africa's chemical and biological warfare program, Project Coast, was a covert weapons of mass destruction program sponsored by the apartheid regime. While the evolution and dismantling of South Africa's nuclear program has been widely discussed, detailed accounts of Project Coast programs and activities did not start to appear until the late 1990s. Many disclosures about Project Coast activities came to light because of the investigations and hearings of South Africa's Truth and Reconciliation Commission in 1997 and 1998; the 1999–2002 criminal trial of Dr. Wouter Basson, Project Coast's director; disclosures associated with the death of the American scientist, Dr. Larry Ford; and more-recent actions by other scientists affiliated with Project Coast.

This chapter identifies the historical roots and international linkages of Project Coast. Our account is based on published documents and interviews with officials and researchers in the United States and South Africa. Assessments of South Africa's chemical and biological warfare program range widely, from the judgment that it was "second-most sophisticated after the Soviet Union" to the analysis that it was a program based on "pedestrian" science and insights developed in the 1950s. The three quotes listed above illustrate some of the more important questions that have not yet been answered about the purpose and scope of Project Coast and its program and the nature and extent of past relationships between the U.S. and South African governments regarding biological research and development. Our account suggests that Project Coast developed some highly novel processes and procedures and state-of-the-art biowarfare research that included the genetic modification of pathogens. However, most of the chemical and biological agents South Africa actually used for crowd control, assassinations, and counterterrorism were well-known agents. There is scant evidence about the widespread use of biological agents for mass attacks in South Africa, but suspicions linger. The large amount of drugs that flooded the South African townships in the late 1980s and more-recent claims about sophisticated lines of genetic-based research suggest that the jury should remain out concerning the full story of what the former government in South Africa developed and used. We conclude the chapter with a discussion of reasons for the widely varying assessments and some of the most important outstanding questions about what was developed under Project Coast and why.

ROOTS OF SOUTH AFRICA'S CHEMICAL AND BIOLOGICAL WARFARE PROGRAM

South Africa's decision in the late 1970s to initiate Project Coast can best be understood within the historical context of a country that participated in early research in chemical and biological warfare as a member of the Western alliance but was subsequently isolated from this community in the 1970s because of its racial policies. The decision to fund a new chemical and biological warfare program, much like the decisions related to research and development on different nuclear-weapons and delivery systems, was a response to the changing status of South Africa within the Western world and changing perceptions about conditions in the region and at home.

Project Coast, which was officially initiated in 1981, was the most sophisticated chemical and biological warfare program undertaken by the South African government. However, it was not the first such program in South Africa. South African troops faced the threat of chemical and biological warfare in the two world wars. South Africa's scientific and military communities kept pace with developments in chemical and biological warfare.

South Africa participated in these early chemical and biological warfare research and development programs primarily because of its close ties to the United Kingdom and as a member of the Western alliance. In the 1940s, South Africa produced mustard gas for possible use in World War II. In the 1930s, South African companies in the mining industry, including the Anglo-American Corporation, Anglo-Vaal, and other companies, developed explosives that were linked with chemical agents.[2] Director-General of War H. J. van der Bijl oversaw the production of chemical weapons and defensive measures that would protect South African troops against chemical and biological attack during World War II.

As a member of the British War Cabinet, South African prime minister Jan Smuts was also privy to chemical and biological warfare planning. For example, in 1943, the War Cabinet formed a plan to retaliate in case the Nazis used biological warfare on British livestock. The plan was to release anthrax spores using 500-pound cluster bombs, each containing over 100 four-pound spore devices. Trials at Porton Down, the United Kingdom's chemical- and biological-weapons research establishment, indicated that the cluster bombs produced aerosol concentrations of spores that covered nearly 100 acres. The War Cabinet viewed biological warfare as a quick-fix weapon that required no special munitions or hardware. The British planned to simply charge ordinary cattle-feed cakes with anthrax spores. This was a neat and simple example of wholly effective precision delivery, literally down the throat and into the stomach of targeted cattle. By the end of World War II, the British had stockpiled 5 million cakes.[3] South African policymakers learned from this experience that biological warfare was a simple technology that anyone could use and that it could be effective, under certain conditions, in Africa.[4]

Like other Western states, South Africa maintained its interest in military applications of biological and chemical agents after World War II ended. South African military officers continued training in Britain and the United States in chemical and biological warfare strategy and tactics throughout the 1950s.[5] South Africa dumped large quantities of mustard gas out to sea in 1946 but did not roll back its military chemical and biological warfare program entirely. South Africa did not become a party to the 1925 Geneva Protocol that banned the use of chemical and biological weapons in warfare until 1963. This underscores the fact that for forty years, the SADF was prepared to use chemical and biological agents in warfare. South African accession to this treaty did not affect its decision to initiate a new and more-sophisticated chemical and biological warfare program. The SADF maintained a very small military program related to chemical and biological warfare research and development until the onset of Project Coast in 1981.

South Africa's chemical and biological warfare research was supported by research conducted in civilian organizations. Literature about the World War II program was maintained and used in civilian research institutions.[6] The government funded a modest number of basic research projects in the Afrikaans universities and other government-supported institutions. Much of this research was conducted under the umbrella of the Council for Scientific and Industrial Research.

In 1960, a new phase of the chemical warfare program was started when scientists corrected a problem with teargas that made it more effective in controlling riots and dealing with militants hiding in the bush. The new teargas was used extensively to control the 1960 Pondoland uprising in Transkei. That same year, South African scientists were sent for a course on nuclear, biological, and chemical warfare in the United Kingdom. In the 1960s, the Council for Scientific and Industrial Research continued to work on teargas and CX powder for tracking, and it fitted Cessnas so the army could spread the powder.[7]

In the mid-1960s, the council worked on mustard gas and gas masks to replace the World War II–vintage masks of the SADF. The Egyptians had used chemical weapons in Yemen in 1962–1967 and may have passed them on to the African National Congress. South African leaders realized the importance of updating the chemical and biological warfare program. The EMAC (electrical, mechanical, agricultural, and chemical) Department of the Council for Scientific and Industrial Research worked on and innovated weapons, including chemical and biological agents, during the 1960s and 1970s.[8]

In the early 1970s, senior generals of the SADF asked the council for "aggressive" chemical and biological warfare agents and help in starting a chemical and biological warfare industry. Council for Scientific and Industrial Research Director J. W. de Villiers objected to the chemical and biological warfare proposals because he felt that Africa was not the kind of continent for chemical and biological warfare and that it was too "complex" and too expensive to develop. In 1974, de Villiers wrote a ten-page report in which he estimated that it would cost 500 million rand (more than US$500 million in 1974 dollars) to build a chemical and biological warfare program. De Villiers concluded that the Soviet Union was too well armed with chemical and biological and nuclear weapons and would retaliate against any chemical and biological warfare attack.[9] De Villiers's skepticism reflected a widespread concern among military analysts about the usefulness of chemical and biological weapons in Africa given the heat and the possibility that shifting winds could blow chemical agents onto one's own troops or spread biological agents into one's own population through food and water. These types of concerns temporarily slowed the momentum for initiating a sophisticated chemical and biological warfare program. The SADF postponed its plans to develop an offensive chemical and biological warfare program and supported a minimal chemical and biological warfare research and development program. By 1980, its staff had dwindled to only one individual who worked on chemical and biological warfare at the SADF Special Forces complex in Pretoria.[10] In contrast, the momentum to develop South Africa's covert nuclear weapons and medium- and long-range missiles continued unabated throughout the 1970s.

COUNTERINSURGENCY AND
CHEMICAL AND BIOLOGICAL WARFARE
IN SOUTHERN AFRICA

Throughout the 1960s and 1970s, South Africa's apartheid leaders increased their support for and involvement in counterinsurgency programs in several neighboring states. These experiences influenced the direction that South Africa's chemical and biological warfare development took in the 1980s. Involvement in neighboring counterinsurgency programs provided training opportunities, strategies, and tactics that the SADF and covert special police units used against political opponents as unrest increased at home in the 1980s and 1990s. After the political transition in Zimbabwe in 1980, personnel from several Rhodesian military units, including the Special Air Service and Selous Scouts, Rhodesia's elite counterinsurgency force, moved to South Africa. Many individuals in these units were experienced users of chemical and biological warfare, and some of them played key roles in incidents where South African Special Forces and police used chemical and biological warfare agents against opponents during the 1980s and early 1990s.[11]

In the 1960s and early 1970s, South Africa's response to developing guerrilla movements and a changing regional security environment was to increase security-force cooperation with Portuguese forces who were fighting guerrilla insurgencies in the former colonies of Angola and Mozambique; Portuguese tactics influenced the South African military and police. South Africa also increased its cooperation with Rhodesian police and defense forces. Increased involvement in security operations in Southern African states was part of a national-security strategy designed to counter communist-inspired guerrilla campaigns in neighboring states and to protect South African–occupied South West Africa (Namibia). The apartheid regime also wanted to be in a position to launch attacks on ANC Umkhonto we Sizwe (also known as MK) and Pan-Africanist Congress military training camps in Zambia and Tanzania.[12] The South African military was anxious to obtain firsthand experience with counterinsurgency techniques and wanted to explore the potential usefulness of unconventional chemical and biological weapons.[13]

The Portuguese military was the first to use chemical and biological warfare for counterinsurgency warfare in Africa. Portuguese troops poisoned wells and threw drugged prisoners out of aircraft. South African military officers were dispatched to Portuguese army units in Angola to gain experience in counterinsurgency warfare. In general, South African military personnel were not impressed with the overall effectiveness of Portuguese counterinsurgency programs. However, officers who worked in Angola learned firsthand how the Portuguese military used defoliants and napalm, mined trails, and poisoned water holes as tactics to counter their guerrilla enemies without having to engage in direct combat.[14]

In the 1960s, South African police and military personnel started helping the former Rhodesian government deal with an increased "terrorist" threat. In 1967, the SAP sent a contingent to help with border patrols as ANC/MK and ZAPU guerrillas infiltrated the county from Zambia. The South African Police were sent to train Rhodesian intelligence personnel and later the Selous Scouts in laying mines and using other counterinsurgency techniques. The South African Police, who acquired some of their techniques from the French in Algeria, ended up learning a great deal from their experiences in Rhodesia.[15]

SADF military advisors in Rhodesia assisted with the interrogation of captured ANC/MK guerrillas. The South African military became involved in Rhodesia because they were interested in gaining experience in bush warfare and improving their ability to monitor intelligence about ANC/MK and Pan-Africanist Congress political and guerrilla activities in neighboring states. A Corps of Signals detachment of the SADF Monitoring Division, known as V Troop, started intercepting and deciphering coded radio transmissions of Zambian police in 1968. After the high-profile withdrawal of SAP forces in early 1975, SADF personnel remained behind, maintaining a low profile. Their presence was increasingly important to Rhodesian security, and SADF personnel participated in several counterinsurgency operations conducted by the Selous Scouts from 1973 to 1979 in Rhodesia, Mozambique, and Zambia.[16]

The Selous Scouts experimented with the use of poisons. For example, they impregnated blue jeans with toxins and gave the jeans to guerrillas of the Zimbabwe African National Liberation Army (ZANLA) and Zimbabwe Peoples Revolutionary Army (ZIPRA) guerrillas. The Selous Scouts also experimented with poisoned pens to assassinate guerrilla leaders and with bacteriological cultures that they introduced into the Ruya River near the Mozambique border in 1976. Former top Rhodesian intelligence operative Henrik Ellert claims that a Selous Scout operation poisoned the water supply of a town in Tete Province in Mozambique in an attempt to kill ZANLA guerrillas who were reported to be operating in the area. Other accounts allege that Rhodesian military forces used cholera to contaminate rivers and seeded farming areas used by ZANU and ZAPU with anthrax spores in an effort to poison guerrilla food supplies.[17] Finally, Rhodesian forces poisoned wells and were suspected of using chemical and biological agents, especially in Rhodesia's Eastern Highlands and across the border in Mozambique.[18]

As the 1970s developed, the Rhodesian government became increasingly dependent on South Africa for financial support and military hardware. By the end of the 1970s, SADF military intelligence was a principal source of funding for the Rhodesian counterinsurgency program, including the Selous Scouts. The Rhodesian defense budget was very small, and the regime had only one rudimentary chemical and biological warfare plant, which received outside aid from South Africa. In assisting Rhodesia, South African researchers continued to work on chemical and biological warfare and land-mine projects.[19]

After Zimbabwe achieved independence in 1980, South Africa's involvement in the guerrilla war in Rhodesia provided useful personnel connections. Many Selous Scouts and other units of the military of former Rhodesia were quickly integrated into special units of the SADF and the SAP. SADF and SAP officers stationed in Rhodesia studied the organizational structures and tactics used by the Selous Scouts, including the use of chemical and biological agents. Personnel assigned to the 5th Reconnaissance Commandos, the SAP security branch *koevoet* (crowbar) unit (part of the SADF 5th Reconnaissance Commandos), and the SADF Special Forces D40 unit used similar tactics in Namibia and Angola. They were also used in covert support operations for the Union for the Total Independence of Angola (UNITA) and in Operation Barnacle against the ANC throughout Southern Africa in the 1970s and 1980s. Toward the end of the apartheid era, the Civil Cooperation Bureau was routinely using poisons against dissidents. By the time Eugene de Kock took charge of the Civil Cooperation Bureau in 1988, he had a working relationship and regular contacts with Project Coast director Wouter Basson. Whenever the Civil Cooperation Bureau wanted "special tools" for interrogations or to eliminate political dissidents, Basson was available to supply customized orders.[20]

PERCEPTIONS OF A SOVIET AND CUBAN "THREAT"

The collapse of Portuguese colonialism led to the takeover of Angola and Mozambique by revolutionary communist regimes from 1974 to 1976 (backed by the Soviet Union and Cuba). South Africa decided to intervene militarily in Angola in October 1975, which triggered increased interest among South African military and political leaders in chemical and biological warfare for defensive and offensive military purposes. It also fueled research on nuclear weapons and sophisticated launch vehicles. One of the more lasting effects of this military intervention was the sense among senior South African leaders that they had been abandoned by Western allies. Magnus Malan, the SADF chief of staff from 1975 to 1980 and South African defense minister from 1980 to 1991, summarized this view by noting that the United States encouraged the SADF to enter Angola in October 1975 and then left the South Africans to face Cuban forces alone.[21] South African defense experts knew that the Soviet Union possessed nuclear, biological, and chemical weapons. They had gained some indications of the scale and sophistication of the Soviet bioweapons program from Western countries and from the negotiations surrounding the 1972 Biological and Toxin Weapons Convention.

In response to dramatic changes in the regional environment, Prime Minister P. W. Botha and Defence Minister Malan approved a new and more-sophisticated chemical and biological warfare program. Senior South African officials also approved an acceleration of the nuclear-weapons and missile research and development programs. The motivations of senior apartheid officials for developing chemical and biological warfare capabilities were complex. On one hand, the official rationale was the need to "counter the communist onslaught." Malan, General Georg Meiring (chief of staff of SADF 1993–1994 and chief of the new South African National Defence Force 1994–1998), and others claimed that the chemical and biological warfare program was intended to counter the Soviets, the Cubans, and ANC and SWAPO guerrilla groups, who might have used chemical and biological warfare in the 1970s and 1980s, or so South African officials feared.[22] Meiring commented that the SADF sought protection against biological warfare in the 1970s, when biological weapons became known as the "poor man's atomic bomb" and the possibility increased that Soviet-trained SWAPO and ANC/MK guerrillas would use such weapons.[23] Former senior-level South African officials at the Truth and Reconciliation Commission testified about the need to develop defensive chemical and biological weapons because of the Soviet backing of Cuban forces in Angola.

The acceleration of weapons of mass destruction and missile programs during this era was fueled by the sense of abandonment by former allies and the need to find force multipliers that could be used against a host of enemies (that is, Cuban troops in Angola and guerrillas located in hostile neighboring states). The evidence to date, however, suggests that South African policymakers diverted substantial resources to develop chemical and biological warfare capabilities after their intervention in Angola for both defensive and offensive purposes at home and against foes in the region. Definitive conclusions about the most important factors influencing the initiation of South Africa's covert nuclear, biological, and chemical warfare programs cannot be made until official South African documents from the 1970s are released. One conclusion that can be drawn from the continuing charges and countercharges about the possible use of chemical and biological warfare agents in military operations in Angola, Namibia, and Mozambique as well as inside South Africa is that it is difficult to anticipate a chemical and biological warfare attack and identify who initiated it.

From the late 1970s onward, South Africa stepped up its military activities by supporting UNITA in Angola and the Mozambican Resistance Movement (RENAMO) in Mozambique. It launched Operation Barnacle against ANC exiles and MK guerrillas throughout Southern Africa. In May 1978, the SADF launched the Cassinga raid, in which 800 people were killed. SADF soldiers and paratroopers were accused of using chemical warfare in the raid.[24] The reports coming out of Rhodesia and Mozambique about chemical and biological warfare usage led the Cubans, Angolans, Mozambicans, and the liberation movements to suspect that South Africa possessed an offensive chemical and biological warfare program.

In Angola in the 1980s, South African troops faced increased costs and maneuverability problems because of the need to wear defensive chemical and biological warfare masks and uniforms that had to be changed daily. SADF troops routinely avoided local water supplies in Angola and parts of Namibia because they did not have enough intelligence about whether water supplies had been poisoned by SADF Special Forces in secret operations or by SWAPO, ANC/MK, or UNITA guerrillas.[25] The SADF found it very difficult to verify alleged use of chemical gas by Cuban-backed Angolan government forces and were unable to irrefutably rebut allegations that SADF forces used chemical agents against SWAPO and refugee camps in Angola. In addition, reports persisted that in early 1989 in Angola, the SADF was testing organophosphates, new generations of teargas, and new battlefield missile warheads. Supposedly, South Africa was designing the warheads to deliver chemical and biological agents and possibly even a miniaturized nuclear device. Early that same year, UNITA forces in Angola reportedly experienced huge losses.[26] Some sources alleged that the deaths were due to SADF testing of chemical gases. Other sources close to SADF claimed that the deaths were due to an "unexpected shift in the wind" that blew chemical gases onto the UNITA troops.[27]

The question of who used what type of agents in Rhodesia, Namibia, Angola, and Mozambique raises important issues. If South African forces were involved in offensive chemical and biological warfare in Southern Africa in the 1970s, it violated international commitments. These included the 1925 Geneva Protocol, which South Africa agreed to in 1963, and the Bacteriological and Toxin Weapons Convention, which South Africa signed in 1972 and ratified in 1975. Also, it means that the regime might have already developed chemical and biological weapons and used them. Claims that Project Coast was developed in the 1980s as a "defensive" program in reaction to the "Soviet and Cuban threat" in Angola and Mozambique would lose credibility.[28] South Africa would be viewed even more as an "outlaw state," willing to break conventions and subject black victims to inhuman deaths. It would also appear that the regime was prepared to continually violate commitments to international law if threats to its survival continued to grow.

"TOTAL ONSLAUGHT" AND PROJECT COAST

The need to develop chemical and biological warfare capability to support South Africa's military involvement in Angola was one reason Project Coast was developed. At the same time, growing domestic unrest at home in the mid-1970s also fueled research and development of exotic ways to neutralize opponents, large-scale offensive uses of the program, and weaponization. The evidence available to date indicates that plans for large-scale offensive use were not operationalized. The military involvement in Angola and growing political instability at home ensured that the decision-making process of Project Coast would be secretive, controlled by the military, and not subject to routine oversight or accounting procedures.

The Soweto uprisings of 1976 led the apartheid regime to search for ways to control or incapacitate large groups of people, including the use of chemical agents. The eruption of the Muldergate scandal at the end of the 1970s demonstrated that corruption and internal power struggles were eating away at the unified strength of the apartheid regime. Informal norms had become entrenched by the mid-1970s that permitted an extensive level of corruption within the Afrikaner-dominated bureaucracies. The corruption was an important precondition that allowed Wouter Basson and other top officials to use the chemical and biological warfare program in the late 1980s and early 1990s as a cover for their alleged personal gain.

As mentioned in previous chapters, in the wake of these regime-shaking events, Defence Minister P. W. Botha became prime minister in 1978 and initiated his "total strategy." Because Botha was oriented toward the military (and special forces), he initiated a range of reforms to ensure the survival of the regime that included the widespread use of coercive power. Power was increasingly consolidated in the hands of the military and taken away from civilians. Botha was an unwavering advocate of developing advanced-weapons projects and covert operations that would give South Africa additional advantages against its adversaries. During his reign of power, South Africa initiated a series of internal and external military and paramilitary operations. These included assassinations, torture, and smuggling. All were defined as "legitimate" weapons against the "total onslaught" of "red" and "black" forces. These practices were established at the top and legitimized deviant behavior throughout the military, police, and intelligence services.[29]

Within the "any means necessary to survive" framework, preparations began to develop the chemical and biological warfare program of Project Coast to counteract and even rival the Soviet program. P. W. Botha and SADF chief Magnus Malan directed the surgeon general, Air Force Major General N. J. Nieuwoudt, to launch a covert chemical and biological warfare program. Nieuwoudt enlisted a young military doctor, Major Wouter Basson, to be his lieutenant.[30] Basson was "tasked" to develop Project Coast by a "kitchen cabinet" composed of Minister of Defence Malan, SADF Chief Constand Viljoen, Commanding Officer of Strategic Intelligence and Special Forces Kat Liebenberg, SAP Commissioner van der Merwe, and the director general of the National Intelligence Service. Basson was placed in charge of managing all aspects of Project Coast, including defensive and offensive measures.[31] In addition, he continued making trips abroad to make contacts with scientists and to procure supplies for Project Coast.

The new covert chemical and biological warfare initiative quickly became highly compartmentalized in the late 1970s as Nieuwoudt and Basson individually approached South African university scientists and specialists in weapons development to determine if they would be willing to participate in and even lead the different components of a chemical and biological warfare program. Basson contacted Dr. Vernon Joynt of the Council for Scientific and Industrial Research and asked what it would take to develop offensive chemical and biological warfare capabilities. Dr. Joynt estimated that it would take 500 million rand (more than US$500 million) to build a chemical and biological warfare program. He noted that the SADF even lacked modern gas masks. Undeterred, Basson returned the following year accompanied by Surgeon General Nieuwoudt. Basson offered Dr. Joynt four times his current salary to run a chemical warfare program. Joynt turned down the offer. Instead, Basson and Nieuwoudt started a new parastatal, Delta G Scientific, the following year. The extent of secrecy surrounding Project Coast from the onset is illustrated by the fact that even Dr. Joynt did not learn that Delta G had become the basis of a chemical-weapons industry until five years after Major Basson's offer to him.[32] Nieuwoudt and Basson continued to approach scientists and weapons specialists and enlisted many.[33] They also began to make contacts in the international scientific community.

THE ORGANIZATIONAL CONTEXT OF PROJECT COAST

The decision to locate Project Coast within the SADF Medical Service (SAMS) would have important consequences for both the way the program was managed and the direction of research and development over time. At the time Project Coast was launched, the SAMS existed as a separate medical branch of the South African military that had joint ties with Special Forces. The close connection with covert Special Forces operations provided a highly secret and loosely managed organizational context for the new chemical and biological warfare program. Weak managerial oversight and accountability quickly led to personal abuse of authority and corruption by Project Coast manager Wouter Basson.

South Africa's involvement in Angola in the 1970s and 1980s resulted in important organizational changes within the military that ensured that the new chemical and biological warfare program would be controlled by the military. Between 50 and 80 percent of all SADF military-related deaths in Angola happened because of difficulties in getting immediate treatment for combat injuries, accidents, and diseases. Military leaders already understood the importance of having immediate field treatment for

SADF soldiers. This appreciation can be traced back to the large number of battlefield casualties incurred in the Anglo-Boer War.[34]

In Angola, the importance of immediate battlefield medical attention was the primary rationale used to justify elevating and reorganizing the SAMS as a new and separate fourth branch of the military in the 1970s. The operational command and administration of the new medical corps branch was placed on an equal footing with that of the three existing branches of the service (army, navy, and air force). The SAMS received a mandate to develop defensive capabilities to train in protecting the SADF from all types of attacks, including biological and chemical warfare. This mandate was the principal reason why managerial oversight and responsibility for the new chemical and biological warfare program was given to the SAMS 7th Battalion in 1981. The mission of the SAMS changed and became more ambiguous as SADF forces shifted from battlefield operations to policing functions at home in the mid-1990s. The fact that the 7th Battalion was accorded a large degree of autonomy from its inception and operated on a strict "need-to-know" basis meant that relatively few SADF officers, including the majority of senior SADF generals, had detailed knowledge of the activities of the 7th Battalion throughout its existence.[35]

Another important organizational factor that permitted the head of the 7th Battalion to have an unusual degree of decision latitude and autonomy was the fact that this was the medical support organization for special services operations. SAMS medical personal (e.g., doctors and orderlies) were also Special Forces officers who underwent special service training. During the period South Africa was involved in Angola, many of these medical personnel served as members of four-man Special Forces covert action teams. Although the surgeon general was responsible for the operations of seven medical battalions, the secret nature of 7th Battalion operations during incursions into Angola meant that this unit had a high degree of operational autonomy, which continued into the 1980s even though new types of Special Forces operations at home gradually replaced the combat-related functions of the unit. As the SADF increasingly undertook policing and internal suppression of political dissidents at home, the SAMS conducted new basic research projects and developed new chemical and biological weapons.

WOUTER BASSON

Dr. Wouter Basson was a young respected cardiologist who was the personal physician of P. W. Botha. When Surgeon General Nieuwoudt recruited him to direct Project Coast and serve as his special advisor, Basson was promoted from major to lieutenant colonel.[36] He joined the 7th SAMS Battalion and began making trips to Angola with the SADF. In a remarkable departure from normal military promotion cycles, Basson (at the age of 30 and with less than five years of military service) was offered the job of leading the chemical and biological warfare program. Personal connections helped Wouter Basson. When Basson was completing his master's thesis, he was a good friend of Philip Mybergh, the nephew of Defence Minister Magnus Malan. Before his prestigious appointment, Basson worked at the government laboratory that monitored infectious diseases throughout the continent of Africa. While working at the institute, Basson completed a master's thesis in medical virology research.[37]

Although Project Coast was run by the military, Basson proved to be a successful entrepreneur who played a central role in defining the research and development agenda. He capitalized on the secret nature of Project Coast to establish a number of new projects and as a rationale for acting alone. From the start, Basson was a highly charismatic and effective recruiter who was apt at identifying and enlisting some of the most promising and highly skilled medical researchers from the military and from the larger civilian scientific community. Basson also proved to be a master manager of people; he was able to inspire loyalty and respect from employees. Many researchers and scientists joined the program because they were intrigued by the intellectual challenges and opportunities to participate in pathbreaking research in one of several related disciplines such as chemistry, anatomy, and virology. Almost all were Afrikaners who shared a sense of patriotic duty, a nationalistic zeal for the importance of the work, and a sense that their research was critical for maintaining national security.[38]

PROJECT COAST (1981–1993)

From 1979 through 1981, the State Security Council, led by Prime Minister P. W. Botha, General Malan, and other SADF generals, discussed the principles that might apply to the chemical and biological warfare program. Several possible missions were identified for the new program. It became clear that a program designed to defend against a Soviet chemical and biological warfare attack could be built only if the Soviet offensive program was emulated and then tested.[39] Once the need for offensive chemical and biological warfare capabilities was identified, discussions began concerning the possible uses of such a program. Malan proposed that signs of a chemical warfare attack in Angola would force the Cuban and Angolan forces to don suits that would cut combat effectiveness in half. In 1981, General Constand Viljoen, SADF chief of staff, requested that the chemical and biological warfare program provide SADF with ways to control clouds in South Africa. Other possible uses considered included counterinsurgency, assassinations, and controlling the black population. It is noteworthy that during the process of launching the chemical and biological warfare program, no delegation from South Africa appeared at the 1980 review conference for the 1975 Biological Weapons Convention.

In April 1981, a top-level SADF committee meeting finalized the principles for Project Coast.[40] One principle was that chemical and biological warfare should be treated as a top-secret matter in order to conceal it from adversaries. Another was that South Africa had to fend for itself in the chemical and biological warfare arena; South Africa assumed that the West had fallen behind the Soviet Union in this area. The SADF committee decided that South Africa would use front companies to research and produce chemical and biological weapons in top-secret installations. ARM-SCOR was excluded from the initial phases of the project because of the desire for secrecy; it was not brought in until the weaponization phase of the program. One of Malan's suggestions that was adopted at this meeting was that South Africa would experiment with the strategy of forcing the enemy to don protective suits. The chemical and biological warfare program would also investigate ways to deal with massive demonstrations, insurrection, insurgency, and the rapid growth of the black population. Another principle was that biological warfare had to be used with caution. It could be devastatingly effective and therefore attractive. However, the regime was concerned that it was difficult to control and that it could cause tremendous, plague-like damage.

The annual budget for Project Coast was estimated to be $10 million, with a staff of 200 involved.[41] Members of the Project Working Group included Surgeon General Nieuwoudt and his deputy and successor, Dr. Niels Knobel. They were supposed to supervise Project Coast, but Knobel has claimed that they rarely visited the front companies for fear of compromising their cover. Basson and the scientific researchers decided on requirements and costs. Much of Basson's efforts focused on circumventing sanctions against the sale of military-related items to South Africa and into black-market activities. All procurement was undertaken by Basson and approved by Nieuwoudt and by his successor, Knobel, who has claimed that he and Nieuwoudt were told only after the fact about Basson's activities.

The procurement processes the SADF used during this period lacked civilian leadership and supervision. A Special Defence Account was established by the SADF for Project Coast that precluded access by the auditor-general.[42] Thus, although Wouter Basson was required to provide records of financial expenditures for Project Coast activities, there was no effort throughout this period to match these records with those of covert special operations.[43] The rationale of the need for secrecy for covert programs and Basson's unsupervised activities would lead Project Coast into a morass of corruption.

In August 1981, the SADF launched Operation Protea in Angola. Wouter Basson accompanied the SADF during the operation. In Angola, evidence was discovered that indicated that the Cubans might be preparing for chemical warfare.[44] Although the evidence was sketchy, top SADF generals chose to take action to counter chemical and biological warfare any-

Figure 1. SADF Project Coast Hierarchy

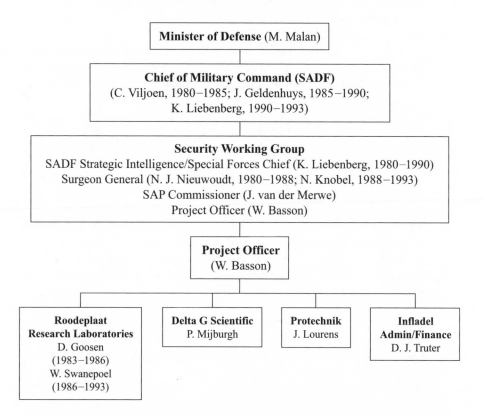

way. Defence Minister Malan took SADF generals to Angola to examine chemical and biological warfare protective suits and demonstrate the problems they created during combat. After the trip, Malan reiterated his proposal that the SADF take measures that would force the Cubans rather than the South Africans to don suits. Accordingly, the SADF developed a strategy of deception by firing smoke that would achieve such a result. In addition, Malan proposed that the chemical and biological warfare program be developed to counteract the ANC and its military wing, Umkhonto we Sizwe (MK), which was in the process of escalating a revolutionary war with more than 3,000 guerrilla forces. During this period, the SADF obtained evidence that some of the ANC/MK troops had been trained in the Soviet Union in chemical and biological warfare techniques.[45]

In 1982, the Delta G Scientific Company began work on chemical warfare agents for Project Coast. The chemicals that Delta G developed for testing were divided into lethal, incapacitating, and irritating agents. Roodeplaat Research Laboratories then tested the biological effects of the agents from Delta G. Roodeplaat was a front company that was primarily responsible for biological warfare. Another parastatal, Protechnik Company, manufactured and tested protective chemical and biological warfare equipment for the SADF.

In 1983, Roodeplaat Research Laboratories opened and began research on biological agents and the biological effects of chemical agents. Dr. Daan Goosen was the first head of Roodeplaat; he served until 1986. Dr. Goosen was one of several veterinarians recruited from the state-run agricultural institute, Ondestepoort, to work for Project Coast as senior managers and research scientists. Veterinarians were aggressively recruited to work for covert projects because they were extremely well trained. Most had advanced degrees in animal health and at least one other field such as microbiology or biochemistry. Many of the veterinarians had already studied and conducted research abroad.[46] Several of the recruited veterinarians initiated sophisticated but bizarre research projects. For example, Dr. Goosen supervised a project designed to implant sensors in rats' brains so that rats, instead of electronic sensors, could be used to find TNT mines. The project required a complicated operation and many rats died too soon to justify the surgical procedure. Moreover, the rats in the field tired quickly. Once this line of research was publicized in the local press in the early 1990s, protests by animal-rights advocates rather than feasibility concerns killed the project.[47]

Covert biochemical research conducted during apartheid was widely dispersed in the 1980s, which made efforts by the post-apartheid government to censor Project Coast scientists on ethical grounds difficult. Project Coast was not just one individual or the several groups working at Roodeplaat.[48] Instead, South Africa developed a sophisticated and dispersed network consisting of several different research and testing centers at universities and companies, and scientists in various parts of South Africa assisted Project Coast. Anthrax, cholera, botulinum, and a variety of pathogens were collected and/or developed at Roodeplaat and elsewhere for testing. Collecting and testing a range of biological agents was a principal objective of Project Coast. The defensive rationale was a need to develop protection from a biological warfare attack by the Soviets. In 1984, Dr. Schalk van Rensburg joined Roodeplaat and started the cholera research program. By the end of 1984, Project Coast and Roodeplaat had tested a range of biological warfare toxins; reportedly, they had acquired anthrax, plague, cholera, E. coli, staph, ricin, botulinum, gas gangrene, and anti-matter bacteria. They had also developed countermeasures to ricin and botulinum.[49]

Eventually, according to a number of sources in the United States and South Africa, Project Coast developed unique processes and procedures for producing biological agents that had never before been seen.[50] Project Coast managed to obtain the Soviet-developed flesh-eating bacteria necrotizing fasciitis as well as the antidote. In 1994, the South Africans surprised a visiting American delegation by revealing that they had the bacteria and then giving it to the United States.[51] However, claims by Basson and former surgeon general Knobel that South African espionage agents penetrated Russian programs during the 1980s remain to be proven. No evidence has emerged to support similar claims by Basson that he was able to penetrate Porton Down in the United Kingdom and Fort Detrick and other laboratories in the United States. During Basson's trial, the fact surfaced that he had married three times in order to get passports (in addition to his two legitimate marriages). He allegedly married three different women from Belgium, Bulgaria, and Russia to obtain passports to travel to and from those countries.[52]

From the start, Project Coast was not just a defensive program.[53] In the early 1980s, fears of a "black tidal wave" drove white scientists to try to develop a variety of means that could ensure the survival of white South Africa. Plans were devised to build a large-scale anthrax production facility at Roodeplaat. The anthrax could have been used either outside or inside South Africa, particularly where guerrillas were present. According to former Roodeplaat scientist Mike Odendaal, who testified in the Basson trial, those plans were nearly operationalized in 1985.[54]

Another important line of research at Project Coast focused on genetic engineering. A priority project worked on developing a "black bomb"; that is, bacteria or other biological agents that would kill or weaken Blacks but not whites. This approach appealed to apartheid strategists since it promised to wipe out or incapacitate an entire area where an insurrection was taking place.[55] Project Coast scientists asked Basson to obtain a peptide synthesizer outside South Africa that would assist in genetic engineering efforts.[56] Just how far South Africa's secret research programs may have progressed by the mid-1990s, when Project Coast was terminated, has been suggested by the fact that research and development involving ethnic-specific genes and proteins is one of South Africa's most promising lines of biological research today.[57]

Project Coast scientists also reportedly worked on controlling black fertility as part of efforts to limit black population growth. One approach involved research on birth control methods to reduce the black birth rate. This research is one of the many aspects of Project Coast research projects that may never be uncovered. Daan Goosen told Tom Mangold of the BBC that Project Coast supported a project to develop a contraceptive that would have been applied clandestinely to Blacks.[58] Goosen claimed that Dr. Knobel, who was SAMS deputy surgeon at the time, knew all about this project. The scientists were told that this was the most important research on which they would work. Goosen reported that the project had developed a vaccine for males and females and that when Project Coast was terminated the researchers were still searching for a means of delivery to make Blacks sterile without their knowledge.[59] Testimony given at the Truth and Reconciliation Commission suggested that Project Coast researchers were also looking into ways to put birth-control substances in water supplies.[60]

Because the HIV/AIDS pandemic grew exponentially in South Africa and throughout the region, many analysts and South African policymakers have wondered whether Project Coast research extended to using the HIV/AIDS virus. Dr. Goosen has been remarkably consistent in his statements on this topic. He has repeatedly acknowledged that while a vial of HIV/AIDS was found at a Roodeplaat facility, Project Coast scientists did not experiment with using HIV/AIDS as a biological weapon.[61] Some people, including some senior officials in the current South African government, do not believe these denials.[62]

Project Coast claimed its first victims at the end of 1982, when Operation Dual was launched in Namibia and Angola. The aim of this operation was to eliminate hundreds of SWAPO prisoners and SADF informants who were deemed dispensable.[63] Colonel Johan Theron, counterintelligence officer in the Special Forces, testified at the Basson trial that he received muscle relaxant pills from Basson in December 1982 and used them to kill approximately 200 SWAPO prisoners, then dumped their bodies from airplanes into the sea.[64]

The Soviet Union accused the SADF of using herbicides in both Namibia and Angola. There were also allegations that the SADF used napalm and phosphorous in Angola during the 1980s, which was a violation of the Geneva Protocol. Basson was allegedly involved in the use of chemical and biological warfare against regime opponents in Dukuduku in KwaZulu-Natal in 1983. He is also alleged to have supplied the poisoned tea and oranges that killed Special Forces member Lance Corporal Victor de Fonseca in a military hospital in Pretoria. Fonseca was said to have started talking about clandestine operations after developing brain cancer. These acts were part of the sixteen murder charges introduced on March 26, 1999, prior to the October 1999 opening of Basson's trial in South Africa.[65]

The mass-action campaigns that spread throughout the country in 1984 were far more widespread, violent, and deadly than those in 1960 or after 1976. The nationwide scope of these protests intensified concerns about crowd control and fueled ongoing efforts to develop weapons, including chemical and biological agents, to deal with the unrest. SADF Chief of Staff General Constand Viljoen, as well as Generals Liebenberg and Meiring, were seeking an offensive chemical and biological warfare substance that would weaken rioters and be more effective than existing teargas, and they consulted Basson and Project Coast. The SADF also sought a chemical that would color the skin for about two weeks and allow them to identify frontrunners in the violence.[66] In response to General Viljoen, Delta G Scientific developed a New Generation Teargas (CR gas). Subsequently, the New Generation Teargas was designed to be more powerful than conventional teargas (CS gas) and to incapacitate without causing death or excessive irritation.[67] CR gas was intended to counteract rolling mass actions led by the ANC or its surrogates. It was used rarely and only on the orders of the chief of the army. When CR gas was used, it was usually mixed with CS gas and dissolved in water to be used by water cannons.

After a state of emergency was declared in South Africa in June 1985, the government's perceived need for crowd-control agents intensified. One proposal was for a "third force" that would combine the military functions of the SADF and the police role of the SAP in suppressing unrest.[68] Another proposal was to use nonlethal chemical weapons, particularly in the form of the new teargas that Project Coast had developed. General Liebenberg revealed that chemical agents were being developed to make people passive and to render weapons unusable. General Lothar Neethling, SAP forensics commander, ordered the development of teargas, gas grenades, and tranquilizing drugs for use in pacifying rioters. Neethling was also an expert in the use of chemical and biological warfare for assassination and worked closely with Basson, who supplied poisons to get rid of individuals.[69]

By 1986, the state of emergency had led to massive waves of arrests and detentions in South Africa. In response, the ANC/MK vowed to "make the streets ungovernable." The SADF proceeded with efforts to develop and apply chemical and biological warfare agents to counteract the "black onslaught." The township unrest of 1984–1986 produced antipathy between military and civilian departments. In essence, the State Security Council, the SADF, and the SAP took over the state. Civilian departments were subordinated to the State Security Council. Even the education departments began to take orders from the State Security Council. At this time, the security forces perpetuated the doctrine of "plausible denial." Security forces carried on activities in secret, which allowed civilians to deny knowledge.[70]

In 1986, the Civil Cooperation Bureau (CCB) was created; it drew on the "dirty tricks" experiences of former Rhodesian Selous Scouts and D-40, an infamous military intelligence unit of the SADF. The Civil Cooperation Bureau became one of the cornerstones of a third force that was dedicated to preventing the ANC/MK from taking power. There was consensus in the Botha government that unconventional methods were needed, according to Malan's testimony before the Truth and Reconciliation Commission, and that Malan personally approved the establishment of the Civil Cooperation Bureau but never gave it instructions to have anyone killed. Malan denied the existence of a third force and refused to apply for amnesty from the Truth and Reconciliation Commission because that would have required him to provide full testimony of his activities. However, he said he would apply to the ANC leadership for "collective responsibility" for acts committed during the violence that started in 1960.[71]

By 1987, the uprisings in South Africa had largely come to an end. At the same time, ANC/MK guerrillas stepped up their armed campaign, which came to include the bombing of civilian targets. The Botha government intensified efforts to eliminate the guerrilla threat, even as negotiations between the apartheid regime and Mandela continued. In 1988, in response to ANC/MK military and political actions and other perceived threats, the Civil Cooperation Bureau started operations. Basson worked with the bureau, had offices in the same building, and supplied them with chemical and biological warfare poisons for assassination purposes. The 1992 Steyn Report found that Basson and the Civil Cooperation Bureau were receiving instructions from Malan and other superiors. However, Basson and the bureau interpreted the instructions as they saw fit.[72]

PLANS FOR A CHEMICAL
AND BIOLOGICAL WEAPONS
OF MASS DESTRUCTION PROGRAM

By 1985, several Project Coast program directors were planning for a massive escalation of the chemical and biological warfare program and working on plans that would have resulted in a program that was even more sophisticated. Roodeplaat scientist Mike Odendaal reported that he received instructions that year to start a factory where biological agents would be produced in mass form and that 200,000 rand ($100,000) had already been spent on the plans.[73] A new wing was added to Roodeplaat for a production-scale laboratory with fermenters that could produce 300 liters and upward of anthrax and other biological agents and a Bio-Safety Lab (BSL) level-4 laboratory. For the first few years, Project Coast used BSL-2 and BSL-3 facilities and two ten-gallon fermenters for growth medium. The BSL-4 facility was added in 1985, when the new wing for Roodeplaat was built.[74] Basson and his superiors in the SADF (Generals Liebenberg, Nieuwoudt, and Viljoen and Magnus Malan) approved the upgrade. According to Roodeplaat scientist Schalk van Rensburg, when Basson wanted the safety level raised to BSL-4, two British scientists on an unauthorized visit from Porton Down (which had been privatized) helped and advised.[75]

In the end, the directors of Project Coast decided not to fund the larger fermenters. According to Odendaal, SADF decided that biological agents would be used in low-intensity regional skirmishes and assassinations but not on a more massive scale.[76] In comparison to the Soviet Union, which had scores of big fermenters, the South African program was quite small in size and scale. However, South African scientists developed several novel processes and procedures and examined a wide variety of pathogens under the auspices of Project Coast research. These aspects of Project Coast may be why several American and South African experts with first-hand knowledge of South Africa's chemical and biological warfare program have described it as the "second most sophisticated program" in terms of the range of biological agents possessed and the science involved; only the Soviets had a better program. Some of these experts emphasized that the South African program was more sophisticated than the Iraqi program that was uncovered in 1995.[77]

Weaponization began in cooperation with ARMSCOR. Several projects were sponsored by different divisions of ARMSCOR, including Kentron Missile and Space Division. Development of the capability to carry chemical and biological agents was a key priority of this line of research.[78] All of these research and development projects were top-secret. Senior Americans and British officials did not become aware of the full extent of South Africa's weaponization efforts until 1994. According to U.S. diplomats, the U.S. and British governments did not insist that weaponization be included in the chemical and biological memorandum because they had no hard evidence with which to make such a demand.[79] The South African Ministry of Defence still denies that weaponization took place.

There are unconfirmed reports that the former South African government tested battlefield weapons capable of carrying biological and chemical agents. It appears that Basson, much like his counterparts in other countries (for example, Iraq), had trouble developing effective delivery systems for biological agents as weapons of mass destruction. Although Project Coast researchers undertook conceptual studies in the aerosolization of biological agents, the evidence available to date indicates that sophisticated delivery systems of aerosolized agents were not developed. However, conceptual studies of such systems were well under way when Project Coast was shut down. Much more progress appears to have been achieved in developing sophisticated artillery warheads and tactical missiles that were capable of delivering nuclear, biological, and chemical warheads. What types of missiles and warheads were built, possibly tested, and sold abroad remains among the most important and yet-unanswered questions related to South Africa's nuclear, biological, and chemical programs.

PROJECT COAST'S
INTERNATIONAL LINKS

Even before the formal biological and chemical warfare program was established, South African covert biological and chemical research and development activities benefited from collaboration with several states.[80] Details of many of these national collaborations remain classified. What is clear from the historical record is that in the early years of the project, Project Coast research relied heavily on open sources of research, cooperative exchanges with foreign governments' officials and scientists at professional conferences, and the purchase of chemical agents that were legal and largely uncontrolled substances. As sanctions against South Africa increased in the 1980s, Basson used procurement specialists paid by ARMSCOR and built his own international network of procurement agents. Basson's network included South African and foreign operatives, an American accountant, and medical researchers and other individuals in the

United States and Europe. It enabled Basson to allegedly move millions of rand offshore and to fund a wide range of illegal activities, including the manufacture of large amounts of Mandrex and Ecstasy. The extent to which some of these illegal activities were unauthorized activities for personal gain or run as government-sanctioned covert operations was a central issue at Basson's criminal trial. Most of the questions remained unanswered because Basson was acquitted of all charges.[81]

What is known is that from 1981 onward, Basson and Project Coast scientists intensified their international contacts, particularly at conferences on chemical and biological warfare. South African delegations made visits to the United States, Britain, Taiwan, Israel, and Germany. From 1981 to 1986, Reagan administration officials, under the administration's policy of "constructive engagement," sent signals to the Botha regime that the United States was willing to turn a blind eye to American industries and scientists who helped the South Africans build up their defense industries. Under Secretary of State William Clark went one step farther and welcomed South African defense officials and experts to Washington and facilitated their interaction with U.S. counterparts. Basson attended a conference on biological warfare in San Antonio, Texas, in 1981; reportedly, this trip attracted the attention of American intelligence, which recommended that he be barred from entry to the United States for scientific purposes.[82]

According to the BBC's Tom Mangold, MI6 opened a file on Basson after he attended the Second World Conference of Toxicologists in Ghent, Belgium, where he reportedly met with scientists, including some from Porton Down.[83] Both American and British intelligence agencies monitored Basson's activities during this time but did little to stop his activities. However, there is no evidence to corroborate Basson's claims that he ever visited Porton Down.[84]

In 1984, the U.S. Centers for Disease Control sent eight shipments of the Ebola, Marburg, and Rift Valley viruses to South Africa. These specimens were part of a wider cooperative relationship between South Africa and United States researchers involved in identifying existing and emerging infectious diseases. In 1977, U.S. missionaries in a remote region of Zaire (the Democratic Republic of the Congo after 1997) fell ill with an infectious disease that researchers feared was Ebola. Officials of the U.S. and South African government cooperated in the evaluation of these and other American citizens who fell ill with serious infectious diseases in remote parts of Africa. A cooperative relationship between the two countries on medical issues continued throughout the latter half of the 1980s.[85] One unintended consequence of the close cooperation among health officials in the two countries may have been that South African researchers got specimens of viruses they did not have, which could have been used with devastating effect in surrounding countries.[86]

Details of the extent and importance of South African cooperation with Israel in chemical and biological warfare research have not been dis-

closed. As detailed in Chapter 3, the two countries started working together on covert research related to nuclear weapons after World War II.
These links had developed into a mature working relationship by the
1970s. Bilateral cooperation between the two states proved especially
fruitful in developing nuclear weapons and testing a number of increasingly sophisticated missiles. Israel and South Africa also cooperated closely in the production of the G5 artillery gun to fight a conventional war.[87]
This line of research, which cost millions of rand, may also have explored
the feasibility of using nuclear, biological, and chemical warheads for the
G5 gun and later the G6 gun. The Israelis also helped South Africa with
armored cars and tanks and the Atlas Cheetah aircraft (a Mirage off-
shoot).

Given the breadth and depth of cooperation, it is quite possible that Israel and South Africa cooperated on chemical and biological warfare efforts. It is significant that Basson went to Israel several times during the
1980s.[88] However, the direction of covert technical exchanges between
South Africa and Israeli involving ethnic-based biological research and development has not been established. As concern mounted about the likelihood that Saddam Hussein was preparing Scud missiles with biological
warheads in 1998, a special report in the respected *Jane's Defense Weekly,*
based on unnamed South African sources, claimed that Israeli scientists
had used South African research on differences in the genetic makeup of
different ethnic groups to construct an "ethnic bullet" against Arabs at
Nes Tziyona, the main research facility for Israel's clandestine arsenal of
chemical and biological weapons.[89]

Throughout the 1980s, Basson continued his visits abroad and interaction with experts from the United States, Britain, and other countries.
Most of these contacts were legal ones between Project Coast scientists
and other scientists and consultants in Europe. Most of the substances
and knowledge relevant to biological and chemical weapons were not
controlled in the 1970s and 1980s, because a high level of concern about
the possible use of biological and chemical agents did not emerge until the
1990s.[90] However, Basson and Knobel subsequently claimed that Basson
visited Iran, Iraq, the Philippines, North Korea, and Croatia and met with
members of Colombian drug cartels to make contacts and collect information.[91] The content of what was obtained or exchanged during these
visits has not yet emerged.

THE STRANGE CASE OF
DR. LARRY CREED FORD

New details about the apartheid government's international connections
and interest in use of birth-control methods and other sophisticated biological warfare methods surfaced in early 2000, after Pat Riley, one of the
owners of a southern California biotech firm called Biofem, was shot in

what appeared to be a contract hit by his partner, Dr. Larry Ford. (Riley survived.) The local police in Irvine had already questioned Dr. Ford about his partner's shooting and were on their way to arrest him for the attempted murder of his partner when Ford shot himself. Immediately after Ford's suicide, the police received a tip from an acquaintance of Ford, warning that he had kept dangerous biological pathogens and an arms cache at his house and at other locations. When the Irvine Police searched Ford's house, they found documents in his house that led them to dig up his backyard. The police removed automatic rifles from a concrete bunker and found tubes of cholera and typhoid fever germs in a freezer in the Ford house.[92]

As soon as biological pathogens were found at Ford's house, the FBI became the lead agency because the case became a weapons of mass destruction investigation, but local authorities remained involved because the attempted murder had occurred in their jurisdiction. Both the local authorities and the FBI investigated claims that Ford had made to several friends and associates that he served as a consultant to the SADF and had close ties with the CIA. Former South African surgeon general Dr. Niels Knobel initially stated that he met Ford at a conference in San Diego, California, in the late 1980s and that they had remained friends ever since. Knobel explained that they shared an interest in HIV/AIDS because they both knew that the epidemic would have a devastating impact in Africa. Later, Knobel acknowledged that he met with Ford and his associates during one of their many visits to the South African trade representative, who was part of the South African Consulate in Los Angeles.[93] In a phone interview, Knobel stated, "Our whole policy of protecting members of the defense force against HIV [educating them to use condoms] came from my relationship with Larry. We both worked toward a cure for AIDS that would be available to the vast population of Africa, [and] there was no political agenda."[94]

At the time of his suicide, Ford was working on several projects. One product was a "microbicide" form of birth control that he had patented in 1997. Ford claimed that his product, which he called Inner Confidence, could prevent millions of people from acquiring sexually transmitted diseases but not necessarily AIDS. His microbicide contraceptive was a vaginal suppository that contained chemicals that kill germs transmitted through sex as well as sperm. The potential advantages of this type of contraceptive was that women could control it, it would protect the user from acquiring the most common sexually transmitted diseases, and it might help reduce the user's chances of acquiring AIDS. However, there was little interest in this approach to birth control until the late 1990s because several technical problems remained unsolved. The results of several small-scale trials and one large-scale publicized study of another microbicide found that the chemicals in it damaged the lining of the vagina, making the user more, rather than less, susceptible to HIV infection.[95]

The results of early microbicide studies raise intriguing questions about Dr. Ford's motives in arranging field tests to assay Inner Confidence in South Africa during the 1980s. According to Dr. Otto Muller, Dr. Knobel brought Ford to the University of the Free State in South Africa and introduced him as an American researcher who was interested in testing the effectiveness of Inner Confidence as a contraceptive and a protection against certain sexual diseases but not HIV/AIDS. Ford initiated and pursued the official process for gaining approval for a field study in South Africa. Three of Ford's protocols were submitted and approved by the Bioethics Committee of the principal body in charge of regulating the use of human subjects, the Medical Control Council. Ford also pursued his initial contracts with Dr. Muller and his associates and signed a contract for a series of field trials. However, these studies were never started, and Dr. Muller and his associates never received any payment for their services from Ford.[96]

It is not clear what else Ford did during his numerous trips to South Africa. According to microbiologist Mike Odendaal, a senior researcher at Roodeplaat, Ford visited South Africa again in 1987 to teach scientists working with an SADF front company how to turn teabags, doilies, and pornographic magazines into "weapons" that could be used against the ANC using a species of clostridium bacteria. Odendaal reported that the scientists found much of Ford's advice confusing, and some went so far as to call him a fraud.[97]

A far different picture of Dr. Ford emerges from accounts about two other lines of research he pursued with South African colleagues. Apparently Ford was working on a biotin analogue to prevent keloid formation in an obsessive attempt to develop a hair tonic for baldness with South African chemist Johan Kohemeyer, although Ford's business partner claims he had no knowledge that he was involved in such a project. Suspicions that the hair-tonic research might be a cover for a covert biowarfare research led investigators working for the prosecution in Basson's criminal trial and several teams of investigative journalists to research Kohemeyer's involvement with Ford. However, few new details about this line of research have emerged. Instead, professional associates of Dr. Kohemeyer claimed that he was innocent and was only conducting biotin analysis for Dr. Ford.[98] Many intriguing questions have been raised about the possibility that this line of research may have been part of a larger effort to develop targeted biological weapons to be used against black South Africans. To date, more questions than answers have been generated.[99]

Another line of research Ford had worked on since the 1970s involved women's amniotic fluid. He continued to pursue this line of research after establishing Biofem. At the time of his death in 2000, he had developed a formula for a commercial product that was developed from an unidentified substance found in amniotic fluid, which he called Unidentified Amniotic Substance, or UFAS. Ford frequently described this substance as having the potential to be as revolutionary a new drug as penicillin. To his closest friends and family, Ford had confided that he hoped that the synthesized substance, UFAS, would be a superantibiotic that would "save lives, and win [him] the Nobel Prize."[100]

Ford was looking for amniotic fluid when he traveled to South Africa several years earlier than Dr. Knobel initially acknowledged. Numerous associates of Ford claim that he, Pat Riley, and others frequently traveled to South Africa during the early 1980s and possibly in the 1970s as guests of senior South African officials.[101] Dr. Scharf, the former head of Military Hospital One in Pretoria, remembered Ford visiting the hospital in the mid-1980s as a guest of his deputy surgeon general, Dr. Knobel. One reason Scharf remembers the visit so well is that he claims that Knobel insisted that Ford be given VIP treatment (at the hospital's expense). Scharf was also extremely offended by Ford's request for human placentas. He refused to cooperate and claimed that he threw Ford out of his office after warning him that such activities would be very controversial if they became public because all Africans view babies as sacred.[102] Apparently, Ford and Riley recognized that Scharf's reaction would be a common one, because they did not tell prospective investors where they were getting the amniotic fluid used to manufacture pre-patent amounts of UFAS.[103]

Dr. Ford was undeterred by Scharf's rebuff and continued pursuing other avenues in his quest to obtain large amounts of amniotic fluid in South Africa. Ford continued working with Dr. Knobel and other longtime South African government officials even after the 1994 transition. Records found in Dr. Ford's possession at the time of his death indicate that with the help of a few officials in the newly formed South African National Defence Force (SANDF), Ford collected large amounts of amniotic fluid at medical facilities and spring clinics run by the South African Medical Services.[104] The collection project continued at least through mid-1995. Collection ceased after a large amount of fluid had been collected and freeze-dried.[105]

Few details have ever been published about this project and it is not known what methods were used to collect this vast amount of amniotic fluid or how many patients suffered adverse effects (for example, spontaneous abortions). When asked about this project, Dr. Knobel said that the program had the approval of senior officials in the post-1994 SANDF. Knobel also stressed that all ethical norms and practices were followed and that all patients involved in this collection project had given their informed consent.[106] Although these claims could not be confirmed by other sources, both Dr. Knobel and Dr. Basson have acknowledged that they were involved in arranging payments to Dr. Ford for AIDS research through Project Coast's Swiss bank account and that they tried to help him find a South African laboratory for AIDS research. Ford's persistence seems to have paid off. As Jo Thomas reported in November 2002, Ford was eventually given laboratory space in an aerospace medicine facility "to work on several projects using amniotic fluid collected from thousands of women in South African military hospitals."[107]

Most of the important questions about the amniotic fluid collection project remain unanswered. For example, it is not known whether there is any truth to allegations that the cooperation of former South African military officials in collecting amniotic fluid at South African military hospitals and clinics was part of a quid pro quo for Dr. Ford's cooperation on biowarfare projects. It is also not known whether Dr. Ford was working as a lone rogue American scientist or as part of a covert intergovernmental program between South Africa and the U.S. government. A third possibility is that this collection project was hatched and implemented by a relatively small number of like-minded individuals who sought, before they left public service, to take advantage of their positions to harvest the resources needed to jump-start a future commercial enterprise. A final, deeply disturbing possibility is that this collection effort was part of a longer-term secret plot by transnational right-wing supremacists that may include individuals within the former apartheid South African government who believe that some day whites will return to rule in South Africa. A fundamentally new type of biological warfare that significantly reduced the size of the black population and wrought havoc in post-apartheid South Africa would be one way to hasten that day.

Police who investigated the Ford case have been unable to explain the nature of his relationship with several South Africans and Europeans or corroborate many of the claims Ford made before his death. For example, he claimed that he parachuted into Southern Africa during the apartheid era to take blood samples from dead guerrilla fighters in order to help the U.S. government determine which biological warfare agents the Soviets were vaccinating their allies against.[108]

Another longtime Ford associate, Dr. Jerry D. Nilsson, was investigated by the Irvine police. Nilsson claimed that he and Ford traveled to Africa together. In 1988, Nilsson organized a group of doctors, including Ford, to buy a defunct Los Angeles hospital. The plan was to turn it into a state-of-the-art infectious-disease research center, the Lake View Terrace Institute. Nilsson told a reporter that the facility was to be "one cog in a complex, far-reaching project" with related facilities in Africa, Germany, Italy, and Britain. The clinic never opened because of financial problems. Several potential backers withdrew after well-established research groups denied that they were backing the venture.[109] The nature of Nilsson's relationship with Ford remains unclear. Police seized considerable material when they raided Nilsson's house and storage lockers but did not release details of the searches. Nilsson's friends claimed that he and Ford stashed chemicals and germs at several locations in southern California. Police acknowledged that the evidence strongly suggested that Dr. Ford was deeply involved in a conspiracy and that he would be in custody today were he alive. Another longtime associate of Ford claimed that only about 1 percent of the story of Ford's activities in Africa has been disclosed.[110]

In July 2000, a closed grand jury in Orange County, California, heard evidence to determine the facts in the Ford case. Press accounts of evidence compiled by local police suggest that Ford had long-standing links to the former South African government and was a member of a larger network that included former South African officials and like-minded individuals in the United States and Europe. Ford claimed to have served as a consultant to the South African government, lecturing scientists on biological topics relevant for making biological weapons. If true, his actions would have constituted a violation of U.S. laws, which prevented such contacts during the apartheid era.[111] The FBI coordinated an international investigation to determine whether any crimes under U.S. law had occurred in South Africa.

The results of the closed grand jury investigation of the Ford case have not been made public, but the discovery of biological agents and toxins in Ford's possession renewed questions about whether Basson called upon former associates to conceal biological agents, poisons, and drugs overseas. Testimony at the Basson trial failed to explain where tons of drugs and smaller quantities of deadly toxins went (whose production Basson oversaw before his retirement from the military in 1993) and why so many drugs were produced in the first place. One of the prosecutors in the Basson case has acknowledged that the prosecution did not have a very clear idea about either the purpose of the drugs or their final destination.[112]

When Basson was arrested in January 1997, investigators found several trunks in his possession that contained documents and items related to Project Coast. The investigators also found a great deal of personal correspondence between Basson and individuals in Switzerland, the United Kingdom, and other countries in the trunks and among Basson's personal effects. One letter was from an individual in the United Kingdom who lived near Heathrow Airport. This letter described what Basson should do if he needed to leave South Africa quickly. The letter said he should contact them when he arrived at Heathrow and that "we will collect you." Other letters from individuals in other countries described similar emergency-exit plans.[113]

The identity of this letter writer and others was not known by the investigators representing the Truth and Reconciliation Commission, the South African president's office, or the National Intelligence Agency, who were all present in January 1997 when the trunks were found. The contents of the trunks were itemized and the National Intelligence Agency took control of them for security reasons. The chief investigator for the Truth and Reconciliation Commission at the time, Dr. Villa-Vicencia, never learned whether these letters were from private individuals or representatives of governments.[114]

The documents are interesting, given statements made by Juergen Jacomet, a former Swiss military intelligence agent who worked with Basson on money-laundering for Project Coast in Europe. He spoke of a right-wing conspiracy and alluded to the existence of an organization of individuals, including Americans.[115] The death of Dr. Ford, the revelations of his South African involvement, and the failed effort to establish the Lake View Terrace Institute raised again the possibility of a right-wing international network united by a vision of a South Africa once again ruled by whites.[116]

No evidence to date has been found to substantiate concerns expressed by some about possible linkages between Project Coast programs and the intentional use of HIV or microbicide contraceptives.[117] However, the revelations since Ford's death are consistent with reports that the former South African government was already concerned about the future impact of the AIDS epidemic by the mid-1980s. The many unanswered questions about past activities sponsored under the auspices of Project Coast may help to explain why current senior officials in South Africa, including President Thabo Mbeki, expressed so many doubts about the causes of the HIV/AIDS pandemic.[118]

The secret right-wing Afrikaner organization, the Broederbond, also acknowledged during the Truth and Reconciliation hearings that they had become concerned about the future size of the black population based on projections they started making in the late 1960s. In order to prevent white areas from being overrun by Blacks, the Broederbond began exploring various ways to reduce the size of the black population in urban areas in the 1960s. The apartheid government plan for independent homelands for different ethnic groups was one effort to manage the problem. By forcing Blacks and Coloureds to marginal areas of the country and then declaring these areas to be independent homelands, the government hoped to reduce the size of the black population in urban areas. Another plan allegedly involved recruiting poor white American miners from West Virginia and other poor areas of America to live and work in South Africa in order to get the Blacks out of the mines. This project was one of several managed by the South African trade consulate in the United States during the 1980s.[119]

By the mid-1980s, the Broederbond's population projections indicated that whites would be in the majority in the future because of the devastating effects of HIV/AIDS. Their projections indicated that AIDS would devastate the black population of South Africa by 2000.[120] Despite the lack of evidence linking Project Coast research with the intentional use of AIDS, allegations that certain individuals in the former South African government used the HIV/AIDS virus as a biological weapon are likely to be raised in the future as the HIV/AIDS epidemic peaks in South Africa. For example, one researcher at the XIII International AIDS Conference in Durban in July 2000 suggested in a paper that projections of huge losses in the black population through AIDS was the real reason why de Klerk had started the transition process. This analysis is based on the assumption that de Klerk, like many other white conservatives, believed that whites had no other alternative but to give up power in South Africa for economic and political reasons in the 1990s but that whites would live to see the day when they would return to power due to the havoc caused by HIV/AIDS and the chaotic conditions and instability resulting from mis-rule by black politicians.[121]

CORRUPTION AND THE
DETERIORATION OF PROJECT COAST

Allegedly, Basson took advantage of loose financial oversight and account-ability requirements to ensure that he acquired large sums of money from the project several years before the actual decisions were made to privatize the state-owned corporations of Project Coast. Starting in the mid-1980s, if not before, Basson was reported to have offered his friends and trusted employees the opportunity to invest in a number of these official front corporations. Basson and other early investors made overnight fortunes when these corporations were privatized.[122] The magnitude of these prof-its, perhaps more than any other action, caught the attention of a nonmil-itary agency, the Office of Serious Economic Offences (OSEO), which started investigating the financial flows associated with Project Coast soon after the shares of these corporations were sold on the open market.

Basson was the central figure who coordinated the funds and the cen-tral point of contact between the scientists, the SADF, and the government. As the project expanded into sophisticated research into genetic engineer-ing and the manufacture of large amounts of Mandrax and Ecstasy (which may have been sold on the black market), millions of dollars were siphoned off into a series of elaborate holding companies. Basson main-tained that state-owned companies produced large amounts of Mandrax and Ecstasy as authorized products intended for use in crowd control. Few observers, including the prosecution in his trial, believed this story.[123] In-stead, a mystery remains about why so many drugs were produced and where they went. However, some South Africans point to the fact that Mandrax and Ecstasy started flooding into the Cape flats and other town-ships about the same time that millions of these drugs were produced un-der the auspices of Project Coast.[124]

As Basson and his closest associates allegedly skimmed millions of rand and dollars from Project Coast activities, he and his American accountant, David Webster, developed an elaborate web of foreign shell companies to launder the money. Several offshore holding companies, such as WPW In-vestments, which was incorporated in Cayman Island in 1986, sold initial share offers at low prices (for example, US$4 per share) to Basson. In this company, as in numerous others, David Webster was the director while

Basson maintained indirect control as a member of the board. Toward the end of Project Coast, new companies were being incorporated and large amounts of assets were being transferred from existing companies to the new ones over a 24- or 48-hour period.[125] The investigation of South African forensic auditor Hendrik Bruwer took nearly seven years to complete. After traveling to the United States, Britain, Belgium, Switzerland, Croatia, and Luxembourg, Bruwer produced an 800-page report that highlighted serious illegalities in the SADF and former government.

Obtaining permission from foreign governments delayed the investigation, as did ongoing investigations by other national and provincial bodies (e.g., the Transvaal Auditor General's office). David Webster, who had acted as a nominee for Basson, at first refused to hand over papers in his possession to South African investigators. He was eventually forced to do so by an American court. The international and transnational character of this case was highlighted by the fact that the Basson trial took the unusual step of holding sessions of the trial in Jacksonville, Florida, during the fall of 2000 in order to establish the exact nature and extent of David Webster's involvement in the case. The complexity of these dealings were such that prosecutors in Basson's trial expected it would take over two years to present evidence to support fraud charges against Basson.

Project Coast ground to a halt in 1988, allegedly because of corruption by Basson and others. According to interviews with Project Coast scientists, between 1982 and 1987 Project Coast was advancing as a sophisticated program.[126] Project Coast had anthrax, cholera, botulinum, and other biological agents; was planning to add a wing to Roodeplaat to produce massive amounts of anthrax; and was proceeding with genetic-engineering research to produce germs that would harm Blacks and not whites. However, as the communist threat receded in 1987–1988 and as it seemed possible that the apartheid regime's days were numbered, Basson and others allegedly took large amounts of money intended for Project Coast programs and diverted it to their own accounts. Elsewhere in South Africa, top government officials were allegedly taking funds on a large scale. As the biological warfare program stopped, Basson and others began to plan how to roll back Project Coast in a way that would be advantageous to them. By 1988, President P. W. Botha, Defence Secretary Magnus Malan, and Wim de Villiers of ARMSCOR had initiated the privatization and liberalization of the defense industry. They envisaged a transfer of power to Mandela and the ANC and saw the need to keep the defense industry out of their hands.[127] The privatization process opened the door to the type of corruption allegedly exhibited by Basson and his colleagues.

In 1988, Basson was supposed to have bought a sophisticated peptide synthesizer for US$2.2 million from clandestine sources. Project Coast researchers were attempting to make significant advances in the field of peptides to alter brain function, which was a key to creating a biological weapon that would affect Blacks and not whites. However, at Basson's trial, Dr. Lucia Steenkamp, a Project Coast researcher, refuted claims that Basson had bought the peptide synthesizer, and the prosecution alleged that Basson had defrauded SADF by pretending he needed the synthesizer but actually used the money for overseas business deals.[128]

In August 1988, Delta G scientists arranged for 1,000 kilograms of methaqualone (a muscle relaxant and tranquilizer) to be produced. The production manager at Delta G approached Dr. Philip Mijburgh, managing director of Medchem Consolidated Investments, and asked him to produce the methaqualone. What happened to the methaqualone and whether or not it was encapsulated remains unknown. The explanation given by witnesses at the Truth and Reconciliation Commission hearings in 1998 was that the methaqualone was to be mixed into CR gas and used for crowd-control purposes. General Lothar Neethling testified that on three occasions Project Coast officials had asked him to provide Dr. Basson with Mandrax tablets confiscated by the South African Narcotics Bureau. He claimed that he gave Dr. Basson approximately 200,000 tablets in total as well as quantities of LSD and dagga (marijuana) on the understanding that they would be investigated to determine whether they would be appropriate crowd-control weapons.[129]

None of the witnesses could provide the Truth and Reconciliation Commission with any information about tests that had been conducted in this regard, and at least one witness stated that these drugs would not be suitable for such a purpose.[130] Medchem's role is noteworthy given the fact that Defence Minister Malan's nephew, Dr. Mijburgh, was on the board. Allegedly, Mijburgh benefited from privatization of both Medchem and Delta G Scientific in the early 1990s.

In 1988, Dr. Knobel became surgeon general after Dr. Nieuwoudt died. Basson briefed Knobel, claiming that he had penetrated facilities in the Soviet Union, Libya, the United States, and Britain (Porton Down), as well as Belgium, France, Switzerland, Germany, and Israel. Knobel still believes Basson's claims. However, in retrospect, Knobel found that Basson's activities were not sufficiently monitored and that supervising by committee was a mistake.[131] Throughout the 1980s, Project Coast was only loosely managed, which left it susceptible to mismanagement and corruption. SADF Chief of Staff Jannie Geldenhuys attended the steering committee for Project Coast on one or two occasions from 1985 to 1990. Usually Geldenhuys was represented by the surgeon general. The problem was that a committee could not control Basson.

According to Geldenhuys, General Kat Liebenberg was convinced that the Project Coast steering committee (of which he was a member) was supplanted by the Small Command Council, especially regarding financial reviews and working with Basson. The Small Command Council was controlled by Malan and dealt with secret projects on a need-to-know basis.

In contrast to his statements to the Truth and Reconciliation Commission about Project Coast, Geldenhuys claimed in 2000 that as SADF chief of staff, he monitored finances and that his chief of finance was good. He claimed that there was not disproportional spending on Project Coast and that secret funds were audited. Geldenhuys pointed out that in the 1980s, South Africa was the "skunk" of the world. This led to an "unconventional arms trade" and to the use of middlemen and secret funds. However, the Office of Serious Economic Offences objected to secret funds as well as "safe houses," clandestine front companies, and clandestine flights.[132] (Project Coast was kept secret from civilians in government but the SADF conducted internal audits.)

The profile of South Africa that emerges is one of a state that initially developed a chemical and biological warfare program in response to isolation from its former Western partners. South Africa faced hostile regimes and movements in neighboring states aided by the Soviet Union, which had a formidable chemical and biological warfare program. Over time the Afrikaner-led regime also felt threatened by the majority of the country's black and Coloured citizens, who refused to accept harsh minority rule. For many of the scientists involved in Project Coast, the existence of adequate funds, sophisticated laboratory facilities, and a sense of pride in the quality and importance of their work served as an impetus for sophisticated research. (Scientists were fed the line that their work was entirely for "defense" in the war against communists at home and abroad.)

The apartheid regime responded to its perceptions of external and internal threats by developing a new chemical and biological warfare program and accelerating the nuclear-weapons program. The decision-making process, which was secretive and controlled by the military, enabled a very sophisticated program to be developed with little outside scrutiny. This was unlike the nuclear-bomb program, which was tightly managed; its program managers reported regularly to an interagency committee. In contrast, Project Coast was loosely run by the military health service and left a great deal of latitude to the program manager, Dr. Wouter Basson.

Military and police units used chemical and biological agents for counterinsurgency warfare, assassination, and the execution of war prisoners. As the regime felt more and more threatened by opposition at home, top political leaders approved plans for research and development of exotic ways to neutralize opponents, large-scale offensive uses of the program, and weaponization. However, the plans were not operationalized.

The information that has emerged to date about Project Coast suggests that a country that possesses chemical and biological weapons is likely to use them against adversaries at home and abroad. The unpredictable and harsh environment of Southern Africa did not deter conventional or counterinsurgency units from experimenting with these weapons. In both the Angolan and Rhodesian conflicts, conventional arms remained the primary instruments of combatants. However, the rumors that chemicals had been used to poison wells and the potential threat of a biological or chemical warfare attack frequently slowed down operations on the ground and made them more costly. The South African case illustrates the importance of understanding how top political leaders perceive threats. The perceptions and beliefs of senior policymakers about the country's secret biochemical program were crucial factors in determining whether they would undertake costly covert programs that produced weapons of mass destruction.

The South African case also dramatically shows how thin the line is between defensive and offensive weapons. First the Iraqi and now the South African case suggest that it is prudent to assume that if a country is suspected of developing covert nuclear capabilities, it is probably supporting research into the offensive uses of chemical and biological weapons as well.

Finally, the South African chemical and biological warfare programs underscore the importance of transparency, accountability, and control by civilians. Some aspects of the apartheid regime's management of their chemical and biological warfare programs may be unique. However, this case vividly illustrates what will happen when there is loose accountability for covert nuclear, biological, and chemical research and development by senior military and political leaders.

SIX

Dismantling the
Nuclear-Weapons Program

The only difference between the rocket that
launched John Glenn into orbit and those the
U.S. used to threaten nuclear destruction against
the Soviet Union was "attitude": One flew directly
into space, the other did so only to reenter the
atmosphere to hit a specific military target.

—Henry Sokolski, paraphrasing a
statement by John F. Kennedy[1]

By 1989, a confluence of factors made the nuclear program less attractive to senior National Party politicians, top national-security officials, and senior military officials. Among military leaders, particularly among the highest echelons of the South African Air Force, there were growing concerns that the projected costs of nuclear-related programs nearing completion would crowd out plans to upgrade key conventional systems such as fighter-bombers. Top National Party leaders recognized that some form of negotiated power-sharing arrangement with the ANC would soon be reached. Security threats in the regional environment had been eliminated with the internationally brokered regional settlement that linked the independence of Namibia with the withdrawal of Cuban troops and Soviet advisors from Angola. The demise of the Soviet Union was imminent and there were growing pressures from Western countries for South Africa to accede to the Nuclear Non-Proliferation Treaty. Similar pressures developed in the early 1990s for South Africa to renounce its space-launch-vehicle program and join the Missile Technology Control Regime.

Shortly after his election and inauguration as state president in September 1989, F. W. de Klerk initiated a series of reviews of policies and spending priorities. The de Klerk regime wanted to cut defense spending in light of the dramatically altered regional strategic context and in order to free up money to pay for social and economic reforms the National Party

government planned to implement as part of a wider political and economic reform initiative.

The SADF, ARMSCOR, and the AEC were all under pressure to cut
expenses. By the late 1980s, defense industries constituted one of the most
significant economic sectors. Defense-related industries accounted for
nearly 10 percent of all manufacturing employment and directly or indi-
rectly employed approximately 130,000 people. Over the next decade, the
resources available for defense would be cut rapidly by more than 50 percent.[2] A concerted effort was made to find alternative employment or negotiate early retirement for personnel involved in the nuclear-bomb program.

The review of the World War II–type bomb program was one of the
first that de Klerk initiated. In February 1990, he issued internal orders to
terminate the nuclear program and dismantle all existing weapons; the Y-
Plant was dismantled that same month.[3] The manufacturing facility was
decontaminated and plans were made to convert it to civilian production.
All the hardware and design information was destroyed. The two test
shafts at the Vastrap test range were sealed off, and the site was abandoned. The South African government was not interested in negotiating
concessions from Western powers and did not seek help from international sources such as the International Atomic Energy Agency to dismantle the program. Instead, the South African Air Force, the AEC, and ARM-
SCOR developed a joint plan for the safe and secure dismantlement of the
bombs.[4]

The bomb-dismantlement process proceeded swiftly. At the beginning
of July 1990, the uranium-enrichment plant at Pelindaba East was decom-
missioned, the six devices were dismantled, the hardware and technical
documents were destroyed, and Advena (formerly Kentron Circle) was decontaminated and converted for commercial use. All the highly enriched
uranium was recast and sent back to the AEC for storage by early September 1991, just ten days before South Africa signed a full-scope safeguards
agreement with the IAEA.[5] Although the dismantlement process happened
quickly, and was audited internally, it is impossible to document that
everything was dismantled because the process took place in secret. After
South Africa signed the agreement with the IAEA, all of South Africa's nuclear plants and all previously produced enriched uranium were placed
under IAEA safeguards. The unilateral dismantlement process was completed by 1992.[6]

As a precursor to signing the Nuclear Non-Proliferation Treaty, South
Africa invited IAEA inspectors to make on-site inspections. During a series of visits, the South African government permitted IAEA personnel unprecedented access to highly enriched uranium facilities and weapon-pro-
duction sites. South Africa and the IAEA established new procedures and
important precedents for the future by working out explicit guidelines for

on-site IAEA inspections and safeguard procedures at nuclear enrichment facilities. South Africa acceded to the Nuclear Non-Proliferation Treaty in 1991.

Thus, by the time President de Klerk officially acknowledged the program's existence in a speech to Parliament in March 1993, the government had already unilaterally dismantled six nuclear bombs and the components for a seventh bomb, destroyed much of the documentation associated with nuclear-weapons programs, and shut down or converted a number of research laboratories and storage and test facilities. On August 19, 1994, the IAEA confirmed de Klerk's statement that one partial and six complete nuclear devices had been dismantled.[7]

De Klerk made history by ending apartheid and entering into multilateral talks designed to end white rule and lead to a peaceful transition. As support for a peaceful political transition gathered momentum, the de Klerk government considered options for eliminating the highly enriched uranium stockpile and for terminating advanced-weapons research and development projects.

Initially, de Klerk made no similar recommendation to cut the satellite-launch rocket program. International pressure to close down the space-launch-vehicle program, particularly from the United States, did not begin in earnest until 1991.[8] Although de Klerk's initial recommendation to terminate South Africa's nuclear-bomb program did not involve a major cut in defense expenditures or defense-related jobs, the government moved swiftly over the next several years to cut the defense budget and privatize much of the defense sector. ARMSCOR started a major restructuring that included spinning off key divisions as quasi-private corporations within the Denel group in 1992. (The Denel group consists of several smaller companies related to the larger Denel company.) Large numbers of civilian military workers were retrenched as an irreversible process of political reform culminated in the first elections that were open to all South Africans in April 1994.

In the run-up to the historical election, and while his National Party was campaigning hard to win as large a share of votes as possible in the forthcoming election, de Klerk informed the public in March 1993 of the existence of South Africa's bomb program and its subsequent dismantlement in a dramatic speech to the new mixed-race Parliament of South Africa. The former president stressed that South Africa had built nuclear bombs without outside assistance.

During the final stage of political negotiations leading to a negotiated transition to majority rule, de Klerk took another step toward denuclearization by agreeing to close down the space-launch initiative. This decision can be viewed as another step toward a full nuclear rollback, since this ostensibly peaceful space-launch-vehicle program masked programs to develop and test a long-range missile system and launchers capable of carrying nuclear weapons. In this chapter we detail the reasons for the reversal of an earlier commitment to develop a domestic space industry. The decision to close down the space-launch vehicle was the result of intense behind-the-scenes bilateral and multilateral diplomatic meetings led by representatives of the United States. The shutdown was the result of a successful attempt by the United States to convince the South African government that the economic imperatives of a marketplace saturated with commercial launch vehicles would make the program a drain on scarce public resources for years to come.[9] In June 1993, South Africa announced that it was canceling the project. In October 1994, South Africa signed an agreement with the United States pledging to eliminate its medium-range ballistic-missile program and to abide by the Missile Technology Control Regime.[10]

In contrast to the international contingent marshaled to ensure the dismantlement of the bomb, the decision to terminate the space-launch-vehicle program was not well publicized. Only a few foreign visitors and local press representatives attended the low-key ceremony marking the destruction of a space-launch vehicle in the spring of 1994. It is ironic that at a time when the technology to build tactical, medium-range, long-range, and even space-based launch vehicles was proliferating worldwide, little notice was taken abroad of South Africa's decision to destroy components of a long-range missile system. The termination of South Africa's space program also meant that the country would be unable to compete for contracts to launch civilian satellites a decade later when demand overtook supply in other countries.

South Africa continued to scale back nuclear capabilities at home and rack up denuclearization milestones in international affairs after the historic elections of April 1994. The interim coalition government was composed of former enemies led by Nelson Mandela and the ANC as the majority partner. The transitional government came to power committed to improving the quality of life for millions of black South Africans. Under pressure to reduce public subsidies to defense and nuclear industries, the government announced plans in early 1995 to close its heavily subsidized uranium-enrichment facility at Pelindaba and begin using imported enriched uranium to fuel its nuclear-energy reactor at Koeberg. It also closed the semi-commercial Z-Plant in March of that year.

The Mandela government demonstrated its commitment to nuclear nonproliferation and an ability to translate its moral clout into policy. As the only country to engage in nuclear rollback, South Africa now has real political clout in a number of international forums. During 1995, Mandela's personal appeals to support indefinite and unanimous extension of the Nuclear Non-Proliferation Treaty at the 1995 Non-Aligned Movement meeting helped to ensure that the extension passed by a consensus agreement rather than a recorded vote.[11] South Africa continues to play an important role as a denuclearization trendsetter in international forums and has implemented stringent safeguards and compliance mechanisms at home to ensure that the national-security apparatus is transparent and accountable and meets international agreements designed to limit nuclear proliferation.

These recent policy changes reflect a sophisticated awareness among key members of the post-apartheid political leadership of the symbiotic nature of the relationships between the nuclear rollback, democratic practices, and political reforms. But these political leaders also appreciate the economic value of maintaining a high-tech defense sector and the importance of a competitive edge in certain niche markets for exports. During the past decade, some members of the Mandela and the Mbeki Cabinets have expressed resentment about the complete dismantlement of past high-tech defense-weapons programs and have pushed for South Africa to resume research and development in a number of dual-use areas, including restarting the civilian satellite-launch program.[12] Consequently, it is difficult to pigeonhole official South African thinking on policies involving nuclear proliferation and arms exports. No one knows if the current denuclearization and democratic trends will continue beyond the Mandela and Mbeki eras. However, events in South Africa to date suggest that once the denuclearization process begins, it is difficult to reverse.

The official story of how South Africa dismantled its nuclear-weapons program is well known. However, as more participants come forward to talk about the dismantlement process, some questions have been raised about whether the nuclear rollback was as complete and secure as once thought. Throughout this descriptive analysis, we identify certain contradictions and gaps in the official story line that will need to be reconciled in future years. We also try to identify the most important variables that explain key decisions and some of the immediate and longer-term consequences of the decision to dismantle the covert nuclear and space-launch-vehicle programs. The concluding section summarizes the major implications of this first known case of nuclear rollback for future trends in nuclear proliferation.

PHASE 1: SOUTH AFRICA DECIDES TO DISMANTLE THE BOMB AFTER F. W. DE KLERK BECOMES PRESIDENT

F. W. de Klerk came to power as the acting state president at the start of 1989 after President P. W. Botha unexpectedly suffered a stroke. One month after the stroke, Botha signaled his intention to resign as party leader but stay on as state president. This announcement created a constitutional crisis, since the two portfolios were combined in the constitution. It also triggered a political crisis, because most members of the party caucus did not believe that he was healthy enough to return to office. Party officials succeeded in blocking Botha by holding a surprise election at an extraordinary meeting of the National Party's federal council in March. De Klerk won this election by a very thin margin of votes.

As the leader of the Afrikaner heartland, de Klerk was widely regarded as head of the conservative (the *verkrampte*, or "closed-minded") faction within the party and throughout the white electorate. Support for the reformist position that the National Party should enter into negotiations with the ANC was increasing; many party leaders favored retaking control of the party from the securocrats who had grown powerful under Botha's rule. De Klerk won a run-off vote against a reformist candidate, Finance Minister Barend du Plessis, primarily because de Klerk was considered to be a "party man," but only by a narrow margin of 69 to 61.[13]

After consolidating his position within the National Party by winning the presidency in his own right in September 1989, de Klerk articulated the belief that the National Party had to reach agreement on a transitional government with their former political enemies.

Almost immediately after assuming office as state president, F. W. de Klerk gave J. W. de Villiers, then head of the AEC, and his deputy, Waldo Stumpf, the following ultimatum: "I have one vision in my term of office. I want to make this country once again a respected member of the international community and we'll have to turn around the politics and we'll have to terminate this program, turn it around and accede to the Nuclear Non-Proliferation Treaty."[14] This announcement was a remarkable turnaround for a lifelong conservative who had dedicated his public career to increasing and maintaining Afrikaner rule through the National Party.

De Klerk also immediately dismantled the structures that the securocrats had developed under P. W. Botha. The National Security Management System (NSMS) was created by P. W. Botha and General Magnus Malan after Botha became prime minister in 1978. The NSMS subsumed and co-opted existing structures, both public and private, in a comprehensive security apparatus. Its mission was to identify and neutralize antigovernment activists and to strengthen public support for security-related activities. At the apex of the NSMS was the State Security Council. In 1979, it became the most important and most powerful of four cabinet committees. Botha chaired the enlarged State Security Council, which also included the minister of defense, the minister of foreign affairs, the minister of justice, the minister of law and order, the chief of the SADF, the chiefs of the military and the intelligence services, the commissioner of police, the chief of the security police, and other senior government officials by invitation. In November 1989, he disbanded the National Security Management System and ordered an investigation into all secret projects. In a dramatic break with the style of his predecessors, de Klerk went public in February 1990 with a commitment to enter into negotiations that would result in "a new and just constitutional dispensation in which every inhabitant will enjoy equal rights, treatment and opportunity in every sphere of endeavor—constitutional, social and economic."[15] After identifying negotiations toward a new political order as the "highest priority" of his administration, de Klerk released senior ANC leaders from prison except for Nelson Mandela, allowed Blacks to march peacefully throughout South African cities, and began implementing his own legislative plan to end apartheid.

At the same time, de Klerk had to implement a new political strategy that would win the support of new voters in an expanded electorate without alienating his National Party support among white voters. One way to gain new voters, especially among Coloured (mixed-race) voters, was to initiate new social welfare programs. In order to free up financial resources for these reforms, one of de Klerk's first acts as president was to order a series of defense reviews. A central question in these reviews was what to do about the costly covert nuclear-weapons program and other unconventional-weapons programs. From the outset, de Klerk saw that cuts in defense programs would likely be one of the best ways to fund massive new social policies. Initially, de Klerk did not have to worry too much about the reaction of the white electorate, since public opinion polls indicated that most white South Africans were adopting a "wait and see" attitude.[16]

De Klerk also did not have to worry much about dissenting views from members of his Cabinet, since most hard-liners had already left the National Party to join the Conservative Party in 1982. Instead, throughout his administration, de Klerk was able to rely heavily on the support and advice of a smaller circle of close advisors within the Cabinet known as his "kitchen cabinet."

The politicians in de Klerk's inner circle shared a number of characteristics, experiences, and beliefs. All were loyal Afrikaners who had served as ministers or deputy ministers in P. W. Botha's Cabinet. All of them, with the exception of Kobie Coetzee, leader of the Orange Free State and a key player as minister of justice since 1980, were regarded as "enlightened reformers." This meant that they shared a belief in the preeminence of the party over the security establishment. They also shared a belief that it was important to reestablish civilian control of the government and that changes in the regional and international environment since the withdrawal of the Soviet Union and Cuba from the region created conditions that facilitated negotiations toward a power-sharing government. De Klerk and his advisors shared a common understanding of the most important problem facing the government—how to manage a negotiated transition to a new order that would allow the National Party to maintain a dominant role in government.[17]

In November 1989, the nuclear review committee recommended that the nuclear-weapons program be ended and that South Africa join the Nuclear Non-Proliferation Treaty. De Klerk and his Cabinet agreed and ordered dismantlement to commence.[18] De Klerk instructed the three agencies involved in running the covert program, the SADF, ARMSCOR, and the AEC, to submit a plan for "safe and secure wind-down."[19] Once de Klerk's Cabinet approved the plan, the process of unilaterally dismantling six bombs and the components for a seventh bomb was very quick. The unilateral dismantlement process began in February 1990 and was completed by 1992.[20] Although all of South Africa's nuclear plants and previously produced enriched uranium were placed under IAEA safeguards during the fall of 1991, de Klerk chose not to disclose this dramatic policy reversal until March 1993. The IAEA gave its official confirmation of the dismantlement on August 14, 1994. De Klerk assured his role in history during the early 1990s because of the key role he played in presiding over the first major rollback of a previously covert nuclear-bomb program.

UNILATERAL DISMANTLEMENT OF THE NUCLEAR-BOMB PROGRAM AND THE ROLE OF THE IAEA

Ensuring a safe and secure wind-down was the top priority of the joint plan devised by ARMSCOR, the AEC, and the SADF. A group of ARMSCOR and AEC officials and their SADF counterparts developed a timetable for dismantling the bombs, signing the Nuclear Non-Proliferation Treaty, and concluding the safeguards agreement with the IAEA. The working group reported that they would need about eighteen months to fully dismantle the country's nuclear capability. De Klerk approved the plan and assigned the responsibility for its implementation to a joint task force of representatives from ARMSCOR, the AEC, and the SADF. De Klerk also appointed an independent auditor, Dr. Wynand Mouton, a respected scientist and former principal of the University of the Orange Free State, to oversee the dismantlement process and report directly to him. Mouton, a respected nuclear physicist with an international reputation, was to ensure that the highly enriched uranium was removed from ARMSCOR's custody and returned to AEC to be diluted with other uranium isotopes so that it could no longer be considered weapons grade.

F. W. de Klerk and the representatives of the AEC, ARMSCOR, and the defense forces in charge of supervising the dismantlement process wanted all facilities used for the manufacture of nuclear devices to be decontaminated, all nuclear material melted and stored, all equipment removed, all technical drawings destroyed, and all facilities mothballed or converted to commercial use before concluding an agreement (a necessary step nations must take before they can sign the Nuclear Non-Proliferation Treaty). Security, safety, and accountability for all extracted materials from the warheads were to be principles of all phases of the dismantlement process.[21] The procedures developed and implemented by the interagency task force were remarkable for their systematic and comprehensive character. Care was taken to ensure that the procedures used to extract radioactive materials from the warheads followed comprehensive accountability requirements drawn up by members of the interagency task force. After de Klerk's March 1993 speech, the IAEA was given access to all facilities previously used in nuclear programs. Safeguard agreements are now in effect and IAEA teams visit South Africa to inspect on a monthly basis. According to Waldo Stumpf, the head of the AEC, the only work left for the IAEA in South Africa by 1994 was to determine the completeness of the declared inventory of less-sensitive low-enriched uranium in the larger semi-commercial enrichment plant.[22]

HIGHLY ENRICHED URANIUM BECOMES A POLITICAL ISSUE

Since the Nuclear Non-Proliferation Treaty was meant to be a forward-looking document, South Africa was under no binding obligation to reveal past nuclear-weapons activities. The treaty requires extensive accounting for nuclear materials and facilities only from the time it takes effect. Nonetheless, South Africa gave unprecedented access to the International Atomic Energy Agency to monitor installations and records, including extensive production data from the Y-Plant that had produced uranium for nuclear weapons.[23]

The IAEA used this information to recreate the Y-Plant's operations on a day-to-day basis. After a two-year investigation, the IAEA reported that "the amounts of highly enriched uranium which could have been produced by the pilot enrichment plant are consistent with the amounts declared in the initial report." The IAEA estimated that South Africa's declaration was accurate within one significant quantity, or the equivalent of 25 kilograms of weapons-grade uranium.[24] The AEC and the IAEA were confident that if significant quantities of highly enriched uranium were hidden or exported secretly, the IAEA would have detected it.[25]

Despite the care taken during the dismantlement process by both South African and IAEA officials, questions have been raised in subsequent years about the total amount of weapons-grade uranium produced by the South African nuclear program. Some independent analysts disagree about how much of the enriched uranium taken from the warheads was diluted with other uranium isotopes to ensure that it was no longer considered weapons-grade material. Some of these disagreements are tied to the use of different statistics: some estimates included only weapons-grade highly enriched uranium and some estimates combined production figures of both highly enriched uranium and low-enriched uranium. South Africa was estimated to have produced about 330–350 kilograms of weapons-grade uranium enriched to 90 percent or higher (that is, weapons grade) and to have had another 55 kilograms of 80-percent enriched uranium on hand.[26] According to South Africa's declaration to the IAEA, the Y-Plant produced a total of about 1,500 kilograms of enriched uranium. This figure included both low-enriched uranium and highly enriched uranium; 350 kilograms of this total was uranium enriched to 90 percent or higher.[27] An unknown amount of the uranium stockpile was used to fuel the Safari reactor. A crude estimate is that about 100 kilograms of highly enriched uranium (45-percent enriched) were irradiated before the reactor shifted to using low-enriched uranium in the early 1990s. In the mid-1990s, South African officials said that the bulk of this highly enriched uranium was slated to be blended down to low-enriched uranium; it is not known whether or not this was done.[28]

De Klerk and ANC officials disagreed about what to do with the enriched uranium stockpile both before and after the 1994 election. It became a serious issue that threatened to be a negotiation roadblock during the multiparty negotiations held between the National Party, the ANC, and other parties to the negotiations. There were reports in 1992 that the de Klerk government offered to sell the entire stock of highly enriched uranium to the Bush administration. When the ANC heard about the possibility that the de Klerk government might sell or remove the highly enriched uranium stockpile from the country, it lobbied hard to leave the stockpile in the country and postpone a decision until after the transition government was in place. By late 1992, the ANC had intensified its efforts to uncover the nuclear-weapons program and charged that the government might have hidden some weapons-grade material from the IAEA. The delays in making a public disclosure about the bomb program fueled suspicions about the nature and extent of South Africa's covert operations and research and development programs.

Finally, the de Klerk regime agreed during the summer of 1992 to wait until after the election to decide what to do with the stockpile of highly enriched uranium. Shortly after the 1992 U.S. presidential election, representatives of the de Klerk government allegedly approached Clinton political appointees with another offer to sell the highly enriched uranium stockpile to the United States, but the Clinton administration did not immediately act on this second offer. When Clinton officials attempted to revive discussions about the possible purchase of the highly enriched uranium stockpile at a later time, South African representatives did not want to resume the behind-the-scenes talks about the HEU stockpile.[29]

By 1993, press revelations about South Africa's secret nuclear projects were hurting its attempts to improve its image internationally. Statements by leaders in neighboring states suggested that no progress in negotiations on the creation of an African Nuclear-Weapon-Free Zone (ANWFZ) would be made until South Africa's previous nuclear status was clarified. South Africa was also under pressure from the ANC to reveal its previous nuclear activities. The tone of domestic criticism also escalated.[30]

After the 1994 elections, most ANC members of the transitional government agreed to retain the highly enriched uranium stockpile for use in the Safari-1 research reactor and in additional commercial applications.[31] South Africa currently has no plans to sell this material, since its value can be increased thirty or forty times by using it in Safari-1 to produce isotopes and for other commercial irradiation services.[32] However, the lack of precise records regarding the amount of highly enriched uranium that was produced while the nuclear-bomb program was under way continues to fuel lingering suspicions in the minds of some ANC members, including high-ranking members of the government. Some of them remain convinced that some amount of highly enriched uranium was shipped out of the country or hidden during de Klerk's term of office.[33]

U.S. officials continued to be concerned that the highly enriched uranium stockpile was a possible source of nuclear proliferation, and it was a topic of periodic discussions between South African and U.S. officials after the 1994 election in South Africa. The United States and South Africa continued to discuss the possibility of converting the Safari reactor from highly enriched uranium to low-enriched uranium throughout 1994. By 1995, it appeared that the two countries had made progress in negotiations to transfer American nuclear technology to South Africa that could help in the conversion of the reactor. However, by late 1995 a group of South African experts decided that "while converting the reactor was technically feasible, it was not practical on economic grounds." U.S. officials dispute this assessment and the two countries continued to talk about the type of nuclear fuel used in the Safari-1 plant.[34] The stockpile of highly enriched uranium remains under the control of the AEC of South Africa and is subject to IAEA inspections.

REASONS FOR DISMANTLING THE NUCLEAR-BOMB PROGRAM

In explaining the unilateral nuclear disarmament decision, President de Klerk emphasized changes in the region. In his statement to Parliament in March 1993, he noted the signing of the 1988 Tripartite Agreement, which led to Namibian independence and the withdrawal of 50,000 Cuban troops. He also mentioned the end of the Cold War, the breakup of the Soviet bloc, and a desire to have South Africa move away from confrontational relations with regional neighbors and the world community. These factors made nuclear deterrence superfluous and an obstacle to peaceful international relations. Many observers have stressed the fact that de Klerk had a genuine commitment to restoring South Africa's reputation and bringing it back into the world community. De Klerk and other Nationalist Party politicians felt that unilateral dismantling of the nuclear-weapons program and acceding to the Nuclear Non-Proliferation Treaty would go a long way toward reversing South Africa's status as a pariah.[35]

De Klerk came to office committed to implementing a reform process that would ensure a leading role for the Nationalist Party in the next government. While most outside observers believed by the beginning of the 1990s that a majority-rule government headed by the ANC would gain power in the near term, leaders of the National Party, including de Klerk, chose to believe that they could maintain control of the process and retain a substantial amount of power in a future coalition government.[36] De Klerk's government did not like the idea of turning over access to nuclear weapons to the ANC. This view complemented a concern widely shared among U.S. government officials that it would be unwise to have nuclear weapons in the hands of a government that maintained friendly relations with Libya's Qaddafi and Cuba's Castro. This U.S. position was communicated quietly through diplomatic and back channels to the de Klerk government,[37] and the de Klerk regime hoped that elimination of the bomb program would result in improved relations with the United States.[38]

Economic factors, especially the macroeconomic factors related to the need to free up money for planned social, educational, and economic reforms, also played a role. Some analysts have cited the high costs of subsidies to the AEC to maintain the uranium enrichment as another factor that may have influenced de Klerk's decision to shut down the bomb program. South Africa's uranium-enrichment process was far more expensive than expected, and it needed access to cheaper sources of enriched uranium. This would be feasible if it signed the Nuclear Non-Proliferation Treaty.[39] During the 1988–1992 period, the average costs of operating the Beva plants that converted, enriched, and manufactured uranium were between ten and twenty times the open-market price. The enrichment plant was inefficient and costly. Thus, there were powerful economic arguments for joining the Nuclear Non-Proliferation Treaty.

The government subsidies needed to support the use of this expensive enrichment process were not continued after the transition election in 1994. In January 1995, less than a year after Mandela became president, his mineral and energy affairs minister, Pik Botha, announced that South Africa planned to close its enriched uranium facility at Pelindaba that had been set up in the face of sanctions to supply the Koeberg nuclear power plants. By 1999, both enrichment plants were slated for dismantlement, he said.[40]

Other costs beyond the straightforward economic costs of the bomb program need to be taken into account in order to understand why there was a lot of support among leaders of the South African Defence Force for dismantling the bomb program. South Africa's World War II–type nuclear-bomb program was small. At its peak, it could produce only one or two weapons a year. Even at the end, the total costs of the bomb program were only a tiny fraction of South Africa's total defense budget.[41] To understand growing opposition to ARMSCOR's nuclear programs within the military, one needs to look beyond direct costs and consider other types of opportunity costs.

At the outset, the SADF was generally supportive or neutral about the nuclear-bomb program. But as the costs for projectiles capable of carrying nuclear warheads increased, certain branches of the military became critical of the program. By the end of the 1980s, South Africa's new mid-range launchers were coming on line. In addition, the projected costs of a planned space-launch vehicle were seen as cutting into the military's capacity to maintain a conventional deterrence force. This was especially true for the air force, which was desperate to modernize its bomber and helicopter fleet. The leadership of the navy also had plans to modernize expensive equipment that had already been delayed throughout the 1980s.[42]

By the late 1980s, the South African Air Force saw the rising costs of government subsidies to ARMSCOR as the main reason it was not obtaining replacement aircraft. The former chief of operations of the SAAF and secretary of defense, Lieutenant General Pierre Steyn, confirmed that the air force never asked for or desired control of these bombs. Instead, they viewed them as part of an agreement between the politicians and ARMSCOR officials. While these weapons may have given P. W. Botha a "warm feeling that he had a deterrent," the air force did not see them as part of a viable deterrence strategy, and it questioned the value and reliability of the weapons and the merits of a proactive nuclear strategy, especially given the growing expense of conventional deterrence.[43]

The modernization concerns of the South African military were reinforced by a confluence of events that dramatically changed the strategic landscape for the last apartheid political leader, F. W. de Klerk. The internationally sponsored agreement that led to the withdrawal of Cuban troops from Angola in the late 1980s and the independence of Namibia, along with the impending collapse of the Soviet Union, made it possible for de Klerk and his colleagues to scale down military defense expenditures.

External strategic considerations combined with the National Party's need to initiate political and social reforms. A number of strategic decisions taken by de Klerk in the run-up to the 1994 election, including the decision to close down the nuclear-bomb program and later the space-launch-vehicle program, were fueled by the overarching needs of the National Party to reposition itself within a changing domestic political environment in order to maintain its dominant position in government in the future.

The termination of the bomb program was an easy decision to make since de Klerk and his advisors felt that the decision had few costs and many benefits. It would not save a large amount of money, but it also would not cause a large number of jobs to be lost from the defense sector. The closure was expected to translate into increased levels of political goodwill and clout for the South African government in the area of nuclear power and national defense both at home and abroad. Thus, when de Klerk approved the plan to dismantle the nuclear bombs, the main issues were relatively easy ones dealing with the "strategic, safe and secure wind-down and dealing with the international dimensions."[44]

DENUCLEARIZATION STAGE 2:
TERMINATION OF THE SPACE-
LAUNCH-VEHICLE PROGRAM IN 1993

After de Klerk ordered the dismantlement of the nuclear-weapons program, lifted the ban on political activities by the ANC, and freed Mandela, he turned his attention to reviewing other covert programs. He also revisited the early review of secret missiles and the space-launch vehicle after receiving extensive pressure from the United States and other Western states to terminate all research and development programs related to weapons of mass destruction.

The United States was concerned about South Africa's possible violations of the Missile Technology Control Regime because of its more-recent covert arms sales and its security-cooperation arrangements with some of its defense partners. The United States had been aware of Israel's assistance to South Africa's medium-range ballistic missile program throughout the 1980s. It was also aware that the South Africans had conducted a test of a medium-range ballistic missile in July 1989 that probably contained components manufactured in the United States. However, despite several alleged violations of U.S. laws, the United States was not prepared to impose missile proliferation sanctions against ARMSCOR until 1991.

During the Gulf War, the United States discovered weapons capable of carrying nuclear shells in Saddam Hussein's arsenal that were made in South Africa. In response to U.S. charges, South Africans replied that they had not announced their unilateral disarmament to the world in 1990 because they had not wanted to be tarred with the same brush as Saddam Hussein. The real reason they did not announce their nuclear capacity to the world is probably more sinister; ARMSCOR was still working covertly with a number of partners to develop intermediate-range missiles and other types of launch vehicles. Because several of South Africa's missile programs relied upon U.S. components or technologies that were obtained in violation of U.S. laws and international sanctions, the United States repeatedly warned the South Africans behind closed doors that these violations would be enforced if necessary.[45]

Mounting pressures from a growing international sanctions movement organized largely by U.S.-based groups led the United States to take official action against South Africa. In September 1991, the United States announced official sanctions against South Africa for importing ballistic-missile technology from Israel. As a former U.S. official, Henry Sokolski, explains, "under U.S. law the President is required to prohibit U.S. exports of aerospace items to any foreign entity exporting or importing missile technology in contravention of international guidelines contained in the Missile Technology Control Regime (MTCR)."[46] Although the United States was aware of Israel's assistance to South Africa's missile program and alleged participation with South Africa in missile tests through 1989, it did not take legal actions against Israel.

The external pressure that accompanied U.S. decisions to get tough on missile violations came at a particularly difficult time for de Klerk in terms of domestic politics. His government was concerned about the increased number of violent incidents tied to an increase in both right-wing terrorism and black-on-black violence. The escalation of violence was particularly serious in KwaZulu-Natal after de Klerk announced the government's intention to negotiate with the ANC and other former enemies. During this time, the ANC and other opponents of the National Party government repeatedly charged that rogue elements of the SADF and the SAP were involved in what came to be widely known as "third-force violence." De Klerk ignored a steady stream of information that suggested that these rogue elements were using chemical and biological agents to assassinate political opponents.

What to do about the increasing violence was an issue that consumed a great deal of time in meetings between de Klerk and his Cabinet and among members of the Congress for a Democratic South Africa (CODESA) multilateral negotiating forum that met on a regular basis to try to reach agreement on how to achieve a peaceful political transition and reconciliation within South African society. Political opponents, the press, and powerful outside countries, including the United States and the United Kingdom, expressed their concerns and demanded action. Concern grew among de Klerk's advisors that talks between the National Party and their negotiating partners in the CODESA multilateral forum would break down.[47] The degree of concern about South Africa's political strife prior to the elections seemed to vary, from extreme fears of outright civil war to encouragement about signs of real progress.[48]

The de Klerk government wanted to complete the nuclear disarmament process and negotiations with concerned governments and the International Atomic Energy Agency before making a formal announcement to the world. The unilateral process was a secret process that involved the shredding of thousands of pages of documents in addition to closing facilities involved in the covert program. Many confidential meetings between South African government officials and representatives of the United States and other concerned national governments and IAEA officials took place. South Africa invited IAEA inspectors in for inspections shortly after the unilateral dismantlement process was completed.

It was against this backdrop that President de Klerk made his March 1993 announcement that South Africa had dismantled a nuclear-bomb program and had joined the Nuclear Non-Proliferation Treaty in 1991. Although de Klerk did not discuss the country's capacity to deliver missiles in this speech, his government issued an announcement a few months later, in June 1993, that South Africa was canceling the space-launch-vehicle program.[49] A few months later, in October 1994, South Africa and the

United States signed an agreement that included a commitment by South Africa to eliminate its mid-range ballistic-missile program and abide by the Missile Technology Control Regime.[50]

After a low-key ceremony to mark the termination of the program, the missile program disappeared from public sight except for a display at the air force military museum outside Pretoria. There is remarkably little evidence available to the South African public today to indicate that their country was developing a multistage missile as recently as the early 1990s. In a similar fashion, there has been a remarkable lack of discussion of the evolution of this covert missile program or the reasons why de Klerk made the decision to terminate the program.

FACTORS THAT INFLUENCED DE KLERK'S DECISION TO TERMINATE THE SPACE-LAUNCH-VEHICLE PROGRAM

In the late 1980s, the South African government started the process of privatizing the various divisions of ARMSCOR. Denel (Pty) Ltd was established in 1992 as a private company incorporated with the state as the sole shareholder. The Denel Company is managed by a board of directors appointed by the minister for public enterprises. Formerly a subsidiary of ARMSCOR, Denel operates today as a holding company with divisions and subsidiary companies, such as Somchem, managed on a decentralized basis. The shift in the status of Denel's legal status is why Denel, rather than ARMSCOR, was named in the ISC lawsuit in the early 1990s.

Several economic and political factors contributed to the South African decision to terminate the space-launch-vehicle initiative. These include sustained U.S. pressure, threatened multimillion-dollar penalties for Denel in the International Signal and Control Company court case (mentioned in Chapter 4), the lack of commercial clients for the space launcher, and the resulting drain on state resources; all probably contributed to the cancellation of the project. Other analysts emphasize domestic politics and the desire of the de Klerk regime and the national security elite to have the defense industry transferred to the private sector before the political transitions. Efforts to sort out the relative importance of these factors are compounded by selective perceptions and knowledge among different participants. While American officials involved in the space-launch vehicle case cite U.S. efforts to convince the South African government to close down the space-launch-vehicle project as the major factor, most South African decision makers in both the de Klerk and Mandela governments emphasize economic considerations.[51]

Throughout the 1980s, South Africa was able to leverage its geographical location and test facilities at Overberg to benefit from a number of covert cooperative ventures with the Israelis and other partners. One of these projects was a multistage long-range missile that put Lagos, Nigeria, within South Africa's firing range as early as 1983.[52]

The principle of building a civilian space-launch vehicle was officially approved by the president early in 1989 after ARMSCOR demonstrated the capability by successfully firing a test booster rocket. Since only minor modifications are needed to turn a space-launch vehicle into a missile, most analysts consider this time frame to be the period when South Africa built multistage long-range missiles. The main difference between a space-launch vehicle and a long-range missile lies in its military offensive front end and, consequently, in the functions expected of its inertial platform. Under the guise of a "booster project" for their civilian space-launch-vehicle program, South Africa developed an engine, a solid fuel, the missile casing, and a nose cone that could be used for military applications. The payload to be carried determines what is expected of the inertial platform and the nature of the platform itself. Thus, the three launches South Africa carried out from the Overberg Test Range were considered launches of a "booster system" because they carried nothing except telemetry equipment. However, when the test facility launched Israel's first satellite into orbit in 1989 it was considered a space-launch vehicle rather than a booster system.

As the demand for missiles grew, South Africa secretly built a homegrown version of the Jericho-2 missile system with extensive Israeli help. Some of the technologies and materials used in this joint South African–Israeli missile project were secured illegally from the West, notably the United States.[53] Collaboration with Israel was crucial to South Africa's efforts to build several missiles, including the long-range RSA-4 missile.

While President de Klerk is widely reported to have killed the long-range missile program in 1990, he initially supported the project and announced that South Africa would develop a commercial space-launch-vehicle initiative.[54] An intense but largely academic debate continued behind closed doors in the government from 1990 until 1992 about the relative merits of continuing the missile-launch program (which could carry nuclear warheads). There were intense internal debates about the wisdom of the satellite program and a secret cruise missile program.[55] Many military leaders were skeptical or outright negative about the space-launch-vehicle initiative. The former South African Defence Force (SADF) was preoccupied with efforts to cope with cuts in pay for defense personnel, cuts in procurement funds, the looming need to integrate black and Coloured soldiers, and the costs of increased police responsibilities in the townships and throughout KwaZulu-Natal province. (In 1992 there were only three black or Coloured officers in the South African Defence Force at or above the rank of colonel.[56])

By the early 1990s, the political and economic costs of maintaining the space-launch-vehicle program had grown exponentially. After Israel admitted to the United States that they had exported Jericho-1 ballistic missiles to South Africa, the United States moved to impose missile-technology sanctions against South Africa. This new round of sanctions in 1991 intensified an ongoing, largely academic debate that had been conducted behind closed doors in the South African government since 1990 about the relative merits of continuing the missile-launch program, a satellite program that was funded from a secret "black" account, and the cruise-missile program. This was because the SADF was preoccupied with efforts to cope with cuts in defense pay and procurement funds, the looming need to integrate black and Coloured soldiers, and the costs of increased police responsibilities in the townships and throughout KwaZulu-Natal province.[57]

In 1990, the budget for a space-launch-vehicle initiative was approved, even though doubts about the feasibility of the project were increasing among officials in the de Klerk government. Some critics have speculated that this shift was due to problems with the first launch vehicle. Other analysts have cited the fact that the South African government began to lose interest in the project after the Russians opened their own mobile launch pad for missiles. Public allegations about attempts to negotiate joint projects with China and India also hurt the image of the project. Finally, there was a problem with economy of scale. Initial plans for the project called for twelve to twenty-four launches per year to make the project economically feasible. But in the early 1990s, the plans had to be adjusted and only four or so launches were envisaged per year.[58]

South Africa did not announce that it had embarked on a major program to enter the commercial space-launch business until 1992; the announcement surprised some industry analysts and proliferation specialists. A RAND corporation report completed for the U.S. Department of Defense in 1993 noted that Brazil, the most advanced of all "emerging space launch nations, could at best recoup only 40 percent of its investment because of stiff competition from Russia, China, and France as well as the United States. South Africa has absolutely no rationale for a space program."[59]

Throughout the period when South African decision makers were trying to decide whether to proceed with a commercial space-launch vehicle, there was intense behind-the-scenes pressure by the Americans to terminate the program. The U.S. announcement of new sanctions against South Africa for illegally importing ballistic-missile technology from Israel resulted in a swift protest from the South African government. U.S. officials at the State Department were reportedly surprised by this response because U.S. exports to South Africa were already embargoed under a variety of congressional and UN anti-apartheid sanctions. Given the sanctions already in place, the State Department had concluded that the additional sanctions against the export of missile technology would impose no additional hardship on the South African economy.[60]

President George Bush was caught off guard by the State Department action and the response of South Africa. Bush was unhappy because he had been trying to get Congress and other countries to lift their sanctions against South Africa. In a meeting between South African Ambassador to the United States Harry Schwartz and Under Secretary of State Reggie Bartholomew, the U.S. government offered to lift the sanctions "if South Africa limited its rocket activities to development of 'peaceful' space launch vehicles, allowed this activity to be 'safeguarded' by some form of inspection, foreswore building any 'military' missiles, and promised to adhere to the export restriction in the MTCR."[61]

This offer prompted extensive disagreements among agencies within the U.S. executive branch. In subsequent discussions, the United States shifted and hardened its position that the space-launch-vehicle program had to be dismantled, since detecting military diversions of space-launch vehicles in a timely fashion was not possible. Such talks would have been the first direct diplomatic talks on any subject between the United States and South Africa. Moreover, many agencies within the national-security community expressed concerns about the difficulties involved in trying to distinguish a long-range offensive missile program from a commercial space-launch vehicle. The final U.S. negotiating position under the Clinton administration was similar to the position John F. Kennedy had taken during the Cuban Missile Crisis; there was no real difference between a long-range missile and a commercial space-launch vehicle other than "attitude."[62]

U.S. officials credit the RAND report as a key factor that persuaded their South African counterparts that launching commercial satellites would not be a profit-making venture. The report underscored the fact that the project would drain public funds for years to come. The study also contained data that demonstrated that South African projections of profits from commercial launches of satellites were unrealistic; the market for space launches was just too small to make the investment profitable. It noted that even U.S. commercial space-launch efforts relied heavily on public financing to break even.[63]

After a series of meetings with the Americans, additional market analyses of the commercial viability of the project, and a great deal of internal debate, senior South African officials decided to cancel the highly valued but costly project on both economic and political grounds. Foreign Minister Pik Botha announced on June 30, 1993, in his capacity as acting state president of the country, that South Africa was abandoning the project to "allay suspicions that South Africa was still working on ballistic missiles."[64]

While Nelson Mandela and his senior advisors ratified this decision shortly after taking office, there was some opposition to this position within the ranks of the ANC and heated discussions about whether the new government should have reversed a decision that essentially eliminated the crown jewel of the country's high-tech defense programs.[65] Residual resentments, discussions about the merits of this decision, and efforts to restart a space-launch-vehicle program have grown more intense over the years as demands for launch capabilities for commercial satellites have outgrown existing supplies of launch facilities.[66]

The space-launch-vehicle program was transferred to Houwteq, one of the divisions of ARMSCOR that was now a quasi-private corporate subsidiary of the Denel group. Even though representatives at Houwteq continued to maintain that the vehicle they were developing was a space-launch vehicle, officials in the United States and other developed countries grew concerned because the pattern of testing indicated a ballistic-missile program.[67] Debate within the South African government ended temporarily after the decision to terminate the space-launch-vehicle program was announced. As noted above, the principal reasons cited by both South African and U.S. officials for abandoning the program were the lack of demand for another commercial space-launch-vehicle program in a market saturated with suppliers (the United States, the European consortium, and Russia) and pressure from the United States to end the program triggered by concerns about the booster-launch system and the nature and extent of foreign involvement.

From 1991 through 1993, the United States lobbied South Africa to abandon the booster-launch project in a sustained diplomatic campaign. The United States is alleged to have threatened to withdraw support for impending credit for South Africa at the International Monetary Fund if the space-launch program was not abandoned. IMF officials communicated to the South African government that they would have difficulty approving new loans if South Africa continued the project.[68] An additional source of pressure on the South African government was the unwavering refusal of a U.S. federal prosecutor to negotiate a deal with ARMSCOR or to drop charges against individual South Africans named in U.S. federal indictments for allegedly working with U.S. companies that were indicted for sanctions-busting activities.

The agreement signed between the United States and South Africa to codify the terms under which South Africa would terminate its space-launch program was similar to ones that the United States negotiated with Taiwan and South Korea in 1990 and 1991. It negotiated a similar agreement, with some additional private incentives, with Argentina. In each of these cases, the economic realities of the marketplace rather than existing international treaties or norms proved critical to reaching an agreement.[69] U.S. officials felt they had successfully "convinced" the South Africans that the marketplace was saturated with space-launch capabilities by showing South African government officials up-to-date data on world supply and demand.

After the two countries signed an agreement to destroy the space-launch vehicle in 1994, the United States provided funds for the dismantlement of the South African launchers.[70] The United States and South Africa also initiated a number of cooperative bilateral nonproliferation measures designed to facilitate implementation of South Africa's agreement to adhere to the Missile Technology Control Regime guidelines.[71] The level of cooperation between the two states continued to grow after 1994. At the end of President Mandela's two-day visit to the United States in October 1994, Presidents Clinton and Mandela announced a series of cooperative programs included in a new three-year U.S. aid package, a $600 million aid package that represented a doubling of U.S. assistance to South Africa. In the field of space technology, the two countries agreed to establish a Joint Working Group on Civilian Space Cooperation, which gave South African organizations and institutions an opportunity to interact with U.S. space-related programs, including areas such as remote sensing, satellite tracking, and meteorology.[72]

LESSONS AND CONSEQUENCES

American diplomats see the U.S.–South African missile nonproliferation agreement as an important win for U.S. diplomacy. From the U.S. perspective, if the program had not been terminated in 1993, South Africa would have developed an intercontinental ballistic-missile capability that the new ANC-led government could have used for their own political goals or to raise cash by working with new partners such as Libya.[73]

In contrast, several South Africans involved in this process viewed the American motive as economic; that is, they feel that the United States got rid of an economic competitor. Many South African officials cite the fact that no indictments were issued against Israel as evidence of the lack of a level playing field in this arena.[74] Moreover, most South African officials claim that economic considerations rather than outside diplomatic pressures led to the decision to cancel the space-launch-vehicle program. There are few signs that the negative reactions expressed by former South African officials have subsided. A recently published account by former South African insiders who were involved in managing several of the covert programs observed that a massive economic downturn coincided with the closure of the programs. The authors noted that "the South African government could have negotiated a better deal!"[75] These statements, even if self-serving, suggest that differing lessons are being drawn about the reasons for this second case of unilateral rollback.

Employment cutbacks that resulted from cuts in the South African defense force budget and the privatization of much of ARMSCOR's production capability in the early 1990s created new concerns among American and other Western governments about proliferation. An attempt during early 1994 by a small group of nuclear scientists to blackmail Denel, and their threat that they would sell their knowledge to the highest bidder underscore the fact that retrenched scientists remained a problem. These disgruntled and unemployed scientists were only a few of the thousands of South Africans who lost their high-paying jobs after South Africa began the process of privatization, downsizing, and defense cuts.[76]

In 1995, additional reports surfaced that unemployed engineers and scientists who had worked on nuclear-weapons or missile programs were offering their expertise to countries in the Middle East.[77] Such reports are hardly surprising. According to some estimates, thousands of people were employed in some aspect of South Africa's weapons-procurement and weapons-production system before the defense cutbacks of the late 1980s. When South Africa's military and arms industries downsized, thousands of individuals lost their jobs or source of income. Desperate for income, a few of these former employees and many more freelance arms dealers and procurement specialists became free agents engaged in finding new patrons and markets.

By the time de Klerk came to power, pressure had grown to rationalize the overlapping components of the military-industrial sector in order to produce more products for export sales. ARMSCOR undertook several new initiatives designed to make a number of weapons systems more competitive by relying more on private defense contractors. Starting in 1992, a number of subsidiaries were converted to private companies. The critical spin-off for research about delivery systems was the Denel Division, which took over twenty-three of ARMSCOR's twenty-six subsidiaries and facilities. Denel now manufactures weapons while ARMSCOR is a pure acquisition organization that provides primarily for the South African National Defence Force (SANDF) and the South Africa Police Service (SAPS) and regulates military imports and exports.

Denel is now organized along the lines of an independent private company with sixteen divisions. It is still accountable to the minister of public enterprises, although the overwhelming majority of the 800 companies that constitute the defense industry are located in the private sector.[78] ARMSCOR, as the acquisition wing of the Ministry of Defence, depends on the defense budget for its funds and is still the chief customer of Denel. The South African government remains the primary customer for most defense companies. The lines of decision-making responsibility between ARMSCOR and private companies within the Denel group and overall relations between the different entities remain very close. What has happened to the hundreds of professionals who used to work on covert weapons programs is unknown.[79]

Similarly, no one seems to know what has happened to the estimated 600 individuals who were employed part-time or full-time by ARMSCOR or other government agencies to procure proscribed technology, expertise, and materials from abroad. According to more-recent estimates, the closure of the space-launch-vehicle and related programs resulted in a loss of 15,000 job opportunities in the defense industry, possibly another 7,000 in the nuclear industry, and a continuing brain drain of engineers, scientists, and entrepreneurs.[80]

The longer-term consequences are more mixed. In the mid-1990s, the commercialization of space was in its infancy. One South African official predicted in 1994 that the lack of a viable customer base for an entire range of products would "probably lead to the demise of Houwteq and even Denel."[81] Such dire predictions have not come to pass. Instead, many companies within the Denel group, including Houwteq, have survived and prospered primarily by specializing in niche markets for defense customers worldwide and by cultivating a wide range of commercial partnerships.[82] South African corporations have continued to work on a variety of unmanned aerial vehicles and battlefield missiles, including a high-speed target drone, the Skua, which is capable of traveling 800 kilometers with a 100-kilogram payload.[83]

Throughout the 1990s, as demand outstripped launch capabilities worldwide, private South African firms continued to pursue research and development designed to develop satellites such as the four-ship "Green Sense" constellation for commercial purposes. Although press reports announced that the satellite deal was on hold during the summer of 1998, there were continuing discussions within the government and negotiations with interested parties in the business sector. As late as 1999, South Africa's minister of posts and telecommunications, Jay Naidoo, announced that South Africa was "on track to launch a satellite programme that will . . . operate its own regional communications satellite." He said that the various users of satellite facilities, such as South Africa's Telkom, Sentech, and Transtel, spend between 450 million and 550 million rand annually to lease satellite time. Naidoo said that South Africa was the eighteenth-largest user of Intelsat services in the world.[84]

In June 2003, Houwteq announced a new program that may result in a full-blown space project within five years. The program calls for two observation satellites that will be called the ZASat satellites. The program will use Houwteq facilities near Grabouw to test the satellites at an estimated cost of 5 billion rand. Earnings from the program are projected to be about 1.2 billion rand. Unlike the first space-launch program, the new space program is a joint venture that will be managed with three other entities: Algeria, Nigeria, and the German state of Bavaria. Each of the participating states will place their own satellite in an orbit around the earth at a later date.[85] The new South African program was announced about the same time that a Nigerian satellite was launched. The Nigerian satellite, called Sat-1, was produced by a British company with the help of Nigerian technicians and was launched by a Russian rocket. These two events in 2003 underscored the fact that the Nigerians, like their South African neighbors, are serious about building and launching their own satellites in the future.

The recent efforts to revive space-based industries in South Africa underscore the importance of political changes and new commitments to nonproliferation norms as ways to ensure that a country will not restart former secret defense programs. F. W. de Klerk played a role in establishing the strong commitment to nonproliferation that exists in South Africa today following the termination of the nuclear-bomb and space-launch-vehicle programs. His government supported a number of other policy initiatives that placed South Africa farther along the path of nonproliferation. In 1993, South Africa passed the Non-Proliferation of Weapons of Mass Destruction Law. The 1993 law committed it to adhere to the Missile Technology Control Regime and to use IAEA control categories to monitor the flow of materials and technologies into and from the country.[86] In order to implement the Nuclear Non-Proliferation Treaty and meet the reporting requirements of the Missile Technology Control Regime, the division of ARMSCOR formerly in charge of building nuclear bombs is now in charge of implementing adequate monitoring and record-keeping procedures required by the Non-Proliferation of Weapons of Mass Destruction Law.

According to this law, ARMSCOR has been empowered as the administering agency to institute measures and initiatives to prevent the proliferation and development of nuclear weapons and to encourage bilateral and multilateral efforts to eliminate weapons of mass destruction.[87] ARMSCOR is using the guidelines listed in the 1993 law and items limited by the Missile Technology Control Regime to approve import and export permits. Under new procedures, two permits—an industrial or commercial permit from the relevant ministry and a technical permit—are required to import or export dual-use items in South Africa. Virtually all permits must go through ARMSCOR. A technical staff that is responsible for monitoring dual-use trade has developed computerized methods to both review and store dual-use permits, licenses, and other relevant information about activities of individuals and companies that produce or trade components capable of being used in weapons of mass destruction. This database promises to become an increasingly valuable tool to monitor dual-use exchange at the national and international levels.

South Africa's policy toward nuclear proliferation strengthened under Mandela after 1994 and under Mbeki after 1999. It has emerged as a leader in the nonproliferation of weapons of mass destruction and promises to play an active role in promoting nuclear nonproliferation in Africa and worldwide. South Africa is now a member of the Missile Technology Users Group and supports the principles of the Missile Technology Control Regime, which seeks to constrain the export of ballistic or cruise-missile technology with ranges of 300 kilometers and payloads greater than 500 kilograms. By joining the Nuclear Non-Proliferation Treaty, South Africa agreed not to export nuclear weapons, plans for nuclear weapons, or nuclear technology to states that do not have nuclear weapons. After dismantling its covert weapons of mass destruction programs, South Africa also expressed interest in joining the Nuclear Suppliers Group, which identifies a "trigger list" of nuclear-related materials, including dual-use materials.

As the first nation to engage in a nuclear rollback, South Africa obtained valuable experience during its negotiation of agreements with the International Atomic Energy Agency. South Africa is now putting these experiences to work in other areas of the world. Along with Canada, Hungary, and Australia, South Africa played a role in a coordinated technical support effort in Belarus and Kazakhstan and was willing to help implement coordinated technical support programs with other countries of the former Soviet Union. The details under the plans, such as hardware needed to protect former weapons facilities, are worked out by teams that visit each site under a "lead donor" program. These activities, which include the opening of National Intelligence Service facilities to foreign visits and the actual modification of facilities, are occurring without final safeguard agreements with the IAEA.

Several aspects of South Africa's experience with denuclearization and the dismantlement of a dual-purpose space-launch-vehicle program may be relevant for understanding the factors that influence when and why a country's political leadership may decide to engage in nuclear rollback. Below we summarize the most important factors influencing the decisions taken by South African government officials and the most important policy lessons that can be learned from the first case of nuclear rollback.

1. Top political leaders play a critical role in taking the lead to initiate nuclear rollback and the dismantlement of high-tech missile programs, despite the direct loss of high-tech jobs.
2. It is important to manage and closely supervise any nuclear dismantlement plan and involve International Atomic Energy Agency inspectors *before* the bomb program is dismantled in order to reduce questions about whether all bombs were in fact dismantled.
3. It is important to ensure the integrity of highly enriched uranium stockpiles and move quickly to eliminate stockpiled highly enriched uranium by blending it with lighter-grade uranium to prevent future threats of proliferation.
4. It is costly to build advanced space-based delivery systems, both in monetary terms and in terms of increasing opposition at home and abroad.
5. Long-range missiles have dual uses and it is impossible to distinguish between programs designed to develop civilian satellite-launch vehicles from vehicles used to launch multistage missiles.
6. Pressures by the international community and key nation-states are important in ensuring that nuclear and missile rollback is implemented.
7. Marketplace considerations are important in determining whether countries will agree to dismantle their long-range missile systems and whether they will decide to restart space-launch commercial ventures as demand increases.

8. Democratic reforms are associated with progress toward nonproliferation; the process of shifting toward democratic governance appears to facilitate the dismantlement process.
9. A commitment to democracy also helps cement allegiance to nonproliferation norms while a commitment to transparency and accountability in government helps make monitoring possible.
10. Norms within the government, the scientific community, the wider society, and the international community are important for sustaining progress toward more nonproliferation commitments over time.

A review of key decisions made by the de Klerk regime underscores the importance of variables at both the macro- and microlevel of analysis. A great deal of attention has been paid in analyses of South Africa's decision to denuclearize to changes in the global and regional strategic environment and the demise of communism. Some analysts have also stressed the role of rising demands for political change at home in creating the context for major changes in the policies of South Africa. However, remarkably little attention has been paid in the nonproliferation literature to the importance of the longer-term effects of economic and psychological factors associated with the increased isolation and economic costs of comprehensive international and national sanctions. In South Africa, international isolation and sanctions took a long time to have a major impact. Over time, these factors became more and more important. The South African economy had shrunk by the end of the 1980s, and it was clear to leaders of the business community and members of the ruling political elite that the time had come to enter into negotiations designed to bring about a gradual and controlled political transition.[88] The remarkable impact of outside pressures, particularly those applied by the United States, to completely dismantle the nuclear-bomb and missile programs underscores the fact that South Africa and presumably other nation-states that are undergoing political transitions are more susceptible to international and domestic pressures to roll back nuclear-weapons capabilities than well-entrenched regimes.

At the microlevel, change in the shared beliefs and perceptions of threat of political leaders was a factor by the late 1980s. The perceptions of political leaders shifted because of changes in the individuals occupying top political leadership positions. A leadership change at the top of the National Party and a collective shift in the ruling-party elite regarding the need for political reform resulted in decisions that led South Africa down a path toward a peaceful political transformation. The need to free up economic resources required de Klerk to make significant cuts in the defense sector. These cuts included the elimination of the nuclear-bomb program. The need to expand foreign investment in an economy that was shrinking due to the impact of sanctions, the dependence of the economy on financial loans from international financial organizations such as the IMF, and sustained pressure from Western countries were important factors in de

Klerk's decision to close down the nuclear and space-launch-vehicle program and related programs.

The first majority-rule election in 1994 in South Africa brought to power a new set of political and military leaders who ruled jointly in a "coalition of enemies." This unusual coalition, led by Nelson Mandela and the ANC, ratified the prior decisions taken to dismantle a sophisticated space-launch-vehicle program and close down related covert missile development. As the leaders of an interim government, Mandela and de Klerk started South Africa along a path of becoming a nuclear nonproliferation trendsetter.

SEVEN

The Rollback of Project Coast

Project Coast had the ability to be very, very
sophisticated. We established the ability to do
genetic engineering and all the fancy type of stuff
that would produce good biological products, but
nothing was really produced. The facilities were . . .
state of the art. The laboratories, the P4 containments,
everything. The scientists assembled there had the
potential of developing really new and fancy biological
weapons. But it was never done. When we got to the
point that we should have produced, there was no
support for the scientists to produce. It was very
ineffective. . . . We produced some knowledge . . . and
crude off-the-shelf assassination devices. . . . It is no
use controlling scientists and laboratories, etc.; the
real control lies in controlling the people who decide
where to apply it or not, and that is the politicians.
And as long as there is no agreement that can be
enforced then you won't control [biological warfare].

—Dr. Daan Goosen[1]

In 1988, as the pace of change accelerated in Southern Africa and South
Africa, conditions for considering the rollback of Project Coast emerged.
President P. W. Botha and the South African Defence Force realized that
the Soviet Union was losing interest in Africa, the SADF was going to win
the war against the Cuban expeditionary force in Angola, and the threat of
chemical and biological warfare was receding. As Botha realized that the
external threat was greatly reduced, he agreed to enter into negotiations. In
1988, the United States, Cuba, Angola, and South Africa negotiated the
withdrawal of Cuban troops in exchange for the independence of Namibia
and by the end of the year had reached a deal. The Soviet and Cuban
"threat" that had helped give rise to Project Coast rapidly receded. However, inside South Africa, the ANC's military wing, Umkhonto we Sizwe
(MK), continued its guerrilla campaign and domestic unrest remained a
concern.[2]

At the beginning of 1989, F. W. de Klerk was selected by the National Party to replace P. W. Botha. Although he was an experienced National Party politician who had held cabinet-level positions in the past, de Klerk was also an outsider to the state security system and knew little about its secret programs, including Project Coast. In September 1989, he was elected and inaugurated as state president and began his own five-year plan of ending apartheid. Part of his task included trying to establish civilian control over the security apparatus and reining in the "securocrats" and secret programs.

De Klerk also moved quickly to initiate political reforms. His February 1990 decision to release Nelson Mandela and lift the ban on the ANC initiated a four-year period of negotiation and contention. In 1991, the process of negotiations began under the auspices of the Conference for a Democratic South Africa (CODESA) that involved the government, the ANC, and other parties. In 1992, the CODESA negotiation process slowed and concerns mounted as the ANC's campaign of rolling violence spread throughout South Africa. Violent clashes continued, especially in KwaZulu-Natal. At the same time, mistrust of de Klerk and the National Party government grew among ANC leaders. There was a real concern by all parties that the situation in South Africa would spin out of control before a negotiated settlement was reached.[3] The fear of collapse provided an important incentive that eventually brought most parties back to the negotiating table. In 1993, negotiations stalled and violence continued. Chris Hani, leader of MK and the South African Communist Party, who was seen as a possible successor to Nelson Mandela, was killed in a right-wing hit operation. Fears of a third force and a right-wing coup grew.

Throughout this period of negotiations, instability, and violence, many in F. W. de Klerk's regime believed that they needed insurance against the ANC/MK and the "black onslaught." With this in mind, Wouter Basson and his associates kept the chemical and biological warfare program intact. Their reasons for doing so were several, but apparently the need for an "insurance policy" for themselves and the need to develop new tools for assassinations and crowd control were prominent in their minds. Experiments with chemical warfare apparently continued, and an alleged attack on Mozambican troops occurred as late as January 1992. At the same time, Basson, his chief associate, Philip Mijburgh, and others were allegedly milking Project Coast for financial gain.

Basson established contacts with foreign governments such as Libya who were interested in purchasing chemical and biological warfare secrets. Soon he became the target of investigation by the South African National Intelligence Service (NIS), SADF counterintelligence, and the Office of Serious Economic Offences, as well as the CIA and MI6. The investigations culminated in the Steyn Reports of December 1992 and January 1993. This chapter details efforts by de Klerk to dismantle Project Coast while attempting to regain control of and reform the procedures for civilian oversight of the military. As the United States and its allies learned more about Project Coast activities, increased pressures were placed on the government to close down the project. Unlike the process leading to the end of the nuclear-bomb program, privatization, corruption, and drugs accompanied the dismantlement of Project Coast. In addition, the many unanswered questions about why drugs were manufactured under the auspices of Project Coast or why smugglers were importing the mysterious substance called "red mercury" into South Africa suggest that we may never know about all of the activities pursued by scientists working for Project Coast or other secret WMD projects. Efforts to learn more about Project Coast during the Truth and Reconciliation process were only partially effective. Numerous efforts to lay criminal charges against Dr. Wouter Basson resulted in acquittals. Today, as Dr. Basson tries to regain his position with the South African military medical service, concerns that the tools of biochemical warfare developed at Project Coast will proliferate have not abated. In fact, such dangers are likely to exist far into the future.

F. W. DE KLERK'S EFFORTS TO ROLL BACK SECRET SADF PROJECTS

When de Klerk became president in 1989, he sought to find out about the secret projects of the SADF, including the covert nuclear-weapons and chemical and biological warfare programs. In July 1989, de Klerk announced the formation of the Kahn Commission. It issued three interim reports and a final report in November 1991. Its mandate was limited: the commission considered only projects that were still ongoing and were brought to its attention by the various state departments, with a view to recommending the cancellation of covert activities wherever possible. Where the commission was of the opinion that projects should be allowed to continue, recommendations were to be made for the possible scaling down and, where necessary, adaptation of such projects. De Klerk asked the commission to ensure that projects did not benefit any particular political party or organization. Projects that were not terminated were to serve what was defined as "the national interest." Such activities were said to include the elimination of violence, intimidation, sanctions, and international isolation.

The Kahn Commission did not investigate Project Coast because of assurances Surgeon General Knobel and Basson gave de Klerk that the chemical and biological warfare program was defensive. According to Dr. Ian Phillips, an ANC defense expert, the explanation for de Klerk's lack of knowledge about the chemical and biological warfare program was institutional. Minister of Defence Magnus Malan was not served by a civilian Department of Defence that administered the SADF. Military personnel held all the top positions that should have been filled by civilians. Consequently, the flow of information was curtailed by secrecy, and de Klerk claimed that Malan and his associates were keeping information about the chemical and biological warfare program secret. Botha and Malan ran the State Security Council with no distinction between strategic and tactical levels. They approved projects and let operatives carry them out as they saw fit. In sum, top apartheid leaders had an abysmal conception of civilian oversight of military affairs.[4]

After de Klerk lifted the ban on the ANC and freed Mandela in February 1990, he addressed the SADF and the SAP. De Klerk stressed that the ANC was becoming a political party and was no longer the enemy. Needless to say, many in the security forces did not like the message. In March 1990, Surgeon General Knobel briefed de Klerk about the defensive side of the chemical and biological warfare program, such as gas masks and protective suits, and told him about work with lethal chemical agents. In response, de Klerk ordered Knobel to stop work on the lethal agents. However, de Klerk claims that he was not provided with all of the details about Project Coast, especially about the offensive aspects of the chemical and biological warfare program and its use in assassination activities. The same was true with other SADF projects and third-force activities. Only with the publication of the Steyn Report at the end of 1992 and the beginning of 1993 did de Klerk become aware of the skill, sophistication, and offensive nature of Project Coast.[5]

Once de Klerk decided to roll back Project Coast, the process was time consuming, partly because of the sophistication of the program. Scientists and researchers had to be phased out over a period of time. Also, South Africa did not want to attract the attention of the United States and other powers to the program.

Another major impediment to the dismantlement of Project Coast was the bloated military that had developed throughout the 1980s. By 1992, the government faced a "situation of insubordination in the military." Security officials continued to believe that the chemical and biological warfare program was necessary for crowd control; they also believed there was a possibility that the ANC/MK might engage in chemical and biological warfare.[6] In response to de Klerk's order, intelligence procedures were restructured and personnel changes were made, but police investigations were never able to determine all the details. Throughout the military, there was stonewalling.

PROLIFERATION AND COUNTERPROLIFERATION

The process of dismantling South Africa's nuclear-weapons program and its biochemical warfare programs were very different. As discussed in Chapter 6, the nuclear dismantlement process followed a systematic plan developed and implemented through an interagency process that involved officials from the AEC, ARMSCOR, and the SADF after it had been approved by de Klerk and his advisors.[7] In contrast, senior officials delegated most of the planning and the details of implementing the dismantlement of Project Coast to Dr. Wouter Basson. But both processes shared one feature; orders approved at the highest political level sought to destroy most of the documentation associated with both programs. From 1990 to 1993, Operation Masada was carried out by the government, which involved the shredding of documents and destroying of hard drives and diskettes relating to the nuclear-weapons program and Project Coast.[8]

Prior to signing the Nuclear Non-Proliferation Treaty in 1991, Minister of Foreign Affairs Pik Botha sought and got repeated assurances from Surgeon General Knobel and the Department of Defence that South Africa no longer had a chemical and biological warfare program. Botha repeatedly asked for clarification on this point, because he had to give assurances that South Africa had destroyed its chemical and biological warfare program before signing the Nuclear Non-Proliferation Treaty.[9]

No international pressure was exerted in 1989 or 1990 with regard to the chemical and biological warfare program, even though the CIA released a report in 1989 that placed South Africa on a list of countries that had developed and stockpiled chemical weapons.[10] Information about Project Coast that the CIA and MI6 possessed was widely circulated and was available within the Bush administration and the Thatcher/Major governments. However, during this time period the main focus of concern for the United States and its allies was nuclear proliferation.

For a brief time between 1987 and 1990, when South Africa sold the G6 155mm gun and chemical warfare agents (including CR teargas) to Iraq, the United States became concerned about the proliferation of a conventional weapon that had the capability to throw "exotic" shells.[11] However, there was little interest among senior officials in U.S. policy and intelligence communities about possible proliferation threats associated with South Africa's chemical and biological warfare program. Most likely, Israeli officials knew more about Project Coast but probably did not want the United States and the United Kingdom to know that they were involved with the program.

This lack of interest changed quickly in the early 1990s as the United States learned more about South Africa's chemical and biological warfare and missile programs. Access to an informant who provided key details about Project Coast increased the interest and concern of the United States, the United Kingdom, and other allies. Wouter Basson's trips to Libya and elsewhere raised the profile of South Africa as a possible proliferator of biological and chemical weapons. The new information led the United States and United Kingdom to issue a démarche in April 1994.

In the early 1990s, friends and associates in Germany, the United States, Switzerland, and Austria asked Lieutenant General Chris Thirion, the head of SADF intelligence, for access to Project Coast secrets. Also, top South African authorities, including Generals Liebenberg and Meiring, asked Thirion if he could put Basson in touch with the right people overseas. He refused to ask his U.S. counterparts to connect the generals with the right people, because he customarily met with these people in groups and thought it would be awkward to ask.[12]

During the 1980s, Thirion had built a good relationship with his U.S. counterparts and cooperated with them in investigating the Soviet-built SA8 surface-to-air missile after the SADF had captured it from Angolan and Cuban forces. He provided information about the G5 155mm gun to American counterparts, even though ARMSCOR was not on good terms with the U.S. government. At the time, Thirion did not want to jeopardize his relationship with U.S. officials by mentioning Basson. However, he did ask a Swiss agent if he would be interested in meeting Basson; the agent replied that the Swiss government was indeed interested. Thirion was interested in defensive chemical and biological warfare measures and encouraged the Swiss, who were experts in defense against such warfare, to put together a team of doctors and send them to Angola.

In 1991, U.S. embassy officials discovered at an arms show that South Africa was running a chemical and biological warfare program that included gas masks and protective suits.[13] The American officials asked the South Africans about the program but elicited little response. Later, an American delegation was invited to visit Protechnik, a state-run corporation that was in the process of being privatized, to view facilities producing chemical and biological warfare protective gear. The South Africans at the arms show were not prepared to comment on the chemical and biological warfare program. Then the South African government decided that the Americans should be shown secret information pertaining to its chemical and biological warfare program. By September 1991, the U.S. government had become aware of the full scope of Project Coast and more concerned about Basson's activities. U.S. personnel began to look for signs of proliferation, especially the passing of secrets to ANC allies such as Libya.

CONTINUED THIRD-FORCE ACTIVITIES AND CHEMICAL AND BIOLOGICAL WARFARE

In 1989 and the early 1990s, violence escalated in South Africa, in spite of the unbanning of the ANC and the release of Mandela. The ANC/MK reserved the right to resume their urban guerrilla warfare campaign, and violence between ANC and Inkatha supporters escalated in KwaZulu-Natal. (The Inkatha Freedom Party was the representative of the Zulu people and was supported by the South African government from the 1970s to 1994.) In this atmosphere of violence, the Civil Cooperation Bureau and other third-force agents intensified their murderous activities.

In April 1989, the Civil Cooperation Bureau attempted to assassinate the Reverend Frank Chikane with poison during a trip he was making to Namibia.[14] The Civil Cooperation Bureau made another attempt to poison

Chikane during a trip to the United States, where one doctor finally diagnosed his malady as organophosphate poisoning. According to the testimony of Roodeplaat Research Laboratories scientist Schalk van Rensburg to the Truth and Reconciliation Commission, the men who tried to kill Chikane with Parathion poison had poor intelligence. He stated, "They were counting on little forensic capability in Namibia. And too little was smeared over his underwear to kill him when he went to the US."[15] Chikane's attempted assassination and several other Civil Cooperation Bureau incidents illustrated the difficulties involved in using chemical and biological agents as methods of assassination.[16]

Civil Cooperation Bureau operative Petrus Jacobus Botes (who claimed to have also directed bureau operations in Mozambique and Swaziland) asserted that he was ordered in May 1989 to contaminate the water supply at Dobra, a refugee camp located in Namibia, with cholera and yellow fever organisms. A South African army doctor provided them to him. In late August 1989, he led an attempt to contaminate the water supply. However, the attempt failed because of the high chlorine content in the treated water at the camp.[17]

In May 1990, the South African newspaper *Vrye Weekblad* reported that the Civil Cooperation Bureau used biological agents against SWAPO members. According to this article, the bureau had nearly 300 people working for it and reportedly consumed about 0.28 percent of the entire South African defense budget. Reportedly, the Civil Cooperation Bureau had authority to operate inside South Africa and in neighboring countries and was disbanded at the end of 1990.[18]

In 1990, violence in KwaZulu-Natal and other parts of South Africa escalated, and Inkatha militants received assistance from the Civil Cooperation Bureau and other third-force agents. In response to increasing evidence of third-force activities, the Harms Commission was established in 1990 and was charged by President de Klerk with investigating third-force agencies, including the Civil Cooperation Bureau and Vlakplaas.[19] As the bureau was being terminated in 1990, its operatives absconded with more than 12 million rand (US$4 million in 1991 dollars) that was due to Mechem (the explosives company) for teaching advanced demolition techniques.[20] These and other third-force activities came as a surprise to de Klerk, according to David Steward, de Klerk's chief of staff.[21] In spite of the evidence it uncovered, the 1990 Harms Commission lacked teeth and was unable to uncover many of the secret projects and third-force activities that were going on in South Africa.

As late as early 1992, Project Coast was still operating against the regime's "enemies." According to Truth and Reconciliation Commission testimony, Jan Lourens of Roodeplaat and Trevor Floyd of the Civil Cooperation Bureau took poisoned screwdrivers to London with plans to kill ANC leader Pallo Jordan and South African Communist Party/ANC military leader Ronnie Kasrils. In addition, Basson allegedly developed "poison beer" to be used against South African Blacks. This testimony was repeated in May 2001 during Basson's trial.[22] However, the veracity of some of this testimony has now been called into question.

PRIVATIZATION, CORRUPTION, AND DRUGS

Roodeplaat Research Laboratories, Delta G, and Protechnik were companies that were part of Project Coast. The three companies were privatized in 1990 as part of a poorly monitored rollback of the chemical and biological warfare program. Rogue directors of these companies allegedly engaged in criminal and murderous behavior to enrich themselves during the privatization and rollback process. In the succeeding paragraphs, their alleged crimes, many of which are still unpunished, are related.

In April 1990, Minister of Defence Malan decided to privatize Roodeplaat Research Laboratories, Delta G Scientific, and Protechnik. After de Klerk made the decision to start rolling back Project Coast, the Ministry of Defence and the SADF could no longer afford to sustain the three companies and their employees. Ownership of Roodeplaat and Delta G was transferred to Project Coast managers, including Basson and Mijburgh.

However, the privatization proceeded with insufficient government oversight. The rapid privatization process of both companies opened the way to massive financial improprieties. Over three years, several individuals affiliated with Project Coast pocketed state assets totaling more than 50 million rand (US$17 million in 1990 dollars). The ten shareholders in Roodeplaat became millionaires overnight when the SADF closed down Project Coast in 1993. The SADF paid the debtors, who were the shareholders, a total of 18 million rand (US$6 million in 1993). The fact that several of these individuals had invested as little as 350,000 rand (US$120,000 in 1990 dollars) attracted the attention of the Office of Serious Economic Offences. However, the details of this multimillion-rand scandal did not emerge in the South African Parliament until 1996. This was almost a year after the new South African National Defence Force, which had replaced the old SADF, forgave Project Coast's debts of almost 22 million rand (US$7.5 million in 1993 dollars).[23] Among the chief beneficiaries was former Special Forces soldier Philip Mijburgh, nephew of Magnus Malan.[24]

In July 1991, commercialization and privatization were put in motion. Magnus Malan ordered that all research stop by the end of August. Contracts with the SADF were canceled. The ownership of Roodeplaat and Delta G Scientific was transferred from the Ministry of Defence to managers and scientists. OSEO investigator Dawie Fouche testified to the Truth and Reconciliation Commission in 1996 that in August 1991, a five-year research contract between the SADF and Roodeplaat was canceled by the SADF on the same day Roodeplaat was privatized and transferred to

Mijburgh and other colleagues. The termination of the contract meant the SADF had to pay these new owners 32.6 million rand (US$11 million at the time) in cancellation fees. In 1992, Denel was created as a privatized arms-production company, although ARMSCOR continued to control acquisitions and maintain tight secrecy about weapons transactions.

Basson did not suffer financially from the changes in his job description. He apparently used money siphoned off from former government projects for his personal projects. In 1991, he began to build Merton House, a multimillion-rand building in Pretoria's plush Arcadia suburb. At the time the project was under construction, Basson claimed he was merely the middleman for a group of American doctors who were developing the property. However, Basson allegedly planned to use the building as a high-class brothel. The new building reportedly outraged local residents. Actual construction started in 1992, and even before the house was completed in 1993, it was up for sale for 8.5 million rand (US$3 million at the time).[25]

In December 1991, the Project Coast Coordinating Management Committee, which included Generals Knobel and Liebenberg, sent Basson to Croatia. There he allegedly purchased 500 kilograms of methaqualone from high-ranking government officials and others ("renegade Croatians," according to Truth and Reconciliation Commission testimony) and brought it back to South Africa.[26] The following year, Basson acquired benzilate and quinazolinone compounds, which were most difficult to develop, in Croatia. During his Croatian transactions, Basson "misplaced" 1.6 million rand.

The Truth and Reconciliation Commission found that the Croatia deal was extremely questionable, leading to a loss of millions of rand. Dr. Basson intercepted Vatican bearer bonds valued at US$40 million (110 million rand) that had been intended for the purchase of weapons by the Croatian government.[27] Basson's activities led to his arrest in Switzerland. The question of why the military was importing such large quantities of methaqualone at such high cost at this late stage of negotiations between the government and the ANC is not clear and was not adequately answered by Dr. Knobel or Dr. Basson at the Truth and Reconciliation Commission. Also, the commission questioned whether the methaqualone was actually destroyed.

In the early 1990s, Delta G Scientific purchased mercury from Thor Chemicals, a SADF front company that was part of the network of corporations working to provide materials for the covert chemical and biological warfare program. What the mercury was used for remains unknown. However, the prosecutor in the Basson trial investigated the purchase in conjunction with the 1997 seizure of Ecstasy, since mercury can also be used in the production of Ecstasy. Others speculate that this purchase was related to the production of Mandrax. However, mercury produced by Thor Chemicals has also been linked to the mysterious nuclear substance called red mercury, a substance said to make it possible to build nuclear devices that were smaller and more effective.[28]

In the mid-1990s, years after the rollback of Project Coast, the South African Broadcasting Corporation program *Agenda* reported that Delta G had carried out research to create nerve gases that could immobilize enemy forces for a number of hours but not kill them, making it possible to overrun strategic installations without exposing friendly forces to dangerous compounds.

Sometimes the actions of former Project Coast employees bought them instant justice. Lieutenant-Colonel Charles Landman, who headed a special police team set up to probe a string of murders apparently connected to red mercury at the time, confirmed that he had evidence that Delta G had bought more than two tons of yellow mercuric oxide from controversial mercury recyclers Thor Chemicals in September 1991. *Agenda* producer Jacques Pauw said there was evidence that yellow mercuric oxide was one of the building blocks of red mercury.

Thor Chemicals executive Alan Kidger was murdered two months after the Delta G deal. Kidger was found completely dismembered and smeared with a black oily substance. Police investigators linked his death to the trade in red mercury. There is some evidence that the 1994 murders of Durban armaments dealers Don Juan Lange (in June) and Dirk Stoffberg (in July) and perhaps others were connected to the trade in red mercury. To date, none of the "red mercury murders" has been solved. The prevailing theory of prosecutors and journalists is that all of these individuals were involved in clandestine arms-procurement deals that had gone bad.[29]

In 1992, Medchem Pharmaceuticals and Delta G Scientific produced 1,000 kilograms of Ecstasy. The Ecstasy manufactured was, in all likelihood, encapsulated by Medchem. This was a subsidiary of the holding company Medchem Consolidated Investments, under which Delta G Scientific also fell (according to Truth and Reconciliation Commission testimony). In 1997, Wouter Basson was arrested for possession of Ecstasy, more evidence of his drug-dealing.

Another incident in 1992 that appeared to be related to illegal drugs involved a South African Air Force jet that frequently flew abroad on top-secret missions. The jet was allegedly carrying designer drugs such as Mandrax. On this occasion, the Mandrax was allegedly used by a group of rugby enthusiasts who went to the first game between the Springboks and England in 1992, when sporting ties were reestablished. The rugby enthusiasts were closely connected to the SADF and the SAAF. Basson and his associates allegedly procured the Mandrax for them. They were flying on the SAAF jet from South Africa to England for the game. Dr. Johan Koekemoer, former research manager at Delta G, provided this information to the researchers at the Gauteng attorney general's office after turning state's evidence in preparations for Basson's trial.[30]

A CHEMICAL WEAPONS
ATTACK ON MOZAMBIQUE?

In January 1992, the SADF reportedly launched a chemical warfare attack on Mozambican troops near the South African border. According to the December 20, 1992, report of Lieutenant General Pierre Steyn, as an experimental training exercise, the SADF launched an attack from Komatipoort, South Africa, into Mozambique. A gas similar to teargas, causing pain and irritation, was allegedly sprayed from reconnaissance airplanes.[31] Investigators from several countries were unable to determine the accuracy of this information, as the use of the Komatipoort airstrip was not regulated. After the incident, scientific teams from South Africa, Mozambique, Switzerland, Sweden, and the United Kingdom conducted a series of investigations. Military personnel from several countries also attempted to determine the cause of death of civilians in Mozambique who were suspected victims of chemical and biological warfare attacks. The reports were inconclusive. The only report that expressed a belief that the troops had been exposed to a chemical agent was that of the British scientist.

These outside investigators had a great deal of difficulty disentangling the proximate cause of deaths since many of the victims were suffering from malnutrition and other diseases at the time of their death. The UN investigated and was also unable to come to any firm conclusions.[32] The reported incident raised American and British concerns and contributed to the decision of the two countries to issue an official démarche in 1994.[33]

South African investigators experienced similar difficulties in their efforts to determine whether a chemical or biological test or attack had occurred in Mozambique in 1992. When the Steyn Report was leaked in 1993, it linked Dr. Vernon Joynt to the reported 1992 attack on Mozambique. Joynt was using unmanned aerial vehicles to locate mines for clearing in the Komatipoort area. One of his planes was accused of dropping chemical agents on Mozambican soldiers; after the alleged incident, approximately forty soldiers began acting strangely. However, Dr. Joynt asserted that the Steyn Report was inaccurate.[34]

ANC defense expert Dr. Ian Phillips asserted that battlefield use of chemical weapons was evident with the Mozambique incident. He alleges that a high-flying airplane launched a chemical attack against Mozambican soldiers on the border near Nkomati. The bomb exploded well above the ground. Many within the ANC noted that the use of chemical and biological warfare against Mozambican troops preceded the whites-only referendum in South Africa in 1992 and felt that the attack was used to demonstrate the resolve of the de Klerk government to persevere in the face of UN pressures.[35]

Dr. Torie Pretorius, a prosecutor in the Basson case, believed that the SADF was carrying out an experiment with a chemical agent in the 1990s

Mozambique incident. One of the drone aircraft that Dr. Joynt was using to locate mines dispersed smoke that could have been a chemical weapon; Pretorius noted that the SADF tested the drone aircraft with yellow smoke after President de Klerk's speech against secret projects in 1990.[36] Retired General Meiring stated that in January 1992, he and General Dias of Mozambique went to the hospital to inspect troops that reportedly had been subjected to a gas attack by SADF.[37] However, the SADF 6th Medical Battalion found no evidence of a gas attack in the 1993 incident and concluded that the troops who were reportedly attacked had deserted in the face of a Mozambique National Resistance Movement (RENAMO) attack.[38]

THE STEYN REPORT

The Steyn Report was the most ambitious attempt to uncover the secret projects of the SADF, including Project Coast. Its goal was to help restore civilian control over the military. The year 1992 was a very sensitive time, and negotiations between the regime and the ANC were proceeding slowly. The behavior of the security forces was a big problem because civilian control of the military was very weak. Attempts at reform met with resistance. In 1990, Lieutenant General Pierre Steyn was SADF chief of personnel and was working with Jakkie Cilliers (now director of the Institute of Security Studies in Pretoria) on civilian control of the military. Together, they produced a code of conduct for SADF that was then rejected by SADF leaders. Later, Steyn proposed completely opening the SADF to Blacks, but this proposal was also rejected. The main obstacle to reform in the SADF was that long-serving leaders (for example, Magnus Malan and Kat Liebenberg), who held traditional beliefs, had acquired an exalted status and were being driven by political convictions. Their underlings were following them blindly. In such a situation, it is difficult to impose a neutral and binding code of conduct.

In mid-1992, Lieutenant General Steyn was transferred and promoted to chief of SADF staff, where he supervised staff functions instead of having any real control over the SADF. However, he was in a position to control SADF programs. He worked with Acting Defence Secretary Roelf Meyer from 1991 to 1992. In the second half of 1992, the Goldstone Commission, an ad hoc committee formed with the support of the president, began investigating violence in South Africa. SADF generals became increasingly concerned that their actions would be discovered and that they would lose control over the situation and then lose their careers.

During the commission's investigations, Justice Goldstone stumbled on damning evidence of secret projects and reported directly to President de Klerk rather than the Cabinet or the SADF. Consequently, de Klerk was compelled to launch an investigation. De Klerk called on Steyn to lead the investigation and report his findings to the Cabinet. In addition, SADF

Army Chief Meiring and SAP Chief van der Merwe asked Steyn to investigate, and he agreed to do so. They thought that Steyn, as SADF Chief of Staff, was loyal and could be controlled. On November 18, 1992, de Klerk officially appointed Steyn to head an investigation of SADF secret projects, including Project Coast and third-force activities around the country. As a result, de Klerk learned about the full extent of activities of Basson, Project Coast, the Civil Cooperation Bureau, and other covert units.[39]

SADF military procedures could not be used in the investigations because the subjects of investigation were not all military personnel and military procedures presupposed full cooperation from all involved. Because of the possibility of a military cover-up, counterintelligence agencies were used to check on the validity of information. The information was reviewed independently by two separate organizations, the National Intelligence Service, headed by Dr. Niel Barnard, and SADF Counterintelligence, led by Joffel van der Westhuizen.[40]

The CIA and MI6 were concerned that Steyn and his associates might find evidence against them and communicated with the National Intelligence Service. While the different organizations often had to rely on information obtained from the same source, most of the information they received was probably valid. The National Intelligence Service had been conducting its own intelligence operation and investigation of SADF and SAP secret projects since 1989. Targets for investigation included Project Coast and Basson, as well as Jan Lourens and Brian John Davey of Protechnik, who were involved in the chemical and biological warfare experiments.[41]

According to a *Weekly Mail & Guardian* account of the Steyn Report, three state-owned companies (Delta G, Roodeplaat Research Laboratories, and Protechnik) were found to be deeply involved in developing chemical and biological weapons. In 1991, SADF Counterintelligence began investigating Basson after he and his associates leaked secrets to the media that might have harmed South African security. Steyn's investigative team found evidence that Basson's team had armed RENAMO with chemical weapons.[42]

The Steyn team quickly investigated secret projects that were subsequently stopped, though financial misdealings were not examined. Their investigations went smoothly until the first report was completed and issued on December 20, 1992, and arrived at de Klerk's desk in the beginning of January 1993. Steyn asked De Klerk to take action, even though there was no legal basis for action, no charges, and no solid evidence. However, de Klerk and his advisors felt that preemptive steps were necessary before a cover-up could be launched. De Klerk was presented with the counterintelligence evidence, which demonstrated that SADF secret programs ran against his stated policy of civilian control over the military. However, he failed to ask SADF Chief of Staff Liebenberg and SAP head van der Merwe if they knew about the illegal activities. Instead, he called in Liebenberg, Meiring, and the SADF chief of intelligence and informed them of the evidence. Liebenberg said he was "shocked" and that he would report back in ten days.[43]

President de Klerk decided that firm and decisive action was needed, even though the evidence of misdeeds by SADF generals and Basson had not been corroborated by a sufficient number of sources. In mid-January 1993, de Klerk called Liebenberg in again and announced that he had changed his mind and that he wanted to act assertively. He told him that he would fire the generals responsible for the Civil Cooperation Bureau and other secret projects. De Klerk asked Liebenberg to ensure that the SADF policed itself. Subsequently, de Klerk launched another, more random investigation. Instead of acting against Liebenberg and van der Merwe, de Klerk let them off the hook and did not oblige them to report back to him about their actions. De Klerk did not even confront van der Merwe about the activities of the Civil Cooperation Bureau of the SAP and its notorious leader, Eugene de Kock. As a result of the second investigation, twenty-seven generals retired early and Wouter Basson was required to leave the SADF at the end of March 1993 and was given a "soft retirement" and reserve status.[44]

By the first quarter of 1993, the sources of investigation were drying up. Steyn had been ostracized by top SADF generals, and none of the generals were prosecuted by the state. The Steyn investigation led to the early retirement of twenty-seven generals and Basson, so it was partly effective. In fact, some generals, such as Chris Thirion, sued the government for defamation of character and won. The Steyn Report found that Project Coast and Basson, Roodeplaat, Delta G, Medchem, and the SADF were all operating completely outside the purview of the civilian government, and the Truth and Reconciliation Commission confirmed these findings. According to David Steward, P. W. Botha was the only civilian who knew anything about the secret projects.[45] Subsequently, the national prosecutor's office (Anton Ackermann and Dr. Torie Pretorius) took up the investigation; they laboriously dug up evidence and built cases against de Kock and Basson. After the investigations and findings of the Steyn and Goldstone Commissions, the SADF began to stonewall further investigations.[46]

The results of the Steyn Commission investigation are still controversial for many former senior military leaders in South Africa. According to retired general Georg Meiring, who was army chief of staff at the time, the "night of the generals" was based on hearsay evidence and the media.[47] There was bad blood between the SADF and the National Intelligence Service, he says, adding that Steyn was the acting chief of the SADF and relied on unconfirmed evidence given to him by military intelligence and the National Intelligence Service. He claims that Steyn and de Klerk often obtained information from only one source.

The Steyn Report found that Project Coast was offensive in nature. It argued that the SADF had created an offensive chemical and biological warfare program in order to test defensive measures and that the lack of civilian control meant that the program was used for nefarious purposes as only a few top leaders saw fit. According to the report, starting in 1985, the ANC/MK escalated its campaign of violence to include civilian targets, and the SADF and the SAP retaliated by using methods such as chemical and biological warfare.

The secret programs persisted after March 1990, when de Klerk was briefed about Project Coast and attempted to assert civilian control. According to the report, Generals Liebenberg and Meiring, in particular, knew about SADF secret programs, including Project Coast, and took an assertive hand in running them. General Liebenberg signed for Project Coast activities, as did Surgeon General Knobel.

At the beginning of 1993, when President de Klerk became aware of the scale, sophistication, and offensive uses of Project Coast, he finally ordered the destruction of all lethal and incapacitating chemical and biological warfare agents and an end to such research and operations. In January 1993, Minister of Defence Kobie Coetzee, acting on de Klerk's order, authorized all chemical and biological warfare research and development stopped. Project Coast documents containing formulas and experiments were to be transferred to CD-ROMs.

According to Dr. Kobus (Jack) Bothma's testimony at the Basson trial, an office secretary scanned the documents from Project Coast onto CD-ROMs. Philip Mijburgh transferred the CD-ROMs to the ministry of defense, where they were placed in vaults. President de Klerk was given a key to the contents so that only the state president could open it, along with the surgeon general, and head of the NIS, Dr. Niel Barnard. All three individuals needed to be present when the vault was opened.[48]

Although it seemed that Project Coast had been rolled back, Mijburgh issued destruction documents. "Destruction documents" were supposed to prove that Project Coast documents had been destroyed. However, the destruction documents were inconclusive. Although the South African government believed that it had rolled back Project Coast, four years later, in January 1997, police investigators found that Basson had taken copies of Project Coast documents home and hidden them in trunks, along with a considerable cache of drugs.

It became clear a decade later that not all chemical and biological warfare agents were destroyed in 1993. Large quantities of drugs were unaccounted for at the time the program was terminated and it remains unclear whether the former regime had a hand in the flood of drugs, including hallucinogenic drugs such as Ecstasy, that entered the Western Cape townships in the early 1990s.[49] Others believe that large quantities of the drugs manufactured under the auspices of Project Coast remained in Basson's possession or were secreted elsewhere.

Senior officials appearing before the Truth and Reconciliation Commission testified that all chemical and biological agents were destroyed.

Retired General Meiring has repeatedly stated that all chemical and biological agents were dumped out to sea 200 nautical miles south of Cape Argulhas in 1993. According to his account, the Forensic Branch of the SAP, which was headed by General Lothar Neethling, placed all agents to be destroyed on a schedule. While lethal chemical and biological warfare agents were destroyed, the irritants, including CR teargas, were kept for crowd-control purposes.[50]

According to Dr. Knobel's testimony to the Truth and Reconciliation Commission, SADF counterintelligence destroyed all chemical and biological warfare agents in January 1993. The accounts of Meiring and Knobel do not match. The methaqualone Basson purchased in Croatia was allegedly destroyed after de Klerk's order that work on all incapacitants should cease. On January 7, 1993, Dr. Knobel advised his superiors that South Africa "should conceal" CR teargas from the inspectors of the Chemical Weapons Convention. On January 14, 1993, South Africa formally acceded to the convention. However, work on the dispersion of CR teargas continued.[51]

After retiring, General Meiring said that the process of rolling back the chemical and biological warfare program took almost three years to complete. The front companies had to be commercialized and the scientists needed to be phased out.[52] In 1993, a forensic audit was conducted to determine the whereabouts of all funds and the availability of chemical and biological agents. The only problem that was detected by this audit was the Croatian swindle and the arrest of a South African agent by the Swiss government.

On March 31, 1993, Basson was retired from active duty in the SADF Medical Service by President de Klerk and became a reservist. Although Basson had been ordered to destroy Project Coast documentation, he took a large amount of Project Coast research documentation out of government files and stored them at his home or the homes of friends. At the time of his "retirement" he immediately joined Transnet, the state-owned transportation and infrastructure corporation that built and maintained railroads, tunnels, airports, and hospitals. As an employee of Transnet, Basson traveled to Libya on contract to give advice on military countermeasures to chemical and biological warfare attacks. When interviewed, retired general Meiring claimed that he did not know if Basson gave away secrets to Libya and other countries. Meiring stressed that the United States especially, but also the United Kingdom and other NATO countries, knew about Project Coast and were worried that information would fall into the wrong hands. Meiring believes that in 1993, American and British officials never knew exactly what chemical and biological agents South Africa possessed.[53]

The United States and other Western countries became more focused on possible proliferation concerns stemming from Project Coast activities after Basson left active military duty. These concerns increased during the second half of 1993, just as peace negotiations between the de Klerk government and Nelson Mandela and the ANC gained momentum. In August 1993, the Office of Serious Economic Offences informed MI6 and the CIA of the misdeeds of Basson and Project Coast. The Americans and British became even more concerned when Basson made his first trip to Libya on behalf of Transnet. This was the first of Basson's five visits to Libya, and it is possible that he sold Project Coast secrets.

During 1993, South Africa submitted a confidence-building measure, as stipulated by the Bacteriological and Toxin Weapons Convention, which provided details on the rollback of the defensive biological side of Project Coast. In November 1993, the United States and the United Kingdom objected to the South African confidence-building measure and began the process of interacting with the South African officials in an effort to ensure that Project Coast would be rolled back to their satisfaction. According to U.S. Ambassador Princeton Lyman, the South African confidence-building measure was not forthcoming on many aspects of the chemical and biological warfare program, including offensive uses, weaponization, and proliferation.[54]

According to Peter Goosen, a proliferation expert in the ministry of foreign affairs, the South Africans lacked the technical expertise to submit an acceptable confidence-building measure and sought British and American assistance. In the meantime, President de Klerk and his colleagues attempted to reassure the United States and the United Kingdom that the chemical and biological warfare program had been rolled back.[55]

On April 11, 1994, Ambassador Lyman and British High Commissioner Anthony Reeve delivered a démarche to President de Klerk.[56] The United States and the United Kingdom demanded that their experts be briefed, that all chemical and biological warfare systems and records (including the CD-ROMs) be destroyed, that abuses of the program be investigated and reported, and that the presumed new president, Nelson Mandela, be informed. According to David Steward, Lyman and Reeve regarded Basson as a "dangerous agent" who needed to be brought under control.[57]

Within the American inspection team, there were differences. Ambassador Lyman was primarily concerned with reducing the threat of proliferation, and State Department and CIA officials joined him in this concern. However, officials from the National Security Council were outraged by evidence of the use of chemical and biological warfare and wanted to see that those responsible were punished. Department of Defense officials were late in joining the U.S. team and felt marginalized. Consequently, they sided with the National Security Council. Ultimately, Ambassador Lyman was able to prevail, and the team focused on proliferation concerns. However, seeking convictions for past chemical and biological warfare use remained as part of the démarche.[58]

According to Knobel, President de Klerk and the South Africans cooperated with the American and British teams. However, Knobel and other South African officials believed that the Americans and the British were acting on the basis of questionable and uncorroborated evidence, some of which came from press reports. On April 21, 1994, South Africa responded to the démarche by asserting that Project Coast records were a "national asset" and that the CD-ROMs would not be destroyed. According to Knobel, he and Basson were told by their supervisors to brief the American and British experts and President Mandela.[59]

After the démarche and the inauguration of President Mandela in May 1994, American and British delegations arrived for the first of several visits to South Africa. Knobel, Basson, and others extensively briefed the delegations over a three-day period and took them on a tour of Roodeplaat Research Laboratories, which had been converted to accommodate commercial production. The SADF compiled a large file on Project Coast and gave it to the Americans and British.

South Africa reassured the British and the Americans that the three keys for gaining access to Project Coast secrets on CD-ROM were in the hands of the South African state president, the surgeon general, and the head of National Intelligence Agency (formerly the National Intelligence Service). The South Africans transferred information they had obtained from the Russian and Iraqi programs (including programs that produced flesh-eating bacteria) to the Americans. Teams from the United States, the United Kingdom, and the United Nations investigated the alleged January 1992 chemical warfare incident in Mozambique. In 1994 and 1995, American and British teams made more visits to South Africa to facilitate the rollback of the South African chemical and biological warfare program.

Wouter Basson and his trips to Libya were the main source of contention between the American and British teams and the South African government. In spite of the démarche, Basson continued to visit Libya in 1994 and 1995, until he had completed five trips. The United States and the United Kingdom kept up the pressure on South Africa to control Basson and suggested that the SANDF, which had replaced the SADF, rehire him. Dr. Knobel claimed that Basson was offered a job and money by the United States and United Kingdom but he declined. Opinion on the degree of damage Basson did varies. According to journalists William Finnegan and Thomas Mangold, American and British officials are certain that Basson was originally invited to Libya to help that country with chemical-warfare facilities at Rabta.[60]

In contrast, South African leaders, such as retired general Meiring, believed that Basson did not pass secret information on the chemical and biological warfare program to the Libyans or to other foreign governments. However, Meiring suggested that Basson gave the Libyans information and defensive chemical and biological warfare techniques. In 2000, it was still unclear how Basson passed information to the Libyans. Meiring stressed that Basson was always under instructions and claimed there was nothing that went unnoticed by his superiors. According to Meiring, much of the information for Project Coast was obtained during the 1980s from nationals from the United States, the United Kingdom, and Germany. He alleged that highly technical and advanced knowledge had passed from American, British, and German scientists to the South Africans, and in 1994 the South African government did not want to cause the American and British governments embarrassment by revealing that fact.[61]

Ambassador Donald Mahley, a U.S. state department proliferation expert, and his British counterpart led teams that examined Project Coast evidence and documents in 1994. Some U.S. officials and outside analysts have characterized the South African biochemical project as "pedestrian." However, the range of biological research programs conducted under the auspices of Project Coast has led several American experts who are very familiar with the details of Project Coast research programs to conclude that South African scientists developed some highly unique processes and procedures in their covert biological research and development.[62] A few U.S. officials have gone so far as to characterize Project Coast as the "second-most sophisticated program next to that of the Soviets."[63] These concerns were fueled further by the fact that by the early 1990s, the South African military had the capability to deliver nuclear warheads to targets in neighboring states and were working on the capability to launch chemical, biological, and possibly even nuclear weapons in tactical launch vehicles.[64]

In August 1994, Knobel briefed President Mandela, Defence Minister Joe Modise, and his deputy, Ronnie Kasrils. The SANDF also provided a large file on Project Coast to Mandela, Modise, and Kasrils. Before April 1994 and the elections, Mandela got only sketchy details from de Klerk about what was developed, according to senior ANC officials.

There had been a debate within the ANC from 1990 to 1994 about whether to keep the nuclear-weapons program. However, the conclusion to roll back the chemical and biological warfare program was unanimous. After coming to power in 1994, the ANC wanted to know where and why the information about that program had disappeared. The ANC believed that white South African scientists and former operatives who emigrated to the Middle East, the United States, the United Kingdom, and Canada sold many of Project Coast's secrets to foreign sources.[65]

After his inauguration, the new secretary of defense, retired general Pierre Steyn, briefed President Mandela on the findings of the Steyn Report. Mandela agreed not to release the report because of concerns that it might jeopardize the transition process. All parties who had access to the information in the report, including the Office of the State President, Deputy President F. W. de Klerk, and two attorneys general, kept it under wraps for more than two years.

In 1997, the *Weekly Mail & Guardian* reported that President Mandela had been in possession of the Steyn Report since 1994. Presidential liaison Parks Mankahlana denied that Mandela had a copy but confirmed that Steyn had briefed the president. The difficulties that de Klerk had in ensuring that his order to dismantle the chemical and biological warfare program was carried out and a widespread tendency among the architects of that program to stonewall politicians made a deep impression on the military leadership appointed by Mandela.

These experiences figured prominently in the mind of the new secretary of defense, Pierre Steyn, and others who were the first leaders of the new Office of Secretary of Defence (OSD). They believed that a ministry of defense led by civilians was critical for developing a professional and fully integrated South African National Defence Force (SANDF). The new OSD, which was patterned closely along the lines of the OSD within the U.S. Pentagon, was created in an effort to ensure coordinated civilian control of the military. An important mission of the newly created OSD from the start was to put in place oversight and accounting procedures that would make it impossible for SANDF personnel to engage in the type of fraud and out-of-control abuses associated with Project Coast.[66] In 1995, according to Dr. Ian Phillips, an ANC defense expert, the establishment of a defense department with the assistance of the United States and the United Kingdom made some progress in clearing up the problem of military dominance and the "security state." The 1994 Defence Act created better structural differentiation and civilian control. However, the Mandela government was forced to find a way to implement the Defence Act in a piecemeal fashion after it was found to be unconstitutional due to certain clauses. The ability of the OSD to effectively perform all of its functions is also limited somewhat by recent budgetary constraints.[67]

At the same time that reforms were being implemented in the South African military during the mid- to late 1990s, the South African civilian justice system was moving forward with its investigation of alleged widespread corruption, fraud, and abuse associated with Project Coast. Public knowledge about the investigation was aided by the fact that all the major local newspapers assigned their top investigative reporters to cover the unfolding story.

In November 1994, the Office of Serious Economic Offences, a special unit attached to the attorney general's department, completed an official report on the activities and financial irregularities of the network of companies (Project Coast) that supplied the SADF with pharmaceuticals and anti–chemical warfare equipment. The report was sent to Justice Minister Dullah Omar marked "top-secret."[68]

At the time, Jan Swanepoel, head of the Office of Serious Economic Offences, confirmed to the *Weekly Mail & Guardian* that the network of companies was under investigation in connection with the "flow of funds connected with an army project."[69] Another report in the *Sunday Tribune* in December 1994 described the network of companies working with SADF on chemical and biological warfare. They named the key directors of this network under investigation as Dr. Wouter Basson, Dr. Wynand Swanepoel, and Dr. Phillip Mijburgh and noted that all three had served in SADF's medical service (SAMS).[70] Using correspondence between Basson and Mijburgh, the *Weekly Mail & Guardian* reported that they were researching the legal aspects of chemical and biological warfare. The same newspaper also reported that SADF military officials used Council for Scientific and Industrial Research facilities to obtain and develop different strains of germs, some of which were highly toxic to humans.[71]

One week before, the *Weekly Mail & Guardian* had reported that ARMSCOR had acknowledged at the end of 1994 that it owned Protechnik, a chemical-warfare research plant. Protechnik described itself as the biggest nuclear, biological, and chemical weapons laboratory in Africa. It was officially designed to develop only defensive equipment against chemical weapons. However, its operations stirred protests (and continue to do so) in the Pretoria metropolitan area because of fears of accidents.[72]

By the end of 1994, more information about the chemical and biological warfare program was emerging from several other sources. They included an investigation by a team from the attorney general's office and reports in the *Sunday Tribune* and the *Weekly Mail & Guardian* based on their independent investigations. Reports emerged of experiments at SADF research firms, including some bizarre experiments involving dogs.[73]

Basson's trips to Libya continued in 1995.[74] In March 1995, the CIA and the Defense Intelligence Agency informed President Clinton of Basson's activities. Clinton authorized a delegation to South Africa, which met with Mandela. It is not certain if the delegation met with Basson or if he was in Libya. The Americans urged both the Mandela and de Klerk governments to bring Basson under control by rehiring him. On April 15, 1995, South Africa submitted a much-revised confidence-building measure. This time, the objections of the United States and the United Kingdom were addressed satisfactorily. Even so, the two countries continued to share concerns that Basson and others would spread the secrets on the CD-ROMs to states and groups of concern.[75]

In early 1995, Generals Meiring and Knobel sat down and discussed Basson after receiving information from the National Intelligence Agency, the CIA, and MI6. Basson had been asked by government and SANDF officials to curb his behavior, but there was no way to make sure that he was under control except to rehire him. Meiring and Knobel went to Deputy Minister of Defence Ronnie Kasrils and urged that Basson be rehired. Kasrils went to Defence Minister Modise and Secretary of Defence Steyn with the same recommendation.[76] In May 1995, in response to extensive pressure from American and British officials to do so, Modise and Steyn took Basson off reserve status and rehired him as a regular SANDF surgeon. Even after that, Basson made one more trip to Libya in October 1995.[77]

The South African government's apparent inability to control Basson was a source of increasing tension with the United States and its Western allies.

A U.S. government lawsuit in Philadelphia, Pennsylvania, against an American firm and ARMSCOR for illegally importing and using American technology created additional tense relations between the U.S. and South African governments and hampered U.S. investigations of possible ARMSCOR involvement in plans for chemical and biological weaponization. However, at the diplomatic and political level, U.S. relations with the Mandela government remained reasonably sound. Cordial relations at the highest level helped to ensure that the investigations into Project Coast were concluded satisfactorily. Finally, in October 1996, Deputy President Mbeki and U.S. Vice President Al Gore worked out an agreement so that ARMSCOR could plea-bargain at a meeting of the US–South African Binational Commission. Defence Minister Modise and the Parliamentary Defence Committee signed the agreement in July 1997.[78]

In February 1996, the Mandela Cabinet finally acted on the Office of Serious Economic Offences report after sixteen months of keeping it secret. This ruling gave OSEO investigators permission to follow the flow of funds overseas but did not agree to the request of the justice ministry that the secrecy on the project, which was regulated by the Protection of Information Act, be lifted. No one was charged immediately, and Project Coast's debts of 22 million rand had already been written off by the SANDF.

In May 1996, the Parliamentary Standing Committee on Public Accounts began its own investigations. This committee and a special parliamentary committee on Project Coast encountered resistance from the SANDF chief, General Georg Meiring, who refused to release information about the chemical and biological warfare program. According to one source, Meiring held the ANC-dominated government and Parliament in "complete contempt."[79] Even though parliamentary committee sessions were held in camera, members were unable to learn many details about Project Coast because of a transitional agreement reached by cabinet members of the Government of National Unity that details of Project Coast should remain secret and that an earlier cabinet decision to lift the secrecy from the project did not apply. The agreement, endorsed by President Mandela and his deputy presidents, Thabo Mbeki and F. W. de Klerk, supported General Meiring's position. There was also some concern that full disclosure might compromise ongoing criminal investigations. Among senior members of the Government of National Unity there were genuine concerns about the fragility of the political compromise that prevailed in South Africa and the possible reactions by the public or paramilitary groups to complete disclosure about Project Coast. At the time, Mandela's spokesman, Parks Mankahlana, explained that "an overall lifting can be considered once the OSEO investigation is over. . . . [T]here is no intention to impose permanent secrecy on the matter."[80] In August 1996, the special committee finally questioned Basson's involvement with the privatization of Roodeplaat. This was almost a year after Project Coast's debts had been written off, and it indicates how weak parliamentary oversight was in practice.

However, with the passage of time, officials in the Mandela and Mbeki governments have chosen to keep details about Project Coast and the dismantlement process secret. The South African government received a great deal of support from several states for these decisions, including the United States, the United Kingdom, Israel, and Germany. It has been alleged that these states are concerned that highly sensitive information about past secret relationships among these governments will be made public.[81]

BASSON'S ARREST AND PROJECT COAST'S EXPOSURE

In 1996, the South African Truth and Reconciliation Commission continued with low-level investigations into Project Coast, but it had so little information at its disposal that it seemed unlikely that anything new would emerge.[82] This expectation changed suddenly in January 1997, when Basson was arrested during a sting operation on charges of fraud and possession of illegal substances based on his alleged effort to sell 1,000 Ecstasy tablets. A subsequent search of the home of Sam Bosch, Basson's friend and business associate, uncovered five or six trunks and several suitcases that contained secret documents related to Project Coast.

Dr. Charles Villa-Vicencia, a senior Truth and Reconciliation Commission researcher; Mike Kennedy, the representative of the National Intelligence Agency; and representatives from the Office of Serious Economic Offences and the Gauteng Province attorney-general's Special Investigation Team went through the contents of the trunks. An agreement was reached that the National Intelligence Agency would take control of the documents and inventory the contents of the trunks.[83] The documents contained information that formed the basis of the commission's investigative work over the next eighteen months. The Truth and Reconciliation Commission called in Professor Peter Folb from the University of Cape Town Department of Pharmacology to serve as scientific advisor.

In March 1998, Commissioner Wendy Orr looked at some of the technical documents that had been found in Basson's trunks and was horrified by what she was able to understand. One of the first documents Dr. Orr examined was the now-infamous *verkope lys* (shopping or sales list).[84] After inspecting the contents of the trunks, one senior Truth and Reconciliation Commission investigator concluded that the trunks contained a "mixed bag" that included memorabilia, sensitive technical information that might prove embarrassing to foreign governments, and information readily available in literature available to the public (e.g., formulas for methaqualone and how to build a bomb). Several senior Truth and Reconciliation Commission officials felt that collectively, these documents confirmed the idea that South Africa's chemical and biological warfare program, particularly the biological side, had developed some very sophisticated processes and procedures.[85]

The beginning months of 1997 were the start of a period of unprecedented public disclosures by South African newspapers. A wide range of the government's most sensitive information about past activities continued to leak and be reported by the press throughout the Truth and Reconciliation Commission deliberations. Thus, despite the fact that many Project Coast hearings were held behind closed doors, the public heard much of this testimony in an almost daily stream of revelations. Many of these articles revealed details about the scope of Project Coast activities and efforts by past officials to use chemical and biological warfare against political enemies.

Throughout this period, Truth and Reconciliation Commission investigators were discovering "pockets of secret documents" that were supposed to have been destroyed by former SADF intelligence, SAP, and prison authorities. As commission investigators conducted spot-checks of police stations in six different areas, they found a wealth of information in documents that had never been destroyed.[86] The option of cooperating with the commission's investigators in exchange for amnesty and assurances that there would be no criminal investigation may have played a role in motivating at least some of the witnesses who later testified to come forward during this period. During 1998, several Project Coast scientists began to talk to authorities about what chemical and biological weapons and knowledge were developed, how the knowledge and weapons were used, and even some details about what was sold after the 1994 elections.[87]

Roodeplaat Research Laboratories scientist Mike Odendaal testified at the Truth and Reconciliation Commission and later at the trial of Wouter Basson that he had received instructions to start a factory where biological agents would be produced in mass form and that 200,000 rand (US$100,000 in 1985 dollars) had already been spent on the plans.[88] A new wing had been added to Roodeplaat for a production-scale laboratory with fermenters that could produce 300 liters or more of anthrax and other biological agents. Basson and his superiors in the SADF (Generals Liebenberg, Nieuwoudt, and Viljoen and Magnus Malan) approved an upgrade to a BSL-4 laboratory. According to Roodeplaat scientist Schalk van Rensburg, when Basson wanted the safety level raised to level four, two British scientists on an unauthorized visit from Porton Down (which had been privatized) helped and advised.[89] Dr. Daan Goosen, who was the managing director at Roodeplaat from 1983 through 1986, acknowledged that biological and chemical weapons had been produced and said that they were justified in the struggle against "the terrorists." Goosen also divulged details about experiments to reduce the rate of growth of the black population.[90]

The Truth and Reconciliation Commission disclosures had international ramifications. In June 1998, MI5 and British police reopened files on six people who had died in the United Kingdom during the 1980s and 1990s of apparent strokes or heart attacks to explore which of these deaths might have been murders related to South Africa's secret germ-warfare program. The dead individuals had all worked in the United Kingdom against the apartheid regime or had knowledge of Pretoria's secret operation in the 1980s to acquire and develop chemical and biological weapons. These investigations required unprecedented amounts of cooperation between South African and British intelligence services.[91] The results of these investigations are still classified.

In general, the Truth and Reconciliation Commission hearings played a critical role in revealing secret government activities by opening up a window on the house of horrors and letting the public know much more about what went on during the apartheid era. A great deal of effort went into the investigation and subsequent efforts to document the work of the commission. Dr. Peter Folb and Chandré Gould, a Truth and Reconciliation Commission investigator, both covered the Project Coast hearings at the commission during June and July 1998 and published their findings.[92] While important, the findings were based primarily on documentation and testimony from the hearings. The researchers did not have access to external sources that confirmed the sophistication and offensive nature of Project Coast. However, these disclosures helped to stimulate a national dialogue designed to allow the nation to start to heal.[93] These disclosures established an important precedent that helped ensure that Basson's trial would be open rather than closed to the public.

However, the Project Coast hearings were only a start, and a frustrating first attempt at that. Despite concerted efforts by Truth and Reconciliation Commission officials to leave adequate time for the Project Coast hearings, the hearings were held only for a few days during the closing days of the commission. There was not enough time to call all witnesses or question witnesses in depth. Many of the senior leaders of the commission have privately expressed intense frustration at the lack of candor or cooperation they received from many senior officials of the de Klerk government. P. W. Botha and many of his associates refused to participate in any part of the commission's investigations. The lack of cooperation was so widespread that there were discussions behind closed doors among senior commission officials about the wisdom of offering amnesty in exchange for testimony by all former government officials, including ones that had shown no remorse.[94]

Time may have softened some of the cynicism expressed by senior ANC officials concerning the Truth and Reconciliation Commission process. Moreover, South Africa's experience with the process and success at avoiding widespread violence among different ethnic groups in ensuing years has led many other parties who were former enemies to model their own efforts at political and ethnic reconciliation after South Africa's Truth and Reconciliation Commission.

Nonetheless, it is important to acknowledge that the commission hearings proved woefully inadequate as a vehicle for uncovering the most important questions related to South Africa's former biochemical programs. For example, it is not clear why Basson stole documents and kept them in his garage. Dr. Daan Goosen claimed that Basson kept the documents in order to have something of value (he was unable to replicate the knowledge on his own) and because he was possibly blackmailing people for protection.[95] Others expressed concerns that he kept the documents so he could sell them to foreign governments (e.g., Libya) in order to maintain his lavish lifestyle after stepping down as head of the project. As time goes by and more information about what was developed under the auspices of Project Coast leaks to the public, it does appear that many aspects of its research were not even mentioned at the Truth and Reconciliation Commission.

BASSON'S TRIAL AND FURTHER REVELATIONS

In March 1999, Wouter Basson was indicted on sixty-seven charges, including the murder of 229 individuals, conspiracy to commit murder, drug-trafficking, and fraud totaling 36 million rand (more than US$5 million in 1969 dollars). The state contended that Basson had turned Project Coast into a death squad and that he had secretly deposited millions of dollars in the Channel Islands and the Caribbean.[96] His trial turned out to be the most expensive in the history of South Africa, yet it was just as ineffective as the Truth and Reconciliation Commission had been with regard to prying details about Project Coast activities from the architect of the programs.

The trial started in October 1999, and immediately Judge Willie Hartzenberg dropped six charges, including one that Basson allegedly supplied drugs that were used to render about 200 SWAPO prisoners of war in South West Africa (Namibia) unconscious before they were dumped in the ocean. Charges of conspiracy to murder top ANC members Pallo Jordan and Ronnie Kasrils in London were also dropped. Crucial evidence, such as the transcript of Basson's bail hearing, which referred extensively to the 1994 interrogation by the Office of Serious Economic Offences, was also excluded.

Several witnesses testified that Basson was the central figure in an international sales and procurement network that included arms deals with the Libyan and Pakistani governments and drug deals. Other witnesses testified about Basson's involvement in manufacturing drugs and his lifestyle. Basson's financial dealings were extremely complex throughout the ten years of Project Coast, and the prosecution's charge sheet covering illegal transactions was several hundred pages long.[97]

What came out in court was that Basson started producing hallucinogenic drugs during the mid-1980s. At some point, he began producing drugs for profit. However, his motives remain unknown, as do the targets (or customers) and the planned or actual methods of distributing these drugs. Despite some lingering suspicions on the part of investigators, there is no hard evidence that Mandrax and Ecstasy were produced for illegal sale in South Africa. Instead, the prosecutors are still exploring the possibility that the bulk of these drugs were destined for illicit sale in Europe, India, and possibly the United States. While the details remain sketchy, one of the most remarkable features of the South African case is the fact that Dr. Basson is alleged to have been both the director of a sophisticated chemical and biological warfare program and a key figure in an international criminal syndicate that was dealing drugs.

In February 2000, senior prosecutor Anton Ackermann demanded that Judge Hartzenberg recuse himself on the grounds of bias in favor of Basson. Hartzenberg had already stated in court that he was "really bored" with the prosecution's examination of bank records that demonstrated Basson's alleged fraud. However, Hartzenberg refused to admit bias or remove himself from the trial.[98]

During the trial, Dr. Larry Ford committed suicide in Newport, California. Revelations of links between Ford and his associates and Basson, Knobel, and Project Coast led the FBI to initiate a "weapons of mass destruction" investigation. FBI agents were sent to South Africa to investigate Ford's activities there.[99] These events did not have a noticeable effect on the trial proceedings. Instead, despite a steady stream of witnesses, in June 2001 Judge Hartzenberg discharged Basson on fifteen of the sixty-one remaining counts, including the attempted murder of ANC leader Reverend Frank Chikane and conspiracy to murder another ANC leader, Dullah Omar.

In July 2001, Basson began giving nine weeks' worth of evidence. During his testimony, he implied that both U.S. and British intelligence agencies helped the SADF develop chemical and biological weapons that were allegedly used to kill hundreds of African guerrillas and civilians. Basson claimed that he had helped American officials find a cure for a fatal blood fever in Zaire (now the Democratic Republic of the Congo) in the 1980s.

Basson asserted that he became an adept sanctions-buster, smuggling the electronic parts of weapons into South Africa inside television sets and CD players. Through front companies, he acquired various properties for his unnamed Libyan, East German, and Russian "financial principals," including a private zoo, a farm, a travel agency, and a luxury guesthouse in Pretoria. Basson's evidence about the private zoo provided insight into the scientific skills and interests of Project Coast scientists and one of Project

Coast's most important objectives, crowd control. According to Basson, the animals in the zoo were to be used for research into the use of pheromones that could control crowds. Animals use pheromones to send messages to one another, especially when danger is sensed. If pheromones were used on a mass of people, it would make them fearful and less likely to riot. After the crowd was intimidated, another chemical could be released that would provide reassurance. Basson also claimed that he had been given a massive 250-gram sample of growth hormones by Russian scientists in 1988 or 1989; he believed the sample could only have come from an estimated 30,000 corpses. After 1989, it became possible to manufacture peptides and growth hormones in laboratories, and Basson set about establishing a peptide-synthesis process at Delta G, the SADF front laboratory. Basson claimed that the process was legitimate and that it was not a way for him to benefit financially.

Basson claimed in his testimony at the trial that in 1992 he was given US$2 million and ordered to obtain 500 kilograms of "Substance M," or methacholine, which is used to make Mandrax, which could be used for crowd control and other purposes. He claimed that the Swiss helped him obtain the shipment from the Russians. He also claimed that the Swiss were secretly negotiating with Russia to obtain nuclear arms in the early 1990s. Basson went on to testify that in December 1992, Project Coast was told to wind down and that he had to destroy his work. The drugs, including cocaine, Ecstasy, and Mandrax, were dumped at sea from an aircraft, he said.[100]

In April 2002, the Basson trial came to an end after more than 300 days of actual trial, almost 200 state witnesses had given evidence, and some 30,000 pages of transcripts had been produced. With many of Basson's former SADF superiors present in the courtroom, including Magnus Malan and Dr. Knobel, Judge Hartzenberg acquitted Basson of all remaining forty-five charges. A charge of possessing thousands of Ecstasy tablets was dismissed when Judge Hartzenberg accepted Basson's version of events and not that of drug dealer Grant Wentzel. The judge found that Wentzel had already been involved in drug-dealing before he met Basson and was not a reliable witness. Judge Hartzenberg also accepted Basson's testimony that he had ordered that all Project Coast documents be destroyed in 1993 and that he believed they had been. The judge accepted Basson's evidence that he had not packed the trunks and could not be found guilty of possession of cocaine, Ecstasy, and Mandrax, because Basson was not aware of the contents of the trunks. Finally, he rejected the evidence of forensic auditor Hennie Bruwer that Basson was the owner of the WWP group (W for Wouter [Basson], W for Wynand [Swanepoel], and P for Philip [Mijburgh]) of SADF front companies that stood at the center of the fraud charges.[101]

Protests against the acquittal came from Archbishop Desmond Tutu, the chair of the Truth and Reconciliation Commission, and from many other prominent South Africans, who were appalled that Judge Hartzenberg had sided with "Dr. Death." Immediately after the ruling, the government sought to appeal the case and retry Basson. In opposition to these moves, Basson and his defense counsel, Advocate Jakkie Cilliers, pointed to the cost of the trial. South African taxpayers had covered the costs of both Basson's defense team and the prosecution. Cilliers estimated that the state had spent "40 million to 50 million rand [US$6.4–8 million in 1999 dollars] a year" on the 30-month trial; expenses totaled 125 million rand (US$16 million in 1999 dollars). Basson gave a lower estimate of 40 million rand (US$5 million) and remarked that the amount would purchase, at retail rates, 5 million doses of the antiretroviral drug nevirapine for HIV/AIDS patients. Chandré Gould of the Centre for Conflict Resolution, which monitored the trial, agreed that the state may have spent 125 million rand ($16 million) over the entire ten or more years during which Basson was investigated and tried, including the initial military intelligence probe into finances of Project Coast, the seven-year forensic audit into the project, and the four-year investigation by the Office for Serious Economic Offences.[102]

In January 2003, the Swiss added a request that Basson and former police chief of forensics Lothar Neethling be interrogated in the presence of Swiss officials about trafficking in arms and nuclear goods. The Swiss government also wanted other records relating to Operation Coast.[103]

In the wake of the trial, Namibian officials considered extraditing Basson to stand trial for the death of more than 200 SWAPO prisoners of war. However, Basson is covered by a blanket amnesty that South Africa's last administrator general in Namibia, Louis Pienaar, extended in February 1990 to all people who had committed crimes in Namibia while exercising their duties as members of the SADF or the police.

The state prosecution started the appeal process for a new trial in April 2002, immediately after Basson was cleared of all charges. On June 3, 2003, the Supreme Court of Appeal in Bloemfontein denied the state's appeal for a retrial of the Basson case. Appeal judges Piet Streicher and Mohamed Navsa ruled that the state did not have the right to appeal against controversial Judge Hartzenberg's refusal to recuse himself.[104] By the end of 2003, the state was undecided about how to proceed and whether a second trial should be pursued. Basson seems to have finally escaped punishment for his alleged misdeeds. Never one to let sleeping dogs lie, Basson guaranteed that the saga would continue by seeking to be reinstated in his past position with the South African National Defence Force.[105]

Like South Africa's nuclear disarmament and dismantlement of its space-launch program, the rollback of Project Coast is explained by the unacceptable costs of continuing nuclear, biological, and chemical weapons and delivery systems research and development, the end of the external threat, and domestic politics (the unexpected leadership change to de

Klerk in 1989 and the regime shift in 1994). Lack of external pressure until the final few years of the program, greater secrecy surrounding the chemical and biological warfare program, and lack of civilian control of the military explain why the program took so long to roll back and why criminality and corruption grew.

Once de Klerk made the decision to assert civilian control over the military, he had to find military officers willing to implement his command. Lieutenant General Pierre Steyn helped de Klerk reassert civilian control in January 1993 and provided invaluable information de Klerk needed about the full scope of the offensive uses of the chemical and biological warfare program. The Steyn Report and the signing of the Chemical Weapons Convention led de Klerk to order chemical and biological warfare agents and documents destroyed. However, the documents were still under the control of Basson, Mijburgh, and the South African Military Health Service. After the documents were transferred to CD-ROMs, they were not destroyed but kept by Basson and, as we learned only in 2003, by several Project Coast scientists. We still do not know who else kept copies of key Project Coast documents.

The United States and the United Kingdom had known about South Africa's chemical and biological warfare program for decades but became really concerned only after discovering South African equipment that could use biochemical weapons in Iraq in 1991 and after seeing equipment that could be used with biochemical agents on display for sale to any interested arms purchasers in Pretoria. Basson's repeated trips to Libya, even after the ANC took power, raised even more alarm bells in Western capitals. Until the early 1990s, politicians and professionals serving throughout the national-security system in both the United States and the United Kingdom were more focused on nuclear-weapons proliferation than on chemical- and biological-weapons proliferation. However, once American and British delegations learned how sophisticated the South African chemical and biological warfare program was, especially the biological side, their interest and actions designed to contain and dismantle the chemical and biological warfare program increased dramatically.

The Project Coast case confirms the importance of psychological variables, including excessive fears and perceptions of external threats on the part of senior political and military leaders, a shared understanding of the nature of the problems the leaders confronted, and high levels of xenophobic nationalism among a wider white elite. All of these factors seemed important in understanding the national-security and foreign-policy decision making related to the development and rollback of nuclear, biological, and chemical weapons programs. The case also indicates the increasing importance, over the past thirty years, of international norms and pressure. International norms become particularly important when they are actively supported by the United States and other major powers. The secrecy accorded the chemical and biological warfare program illustrates that biological and chemical weapons have been considered "dirty" weapons since World War I and especially since the mid-1970s, when most states, including the two superpowers, committed themselves to the Bacteriological and Toxin Weapons Convention and agreed to give up biological weapons.

The South African case also demonstrates the significance of the organizational (or bureaucratic) politics model. As long as the state president and covert military agencies controlled Project Coast and other weapons of mass destruction/nuclear, biological, and chemical programs, they mushroomed. Once civilian control and parliamentary oversight were reestablished and international norms became significant, the ministry of foreign affairs could set about ensuring compliance with the Bacteriological and Toxin Weapons Convention and signing the Chemical Weapons Convention. Nevertheless, the chemical and biological warfare rollback process was tortuous and required sustained pressure by the United States and its allies.

The rollback of Project Coast and other secret programs is explained by the peculiar domestic situation in South Africa in which a regime gradually surrendered power to its enemy through negotiations. The realization that power had to be passed to the black majority, represented by the ANC, led the regime to strive to prevent the transfer and proliferation of its nuclear, biological, and chemical programs; pressure from the United States and other Western allies played a key role in this process. The regime and the United States feared proliferation, but there was an additional psychological motivation. The enmity toward and fear of the ANC among Afrikaner leaders, including de Klerk, led them to reject the concept of nuclear, biological, and chemical weapons in the hands of an ANC regime.

Basson's alleged illegal activities continued even after Project Coast was officially terminated. The behavior of Basson and other South African officials and Project Coast scientists even after they left the government payroll suggests that measures designed to limit the proliferation of chemical and biological warfare in the future are likely to be complicated political and bureaucratic undertakings. The South African case illustrates that it will be very important to effectively coordinate defense, counterproliferation, and crime-solving and crime-prevention agencies within and between countries in future rollbacks.

South Africa's experience with using the Truth and Conciliation Commission approach to a vast number of issues related to the old political order, including the dismantlement of covert weapons of mass destruction, illustrates the strengths and weaknesses of that approach. The Truth and Reconciliation Commission stands as a model and source of inspiration to other war-torn societies who are seeking to achieve a peaceful transition to a new political order. However, the commission's practice of granting amnesty to witnesses was not an effective mechanism for obtaining a complete picture of the former regime's covert weapons of mass destruction programs. In a similar vein, the Basson trial failed to uncover the full truth about Project Coast activities and highlighted the limitations of a judicial approach for resolving nonproliferation or counterproliferation issues.

However, the Basson trial was helpful in highlighting some of the complex ways that chemical and biological warfare project managers exploit transnational financial flows and international corporate instruments to quickly move, launder, and house large sums of money for either political or personal motives. New types of difficulties in penetrating complex international entities have already emerged as a major problem in countering transnational crime. Nonproliferation experts may have a new set of problems to worry about in this era of globalization. Thus, the Basson trial can serve as a cautionary reminder of what may become a more general trend: the initiation or continuation of covert chemical and biological warfare programs primarily as a means to cover illegal personal gains from the sale of chemicals and weapons (including chemical and biological warfare) and drugs.

Finally, the incomplete efforts to dismantle Project Coast illustrate how difficult it will be in the future to completely dismantle the expertise and pathogens produced from past covert biological or chemical weapons research and development. In 2003, a group of former Project Coast scientists tried to secure employment and money from the United States for personal reasons and to ensure that their expertise and the pathogens they had been keeping in their homes for over a decade would not fall into the wrong hands. The South African scientists offered the American government dozens of pathogens, including genetically modified specimens, and their services as biological warfare scientists in exchange for $5 millions' worth of employment contacts and cash. Most of the pathogens developed by Project Coast scientists, including the genetically modified agents, were agents that were familiar to scientists in the West. The Americans declined the offer on the grounds that the South African scientists were offering "nothing new."[106] At least this was the public rationale U.S. officials gave when they declined the offer made by Project Coast scientists. The claims that these scientists had been approached with offers of employment by countries in the Middle East and possibly by an agent for al-Qaeda did not prompt the United States to accept these scientists' offer. Perhaps that was a wisest course of action in a world where it is nearly impossible to control the flow of knowledge or resources needed to manufacture generically enhanced biowarfare agents. However, this recent incident involving biowarfare scientists, who are still seeking employment, and other recent stories about alleged efforts by Middle East countries and terrorist groups affiliated with al-Qaeda as well as efforts by right-wing supremacists to bring back white rule using whatever means necessary should all serve as cautionary tales about how serious and widespread a threat the use of biological and chemical agents is likely to become in the future.

EIGHT

Disarmament Trendsetter

The NPT [Nuclear Non-Proliferation Treaty]
provides us in Africa and the general community
with greater security than did the nuclear weapons which were destroyed. Southern Africa, until
very recently, was in a state of conflict, war, and
destabilization. Nuclear weapons were thought
to be providing security. I believe that security
is provided by nuclear disarmament rather than
by nuclear proliferation.

—South African Foreign Minister
Alfred Nzo, 1995

The economic history of the Afrikaner held many
lessons for South Africa's future growth. . . . Of
particular interest was the manner in which they
tackled the problem of the poor white Afrikaner
—brought about by English domination.

—President Thabo Mbeki, 2002[1]

In the 1990s, the first nonracial democratic South African government,
headed by Nelson Mandela, opted to become a disarmament and nonproliferation trendsetter. In less than five years, South Africa evolved from the
security-obsessed regime of the 1980s to one that eliminated nuclear, biological, and chemical weapons and ballistic missiles in the early 1990s.
The "new" state actively promoted weapons of mass destruction disarmament, nonproliferation, and conventional arms control after 1994. After
establishing a nonracial democracy in 1994, South Africa took a lead role
in the final stage of negotiations that led to a permanent Nuclear Non-
Proliferation Treaty in 1995. South Africa also played the lead role in creating an African Nuclear-Weapon-Free Zone (ANWFZ) in 1996 and required its sophisticated arms industry to control and monitor arms sales.
The first quote given above illustrates the spirit that permeated ANC leaders during the early years of majority rule in South Africa. ANC political
leaders were proud to be disarmament trendsetters.

Since these heady first years as a "new" state, South Africa's foreign and domestic policies have evolved and now more closely resemble a more "normal" nation-state. In 1999, South Africa took another step toward becoming a permanent democratic state by holding its second national election. Power was transferred peacefully from Nelson Mandela to his hand-picked successor, Thabo Mbeki. Peaceful leadership changes are rare enough in Africa that the South African election was a major event for the entire continent. President Mbeki is less charismatic and more controversial than Mandela. He is noted for making controversial statements about such disparate topics as the causes of HIV/AIDS and the best way to improve the living conditions of black South Africans.

The second quote above illustrates Mbeki's tendency to make provocative and controversial statements; he implies that the ANC regime might do for poor black South Africans what the Afrikaner National Party regime did for poor Afrikaners, who had been neglected under English domination. Continuing high levels of crime, the rise of Muslim vigilante groups, a resurgence of political violence by white right-wing extremists, and an unprecedented HIV/AIDS pandemic are issues that take precedence over weapons of mass destruction nonproliferation policies in South Africa today. It is hardly surprising that there has been only limited progress in recent years in implementing the monitoring procedures and domestic inspections required by the 1993 Non-Proliferation of Weapons of Mass Destruction Act. However, the many problems facing South Africa today also raise questions about the ability of the South African government to effectively control weapons of mass destruction proliferation threats inside the country and the region in the future.

Even more disturbing for those worried about proliferation issues are recent indications that the dismantlement of South Africa's nuclear program and Project Coast may have been less complete than was originally thought. Several questions remain unanswered about who might have been involved in past or ongoing efforts to pirate and possibly use or sell nuclear, biological, and chemical weapons, including biological pathogens. Recent moves to resurrect the space-launch program, albeit with several international partners, and to launch a civilian biotechnology initiative are both designed to promote economic growth by creating more high-tech jobs.

Job creation is a major priority for the government because it must meet the unfulfilled expectations of the South African electorate of the better life promised them in 1994 or risk losing a future election. While the motives behind these recent initiatives are economic, a new space-launch program and more new high-tech firms that use state-of-the-art biotechnologies increase the number of potential dual-use activities that will need to be monitored. As the country's foreign priorities and policies have evolved over the past decade, there have also been concerns expressed about potential conventional proliferation problems stemming from South Africa's conventional arms sales to human rights violators.

These sales and increased charges of patronage and corruption among senior ANC politicians tainted by the scandal have tarnished the government's image as a disarmament and nonproliferation trendsetter.

The peaceful election of another ANC-dominated government in the 1999 elections was touted as another democratic milestone. However, the weak showing of the National Party and subsequent realignments of opposition political parties in an effort to increase their strength underscored the fact that South Africa, while still a democracy, will be dominated by the ANC for years to come.[2] Against this context, Mbeki's comments about what can be learned from the Afrikaner architects of apartheid fuel concerns among many whites about whether they have a future in the new South Africa; clearly the focus of the ANC is on black and Coloured South Africans. Although no mainstream analyst expects the demise of the current government any time soon, the prediction of the Broederbond in the early 1990s that a majority-rule government would collapse looks much less absurd today than it did a decade ago.

This chapter discusses recent trends in detail in order to highlight changes in the pattern of South African foreign policy as the country evolves from a disarmament trendsetter toward a more "normal" state. Some residual concerns associated with the rollback of South Africa's nuclear, missile, and biochemical programs are also discussed, along with some new threats regarding weapons of mass destruction that have emerged since September 11, 2001. Each of these topics seems to support our general conclusion that while nuclear, biological, and chemical disarmament is difficult to reverse once the process has started, it is next to impossible to achieve complete nuclear, biological, or chemical nonproliferation. The proliferation of conventional weapons and illegal arms sales may be even harder to control.

SOUTH AFRICA AS A WEAPONS OF MASS DESTRUCTION DISARMAMENT TRENDSETTER

One might expect that a disarmament trendsetter would have an ideological, almost pacifist commitment to the elimination of nearly all weapons. The ideological past of the ruling party or parties would help explain why a state would become a disarmament trendsetter.[3] Furthermore, a democracy, particularly one that has recently made a transition from authoritarianism, would be more likely to become a disarmament trendsetter, because democracies tend to be more transparent and accountable than authoritarian regimes and more susceptible to social pressures to disarm.[4]

The most obvious example of a disarmament trendsetter was the United States during the late 1960s and early 1970s; in those decades, it destroyed its biological-weapons program and led in the promulgation of the Bacteriological and Toxin Weapons Convention and the Nuclear Non-

Proliferation Treaty process from 1965 onward. The role of democracy in the U.S. disarmament process was evident in the growing opposition in the 1960s to biological weapons in public opinion, in Congress, and in the media; these groups exerted pressure on the Nixon administration to end the offensive biological-weapons program.[5] After concluding that biological weapons were no longer morally acceptable and not particularly useful in military operations, the Nixon administration decided to end the program and headed the negotiation process of the Bacteriological and Toxin Weapons Convention to induce other states to sign and ultimately eliminate their weapons. The influential role that American public opinion, the legislative branch, and the media played in biological-weapons disarmament indicated that the United States was a democratic disarmament trendsetter.[6]

Middle powers, especially those that have undergone a democratic transition or are already democracies, tend to be more inclined than great powers or authoritarian states toward international cooperation, multilateralism, and disarmament. They are also more likely than great powers to combine their efforts and resources in order to make an impact on international affairs. Public opinion and peace movements influence governments in middle-power democracies. Other middle powers that have promoted disarmament include Sweden, the Netherlands, Canada, and New Zealand. Middle powers worked collaboratively through the UN Commission on Disarmament to promulgate the 1993 Chemical Weapons Convention and cooperated with nongovernmental organizations in realizing the international land mines treaty in the 1990s.[7]

Japan is a prime example of a middle power that underwent a transition from an authoritarian, aggressive state with weapons of mass destruction to a democratic disarmament trendsetter. In August 1945, Japan was the target of two nuclear attacks and subsequently was disarmed. In September 1945, Japan began a transition to democracy with a pacifist constitution. A decade later, the Liberal Democratic Party dominated Japanese politics and maintained Japan's commitment to a modest military that was armed only for defense. In Japan, survivors of the nuclear bombing and their families as well as public opinion have played a significant role in maintaining Japan's disarmament posture, and the country has taken a leading role in the UN and other international organizations on disarmament matters.[8]

Democratic peace theory helps to explain why democracies are less likely to fight each other; leaders must convince the public and legislatures that all other measures short of war have been exhausted before war is undertaken.[9] Also, middle-level democracies do not develop weapons of mass destruction because they are more open and transparent than authoritarian regimes. Most states that have weapons of mass destruction are authoritarian states that have been better able to maintain secrecy about their weapons. Transition to democratic government results in greater public scrutiny and accountability and ends authoritarian secrecy and can result in parties coming to power that are ideologically committed to disarmament, which in turn can enable a country to become a disarmament trendsetter.

LIBERALIZATION AND TRENDSETTING, 1989–1990

In previous chapters, it has been demonstrated that South Africa under apartheid developed into a "security state" in the 1970s that covertly produced weapons of mass destruction and missiles in the 1980s. With the end of the Cold War, resolution of the conflict in Namibia in 1988–1989, and transfer of power from President P. W. Botha to F. W. de Klerk, a more civilian-oriented South African government began the process of political liberalization, dismantling the security state, and ending the programs that produced weapons of mass destruction. The road to becoming a disarmament trendsetter began in November 1989, when President de Klerk ordered the dismantling of South Africa's nuclear-weapons program and initiated the process of accession to the Nuclear Non-Proliferation Treaty. South Africa became the first state to dismantle its nuclear-weapons program and was the first to end all weapons of mass destruction programs with the rollback of the chemical and biological warfare and missile programs in 1994.

De Klerk took dramatic steps to end weapons of mass destruction in part because he wanted to bring South Africa back in line with the United States, the West, and international law. Before the apartheid regime came to power in 1948, South African Prime Minister Jan Smuts had been a leading force in the founding of the United Nations and in drafting the Universal Declaration of Human Rights. When de Klerk became president, he sought to accommodate the United States and the West by initiating the disarmament process in South Africa. In November 1989, the de Klerk government informed the United States and the International Atomic Energy Agency about its nuclear-weapons program and its plan to disarm. However, de Klerk did not inform the South African public or Nelson Mandela and the African National Congress that its nuclear weapons were being destroyed and that South Africa was acceding to the Nuclear Non-Proliferation Treaty. It appeared that he wanted to deliver a fait accompli that could not be reversed by the ANC and that would support the nonproliferation goals of the United States. After most of the program was dismantled, the South African Parliament ratified the Nuclear Non-Proliferation Treaty in July 1991.

THE AFRICAN NATIONAL CONGRESS AND DISARMAMENT

Once the ban on the ANC was lifted in 1990 and the difficult period of negotiation and confrontation with the de Klerk government began, the

ANC spoke out strongly against the security state and its weapons programs and argued that a peace dividend would direct former military resources toward socioeconomic development. De Klerk favored a more gradual approach which would not cause even more layoffs in the defense sector, which was already being downsized and restructured. In the 1990s, the ANC joined forces with the Non-Aligned Movement to promote the ANWFZ and other disarmament initiatives. Therefore, it was influencing the security and development debates in South Africa even before the 1994 elections. In these elections, the ANC became the majority partner in the interim government.

Because the ANC party won the majority of seats in the 1999 election and promises to remain the ruling party of South Africa for the foreseeable future, it is important to understand its motivation and rationale for promoting a peace and disarmament agenda. From its inception in 1912, the ANC developed as a movement that was devoted to nonviolence and peaceful change. Before 1912, Mohandas Gandhi and the South African Indian Congress played a role in founding the ANC, and it continued to play an influential role in the new party. In the late 1940s, the ANC and the South African Indian Congress interacted with the newly independent India and its leaders, Gandhi and Nehru, and that influenced their commitment to nonviolence, civil disobedience, and pacifism. The ANC's 1952 Defiance Campaign, led by Nelson Mandela, was modeled on Gandhi's civil disobedience campaigns of the 1920s and 1930s in India.[10]

In the 1950s, the ANC established working relations with religious-based social activists in the United Kingdom and United States who were also connected to peace and disarmament movements and organizations. The most notable were George Houser of the United States and Canon John Collins of the United Kingdom. Houser led the Fellowship of Reconciliation, a pacifist organization that later formed the basis for the American Committee on Africa, while Collins headed Christian Action (U.K.), which evolved into the International Defence and Aid Fund for Southern Africa. From 1956 to 1961, Collins and Houser organized religious and political protests of the "treason trial" of Nelson Mandela and dozens of his associates in South Africa. In the United Kingdom, the movement against treason trials evolved into the Anti-Apartheid Movement (AAM-UK). In the 1960s, the ANC-in-exile joined forces with the AAM-UK, the British left, and the Campaign for Nuclear Disarmament.[11]

In the 1960s, the ANC joined the Non-Aligned Movement, which called for nuclear-free zones in Africa, Asia, Latin America, and Europe. Through the South African Communist Party and the training and education of ANC personnel in Eastern Europe, the ANC began a working relationship with the World Peace Council, which became a significant supporter of the anti-apartheid struggle. Many ANC exiles were strongly influenced by the peace and disarmament agenda of the World Peace Council.[12]

In 1961, the leader of the ANC, Chief Albert Luthuli, won the Nobel Peace Prize. Luthuli's award strengthened the movement's status among European peace activists. In addition, many West European governments, the World Council of Churches in Geneva, and national anti-apartheid movements in various countries began to work on behalf of the ANC's anti-apartheid struggle and against South Africa's militarization and weapons of mass destruction programs. The pacifist leanings of these organizations, actors, and institutions significantly influenced members of the ANC in exile.

South African expatriates Abdul Minty, who headed the AAM in London, and Kader Asmal, who led AAM in Ireland, were outspoken critics of weapons of mass destruction. In the 1970s, both Minty and Asmal became leaders of the campaign against apartheid South Africa's secret nuclear-weapons program. Their claims that South Africa had nuclear weapons were denied by the South African government. When they returned to South Africa in the early 1990s, they spearheaded efforts to make that country a democratic disarmament trendsetter. As senior governmental officials in both the Mandela and Mbeki governments, both Minty and Asmal continued their commitment to weapons of mass destruction nonproliferation; more recently they have devoted their efforts to conventional-weapons nonproliferation.[13]

In the 1970s and 1980s, the ANC-in-exile and anti-apartheid movements helped expose the South African nuclear-weapons program and strongly criticized the security state. In South Africa, a strong anti-militarist and anti–security state movement developed that included members of the Black Sash,[14] the Anglican Church (led by Archbishop Desmond Tutu), and a number of academics, including Renfrew Christie, an expert on the nuclear-weapons program who spent years in jail for his efforts to expose South Africa's program. In the late 1980s and early 1990s, as protests against the apartheid regime increased and the government banned established organizations, new organizations quickly formed under the banner of the United Democratic Front. Many of these new organizations were supported by grants from the U.S. and European governments and money from private organizations that were committed to supporting anti-apartheid activities in South Africa.

As members of the ANC returned from exile, they established the Military Research Group that helped formulate ANC defense and disarmament policy. The Military Research Group was composed of a number of defense and security experts who were primarily opposed to a large military establishment and to weapons of mass destruction and who also strongly supported civilian control over the military and a more defensive security strategy.

In the early 1990s, there were debates among ANC leaders about whether to keep the nuclear-weapons program or not. When the ANC began to learn about the existence of Project Coast in 1993, the unanimous conclusion was to roll back the chemical and biological warfare program because of its notoriety.[15] The weapons of mass destruction programs violated basic ANC pacifist principles. But it was divided about giving up nuclear weapons. Eventually, the ANC's disarmament wing prevailed; few ANC voices favored a strong military and the possession of nuclear weapons. No one in the interim South African government (1994–1999) openly supported the development of a nuclear bomb. If there was an Africanist faction among ANC leaders that might once have argued for obtaining a "black bomb" (an African nuclear weapon), it was only a fringe element in the party by 1994.

By late 1992, the ANC had intensified its efforts to uncover the nuclear-weapons program and charged that the government had hidden weapons-grade material from the IAEA. Under considerable pressure by the ANC, the United States, and other nation-states, de Klerk described in detail to the South African Parliament and the world in March 1993 how the Botha regime developed nuclear weapons and how the de Klerk government had begun the process of dismantling and destroying the bombs in early 1990 and had completed it in mid-1991. The ANC criticized de Klerk for his failure to fully disclose the details of the nuclear-weapons program and for the erroneous claim that the program had been fully rolled back by the time the Nuclear Non-Proliferation Treaty was ratified in July 1991. After de Klerk's speech, the IAEA gained access to all facilities previously used in the nuclear-weapons program.[16]

While de Klerk was a disarmament trendsetter in the nuclear-weapons arena, he agreed with the SADF and SAP position that South Africa should keep its New Generation Teargas in violation of the Chemical Weapons Convention that South Africa had just ratified.[17] After 1990, the ANC's ties to Libya and other non-aligned states continued, which concerned the United States and its allies. Moreover, as the ANC moved toward assuming power in 1994, ANC/MK military leaders argued against major cuts in defense spending and the defense establishment and in support of strengthening the military's role in peacekeeping and enforcement in Africa.

Arguments by the ANC's Military Research Group for a smaller and more defensive military eventually proved to be persuasive. The Military Research Group argued that the "peace dividend" should be spent on socioeconomic development. Their argument prevailed over that of the ANC/MK military leaders and other hawks, as did the intense lobbying by the business community and government officials who were working on the economy for policies that would attract more foreign investment. The resulting national strategy devised by the ANC, the Reconstruction and Development Program, was based on neo-Keynesian rather than socialist principles.[18] The Military Research Group and other groups that favored cuts in defense and an expansion of social welfare programs played major roles in the ANC's work on a broadly defined security strategy. The work of these groups culminated in the 1996 national defense white paper, which provided a blueprint for restructuring the military and the defense establishment and for expanding the peace dividend.[19]

The de Klerk government helped to create a substantial peace dividend by ordering the termination of the weapons of mass destruction programs and major cuts in defense industries and the military. These were difficult decisions; many people lost their jobs in the midst of a severe recession. However, many of the leaders, engineers, and scientists who ran and designed the weapons programs understood that the time had come to terminate these programs, even if it increased unemployment. Many believed that the nuclear-weapons program and the chemical- and biological-weapons program had been developed by the apartheid state to stop "communism" and the "black onslaught," and both of those "threats" had subsided.[20]

Many of the professionals who worked on covert weapons programs shared the concern of apartheid politicians about allowing these weapons and state secrets to fall into the hands of the ANC/MK. While many white professional engineers or scientists who had worked on the secret projects emigrated, others have been able to continue working successfully as government employees or employees of privatized defense companies affiliated with Denel. However, some former governmental officials and professionals who worked on weapons of mass destruction programs who left public employment voluntarily or lost their jobs before or shortly after the political transition may be proliferation risks.

By late 1993, negotiations propelled the ANC toward assuming power. As elections and the handover of power to the ANC approached, the United States and the United Kingdom became increasingly concerned about the proliferation of chemical and biological warfare secrets by South Africa and issued their démarche of April 1994.[21] The United States and the United Kingdom demanded that their technical experts be briefed, that all chemical and biological warfare systems and records (including the CD-ROMs containing sensitive material) be destroyed, that abuses of the program be investigated and reported, that Nelson Mandela be informed of the existence of the programs and their destruction, and that Wouter Basson be brought under control.[22] The South Africans believed that the Americans and British were acting on the basis of questionable intelligence and uncorroborated evidence, some of which came from press reports.[23] South Africa responded to the démarche by asserting that Project Coast records were a "national asset" and that the CD-ROMs would not be destroyed.[24] This refusal and subsequent events, such as disclosure by a group of former Project Coast scientists in 2003 that they had retained many samples of biological agents from the dismantled program, continue to raise questions about the effectiveness of the efforts of the current South African government to monitor potential proliferation risks.

De Klerk was not completely forthcoming about the weapons of mass destruction programs and their partial rollback; he knowingly violated the Chemical Weapons Convention and proved incapable of controlling Wouter Basson and potential chemical and biological warfare proliferation. The United States and the United Kingdom monitored the de Klerk government in the nuclear-weapons disarmament process and later the dismantling of the chemical and biological warfare program. The ANC disarmament camp's initiatives were an important factor that pushed de Klerk to become more transparent and accountable and to completely disarm. In 1994, President Nelson Mandela and the ANC-led government hoped to go well beyond the de Klerk government's record as a disarmament trendsetter.

ANC RULE AND DEMOCRATIC DISARMAMENT TRENDSETTING

In the general election in April 1994, a South African government was elected by the majority and not just by the white minority for the first time. The interim government, the Government of National Unity, headed by President Nelson Mandela and the ANC with Deputy President de Klerk and the National Party as junior partners, was committed to implementing new norms of transparency and accountability in all areas of policymaking that would make it impossible for the government to engage in large-scale programs to develop and sell weapons without first obtaining the consent of elected officials. Furthermore, the Military Research Group and a broad range of anti-militarist groups and individuals exerted pressure on the ANC-led government to continue South Africa's disarmament policies and reduce the military. However, the "new" South Africa manifested many of the same problems and conflicts that were present before 1994, particularly in the area of defense and security. What had changed were heightened perceptions of legitimacy and increased expectations about what the government would deliver toward socioeconomic development.

President Mandela endeavored to maintain a political consensus among an uneasy alliance of former adversaries, particularly between the ANC and the National Party. Communication and cooperation between ministries and inside the government were low. Mandela was frequently called upon to personally intervene in conflicts that threatened to divide the Cabinet. His importance and stature maintained the uneasy coalition government. Progress was slow in implementing the Reconstruction and Development Plan that was designed to bring tangible improvements to the lives of millions of black South Africans. Racial integration within the armed forces and the restructuring of the civilian police proved to be problematic.

Many of the delays and problems encountered in establishing a new South African National Defence Force throughout the latter half of the 1990s were tied to the fact that the new government had to integrate and train members from seven different liberation and homeland defense forces into a cohesive force. Historically, both the South African air force and the South African navy were off-limits to black South Africans. The SANDF had to formulate and implement new affirmative action programs in an effort to try to recruit more black and Coloured recruits into all the services.

Many other activities of the new "rainbow coalition" government were delayed or put on hold while the new government addressed more pressing issues and priorities. The ongoing work of the Truth and Reconciliation Commission, which was empowered to investigate the political crimes committed by apartheid state security forces, was delayed by nearly a year. This meant that during this period, arms control and acquisition matters were centralized and placed under civilian control.

In May 1996, the government released *Defence in a Democracy: White Paper on National Defence for the Republic of South Africa*.[25] For more than a year, parliamentarians, civil society representatives, academics, and other experts had been closely involved in the debate that led to the drafting and finalization of the white paper.[26] It represented the most important expression of the anti-militarist camp; it called for further disarmament trendsetting, controls on arms sales, and direction of the peace dividend toward development.[27]

A number of policy shifts demonstrated the Government of National Unity's commitment to nuclear disarmament at home and facilitated its constructive role in strengthening the nuclear nonproliferation regime abroad. The South African government decided in 1995 to end its subsidy of the uranium-enrichment program; it shifted to cheaper foreign sources for highly enriched uranium that would make it more difficult to revert to building nuclear weapons in South Africa. The government attempted to regulate more tightly the activities of ARMSCOR, the AEC, and other agencies. It demoted ARMSCOR from its position as the lead implementing agency in nuclear nonproliferation matters. Government efforts to transform those agencies and turn over top leadership at ARMSCOR, the Atomic Energy Commission, and other agencies were slowed by the high cost of "golden handshakes" that promised high-level bureaucrats lucrative early retirement benefits that could not be readily delivered.

The government also moved to implement the domestic monitoring of the requirements of the 1993 Non-Proliferation of Weapons of Mass Destruction Act. The Ministry of Trade and Industry was designated as the implementing agency for the Non-Proliferation Council, a Cabinet-level body that has the authority to implement the Non-Proliferation of Weapons of Mass Destruction Act. The Non-Proliferation Council reports directly to the president and acts as South Africa's control mechanism over all chemical and biological agents that have the potential to be used as weapons of mass destruction. Although a number of major industrial sectors are excluded from provisions of the act, the inspection regime authorized by this law has established important new precedents in the government's ability to engage in on-site inspections of civilian industrial facilities capable of producing agents of chemical or biological warfare.[28]

It was clear that after 1994, the top political leadership in South Africa was committed to establishing norms of democracy in domestic affairs and working toward nonproliferation. President Mandela pledged to abide by the Nuclear Non-Proliferation Treaty and to make Africa free of nuclear weapons.[29] He promised to open the records of the apartheid state to public scrutiny, including any additional existing information on secret weapons programs. A number of new or revised laws pertaining to national security were implemented that would make it increasingly difficult for the government to undertake future secret weapons of mass destruction or missile programs. The new government actively worked to strengthen and expand South Africa's commitments to nonproliferation.

In the spirit of international cooperation over chemical and biological warfare issues, the Mandela government welcomed and cooperated with American and British delegations. The first delegation was briefed and taken on a tour of former chemical and biological warfare facilities that had been converted to commercial production. South African officials reassured the American and British delegates that the keys to the vault that contained the CD-ROMs with Project Coast secrets were in the hands of only President Mandela, the surgeon-general, and the head of the National Intelligence Agency. In the spirit of full disclosure, the South Africans also admitted to transferring information that they had obtained from the Russian and Iraqi programs to other countries. After seeing the range of pathogens Project Coast had developed, the Americans found that South Africa had developed some unique processes and procedures that could pose proliferation dangers if not controlled.[30]

The Nuclear Non-Proliferation Treaty Review and Extension Conference in April and May of 1995 at the United Nations in New York brought South Africa onto the world stage as an influential democratic middle power committed to disarmament. South Africa played a lead role in building support among non-nuclear nations for the indefinite extension of the Nuclear Non-Proliferation Treaty. In addition, South Africa played a key role as a diplomatic bridge-builder, which resulted in the Non-Aligned Movement's support for the indefinite extension of the Nuclear Non-Proliferation Treaty. The South African delegation advocated the position that the continued support of the Nuclear Non-Proliferation Treaty should not be jeopardized by an incipient struggle between the nuclear "haves" and "have-nots," particularly between Egypt and Israel. South African diplomats also stressed that the review and extension process should be strengthened, which would reinforce the nonproliferation regime. South

Africa also played an active role in discussions that resulted in the adoption of a set of Principles and Objectives for Nuclear Non-Proliferation and Disarmament, which focus on compliance with the provisions of the Nuclear Non-Proliferation Treaty, nuclear disarmament, conclusion of the Comprehensive Test Ban Treaty, and the establishment of regional nuclear-weapon-free zones. South Africa viewed the decision to adopt these proposals as initial steps toward the achievement of the goals of the Nuclear Non-Proliferation Treaty and total nuclear disarmament.[31]

South Africa also played an active role in the successful Nuclear Non-Proliferation Treaty Review Conference in 2000, helping to bring together states as partners in the New Agenda Coalition for the elimination of nuclear weapons; members included Brazil, Egypt, Ireland, New Zealand, Mexico, and Sweden. The New Agenda Coalition lobbied nuclear-weapons states for a commitment to eliminate nuclear weapons. South Africa and the other members of the coalition also focused on that agreement as a step toward implementing the nuclear disarmament provisions of the Nuclear Non-Proliferation Treaty's Article VI.[32]

The ANC undertook initiatives in the 1990s to ensure that Africa became a nuclear-free zone. From its founding in 1961, the Non-Aligned Movement and member states such as India and observers such as the ANC have promoted the concept of nuclear-weapon-free zones in the Indian Ocean, Latin America, the South Pacific, and elsewhere. In 1969, the first nuclear-weapon-free zone was created with the ratification of the Treaty of Tlatelolco and the Latin American and Caribbean Nuclear-Weapon-Free Zone. In 1964, the Organization of African Unity, with the ANC as an observer, adopted a Declaration on the Denuclearization of Africa. This was a significant agreement because Egypt and Algeria had the potential to develop nuclear weapons.

After extensive negotiations, the African Nuclear-Weapon-Free Zone (ANWFZ) Treaty was adopted on June 2, 1995 at Pelindaba, site of the AEC of South Africa. African states agreed that the headquarters of the African Commission on Nuclear Energy would be situated in South Africa. Later that month, the OAU Assembly of Heads of State and Government meeting in Addis Ababa, Ethiopia, approved the ANWFZ Treaty. The treaty was subsequently endorsed at the 50th Session of the United Nations General Assembly in the fall of 1995. The ANWFZ Treaty was opened for signature on April 11, 1996, at a special summit in Cairo, Egypt. At the summit, African states declared their intention, through an international agreement to be concluded under UN auspices, not to manufacture or acquire control of nuclear weapons. All of the nuclear-weapons states signed the relevant protocols to the Pelindaba Treaty. The treaty was broad-ranging in scope; it declared Africa a zone free of nuclear weapons, strengthened the nonproliferation regime, and promoted cooperation in the peaceful uses of nuclear energy, disarmament, and regional peace and security. Since 1996, one drawback has been the slow ratification of the treaty by the fifty-four African states. Twenty-eight states have ratified the treaty, but it has still not come into effect. South Africa has taken the lead in trying to persuade African states to speed up the ratification process.[33]

One reason for the delay in ratifying the Pelindaba Treaty is that the treaty includes the prospect of establishing unprecedented new powers under international law to regulate the flow of shipping to the South Atlantic and South Indian Oceans and the exploitation of natural resources found in the South Pole. The treaty, if it comes into effect, may also lead to new restrictions on the movement of nuclear materials though the southern Indian and Atlantic Oceans. This future possibility is why some actors within the U.S. military initially wanted the U.S. government to oppose South Africa's efforts to establish an African nuclear-free zone. The fact that the U.S. government decided to support the treaty was an important indication of how useful and valuable it felt the Mandela government's international nuclear nonproliferation policies and behavior were as a nuclear trendsetter during the 1990s.[34] Whether the U.S. government will continue to support this precedent-setting treaty in the future remains to be seen.

PROBLEMS OF
CONVENTIONAL ARMS CONTROL

When the ANC came to power in 1994, the South African government sought to control exports and limit imports of conventional arms and build on its record as a weapons of mass destruction disarmament trendsetter. However, control of conventional arms proved more difficult to achieve. The problem was that control of conventional arms hurt the South African economy and displaced workers in a country burdened with high levels of unemployment. By April 1994, South Africa had established itself as the tenth-largest arms producer in the world; it had approximately 800 manufacturers of weapons and arms components that employed a workforce of 50,000. Exports accounted for approximately 1 percent of global arms trade, valued at an estimated US$225 million.[35]

In May 1994, the interim government came to office with a policy not to sell arms to states that violated human rights. However, the effectiveness of this policy was called into question in September 1994, when ARMSCOR delivered weapons to Yemen, a human rights violator, in defiance of national policy. The incident demonstrated how easily documentation of arms exports could be falsified, and it was another reminder that ARMSCOR, Denel, and other defense industries were skilled at avoiding public scrutiny and accountability.

In October 1994, President Mandela appointed the Cameron Commission to investigate this violation and other illegal acts by ARMSCOR. In June 1995, the commission's first report called for the transformation of ARMSCOR and for a more effective policy to control and monitor arms sales. In March 1995, Defence Minister Joe Modise was named to head a commission on South Africa's arms trade policies. In August 1995, the findings and proposals of these two commissions resulted in the establishment of the National Conventional Arms Control Committee (NCACC), which was headed by Kader Asmal and composed of ministerial-level officials, as well as the creation of other arms-control bodies.[36]

The 1996 white paper on defense strongly linked human rights performance and arms control, stating that "South Africa shall not transfer arms to countries which systematically violate or suppress human rights and fundamental freedoms."[37] The government sought to prevent unauthorized diversions of weapons sold by South Africa, and it also worked to strengthen the implementation of arms controls through enhanced transparency, public scrutiny, and accountability. The NCACC raised expectations that South Africa would be able to enforce government controls of arms sales by its sophisticated weapons industry.

In the aftermath of the Yemen scandal, South Africa refrained from selling arms to a number of states with questionable human rights records, including Nigeria after the execution of human rights activist Ken Sara-Wiwa in November 1995, and Pakistan after the military coup in October 1999. South Africa stopped providing maintenance for previously purchased South African helicopters in Sudan, albeit under U.S. and international pressure. South Africa also refused to supply riot equipment to the Kenyan police in 1997 and teargas to Zimbabwe in 2000 for suppressing demonstrators and riots.[38]

While South Africa demonstrated restraint in some cases, its track record was uneven. Consequently, South Africa cannot be classified as a trendsetter in conventional arms control or disarmament. In 1996, Kader Asmal rejected two proposals from the Cameron Commission's second report to categorize potential customers according to their human rights records and to give Parliament the right to review and veto all arms sales. Asmal's decision to reject these recommendations raised questions about his and the NCACC's commitment to arms control.[39] Asmal and the NCACC were accused of being ineffective and of producing falsified paperwork in monitoring South Africa's arms trade.[40]

The interim government failed to be fully transparent in its reports to the UN Register of Conventional Arms, which collates information on seven major weapons categories and represents an important transparency and confidence-building instrument. South Africa reserved the right to withhold the reporting of arms exports when necessary to protect the confidentiality of its clients. Moreover, South Africa stated that it would only disclose such transfers "once the full contractual obligations with regard to full [weapons] systems have been achieved."[41]

In September 1996, the NCACC approved arms sales to Rwanda despite its questionable human rights record. Rwanda was fighting against

Hutu extremist forces that had been responsible for the 1994 genocide. In January 1997, the NCACC approved the sale of electronic tank sightings for T-72s to Syria, which resulted in protests from both Israel and the United States. Similarly, it sold Algeria a remote-piloted Seeker vehicle in 1997; Algeria quickly became South Africa's largest arms customer. Although Algeria and Syria were major human rights abusers, they had historically been supporters of the ANC during the anti-apartheid struggle, and the ANC government was repaying a debt to two stalwarts of the Non-Aligned Movement.[42]

In July 1997, three South African newspapers disclosed a US$1.6 billion arms sale to Saudi Arabia, the biggest South African weapons transaction ever. Subsequently, the arms manufacturer Denel sought but failed to block further revelations by suing the three newspapers and a journalist under the 1968 ARMSCOR Act, which prohibited the disclosure of any information relating to the supply, marketing, and export of armaments.[43] Defence Minister Modise commented: "We were placed in this humiliating position because of our own press, which is supposed to be working in the interest of South Africa."[44]

In 1998, South African–produced phosphorus artillery shells invoiced for Malaysia ended up in Sudan. A government official revealed that a diversion had clearly occurred, but Asmal and the NCACC did not investigate the incident. It subsequently transpired that Denel was actively pursuing a lucrative weapons deal with Malaysia and had asked former President Mandela to help them win the sale.[45]

Efforts at arms control confronted multiple problems of entrenched interests and a military-industrial complex in which ARMSCOR and Denel interacted with the Department of Defence and the Department of Trade and Industry. Civil society forces in favor of human rights were comparatively weak. For example, Barney Pityana, head of the constitutionally established South African Human Rights Commission, complained that the government seldom consulted his commission. The human rights unit within the Department of Foreign Affairs remained underdeveloped.[46] In a similar vein, several members of the South African Office of the Secretary of Defence complained about the limited resources available for obtaining the skills and equipment necessary to monitor procurement, acquisition, and training procedures.[47]

From 1997 to 1999, the process of scrutinizing defense-related industries was relatively closed, especially when compared with the review process that led to the white paper on national defense. On December 1, 1999, the cabinet approved the *White Paper on Defence Related Industries,* which emphasized enhancing the viability of the defense industry and the importance of arms exports to the industry's future. At the same time, it managed to pay lip service to a restrained arms-trade policy and the NCACC's 1995 code of conduct and the call for an independent inspectorate featured in the earlier white paper on national defense.

In 1998, the Conventional Arms Control Bill, which was drafted to replace the opaque ARMSCOR Act of 1968, was submitted to the National Assembly. As in the case of the review process for the *White Paper on Defence Related Industries,* the review of the legislation was secretive, with closed parliamentary hearings. The bill was submitted in order to provide the necessary legal framework to the NCACC and to establish an independent inspectorate to oversee South Africa's defense industries.[48] It was also hoped that the bill would prompt the South African government to end its restrictive policy on reporting to the UN Arms Register and publish details of arms sales, including the quantities and specific types of weapons sold. Unfortunately, the Conventional Arms Control Bill was tabled in Parliament in late July 2000 and has yet to be revived, representing another setback for the anti-militarist camp.

In 1998, the interim government announced a US$5.35 billion arms purchase (including four corvettes, three submarines, and sixteen jet fighters) from several European states (Britain, Germany, Italy, Sweden, and France) that contravened the commitment to further disarmament, a defensive military, and the peace dividend of the Military Research Group and the white paper on national defense. The South African navy and air force articulated strong arguments for the arms purchases and skillfully lobbied the government. The arms purchases included more than US$20 million in offsets, which resulted in subcontracting to the South African defense industry. For example, South African industry is producing the guidance systems for the corvettes. The offsets also provided European companies with the opportunity to acquire South African defense industries. For instance, British Aerospace was interested in buying Denel Aviation.[49] However, the offsets also opened the door to corruption investigations involving top ANC officials, including former ANC/MK officers; the chief whip of the National Assembly, Tony Yengeni; and two cabinet ministers, Moses Mayekiso and Esop Pahad. More than thirty Mercedes-Benzes were shipped to ANC officials. In 2000, the Heath Commission was authorized to investigate the linkage between arms purchases and corruption but quickly came under pressure from the Office of the President not to pursue its investigation too diligently. The Campaign against Arms Trade (U.K.) challenged the offsets, but a British court found that it was not illegal to bribe foreign (South African) nationals in the U.K. The arms purchases raised serious doubts about South Africa as a democratic disarmament trendsetter in the conventional arms arena.[50]

Allegations of bribery, corruption, and wrongdoing among senior South African politicians related to the arms-for-investment deals have not gone away. Instead, investigations into wrongdoing expanded in South Africa and in several European countries and started to have far-reaching political implications beyond the charges associated with the original purchase agreements. During 2002, new allegations were made that involved former defense minister Joe Modise. By 2003, the current defense minister, Mosiuoa Lekota, who had escaped allegations of wrongdoing in past investigations, was accused of covering up past illegal activities by government officials. Even President Thabo Mbeki found himself on the defensive by having to address pointed questions about why the government was going ahead with the controversial arms-for-investment deal whose costs had risen to 52.7 billion rand (about US$6.5 billion) when the government was claiming that it was unable to afford the costs of supplying antiretroviral drugs to HIV/AIDS patients as mandated by a recent court decision.[51]

In spite of domestic criticism over the costs and new allegations of corruption involving high-level ANC party officials and Cabinet-level government officials, the ANC-led government remains dedicated to past commitments to modernize defense. Instead of exercising an option to cancel the purchase of twelve more fighter jets in 2002, Defence Minister Mosiuoa Lekota and Trade and Industry Minister Alec Erwin emphasized that the government remained committed to reequipping the national defense force. Erwin stressed that South Africa could afford to pay for the military modernization plan because the country's finances had improved in recent years.

Sounding very much like the defense minister of a "normal state," Lekota stressed that "the government was committed to equipping SA's armed forces so they could deal with a threat of war or with other demands such as peacekeeping or combating piracy at sea." Lekota noted "the defense spending had fallen as a proportion of the government's budget from 9 percent in 1994 to 6 percent." He went on to suggest that "Al-Qaeda had a budget higher than that of some nations and that some drugs syndicates had better ships than those of the SA navy" and noted that "the national defense force was facing block obsolescence in seven strategic areas of its main equipment, due to the effect of continued sanctions." His pre-1994 revolutionary rhetoric was evidenced when he went on to blame the poor state of South Africa's military equipment on the previous regime and suggested that one reason the apartheid government had agreed to negotiate with the African National Congress was because it no longer had a viable defense force.[52]

Few military analysts dispute the assessment that South Africa needs modern equipment and an expanded national-security force. In addition to maintaining border security along the Mozambican and Zimbabwean borders and offshore patrols spanning two oceans, South Africa has taken on greatly expanded peacekeeping missions throughout the region. South Africa deployed a second battalion to Burundi as part of the African Union's first peacekeeping force. South Africa is also committed to playing a major role in peacekeeping efforts in the Democratic Republic of the Congo and played a decisive role in bringing a new Southern African Development Community defense pact into existence in August 2003. South African defense forces are also expected to contribute to a planned African standby force. These and other new national and regional defense force commitments, which are supported by funds and cooperative defense agreements with the United States and other Western countries, illustrate that South Africa is increasingly adopting the responsibilities associated with being a regional hegemonic and "normal" middle-level power.

South Africa is likely to continue to adopt more-conventional national-security and arms-sales policies as it renews long-frozen ties with former allies in the West. New national-security interests and commitments are being reinforced by the increased contribution defense export sales and cooperative agreements now make to the country's foreign export account. In recent years, South African arms manufacturers and defense corporations have continued to expand their markets and have been remarkably successful at negotiating a number of lucrative contracts in several niche markets abroad. Many of these recent exchanges involve the sale of defense components to foreign companies or co-production deals with large foreign defense contractors. These deals include several multi-billion-dollar deals to co-produce and sell ammunition to both the British and American militaries.

One indication of how important the new national commitment to expanding defense co-production agreements has become was the fact that in March 2003, Kader Asmal, the minister of education and head of the National Arms Control Committee, was back in the public eye defending military export contracts. This time he was defending a multibillion-rand military contract between Denel and the British government for artillery propellants estimated to be worth 1.3 trillion rand (approximately US$200 billion). At the same time, South Africa was finalizing the details of another multibillion-dollar co-production ammunition deal between South African and U.S. defense corporations.[53]

At the same time that the government is shifting more into the role of a "normal state," it has retained its prior commitment to weapons of mass destruction nonproliferation and responsible sales of conventional arms. The existence of a vigorous free press, several groups committed to monitoring government national security and arms sales activities, and individual "revolutionary icons" who remain committed to the goals of human security and disarmament is likely to ensure that the country will continue its efforts to maximize what seem to many to be conflicting goals. Former president Nelson Mandela played a pivotal role in pressuring the Mbeki government to change its policies related to providing drugs to HIV/AIDS-infected mothers by publicly lecturing Mbeki. In a similar vein, in a recent speech after receiving a honorary doctorate from the faculty of theology at the University of Pretoria, Archbishop Desmond Tutu launched a scathing attack of the government on several issues including its AIDS policy and the billions that the government is currently spending on arms.[54]

RESIDUAL CONCERNS ABOUT
THE PROLIFERATION OF
WEAPONS OF MASS DESTRUCTION

Despite South Africa's continuing commitment to the nonproliferation of weapons of mass destruction and promotion of conventional arms exports, several issues related to weapons of mass destruction proliferation remain. This section reviews three issues that have recently raised additional concerns about possible proliferation problems that are tied to South Africa's past history as a developer of weapons of mass destruction and missiles during the apartheid era.

AL-QAEDA AND OTHER TERRORISTS
USING WEAPONS OF MASS DESTRUCTION

A relatively recent set of concerns relates to the possibility that al-Qaeda or its local affiliates may be increasing their presence in South Africa. Authorities now worry about several different but related issues, including the possibility that radical Islamic groups will succeed in efforts to obtain components, materials, or expertise related to weapons of mass destruction from South Africa; that al-Qaeda or affiliate cells will be established in South Africa; and that al-Qaeda or affiliates will increasingly be successful in efforts to recruit new foot soldiers from among the poor and disaffected youths in poor Muslim neighborhoods in several cities in South Africa.

Most Westerners are unaware that al-Qaeda and other terrorist groups might be operating in Africa. However, the suicide bombing in Kenya directed at Israeli tourists in Kenya in November 2002 made many individuals aware that Islamic fundamentalist terrorists have been operating in several African states for years. Extensive press coverage of documents seized at al-Qaeda camps in the mountains of Afghanistan by U.S. military personnel in 2002 alerted many to the fact that al-Qaeda members were interested in obtaining or building a nuclear bomb or an enhanced-radiation device. However, reports posted on the NIS Nuclear Trafficking Database web site note that the CIA had been intercepting messages throughout the 1990s that indicated that al-Qaeda members were trying to obtain a nuclear weapon to carry out a plan for a "Hiroshima" against America. Several African countries, including South Africa, were targeted by terrorists as possible sources of materials or components for weapons of mass destruction.[55]

Much of the evidence for this claim comes from press accounts about information obtained during a grand jury of accused terrorists held in New York in 2001. The indictment by the U.S. Department of Justice of individuals accused of being involved in the 1998 bombings of American embassies in Kenya and Tanzania noted that "at various times at least since early 1993, Osama bin Laden and other known and unknown terrorists made efforts to obtain the components of nuclear weapons." According to press accounts, the indictments provided evidence from a former al-Qaeda member of attempts by group members to buy uranium of South African origin. These efforts were in addition to other efforts to buy a complete warhead or weapons-usable materials from Central Asian states or from Chechen criminal groups in a deal involving money and drugs in exchange for nuclear weapons.[56]

Additional details about al-Qaeda's efforts to obtain weapons of mass destruction materials came from the testimony of the suspected al-Qaeda terrorists before the New York grand jury. Testimony was taken from each of the alleged conspirators in the 1998 bombings of the U.S. embassies in Kenya and Tanzania, which killed 224 people. However, one suspect named Fadl, who turned state's evidence, provided a detailed account of how the group's desire to acquire chemical weapons and uranium for an atomic bomb brought them into contact with officials in Sudan. Fadl testified that his group expressed their interest in buying chemical weapons and told how a Sudanese military officer had offered to sell uranium to al-Qaeda for $1.5 million. Fadl claimed that the Sudanese military officer showed bin Laden's agents a two-foot cylinder that purportedly contained the fissile material and documents that were allegedly from South Africa. Fadl said he received a $10,000 bonus for arranging the sale but did not know whether it was ever consummated. Nor did he know whether the cylinder held bomb-grade uranium, leaving open the strong possibility that the deal was a scam.[57]

Even more attention has been directed toward South Africa by authorities involved in the U.S. War on Terrorism campaign after the suicide bombing in Kenya in November 2002. A previously unknown group, the Army of Palestine, claimed responsibility for the suicide attack on a hotel in Mombassa and a failed missile attack on an Israeli airliner conducted at nearly the same time in Kenya. At the time of the attack, Dr. Abdel-Fattah, assistant director of the Cairo-based Al-Ahram Center for Political and Strategic Studies, alleged that al-Qaeda was behind the attack. He claimed that the attack was an attempt to mobilize support from Arabs who have questioned why al-Qaeda has attacked sites in the United States but not Israel. Much of the press coverage of the attack described it as one of several attacks on tourists and other innocent civilians that occurred in 2002 in Djerba, Tunisia, Bali, Indonesia, and Africa. However, the 2002 Kenyan bomb attack and the bombings of the U.S. embassy in Kenya in 1998 were interpreted by U.S. and South African officials as the work of al-Qaeda or affiliate groups. Concerns have been expressed in both countries since the 2002 attack about the possibility that South Africa and several other African states are being used as "potential breeding grounds, as well as safe haven for terrorist networks."[58]

Since the 2002 attacks in Kenya, South African officials have acknowledged that al-Qaeda operatives may have been operating out of South Africa for years. During 2001, the main concern of authorities in the United States and South Africa was the possibility that several militant Islamic organizations were smuggling gold, diamonds, and cash via Durban and Mozambique to Pakistan and Dubai. President Mbeki also warned the public that al-Qaeda operatives might be establishing a presence in South Africa after the September 11, 2001, attacks in the United States. Mbeki noted that the success of American and European authorities in routing out al-Qaeda cells in other countries may have led many members of these covert networks to find new bases. In the same statement, Mbeki acknowledged that after the 1998 bomb blast at Planet Hollywood in Cape Town, the South African National Intelligence Agency had warned him that foreign Islamic extremists were hiding in South Africa.[59] An unnamed source reported in one local South African press account that members of both Palestinian Hamas and the Lebanese-based Hezbollah underwent paramilitary training in South Africa.[60] The seriousness of these warnings acquired more credence after Khamis Khalfan Mohamed, an al-Qaeda operative from Tanzania who was allegedly involved in the 1998 bombing of the American embassy in Dar es Salaam, took refuge in South Africa before he was arrested in Cape Town and extradited to the United States.

There have also been several public reports in recent years that al-Qaeda and other Islamic extremists are using South Africa as a base from which they can regroup, raise and launder money, and plan more terror attacks. The United States and authorities in other Western states remain concerned about the prospect of terrorists using South Africa as a base of operations. The country has a world-class banking system and stock market, a modern telecommunications system, a good road and rail system, and broad civil liberties, all of which make it easy to move people and money. During 2002 there were reports that al-Qaeda was buying gold and diamonds to make it more difficult to trace the organization's wealth in Africa. Concern in South Africa also increased during 2002 after 35 tons of gold worth $360 million were reported lost. These concerns were no doubt fueled by a widely held belief that Muslims control the bulk of precious-metal smuggling in the country. In 2002, Mohamed Suleman Vaid and his wife Moshena were arrested at a Swazi border post with more than 1 million rand hidden in their clothing. Vaid denied that the money was meant for al-Qaeda, but authorities claimed that the money was on its way to a Mozambican thought by South African investigators to be working with an al-Qaeda-affiliated group.[61] In recent years, the South African government has responded in several different ways to these reports of radical Islamic terrorist groups operating in South Africa. For example, the South African special police unit called the Scorpions has increased its cooperation and coordination with its role model, the FBI. The

Scorpions have also increased their cooperation with counterparts at similar investigative services in several European and Asian countries.

Many observers who are familiar with local conditions in South Africa downplay the importance of recent counterterrorism initiatives by the Scorpions and South African Police Service. Instead, many local analysts emphasize the importance of understanding the role played by ongoing gang wars in the Cape Flats as well as the continuing drug trade and the lack of economic opportunities or jobs in alienating large numbers of Muslims in poor residential areas from their government. These continuing social problems and the breakdown of local order will inevitably fuel support for more-radical brands of Islam among the poor, particularly in the Western and Eastern Cape. As crime and drugs flooded into the townships and local authorities failed to stop the breakdown of law and order in the late 1990s, several vigilante organizations sprang up to try to maintain law and order. Many of these leaders share a deep distrust of the ANC-led government.

The two best-known groups operating in Indian and Coloured townships are People Against Crime and Drugs (PAGAD) in the Western Cape and People Against Drugs and Violence (PADAV) in Port Elizabeth in the Eastern Cape. Leaders of these groups organized citizen patrols and vigilante justice because they argue that the local police and authorities have done nothing to stop gang wars or criminal violence. Both organizations have received substantial support from their local communities since the late 1990s because many residents in these neighborhoods are the victims of gang violence and crime. These organizations are especially attractive to young Muslims because of the lack of economic opportunities and a growing belief among many Muslim youths that the Mbeki government is not doing much to stop drug-trafficking because he is involved in the drug trade.[62] Some of the more militant acts of PAGAD and similar groups have declined in recent years because several leaders were arrested or killed. However, militant brands of Islam continue to spread, especially among youths in poor Muslim areas. When asked by local leaders, several South African Muslims volunteered to go to Iraq to serve as human shields on the eve of the 2003 U.S.-Iraqi war.[63] The continuing drug trade, the lack of economic opportunities for young Muslims, and the general breakdown of law and order evident in several poor areas in South Africa will likely fuel support for more-radical brands of Islam in the future.

WEAPONS OF MASS DESTRUCTION AND CONVENTIONAL-WEAPONS THREATS

A more enduring set of concerns relates to the possibility of illegal sale of arms, components of weapons of mass destruction, and expertise developed by scientists and engineers who worked on one or more of South Africa's weapons of mass destruction or missile programs. Former Project Coast scientists have tried to obtain work in the United States, and there have been reports of another group of former weapons scientists who retained pathogens from covert programs and have recently threatened the government that they too will sell their expertise abroad if they do not receive adequate compensation from the South African government. U.S. and South African officials are concerned about what Project Coast scientists will do for a living, regardless of whether they stay in South Africa or emigrate. Scientists who worked on missile programs are also cause for concern. In 2000, South African engineers who had allegedly sold weapons secrets to Pakistan helped that country overcome restrictions on arms sales imposed since the 1999 coup by General Pervez Musharraf. A Pinetown air-weapons specialist was tried on twenty-one counts that ranged from fraud to theft to contraventions of several laws, including the ARMSCOR Act and the Copyright Act.[64] One gets the impression from the regularity of these reports that unemployed scientists and engineers will be a possible source of illegal weapons proliferation for years to come.

Now South African officials are worried about conventional weapons that were developed by many of the same scientists and engineers who worked on South Africa's nuclear-weapons and missile programs. They are concerned that al-Qaeda and affiliated terrorist groups may seek ways to enhance conventional bombs. Their interest in such weapons has redirected more attention to several conventional warheads that South Africa developed during the apartheid era. These bombs include a very small fuel-air bomb that could penetrate a two-meter-thick bunker roof, and a flag bomb, a deflagration bomb based on the same principles as a thermalberic warhead.[65]

Final work on these bombs was conducted during the period when South African weapons designers were still working on missiles. The weapons researchers started developing many of these new conventional bombs initially because they were unable to buy new types of bombs from foreign suppliers because of end-user restrictions in place since the late 1970s. For example, they developed the Kentron Raptor 1, a precision-guided munition, in the late 1970s.[66] Later on, according to one weapons designer who was involved in developing most of South Africa's rockets, South African weapons builders decided to finalize new conventional bombs rather than focus their efforts on developing biochemical warheads because they were prohibited by international conventions.[67]

At the time South Africa developed a fuel-air bomb in the early 1980s, only three other countries were officially known to deploy them; the United Kingdom, the United States, and the Soviet Union. The defense company Mechem manufactured the warhead and Somchem developed a liquid explosive for the bomb. The bomb was not ready for use until the end of the war in Angola. However, a prototype fuel-air bomb was used in counterinsurgency campaigns against SWAPO rebels in South West Africa (Namibia). By the time the fuel-air bomb program was stopped in 1989, the bomb could be demonstrated but there was no rocket to deploy it.[68]

In recent years, governments around the world have shown a lot of interest in South Africa's cluster, fuel-air, and flag bombs. It is difficult to build a fuel-air bomb and get the right mix of fuels. A flag bomb is easier to make because it is an enhanced normal explosive. This characteristic makes a pseudo–fuel bomb that uses TNT an attractive weapon to terrorists; it can cause a great deal more damage than the conventional bombs used in recent explosions in Saudi Arabia and Beirut. Despite the high demand for conventional bombs, the South African government has adhered to international prohibitions on conventional arms sales. After the September 11, 2001, attack in the United States, the South African government, much like other governments worldwide, began to review its arms-sales polices to be sure that they were strict enough to ensure that terrorists could not purchase more exotic bombs or a host of other weapons systems developed in conjunction with the former nuclear and missile programs—for example, gravity bombs, atomic demolition munitions, low-yield miniaturized devices for artillery pieces, and tactical standoff weapons.

RIGHT-WING TERRORISM
AND RESIDUAL THREATS
FROM THE APARTHEID REGIME

Terrorist threats from white right-wing supremacists who are unwilling to accept the new political status quo and are willing to use violence to unseat the ANC government have escalated in recent years. While all of the incidents reported to date have involved the use of conventional weapons, there are a few scattered reports that some of these right-wing groups, much like their counterparts in the United States and Europe, are interested in obtaining weapons of mass destruction.[69]

Several of the more recent incidents have come as a surprise to most South Africans because until a few years ago most people believed that the threat of violence by extreme right-wing Afrikaner groups had passed with the peaceful transition in 1994. This view was based on the fact that the most serious threat to a peaceful transition on the eve of 1994 was a coup plot organized by the far-right white organization, the Afrikaner Volksfront. Once the leader of this group, General Constand Viljoen, joined the Freedom Alliance and agreed to participate peacefully in the 1994 election, the most serious threat of a white right-wing coup that was to involve as many as 70,000 members of the former armed forces was felt to be over.[70]

While a few violent incidents by right-wing dissidents had occurred since 1994, the police and the military were surprised by the extent of right-wing cells uncovered in 2002 that were planning a series of terrorist acts that would culminate in an attempted coup. One plot involved four men in the Free State who were members of an ultra-right-wing Afrikaner religious movement called Israel Vision. Police alleged that they were planning to blow up the wall of the Vaal Dam. Ten days later, the police arrested three men on charges of treason and terrorism for their alleged involvement in a plan by another right-wing group called the Boeremag (Boer Force). This group had a five-phase plan that involved 4,000 ultra-rightists who planned to seize power after creating chaotic conditions that could be blamed first on the Jews or the Muslims and later on the Blacks. National politicians called both groups fringe groups. However, the trial of the members of the Vaal Dam plot was held in camera and few details about the case were leaked to the public.

Many more details were available to the public through the press about the trial of Boeremag members. This group was widely viewed as the less serious of the two groups. Security forces and police have continued to uncover cells of right-wing terrorists and there have been additional threats and acts of violence, and the authorities have made arrests and seized arms. One of the more widely covered thwarted incidents involved a plan to detonate bombs during the 2002 Summit on Sustainable Development. Many of the members of these different groups share a belief in the prophesies of an Afrikaner visionary named Siener van Rensburg, who predicted in the 1920s that there would be a black president and that seven days after he died a war would erupt which the Blacks, weakened by disease, would lose. Today the disease is widely interpreted to be AIDS.[71]

Several of the accused also looked to former white politicians, including P. W. Botha, for inspiration and had plans to "liberate" such infamous apartheid assassins as Eugene de Kock, who is currently serving a jail sentence for his past crimes. Apparently the Boeremag leaders hoped that de Kock and other freed prisoners would serve as future military commanders. The bail application of Lourens du Plessis, one of the right-wingers accused of high treason and terrorism, alleged that the plot was discussed at a meeting held in Lichtenburg in 2001. Former president P. W. Botha allegedly told him that a white government would never return to South Africa through elections.[72] Lourens also claimed that Botha told him that "F. W. de Klerk had more rightist leanings than himself but that he was bought during his term as president by, among others, America for several million rand, and that this was the reason why he sold out the country."[73]

Although no evidence has been presented to date to corroborate de Plessis's claims, the resurgence of right-wing white violence in recent years is particularly disturbing for those observers who had concluded by the late 1990s that de Klerk and many of his associates were not forthcoming in their statements to the Truth and Reconciliation Commission once their requests for blanket amnesty were turned down. Senior commission officials were so convinced that de Klerk's statement did not provide full disclosure that they left a blank page in their first report where de Klerk's official statement was supposed to appear.[74] After the hearings, many of the official files were taken by the National Intelligence Agency and are no longer available despite an ongoing court challenge. The final Truth and Reconciliation Commission report was not handed to President Mbeki until Human Rights Day, March 19 of 2003. Human rights advocates hope that this final version will finally clear the way to settle the issue of reparations for the thousands of financially desperate South Africans who were victims of past apartheid crimes, have applied for promised reparations, and have been waiting for promised payments since the late 1990s. For researchers and individuals interested in a fuller explanation of what was developed and what was dismantled during the rollback of the nuclear-weapons, missile, and chemical and biological warfare programs, this final act was disheartening since it signaled the commission's ultimate failure to obtain full disclosure about past covert weapons programs.

A similar sense of a forced ending before full disclosure accompanied the recent ruling on the appeals filed by the state prosecution in the Wouter Basson trial. On June 3, 2003, the Supreme Court of Appeal in Bloemfontein denied the state's appeal for a retrial of the Basson case on the grounds that the trial judge, Judge Hartzenberg, had refused to recuse himself. At the close of 2004, the state was undecided about how to proceed and uncertain about whether a second trial should be pursued.[75] The apartheid generals who had told us back in 2000 that Basson would walk away a free man from his trial because he had done nothing that was not authorized by his superiors turned out to be correct.[76]

However, a number of unanswered questions about the past refuse to go away.[77] The arrests of white right-wing coup plotters in 2002 who claimed to have received inspiration from former apartheid leaders raise a few new and several old questions about whether some members of the former government used government financing to obtain the resources needed to provide support for efforts to disrupt or overthrow the ANC government.

Even more troubling questions were raised by the sudden death of Tai Minaar, the former South African operative who was involved in arranging the attempted sale of Project Coast pathogens to the Americans. When the deal stalled, he reportedly sought other buyers. While Minaar's death in 2002 was ruled a heart attack, to those present at his death his symptoms looked more like poisoning from some of the dangerous pathogens he was trying to sell.[78] In a manner reminiscent of the red mercury murders of the 1980s, some observers began to quietly mention the possibility that Minaar had been the victim of another arms deal gone bad.

At least some observers now question whether these recent deaths and reports of right-wing violence are related to some of the unanswered questions about South Africa's past weapons of mass destruction, especially some of the questions about the extent and types of links among former South African officials, scientists, and engineers and their counterparts in the United States, the United Kingdom, and other Western countries. Doubts about the official script of how South Africa dismantled its nuclear, biological, and chemical weapons and missiles during the 1970s and 1980s are likely to fuel concerns that at least a few former Broeders from the old order, including a few high-ranking former Afrikaner politicians, may have moved as many assets as possible offshore in order to wait until majority-rule governments in South Africa "screwed up" politics so much that whites could return and retake political control.[79] What is particularly disturbing about this alternative story is that the new network of white supremacists differs from the old South African Broederbond in one important detail: it is international in scope and includes South Africans, Europeans, and Americans. This loose international network has been called different names including a Fourth Reich, the Phalanx Organization, or simply the Organization.[80]

DISARMAMENT TRENDSETTING? SOUTH AFRICA AND IRAQ

In early 2003, the Bush administration used South Africa under President de Klerk as a prime example of disarmament cooperation and transparency.[81] However, South Africa did not admit that it had nuclear weapons until March 1993, more than three years after deciding to destroy them and almost two years after acceding to the Nuclear Non-Proliferation Treaty. These delays occurred in part because de Klerk and his cabinet members feared confrontational inspections similar to those occurring in Iraq and objections from Nelson Mandela and the African National Congress. Similarly, South Africa did not admit that it had a sophisticated chemical and biological warfare program until 1994, and it did not decide to dismantle its space-launch or long-term missile program until just before power was to be transferred to Mandela and the ANC and under considerable pressure from the United States and the United Kingdom. Therefore, South Africa did not provide full cooperation and transparency and is not a paragon of disarmament.

In March 2003, South Africa sent a delegation of weapons of mass destruction experts to Iraq to assist in the disarmament process. The experts included Deon Smit, formerly South Africa's leading official dealing with the International Atomic Energy Agency during the nation's disarmament, and before that the general manager of the nuclear and missile program at ARMSCOR; Colonel Ben Steyn, advisor to South Africa's surgeon general and an expert on nuclear and chemical weapons; Super Moloyi, who earlier had traveled to Iraq with the deputy foreign minister as part of a presidential support group dealing with peace initiatives; Pieter Goosen, a disarmament expert who works in the South African foreign affairs department; scientist Philip Coleman of Protechnik (the chemical and biological warfare defense firm); and scientists Daan van Beeck and Tom Markram. Not invited to go to Iraq were Project Coast scientists such as Daan Goosen and Wouter Basson. The South African delegation did not succeed in changing the recalcitrant approach of Iraq; this opened the door to the U.S.-led invasion of March and April 2003.

South Africa is a middle power that underwent two transitions in 1989 and 1994 and became a democratic disarmament trendsetter, particularly in the area of disarmament of weapons of mass destruction. President de Klerk's desire to have South Africa rejoin the West, the introduction of relatively greater transparency, and the realization that he might have to transfer power to Nelson Mandela and the ANC inspired moves toward nuclear, biological, and chemical and missile dismantlement. The domestic situation in South Africa at the time was extraordinary. After the National Party agreed to enter into political negotiations it initially thought it could control, the party's leaders had to face the reality that it would lose power to its former enemy, the ANC, at the ballot box. The realization that power would be transferred to the ANC, an ally with many states of concern to the United States, increased the importance of an ongoing U.S.-initiated campaign to preclude the proliferation of South Africa's weapons of mass destruction programs. There was also a psychological motivation. Afrikaner leaders, including de Klerk, felt both enmity and fear toward the ANC, and they did not want weapons of mass destruction to come under the control of an ANC-led regime.

From 1994 onward, the ANC's anti-militarist ideology enabled South Africa to become a democratic trendsetter in the disarmament of weapons of mass destruction that played a key role in the extension of the Nuclear Non-Proliferation Treaty and the establishment of an African Nuclear-Weapon-Free Zone. However, the anti-militarist camp was unable to influence the conventional arms industry sufficiently to enable South Africa to become a trendsetter in the disarmament of conventional weapons as well. Industrial, bureaucratic, military, and political interests in sales were too entrenched and too strong to be overcome.

South Africa's political experience suggests that implementing democratic norms of accountability, public scrutiny, and transparency in government can be effective ways to ensure that disarmament and nonproliferation become permanent features of a state's foreign policy. However, a distinction must be drawn between weapons of mass destruction and conventional arms. Today, South Africa remains a poor democratic middle power which finds that it needs to sell arms to sustain economic growth and which has found it difficult to resist the military-industrial complex. After nearly a decade in power, the leaders of the ANC-dominated government headed by Thabo Mbeki are acting much more like leaders of a "normal" regional hegemonic state that is also a middle-level global power. At the same time, its reputation and role as a disarmament trendsetter is an important one for South African politicians and is highly valued among many members of the active and informed public. South Africa may continue to be a source of surprise for observers of the international system.

Today's states that have weapons of mass destruction are not likely to replicate South Africa's democratic disarmament. If other authoritarian and militarized states were to undergo similar democratic transitions, the chances for disarmament would increase. If a party should come to power that values disarmament ideology, the likelihood of further disarmament would increase. If replication is to be achieved, particularly on the Asian continent, peace processes must advance far beyond where they are today and regimes that are driven by excessive nationalism must be replaced. Given current impasses between Arabs and Israelis and between India and Pakistan, one can conclude that unilateral nuclear, biological, and chemical disarmament is unlikely to occur any time soon.

NINE

Emerging Issues and
Residual Concerns

In the fall of 2001 prior to meeting with President Bush, Prime Minister Putin of Russia said
his "most serious concern was the possibility
that tactical nuclear weapons would fall into
hands of terrorists."

—Gavin Cameron[1]

Throughout this study, we identified unanswered questions about past
covert weapons programs in South Africa. These questions are rarely discussed or analyzed in discussions of foreign-policy, national-security, non-
proliferation, and counterproliferation problems. Unanswered questions
from South Africa's past experiences with weapons of mass destruction illustrate gaps that currently exist in public discourse about such weapons.
Prior to the late 1990s, politicians in the United States, the former Soviet
Union, South Africa, and other nation-states that have had or do have
weapons of mass destruction didn't even acknowledge the existence of
"pocket nukes."

THEORETICAL IMPLICATIONS

A close look at South Africa's past behavior in building and dismantling
covert weapons of mass destruction and long-range missiles adds to our
general understanding of why states build these types of weapon systems
and the conditions and the factors that facilitate disarmament. Our case
study detailed that South African leaders approved covert weapons of
mass destruction programs for several reasons and that the relative importance of the many factors and events that influenced the decision making of the country's top political leaders changed over time.

One important factor was South Africa's military, scientific, and industrial interest in developing the country's natural uranium resources and

exploiting this resource to help develop the capabilities needed to produce nuclear energy. The close working relations among South African political and military leaders with the United Kingdom and the United States created numerous opportunities to increase the country's capacity to develop weapons of mass destruction. From 1960 through the 1980s, Afrikaner nationalist leaders increasingly felt betrayed and isolated by the sanctions that the United Nations and their former allies, the United States, Great Britain, and other European countries, imposed.

A collective sense of abandonment by Western friends proved to be a powerful motive and rationale for embarking on early weapons research and development. Increased political protests at home and the development of the first signs of guerrilla warfare in neighboring states fueled perceptions that the nation was threatened and ensured continuing support throughout the government for sophisticated but costly defense research and development for nearly two decades. A generalized fear of losing control of South Africa's political and economic position among most Afrikaner politicians and members of the white elite fueled this shared sense that the government had to build up defenses using all available means and at any cost in order to protect a cherished way of life and a political status quo. Prime Minister Vorster and, later, P. W. Botha drew upon this reservoir of support for collective survival to develop nuclear and launch vehicles and later to initiate Project Coast and the space-launch programs.

In reality, South Africa during the 1970s faced less threat of invasion or attack than any other state seeking to develop weapons of mass destruction. South Africa was far removed from Soviet weapons of mass destruction and the chances of an invasion were remote. The remoteness of any threat to its survival demonstrates that the South African case is explained less by neorealism theory than any other case involving weapons of mass destruction and points to other models, especially those that draw from political psychology and organizational and domestic politics. South African leaders demonstrated an excessive fear of adversaries as well as a xenophobic form of nationalism. These emotions led South Africa's leaders to exaggerate the severity of security threats. Once the weapons systems were under development, the need to keep scientists and engineers employed provided another powerful reason for embarking on ever-more-sophisticated weapons of mass destruction research and development throughout the 1980s. As time went by, security threats at home and in the region increased and provided additional incentives for building a vast array of sophisticated systems of weapons of mass destruction and conventional weapons. Other factors such as personal greed and corruption also begin to exert a more influential role in the decision-making calculus of government officials.

The result is that South Africa in the 1980s spent excessively on weapons of mass destruction, to the detriment of other defense and security requirements. Resource constraints were intensely felt by the military, which was struggling to fight an increasingly well-armed opponent in Angola and was forced to delay their programs to modernize equipment. Eventually, even the architects of the national-security system, P. W. Botha and his closest advisors, came to realize that the continuation of their political power required some political and economic changes, including more spending on the education of the majority of South Africans. The result was that Botha announced a series of domestic reforms designed to expand the number of skilled black and Coloured workers in urban areas, while others who were not needed as laborers would be shunted off to the internally "independent" black homelands. One of Botha's main political reforms accelerated the independent black homeland scheme. At the same time, Botha secretly instructed his trusted head of the biological and chemical weapons program, Dr. Wouter Basson, to develop novel ways to control the black population. Thus, for Botha and other senior securocrats, the rise of a growing and increasingly unmanageable black population that threatened to overtake urban areas provided a compelling rationale for increasing the budget for research and development and the scope of the sanctions-busting activities of both Project Coast and ARMSCOR.

The organizational politics model helps to explain several aspects of how and why the development of weapons of mass destruction proceeded in South Africa. The civilian nuclear-energy bureaucracy and weapons scientists and managers at ARMSCOR succeeded in convincing government leaders to move from peaceful nuclear explosion and peaceful nuclear-energy programs toward a nuclear-weapons program. Once covert nuclear, missile, and biological and chemical programs were in place, the need to keep the weapons scientists and engineers working provided an additional rationale for continuing and expanding these programs. Also, the high degree of military secrecy associated with the chemical and biological warfare program and the wide latitude given Wouter Basson as Project Coast manager allowed the covert program to be developed in violation of the biological-weapons convention and without close organizational supervision. Over time, accountability procedures were relaxed for Project Coast but not for nuclear- and missile-related research programs, with the result that very different levels of corruption and subsequent proliferation threats were associated with each covert program.

Additional factors that influenced domestic politics during the decade of the 1980s included changes within the ruling party, a significant increase in the scope and level of domestic protest, and the domestic impact of increased external economic and financial sanctions on white voters. Unforeseen factors also played a role. P. W. Botha's massive stroke paved the way for supporters of F. W. de Klerk to prevail over the National Party's hard-line securocrats. De Klerk was a compromise National Party candidate who was chosen because the majority of party leaders had confidence that he would carefully manage political negotiations with the

ANC; most National Party leaders had decided by the late 1980s that they had to enter into negotiations with the ANC in order to maintain their power and influence in the future political order.

Thus, F. W. de Klerk entered into negotiations with leaders of the ANC and other movements with the full support of the majority of National Party politicians. The process of rolling back South Africa's weapons of mass destruction programs was part of this effort to remain a dominant political party. What National Party leaders did not foresee was that de Klerk would not be able to maintain control of the political transformation. Instead, a groundswell of popular support for the ANC and growing confidence in Nelson Mandela as a future political leader meant that the National Party lost control of the transformation process and would not be a dominant party. Nevertheless, once the process started, the de Klerk government and successor governments would remain committed to dismantling the country's weapons of mass destruction.

A desire to rejoin the West was another important reason for de Klerk's policy of dismantling the nuclear program and later the space-launch program and Project Coast. The desire of de Klerk and National Party leaders to retake control from the securocrats and the need to free up economic resources by cutting defense programs were additional factors. However, as political circumstances changed within the country and the ruling National Party faced an increasingly hostile set of political and economic actors abroad, de Klerk and his advisors became even more determined to close down the covert weapons of mass destruction programs before the ANC took power. This goal complemented the desire of the United States to see South Africa dismantle its nuclear, missile, and later its biochemical secret programs; the United States and the ruling National Party had a shared political interest in keeping weapons of mass destruction out of the hands of the ANC.

Outside pressures by the United States were even more important in the decision-making process that led to the dismantlement of the space-launch vehicle. The United States had a determined interest in seeing that the space-launch-vehicle program was dismantled during F. W. de Klerk's government because it was concerned about future proliferation threats from Libya and other friends of the ANC. It devoted an extraordinary amount of time and effort to convincing the de Klerk government that this program should be terminated as well. According to published accounts, U.S. efforts were the decisive factor. U.S. officials convinced members of de Klerk's government that they had shared political interests in overseeing the dismantlement of the space-launch vehicle before a regime change. The logic of the economic arguments the Americans presented to the South Africans was very persuasive for de Klerk and his advisors.[2] Assessments of the importance of U.S. pressures must be tempered by the fact that the de Klerk regime was already searching for ways to reduce national-security spending in order to free up resources for domestic reforms they knew they had to implement if the National Party was to have any hope of playing a leadership role in the next government. While the space-launch dismantlement was viewed as a win for the United States in the short run, the two sides learned different lessons from their experiences.

In regard to the chemical and biological warfare program, the extreme levels of military secrecy, the need to maintain domestic security, and allegations of fraud and abuse made disarmament a more protracted and painstaking process. Repeated diplomatic interventions by the United States and the United Kingdom, including such interventions at a very late stage in the transition to ANC rule, were required to ensure that Project Coast was dismantled. As we have seen in recent years, the dismantlement process was incomplete and numerous proliferation threats are still with us today.

The South African case also demonstrates the significance of political factors and certain factors associated with the organizational politics model. As long as the weapons of mass destruction programs had the full support of the head of government, the programs mushroomed. Once civilian control and parliamentary oversight were reestablished, international norms became a more significant factor in the formulation of South Africa's foreign policies. The ministry of foreign affairs played a greater role than the military in implementing policies designed to ensure compliance with certain international treaties, such as the Nuclear Non-Proliferation Treaty. In the case of the chemical and biological warfare program, the shift to civilian control and compliance with international conventions was a tortuous process. South Africa's shift in decision-making authority from hard-line political securocrats in concert with friends in the military-industrial complex to a more civilian and democratic administration helps explain its disarmament. Psychological factors also played a role. As perceptions of external threats decreased with the settlement of the Angolan and Namibian conflicts, there was a concomitant reduction in the high levels of paranoia and xenophobia and extreme nationalism among political leaders and the majority of whites in South Africa.

A combination of organizational and domestic political and economic factors and the increased prominence of beliefs shared by a new set of political leaders explain why South Africa has been a trendsetter in the disarmament of weapons of mass destruction since 1994 but has fallen short in the conventional-weapons realm. Once South Africa rolled back its weapons of mass destruction program, the disarmament wing of the ANC and government pressed for international control of weapons of mass destruction and looked for ways to prevent the proliferation of nuclear-weapons, biochemical-weapons, and missile secrets. However, on the conventional arms control front, the South African arms industry had too much clout within the government to be regulated by the National Conventional Arms Control Committee and other bodies. Furthermore, the South African government could not give up one of its major industries because of high unemployment and low economic growth rates. The South African navy and air force, along with their allies on various state science councils and throughout the defense industries, proved to be skilled lobbyists for warship and aircraft purchases.

Several important unanswered questions related to what weapons systems were developed, how these weapon systems were used, how they were dismantled, and resulting proliferation threats do not fit neatly into the neorealist, organizational politics, or domestic politics models. The nature of the past relationships between the former South African government and foreign governments, especially the United States, and links between the intelligence services of different countries are also not addressed. We still do not know the extent of links between al-Qaeda and radical Islamic fundamentalists in South Africa today and whether either of these actors poses a serious security threat to South Africans or their neighbors. Policy analyses rarely address whether an international right-wing white supremacist group exists that is willing to use political violence to achieve its political goals, including weapons of mass destruction.

These questions are not widely discussed because there is very little information available in the public domain. National leaders did not even acknowledge the existence of "pocket nukes" until the end of the 1990s. While it is difficult to speculate about many of these questions in the absence of information, the South African case is useful for illustrating the significant gaps that currently exist in public discourse about weapons of mass destruction, missiles, and many other national-security issues today.

COMPARISONS OF THE NUCLEAR PROGRAM AND PROJECT COAST

The motivations and factors facilitating the development and ending of South Africa's nuclear-weapons program and Project Coast were largely the same. The psychology of fear and xenophobic nationalism helped to create the conditions for the establishment of the programs. The end of the external threat, the impending political change inside South Africa, and growing pressures to free up economic resources for other domestic programs fueled the momentum and support to end the programs. Xenophobic nationalism was displayed in South Africa's defiance of the Nuclear Non-Proliferation Treaty. Prime Minister Vorster's 1970 statement that South Africa would not be limited to the promotion of peaceful applications of nuclear energy is an example of a top political leader who did not appreciate the treaty's growing authority.[3]

Dramatically increased threat perceptions and xenophobic nationalism in the mid-1970s led to the acceleration, militarization, and concealment of the nuclear-weapons program within the state-owned arms industry and moves to launch a new and more sophisticated ultra-secret chemical and biological warfare program, Project Coast. Project Coast was placed within the South African Military Health Service. However, organizational political factors helped shape the procedures used to manage the new program. Ever since the Boer war, when South Africans experienced very high rates of casualties, the military medical service has played a central role in battlefield operations. Over time this led to the establishment of a South African Military Health Service (SAMS) as a separate branch of the military on a par with the other three services. Because of its status and important organizational mission, SAMS had the resources and political clout to serve as a front for a secret chemical and biological program. P. W. Botha wanted the chemical and biological warfare program to be even more secret than the nuclear-weapons program. Botha and his cabinet advisors feared that disclosure, even of a defensive program, would bring Western condemnation and perhaps even Soviet-led reciprocation. Parliamentary ratification of the Bacteriological and Toxin Weapons Convention made biological weapons illegal in South Africa. Botha was willing to violate the biological-weapons convention in the interest of what was perceived to be national security, but he needed to be sure of the institutional loyalty of the program manager who headed the secret biochemical program. Thus, he reached outside of normal military channels on the advice of his minister of defense, Magnus Malan, and hired a friend of Malan's nephew who had a medical degree, Dr. Wouter Basson.

The two programs were different in terms of their origins and the procedures used for managerial oversight and accountability. The nuclear-weapons program grew out of a civilian economic program designed to develop an indigenous nuclear power industry and explore the use of nuclear explosions in mining operations. However, Prime Minister Vorster and his associates were aware from the outset that the same capacity could also be used to develop nuclear weapons. Once the Atomic Energy Board had demonstrated that it had the capacity to produce highly enriched uranium, the president quickly approved further secret weapons research.

Full-scale weaponization of the nuclear-weapons program and research and development of more-sophisticated launch vehicles, including the space-launch-vehicle program, did not occur until after external threats intensified in the mid-1970s. To ensure tighter control and accountability, the research and development programs were centralized at a new facility and tightly managed by an interagency team located at ARMSCOR. However, the principal oversight committee included representatives from ARMSCOR, the South African Defence Force, and the Atomic Research Board.

This managerial oversight system contrasted markedly with the oversight of Project Coast, which was run in a highly informal and loosely managed fashion from the outset by Wouter Basson and a handful of his handpicked associates. While there was a nominal Cabinet-level committee in charge of Project Coast, Dr. Basson from the beginning and even more so as time went by had greater latitude and fewer accountability requirements than other managers of covert weapons programs during the same time period. Wouter Basson used this latitude to establish a program that was so highly compartmentalized that only he and a few close associates had a full picture of what was being developed and how the chemical and biological warfare agents developed under the auspices of Project Coast were used.

The greater organizational control, accountability, and management of the nuclear-weapons and missile programs is partly explained by the heavy and open investment in nuclear power and peaceful nuclear energy before the 1970s. In contrast, Project Coast was started in violation of the biological weapons convention and was run in a highly personalized fashion rather than as an institutional program with the normal requirements and institutional checks and balances. The nuclear and space-launch-vehicle programs were managed and dismantled based on carefully worked-out interagency plans. An outside independent auditor was appointed to verify the procedures used to dismantle the bomb program. No similar independent auditor was appointed in the case of Project Coast.

The intended uses of the nuclear-bomb program and Project Coast were also different. The inability to deter the Soviet Union and its massive nuclear-weapons stockpile, the lack of a long-range delivery system, the limited number of retaliatory targets, and the lack of any enemies in the region with comparable weapons systems forced South African leaders to develop a strategy for using nuclear weapons that could serve as a rationale for the bomb program. The "nuclear blackmail" strategy that subsequently emerged was not very logical, and the argument that developing real-time regional surveillance was a rationale for the costly space-launch program was not very persuasive either.

In contrast to the nuclear-weapons and long-range missile programs, Project Coast had a wide range of immediate possible uses. The original rationale for the program was to defend the South Africans and their UNITA allies against the Cubans in Angola. The program was also tasked with the mission of developing new types of nerve agents for crowd control and other internal security purposes. Reports about research efforts into how to design a "black bomb" and other ways to control the black population and the development of the facilities necessary for large-scale anthrax production demonstrated the fears of Afrikaner politicians and many of the scientists that they would be overwhelmed by their own black population or by communists. Project Coast also used well-established methods and newer techniques of genetic modification to produce a wide range of viruses, bacteria, and poisons. Several of these agents were placed inside James Bond–type delivery devices such as umbrellas. Some novel ways to deliver pathogenic agents were also developed for use as assassination weapons to eliminate political opponents at home and abroad.

The differences between the intended uses of the two programs are partly explained by the enormous power of nuclear weapons, which paradoxically limits their possible uses, and the wide range of possible uses of chemical and biological weapons, from mass destruction to assassination. The available evidence suggests that several sophisticated weapons systems that were intended to carry tactical nuclear, and possibly also chemical and biological warheads, were still being developed or just coming on line at the time the nuclear-weapons program was dismantled. The weaponization and mass production of products developed by Project Coast scientists had not yet occurred at the time Project Coast was dismantled. Whether any of these weapons would have been used if the programs had not been terminated remains a matter of speculation.

The timing of the completed nuclear rollback was tied to the mutual interests of the United States and the de Klerk government. Both parties wanted the process to be completed before the ANC took over. The leaders of both countries also shared an interest in having South Africa join the Nuclear Non-Proliferation Treaty and return to the West and the IAEA. An additional factor was the high cost of the nuclear-weapons and missile programs and a growing need to purchase new equipment for the South African Defence Force. These factors led de Klerk and the SADF to overrule objections from ARMSCOR and other quarters within the government that objected to closing down these programs. The failure to publicly disclose the nuclear-weapons rollback until March 1993 is partly explained by de Klerk's desire not to enrage the ANC and complicate the transition process. Other possible reasons remain a subject of extensive debate among South African weapons experts.

The decision to roll back the space-launch-vehicle program, even more than the rollback of the nuclear-bomb program, illustrates the large role that outside countries can play. The United States, and to a lesser extent the United Kingdom and other European countries, played a critical role in influencing the de Klerk government to terminate the space-launch vehicle. The saturation of the market with alternative civilian launch platforms also played a role. The program had been dismantled by the time the Mandela government assumed control of the government. There was still some internal debate within the ANC about whether or not to resurrect the space-launch-vehicle program. The fact that Mandela and his closest advisors ratified this agreement illustrates the influence of the United States, the logic of economic arguments, and the extent to which the ANC leadership was willing to compromise in order to ensure a peaceful transition of power.

In contrast, the rollback of Project Coast was slower and more difficult to consummate. The greater secrecy surrounding the chemical and biological warfare program and the lack of civilian control partly explain why the program took so long to roll back and why there was a lack of external pressure. According to President de Klerk's account, he was not briefed about the chemical and biological warfare program until March 1990, six months after he was inaugurated and several months after he had begun the process of dismantling the nuclear-weapons program. When briefed, he was told that the Project Coast program consisted of lethal, incapacitating, and irritating agents. De Klerk claims that he was told that the program was strictly defensive. Instead of ordering the entire program ended, he ordered only lethal chemical agents to be destroyed. He wanted incapacitating and irritating agents to be kept for purposes of crowd control.

In sum, international pressures to prevent nuclear-weapons proliferation were stronger for the dismantlement of the nuclear-bomb and space-launch-vehicle programs than for the elimination of Project Coast. The United States and its allies knew about the nuclear-weapons program in the 1980s and strongly intervened from 1987 to 1990 to preclude nuclear proliferation by South Africa. Although some elements of the U.S. government were aware of South Africa's chemical and biological warfare programs, the greater focus on the problems presented by nuclear proliferation threats helps to explain why it wasn't until the early 1990s that enough evidence was gathered to induce diplomats and White House staff to protest. President de Klerk also had an incomplete picture of the extent of programs developed by Project Coast scientists until January 1993, when he received the Steyn Report. After he received a more complete picture of the offensive uses of Project Coast, de Klerk ordered most remaining chemical and biological warfare agents destroyed and documents transferred to secure CD-ROMs. However, he went along with the proposal to violate the Chemical Weapons Convention in order to keep tear-gas to control crowds.

Until 1993, the United States and the United Kingdom were more concerned about threats of nuclear proliferation and missile proliferation in South Africa than the spread of chemical and biological secrets. They became much more concerned about South Africa's covert biochemical program as the ANC positioned itself to take power. Another important trigger for the concerns of officials from the United States and the United Kingdom was the fact that Basson began traveling to Libya. After the U.S. and U.K. delegations learned how sophisticated the South African program was, their concerns about the chemical and biological warfare program increased dramatically. One of the lessons from South Africa's experience is that it is important to properly estimate the dangers that chemical and biological weapons will proliferate as well as to understand the broad range of uses of those weapons.

SOUTH AFRICAN WEAPONS OF MASS DESTRUCTION PROGRAMS COMPARED WITH OTHER CASES

Throughout the book, variables taken from several different approaches or models have been used to explain and compare weapons of mass destruction production and disarmament. The development of weapons of mass destruction in the 1970s and 1980s in South Africa, the Middle East, and Asia demonstrated the importance of a combination of models (neo-realism, domestic politics, organizational politics, and psychology). With one exception, all of the cases discussed in Chapter 2 shared the characteristic of being isolated from the international system and were considered to be pariah states. Each of these covert-weapons states was also judged to have aggressive foreign policies and limited civil liberties at home. The South African case, perhaps more than any of the cases discussed in Chapter 2, demonstrates the importance of shared perceptions and beliefs among political leaders and the wider ruling elite. South Africa's apartheid leaders used these shared beliefs as the justification for building weapons of mass destruction. Shared perceptions and beliefs are also important for understanding when, and if, such weapons will be dismantled. The South African case illustrates the long-term impact that international sanctions can have on promoting decisions to dismantle weapons of mass destruction programs. The South African case also illustrates the increased importance of international norms regarding nonproliferation, especially those bolstering the Nuclear Non-Proliferation Treaty.

South Africa's weapons of mass destruction programs produced six nuclear bombs, several different launch vehicles, and a sophisticated chemical- and biological-weapons program. Much of the research and development for these programs was aided by covert relationships with Israel and other partners and illicit arms deals. South Africa's covert weapons of mass destruction placed it near the head of the weapons of mass destruction class. In comparison, Iraq and North Korea fell short of producing a nuclear bomb but produced sophisticated chemical- and biological-weapons agents. The sophistication of the South African nuclear-energy program was similar to that of the programs of India, Israel, Brazil, and Argentina. South Africa, India, and Israel actually developed nuclear weapons whereas U.S. pressure helped to deter Brazil and Argentina.

South Africa is similar to states in the Middle East and Asia in terms of developing chemical and biological warfare programs. All of the states maintained high degrees of secrecy, were authoritarian to varying degrees, and placed limits on the press. All perceived asymmetrical threats that required unconventional weapons. Most signed and then violated the Bacteriological and Toxin Weapons Convention by developing highly secret biological-weapons programs.

Disarmament of weapons of mass destruction, including what happened in South Africa, is partly explained by neorealist theory, which contends that disarmament occurs when former adversaries end threats and roll back their weapons of mass destruction programs. However, the cessation of threats did not fully apply in the case of the ex-Soviet states of Ukraine, Belarus, and Kazakhstan. Instead, the dissolution of the Soviet

Union, changes in political leadership, and external pressures from the United States and other actors were more important factors.

These cases, much like the South African case, illustrate well the fact that nation-states that have gone through major political changes and have new regimes may be the most vulnerable of all nation-states to outside pressure to dismantle secret weapons of mass destruction programs. In each of these cases, the country's leaders decided to join the Nuclear Non-Proliferation Treaty and disarm in exchange for international prestige and the buttressing of sovereignty.

In contrast to other cases, South African disarmament demonstrates the significance of the organizational politics model, especially in implementing new political priorities. As long as the weapons of mass destruction programs were controlled by the head of government and military agencies and kept secret, the programs mushroomed. Once narrow control and secrecy were ended, disarmament commenced.

Since the Nuclear Non-Proliferation Treaty entered into force in 1970, the nuclear nonproliferation regime has become increasingly powerful. However, the desire to join the nuclear club and the massive power of nuclear weapons still entice middle powers to reject the Nuclear Non-Proliferation Treaty and develop nuclear weapons. India and Pakistan openly tested their nuclear weapons in 1998. The experiences of IAEA weapons inspectors in Iraq and in Libya illustrate the value of surprise spot inspections and the need for the Nuclear Non-Proliferation Treaty regime to have more-intrusive inspection powers.

External pressure from the United States and others made it impossible for South Africa and the new states of Ukraine, Belarus, and Kazakhstan to resist the power of the Nuclear Non-Proliferation Treaty regime. The four cases demonstrate that the factors that facilitate the disarmament of weapons of mass destruction include the decline of security threats, changes in domestic politics, and anti-proliferation pressures on vulnerable states undergoing change.[4]

It is not likely that South Africa's unilateral disarmament of weapons of mass destruction will be replicated. However, other aspects of South Africa's experience are very likely to be replicated. The experience of delays in plans to modernize conventional weapons and inadequate resources for other domestic priorities because of the high cost of weapons of mass destruction programs may increasingly be replicated in countries such as Libya that are interested in reintegrating into the modern world economic system. In such cases, economic factors may become more important to leaders of nation-states as the world economic system becomes increasingly integrated.

Regional political peace also appears to be an important precondition to the dismantlement of weapons of mass destruction. Thus, if replication of the South African experience is to be achieved, particularly on the Asian continent, peace processes must advance far beyond where they are today, and regimes that are driven by extreme nationalism must be replaced. Because of the impasses between Arabs and Israelis and between India and Pakistan, unilateral disarmament of weapons of mass destruction is unlikely to occur any time soon.

The clandestine weapons of mass destruction programs and the disarmament processes evident in recent international relations also underscore how international norms and sanctions have become more powerful over the past three decades. The Nuclear Non-Proliferation Treaty regime has become increasingly powerful, backed by the threat of sanctions by the United States and its allies. Still, the desire to join the nuclear club and the incredible power of nuclear weapons have enticed aspiring powers to reject the Nuclear Non-Proliferation Treaty and risk sanctions in attempts to develop nuclear weapons. The secrecy accorded biological and chemical weapons programs, especially since the 1970s, underscores the fact that such weapons have been seen as illegitimate since the 1920s. This consensus was strengthened in the 1960s, when most states, including the two superpowers, committed themselves to the Bacteriological and Toxin Weapons Convention, and again in 1993, when many nations signed the Chemical Weapons Convention. The leaders that ordered the covert development of weapons of mass destruction came to the conclusion, correctly or incorrectly, that the threats they faced outweighed the risk of sanctions and that they had the capacity to conceal their weapons of mass destruction programs and to cheat.

Throughout the post–World War II period, only two states, Iraq and South Africa, committed to eliminating existing nuclear, biological, and chemical weapons and missile programs. The outcome for Iraq was recurring conflicts for thirteen years after the first Gulf War. After losing the first Gulf War, Iraq agreed in March 1991 to eliminate its weapons of mass destruction. UN sanctions ensured Iraqi compliance. From 1991 to 1995, the UN Special Commission on Iraq made progress in eliminating most of the nuclear-weapons, chemical-weapons, and missile programs. On August 7, 1995, General Hussein Kamel al-Majid (Saddam Hussein's son-in-law) revealed the extent of Iraq's weapons of mass destruction program, including bioweapons (he was the director of the program). Iraq was forced to dismantle some of its biological-weapons program by 1998, when the UN special commission was expelled. The Iraqi case demonstrated the difficulties with disarming weapons of mass destruction and the dangers of counterproliferation during and after the disarmament process. In Iraq, the chemical- and biological-weapons programs were more widely dispersed and easier to conceal and shift than the nuclear-weapons program. The U.S.-led military intervention in 2003, which was mounted in the face of opposition by most European allies, Russia, and China, underscores how difficult it may be to gain widespread agreement on how to develop a disarmament regime in future international relations.

In South Africa, the HIV/AIDS epidemic that has not yet peaked, widespread frustration with the lack of improvement in the standard of living of most South Africans, and a renewed threat by right-wing white supremacists willing to use any means necessary in futile efforts to return to a white-ruled state are formidable challenges to the first nation-state to voluntarily dismantle its weapons of mass destruction. The South African case is an important precedent because South Africa today remains the regional hegemonic power in Southern Africa, a key actor in continental politics, and an important middle-level power in international relations.

It is important to learn the correct and most relevant lessons from past dismantlement cases. Past nonproliferation efforts have focused primarily on limiting access to the fissile materials and scientific expertise necessary to build large fission and fusion bombs. Early success with these goals in the past has gradually eroded over several decades and today we have dozens of countries pursuing weapons of mass destruction research and development. Today, in addition to struggling with the issue of how to control technology and expertise that has proliferated around the world, we are also facing a new set of problems brought on by the rise of a huge black market that is accelerating proliferation worldwide to additional nation-states and to nonstate actors.

Documents seized during the War on Terrorism, especially in the caves of Afghanistan in 2002, make painfully clear that a new set of proliferation threats tied to the future use of biological, chemical, or nuclear materials by terrorists is already here. Documents seized by the United States in Afghanistan indicated that al-Qaeda operatives were working to build at least crude radiation bombs. In 2003, U.S. officials learned from documents and statements made during the interrogation of Khalid Sheik Mohammed, the operational chief for al-Qaeda who masterminded the airline attack on September 11, 2001, that al-Qaeda was much farther along in its efforts to obtain biological and chemical weapons than was previously thought. By the time U.S. forces seized al-Qaeda's lab facilities in 2001, the group had completed plans and obtained the materials required to manufacture two biological toxins—botulinum and salmonella—and the chemical poison cyanide. They were also much closer to producing anthrax than U.S. officials had believed. Although the possibility that al-Qaeda had completed their manufacturing plan could not be ruled out, U.S. officials remained most concerned about the possibility that one of the group's state sponsors was supplying the organization with advanced biological weapons or nerve agents.[5]

The revelations about the advanced state of al-Qaeda plans to use biological and chemical weapons against their enemies came at the same time that the United States was preparing to wage war in Iraq. Against this backdrop, the South African case, in which a country peacefully dismantled covert weapons programs, is an important one for those interested in learning how to promote peaceful disarmament. Residual concerns about continuing proliferation threats associated with past South African weapons of mass destruction programs illustrate how difficult it can be to completely dismantle and secure the materials, technology, and expertise developed to build these weapons. The South African case is also useful for identifying some of the new weapons of mass destruction that may be developed in the twenty-first century as researchers, weapons designers, terrorists, and even disaffected individuals attempt to exploit advances in manufacturing new chemicals and biological agents for political or personal reasons.[6]

Appendix: Policy Lessons from the South African Case

South Africa's past experiences with weapons of mass destruction and contemporary efforts by the South African government to monitor and control the proliferation of such weapons suggest some policy lessons that may be applicable to other countries. These are presented as a basis for further consideration rather than as definitive lessons from the past. Proliferation threats throughout the world are changing rapidly. Continuing acts of violence by right-wing white supremacists in South Africa and elsewhere, the alleged overtures by agents for al-Qaeda to former weapons scientists in South Africa to induce them to sell their expertise abroad, and increased support for radical Islamic fundamentalism should all serve as cautionary tales about the many difficulties involved in controlling the proliferation of weapons of mass destruction and missiles. Generalizations about such a dynamic environment are difficult because the technology needed to produce both crude and very sophisticated nuclear, chemical, and biological weapons has spread around the world.

There is also a lively black market in weapons of mass destruction and missiles that makes it relatively easy for interested parties—whether they represent nation-states or terrorist groups—to purchase a wide range of weapons. Given this dynamic environment, we believe that it is important to consider a number of new approaches to the problem of proliferating weapons of mass destruction and missiles. Some of the policy lessons may contain ideas that are useful for understanding enduring and emerging weapons of mass destruction and missile threats in this dynamic environment.

> Policy Lesson 1: Programs designed to promote the peaceful use of nuclear, chemical, and biological technologies carry with them longer-term unintended proliferation risks by spreading the expertise and materials needed to build weapons of mass destruction.

The U.S. Swords into Plowshares program and other programs that promoted the peaceful use of nuclear energy during the 1950s facilitated South Africa's ability to produce indigenous highly enriched uranium and develop the critical mass of scientists and engineers needed to produce indigenous highly enriched uranium and build modern weapons systems. South Africa's ability to exploit the resources and expertise acquired through peaceful energy programs has been replicated in many other countries around the world. The proliferation threats that accompanied early peaceful nuclear-energy-sharing programs are now widely recognized as having had profound and unexpected consequences in enabling some states to become covert nuclear powers.

Scientists and engineers throughout the world have recently realized that there are potential parallel problems embedded in international collaborative research in chemical and biological basic science and industrial research projects. Proliferation concerns about scientific research that uses genetic modification are one reason why a recent recommendation of the U.S. National Academy of Science called for individuals who are more familiar with proliferation issues, especially biowarfare concerns, to serve on peer-review panels that approve biological research involving genetic modifications. How to manage potential proliferation problems without impeding the free flow of scientific knowledge or infringing on individual civil liberties promises to be one of the most challenging national-security issues of the twenty-first century.

> Policy Lesson 2: A country requires a minimal level of industrial infrastructure and a core group of creative scientists and engineers to develop adequate supplies of highly enriched uranium and develop the unique processes and procedures that are required to develop nuclear weapons, new forms of chemical weapons (i.e., nerve gas), and novel forms of biological warfare.

South Africa's early participation in the Atoms for Peace and other peaceful nuclear-energy programs allowed the government to train a core group of scientists and engineers in the new field of nuclear weapons. This group formed the nucleus for early nuclear research. The fact that the nuclear, missile, and biochemical programs enjoyed widespread support among white South Africans meant that all the programs were able to attract some of the brightest scientists and engineers of subsequent generations. The South African experience with developing secret nuclear weapons underscores how important human capital is to the development of sophisticated weapons of mass destruction. Libya recently declared that it had a nascent covert nuclear program, but it failed to develop the indigenous capacity to produce highly enriched uranium, underscoring the necessity of having both a minimal level of industrial infrastructure and the human capital necessary to develop sophisticated weapons of mass destruction. However, most terrorist attacks to date that have involved biological or chemical agents have used readily available poisons or chemical and biological agents. Today, an increased number of nongovernmental actors (i.e., terrorists) are seeking to purchase new or used missiles or seize control of civilian aircraft in order to deliver an illegally obtained weapon of mass destruction from the black market. In this global environment, human capital and industrial infrastructure may be irrelevant for coping with weapons of mass destruction proliferation threats by nongovernmental organizations.

> Policy Lesson 3: Isolated nation-states that are subject to comprehensive sanctions are more likely to initiate or accelerate weapons of mass destruction and missile programs.

International isolation and UN and national sanctions were important triggers that prompted South Africa's shift from early peaceful nuclear-energy research to covert nuclear-weapons research and development. Over time, senior political leaders used South Africa's status as an international pariah as the main justification for undertaking more-sophisticated nuclear and missile programs and for launching Project Coast. In our study, we quoted one former manager of a covert weapons of mass destruction program who noted that the birthday of UN Resolution 418, the mandatory international arms embargo of November 4, 1977, was celebrated in the South African defense family as the onset of the growth of the military-industrial complex in South Africa.[1] However, much more systematic research is needed to determine whether international sanctions and policies designed to isolate other would-be nuclear states will trigger a similar set of dynamics within the national security establishment of other "pariah states."

> Policy Lesson 4: The proliferation of chemical and biological weapons is more difficult to prevent than the proliferation of nuclear weapons.

The knowledge and resources needed to build a range of biological weapons from the most sophisticated to the very crude (i.e., using industrial cyanide or naturally occurring bacteria such as anthrax) have already spread around the world. This condition suggests that it will be much more difficult to control the use of biological warfare with the control strategies employed in the nuclear nonproliferation regime. The history of South Africa's biochemical program illustrates that a country can develop a sophisticated covert program, such as their Project Coast, with little fanfare. In contrast, South Africa's nuclear-weapons program was known and monitored by the international community.

> Policy Lesson 5: A country's public statements related to changing perceptions of threats and patterns of foreign-policy behavior can be useful indicators that a regime may be pursuing covert nuclear, chemical, or biological programs.

Immediately after approving preliminary nuclear research, Prime Minister Vorster made a series of highly bellicose statements in public speeches. In a similar fashion, P. W. Botha's rhetoric became more aggressive as new launch platforms and new ways of assassinating political opponents came on line. The central role that threat perceptions play in a leader's decision to undertake covert weapons of mass destruction suggests that public rhetoric and systematic changes in the pattern of a country's foreign-policy behaviors can be used as indirect indications of changes in research and development related to weapons of mass destruction programs.

> Policy Lesson 6: A country that engages in covert nuclear-weapons research is likely also to be engaged in covert research into the use of chemical and biowarfare weapons.

In South Africa, the factors that fueled support for the development of nuclear-weapons research also prompted covert weapons of mass destruction research. The South African case, much like the Iraqi case and several other cases, suggests that national efforts to build nuclear-weapons capabilities go hand in hand with efforts to develop biological and chemical weapons.

> Policy Lesson 7: Whether or not a government uses chemical and biological agents as weapons depends in part on what the leaders believe about their enemy and the past experiences of the country's military and police. The use of chemical and biological weapons for either defensive or offensive purposes is a learned behavior. Government leaders often claim that chemical- and biological-weapons research and development is strictly for defensive purposes to prepare against foreign enemies. However, the historical record suggests that if officials perceive significant threats from domestic enemies they are likely to use chemical and biological weapons against them as well. Distinctions between defensive and offensive chemical- and biological-weapons capabilities are often blurred in practice. Thus, if a country has defensive chemical- and biological-weapons capabilities it is prudent to assume that it also has offensive chemical- and biological-weapons capabilities as well.

South Africa's commitment to develop defensive and offensive chemical- and biological-weapons capabilities was influenced by events on the ground and what Special Forces troops learned from other counterinsurgency forces in the region. As the tempo of guerrilla activities in Rhodesia increased, South African financial support and the involvement of South African security forces and police in counterinsurgency operations also increased. There is considerable evidence that South African military and police personnel learned firsthand from their involvement in Rhodesia's counterinsurgency operations in the 1970s how they might use poisons and biological viruses for assassinations just as they had learned from the Portuguese in the 1960s how effective the strategy was of contaminating water supplies used by guerrillas. South African involvement in the Rhodesian anti-guerrilla war provided training opportunities, strategies and tactics, and personnel connections for subsequent defense and police special covert units. This learning process influenced how the South African government dealt with domestic enemies. Although the threat of chemical- and biological-weapons use by troops supported by Cubans and the Soviet Union was the primary rationale for launching a major covert chemical- and biological-weapons program in South Africa, the primary uses of chemical- and biological-weapons agents developed under the auspices of Project Coast were against domestic opponents. Many of the SADF and SAP assassins associated with Project Coast had learned their trade in the Rhodesian bush war.

Policy Lesson 8: The effectiveness of biological agents as counterinsurgency weapons is highly variable and difficult to confirm.

Although the extent to which South Africa was involved in developing
and using chemical and biological weapons in Rhodesia is not clear, its alleged use of such weapons in the 1970s highlights several aspects of chem-
ical- and biological-weapons warfare. In the war in Rhodesia, the effectiveness of biological and toxic agents as counterinsurgency weapons was
highly variable. This suggests that difficulties in identifying the perpetra-
tors of biological attacks distinguish biological from nuclear or chemical
warfare. Several biological agents, such as anthrax, are found in nature.
Others, such as cholera, can be caused by factors other than a biological
attack. We could not substantiate long-standing charges by Zimbabwean
officials that South African and former Rhodesian forces planted anthrax
spores in grain fed to cattle in guerrilla-held areas. Recent statements by
Zimbabwean officials that South Africa planted anthrax found today in
rural areas underscore the fact that allegations of uses of biological agents
can also be used as a political disinformation technique against unpopular
regimes. (The Zimbabwean government made these charges against an
unpopular South African government in the 1980s and early 1990s. South
Africa's responsibility still has not been proven.) Continuing uncertainties
about these incidents underscore that we should expect difficulties in future efforts to verify allegations of biological agent use.

Policy Lesson 9: Allegations of chemical agent use can be veri-
fied more readily than the use of many biological agents, but
verification difficulties should be anticipated in areas where
victims are already suffering from malnutrition, diseases, or
general poor health.

National and international teams of experts investigated a number of
incidents of alleged use of chemical weapons. In one incident involving villagers in a remote area of Mozambique, it proved especially difficult to determine the exact causes of death. The problem was that many of the victims suffered from malnutrition and several diseases at the time they died.
This and several other incidents with cases of large numbers of deaths
should serve as a warning to military troops, humanitarian workers, and
human rights advocates who in the future are tasked with determining
whether chemical (or biological) agents were used or if large numbers of
individuals died at about the same time from natural causes.

Policy Lesson 10: Unintended consequences should be expected
when chemical weapons are used in harsh terrain and unpredictable climate zones.

Despite numerous international and national investigations, it is still
unclear who used what chemical agents in bush warfare in Angola. An al-
legation that the Cuban-led troops in Angola used chemical weapons has
never been substantiated. However, rumors persist about a horrible acci-
dent when the Angolans accidentally wiped out an entire brigade of their

own troops with chemical bombs toward the end of 1988. Similarly, rumors that a large number of UNITA troops were killed when there was an unanticipated shift in the wind have never been confirmed. What is clear from the threat of chemical weapons in Angola is that the threat greatly increases the costs and reduces the maneuverability of troops. In Angola, SADF troops faced increased costs and maneuverability problems if they had to wear defensive chemical- and biological-weapons masks and uniforms that had to be changed daily. In addition, it is expensive for troops to carry water and they must rely on local water supplies, but SADF troops avoided water supplies in Angola and Namibia because they lacked intelligence about whether water supplies had been poisoned.

> Policy Lesson 11: Once a country gains experience with using chemical and biological weapons as a counterinsurgency warfare tactic abroad, it is also likely to use these capabilities against political enemies at home and abroad. If a government believes its enemy may posses chemical and biological weapons, it is likely to develop both defensive and offensive chemical- and biological-weapons capabilities. Since distinctions between offensive and defensive chemical- and biological-weapons capabilities are difficult to maintain, any country that is developing defensive chemical- and biological-weapons capability is probably also developing covert offensive chemical- and biological-weapons capabilities.

The history of Project Coast's chemical- and biological-weapons development illustrates how tightly coupled the use of chemical- and biological-weapons agents was at home and abroad. One of the most important provisions sought by former SADF leaders during the negotiations to end the Angolan and Namibia conflicts was blanket amnesty for SADF officers. The judge in the Basson trial threw out murder charges against Dr. Basson because of this amnesty. These charges involved the alleged killing of SWAPO guerrillas. There are several still-unproven charges that Basson and other members of the Civil Cooperation Bureau frequently used SWAPO guerillas as guinea pigs for agents developed by Project Coast. Many agents used for assassination were allegedly also tested on detained guerrillas before being used on domestic opponents or for foreign assassinations. These incidents highlight how difficult it can be to monitor and regulate the use of chemical or biological agents when the state authority is an authoritarian regime that limits press access to areas where fighting is taking place.

> Policy Lesson 12: The organizational context matters. The location of South Africa's chemical and biological weapons program within a separate medical corps that was equal in status with other branches of the armed forces appears to be a unique feature of this case. The importance of the organizational context should be carefully explored in other case studies.

The existence of a separate medical branch, the SADF Medical Service (SAMS) that worked with Special Forces in Angola, created the organizational basis for developing a highly secretive and loosely managed chemical- and biological-weapons program. South Africa's involvement in Angola provided the rationale for the reorganization within the military that ensured that these new chemical- and biological-weapons programs would be controlled by the military. A fear of attacks in Angola using chemical and biological weapons led the government to issue a mandate to SAMS to develop defensive capabilities and train SADF forces to protect themselves from all types of attacks, including biological and chemical. This mandate was the principal reason why managerial oversight and responsibility for a new chemical- and biological-weapons program was given to the 7th Battalion of SAMS. After South African troops left Angola, the SAMS mission expanded and became more ambiguous. As SADF forces shifted from battlefield operations to policing functions at home, Project Coast research and development activities focused more on offensive uses of chemical and biological weapons against political opponents and guerrillas.

> Policy Lesson 13: The organizational context of a weapons of mass destruction program is an important determinant of the type of standard operating procedures, the extent of transparency or compartmentalization, and the degree of accountability of that program.

The South African case illustrates that the practices used to manage a covert weapons of mass destruction program can range from standard public administration principles and practices for managing personnel and activities in complex organizations to procedures used by modern crime syndicates. There are well-established principles for managing, reporting, and holding program managers accountable for their budgets. In contrast, a management style characterized by highly personalized forms of management, high levels of compartmentalization, and limited accountability requirements resembles the management practices of patrimonial governments or transnational crime syndicates.

In the South African case, the nuclear-bomb program was well grounded and used well-established budgeting and accounting practices. When the time came to dismantle the program, an outside auditor was appointed to oversee the process. In sharp contrast, the highly personalized nature of Project Coast provided Wouter Basson with a great deal of latitude in corporate business practices. Basson used state-owned and private corporations, international holding companies, and foreign bank accounts to operate projects under the auspices of Project Coast in a highly compartmentalized fashion. He set up his own independent network of procurement agents and contacts in foreign countries. These practices ensured that only Basson and a handful of his most trusted associates had complete knowledge of the full scope of Project Coast research and development activities and access to all financial accounts. Basson took advantage

of the loose financial oversight and accountability requirements to purchase shares in the front companies and earn huge profits when they were
privatized. These operating procedures meant that there was no general
reconciliation or independent accounting between the amount of money
spent on individual programs and other types of expenditures. When it
came time to dismantle Project Coast, no outside auditor was appointed.

Policy Lesson 14: The full scope of a nation's covert nuclear,
biological, and chemical efforts is likely to be known by only a
small group of politicians, military leaders, and senior research
scientists.

While rumors could not be substantiated that the apartheid South
African government tested battlefield weapons capable of carrying biological agents and chemicals, we did find evidence that such weapons were
planned and developed. Basson, much like his counterparts in other countries (e.g., Iraq), had difficulties developing effective delivery systems for
using biological agents as weapons of mass destruction. While Project
Coast researchers undertook conceptual studies in the aerosolization of
biological agents, the evidence available to date indicates that sophisticated aerosolization delivery systems were not developed. Much more
progress appears to have been achieved in developing sophisticated artillery warheads and tactical missiles that were capable of delivering nuclear, biological, and chemical warheads. One important reason for the
limited understanding of South Africa's past nuclear, biological, and chemical programs, particularly Project Coast, is the highly compartmentalized
nature of the program. Only Basson and a handful of his associates had a
complete picture of what was developed and where products went.

Another reason for our limited understanding of the full scope of these
secret programs is that top political leaders approved increasingly expensive and exotic chemical- and biological-weapons programs based on
promises that they could be used to cope with domestic unrest. The senior
political and military officials who authorized these programs did not
want to know details about many programs designed to eliminate political
opponents using chemical and biological weapons or more conventional
means. Instead, the inner circle of securocrats who authorized research on
genetic engineering, birth-control methods, and the use of chemicals to
neutralize domestic opponents operated on the basis of a largely informal
system of norms and procedures. In some cases, approval was given using
nonverbal communication, such as gestures or nods. There is also evidence that no explicit orders were necessary to prompt many military, police, and political officials to start destroying documents when the end of
apartheid was in sight. Managers of several secret projects run under the
auspices of Project Coast started destroying documents several years before these projects were ordered closed down. Thus, we may never know
the full scope of activities conducted under Project Coast. South Africa's
past covert weapons programs provide important examples of some of

the different types of challenges that are likely to be faced by those working to verify past chemical- and biological-weapons activities in other countries.

> Policy Lesson 15: Covert links among intelligence agents and scientists in one era may be a source of proliferation problems in subsequent eras.

The strange case of Larry Ford, who claimed to have worked as a U.S. intelligence operative throughout the 1970s and 1980s, and a number of unanswered questions about the nature of the collaborative research that he conducted with South Africans serve to remind us that covert projects in one era often carry unintended consequences that are not apparent for many years. Most of the important questions about what Ford was doing with the amniotic fluid collected from South African women who attended military hospitals and spring clinics are not yet known. It is also unknown whether Dr. Ford was working as a rogue American scientist, along with a few other American doctors, or was part of an intergovernmental covert program between South Africa and the United States. The questions about Dr. Jerry Nilsson, who claimed to have worked with the Selous Scouts in Rhodesia during the 1970s and to be one of many "cogs in a complex, far-reaching project," have also not been answered. The possibility that he too was a member of an international group of like-minded white supremacists who might be willing to use unscrupulous methods to achieve their aims raises a number of important issues for both South Africans and Americans who now live in fear of being the victim of a biological warfare attack.

> Policy Lesson 16: A major factor in determining the types of proliferation issues related to weapons of mass destruction that interested international actors focus on at any given time is their shared perceptions about the nature of a threat.

Throughout the 1980s, the United States, the United Kingdom, and other Western countries were primarily interested in the development of South Africa's nuclear program. It took time for the U.S. government to grasp the nature and extent of the threat posed by the space-launch program and Project Coast. Only after finding sophisticated weapons systems, such as a modified G6 gun found in Iraq in 1991 that was manufactured in South Africa and that may have been capable of carrying chemical and biological weapons and possibly nuclear warheads, did U.S. interest in South Africa's chemical- and biological-weapons program change substantially. These concerns were heightened further by the frequent trips that Basson took to Libya in his capacity as a consultant for a South African parastatal, Transnet. However, once the United States did become engaged in shutting down proliferation threats, it was able to play an important role in helping to convince the de Klerk government that it should also dismantle its space-launch and Project Coast programs. Therefore, one of the lessons from South Africa's experience is that it is important to properly estimate the dangers of chemical- and biological-weapons proliferation and to understand the broad range of uses of those weapons in each country and to constantly reevaluate these capabilities.

> Policy Lesson 17: The procedures a regime follows in disman-
> tling its nuclear, biological, and chemical weapon programs
> matter. Unilateral disarmament will not allay proliferation fears.

The initial disclosures about the rollback of South Africa's nuclear-bomb program were widely accepted without many questions. However, over time, claims by a number of employees of the former regime have suggested that some aspects of the official story about nuclear rollback may have been incomplete.

In a similar vein, revelations at the Truth and Reconciliation Commission, Basson's arrest on drug charges, and testimony at the Basson trial suggest that there was extensive fraud and that chemical- and biological-weapons facilities were used to produce illegal drugs. More recent revelations that one and possibly other Project Coast scientists kept documents and agents developed under the auspices of the project have raised additional questions. Still unknown are the intended uses of the drugs, where they went, and who authorized and benefited from their production. This case suggests that chemical- and biological-weapons programs may be used as covers for a wide range of covert activities, including the illegal production and sale of drugs.

Basson's links with individuals in the United States and Europe suggest an important but poorly understood set of transnational connections. The South African case highlights the possibility that there may be transnational criminal links associated with future chemical- and biological-weapons programs. Revelations during the Basson trial underscored a new complication in modern nonproliferation and rollback efforts—transnational criminal networks. These revelations led several European countries and the U.S. to initiate new investigations into Basson and transnational networks of criminals. Future nonproliferation investigations are likely to require coordination among several agencies in many different countries. New methods and approaches may need to be developed to monitor and control future chemical- and biological-weapons programs that may operate as covers for illegal operations.

Revelations about Basson's secret dealings with individuals in the United States and Europe suggest the possibility that the illegal activities of transnational criminal networks, including the manufacturing and distribution of drugs, are likely by-products of covert national chemical- and biological-weapons programs in the present era of globalization. As new revelations about Basson's international activities were made public, authorities in several European countries and the United States opened investigations in order to determine whether any national or local laws related to fraudulent activities or illegal drug production had been broken. While no new charges were filed against Basson or his colleagues, the many still-undisclosed dealings of Project Coast managers that occurred as routine exchanges of virtually hundreds of offshore shell companies registered in islands around the world should serve as a cautionary reminder to all government authorities that they may need to develop new methods and approaches to monitor and understand the actors and activities associated with and triggered by covert national chemical and biological warfare programs.

> Policy Lesson 18: Verification of past nuclear-, biological-, and chemical-weapons programs is also difficult for a variety of other reasons, including the intentional use of verbal rather than written instructions, the intentional destruction of documents long before national or international weapons inspectors arrive on the scene, and the lack of central control of rogue elements in the government.

De Klerk claims that after assuming the presidency in 1989, he only gradually obtained evidence about South Africa's involvement in third-force activities that could not be ignored. Rumors of coups and a right-wing conspiracy to take control of the government and a growing fear during the early 1990s that the country might descend into civil war created uncertainties and difficulties in terminating chemical- and biological-weapons programs. The Steyn Report presented de Klerk with evidence of extensive abuse of power by the police and military, including operations run by Wouter Basson. De Klerk's reaction was to fire dozens of senior military officials. This move prompted a defensive reaction on the part of many military leaders and fueled additional efforts to cover up past misdeeds. As a top former general told us, "the shutters went down inside the South African military."[2] De Klerk's difficulties with regaining full civilian control of the military and ensuring that all chemical- and biological-weapons agents were destroyed and secrets secured suggest that comprehensive dismantlement of former covert biological and chemical programs may be impossible.

> Policy Lesson 19: Rollbacks of weapons of mass destruction are likely to require extensive outside pressure; they are also likely to take several years to complete and even then they are likely to still be incomplete.

A number of outside actors, including the United States, the United Kingdom, and Israel, shared the de Klerk government's concerns about what an ANC-dominated government might do with weapons of mass destruction. These concerns led to a series of outside pressures and moves that were designed to ensure that the South African government completely dismantled their nuclear, chemical, and biological programs. As the ANC was poised to take power in 1994, the United States and the United Kingdom were not satisfied that the chemical- and biological-weapons program had been rolled back and feared that secrets would fall into the hands of adversaries. These two countries took the unusual step of issuing a démarche that demanded investigation of Project Coast. A great deal of diplomatic effort was also directed at ensuring the completion of two South African confidence-building measures. In South Africa, the rollback took several years to complete. Although the South African government assured the United States that knowledge about chemical and biological weapons was under lock and key, the January 1997 discovery that Basson had in his possession large amounts of Project Coast–related documents that were thought to have been destroyed renewed fears that Basson and his associates might become agents of proliferation. Thus, the extent of official or unofficial proliferation from South Africa's chemical- and biological-weapons program remains unknown.

> Policy Lesson 20: A country's adoption of dual-use civilian technology—for example, nuclear energy using highly enriched uranium or a space-launch vehicle—is an important indicator that a country may be developing covert weapons of mass destruction.

In South Africa, once the nuclear-power industry had developed and demonstrated the capability to produce highly enriched uranium, politicians were quickly approached to approve preliminary secret work on the feasibility of using the enriched uranium for weapons development. Prime Minster Vorster wasted little time in approving this line of research. We have seen a similar response by leaders of other countries, including Israel, France, and more recently, Iraq, Iran, and North Korea. The relationships between peaceful energy research and covert nuclear-weapons research are so close that it is a useful rule of thumb to assume that once a country has developed the capacity to produce highly enriched uranium, they either have or will shortly initiate a covert weapons program.

In a similar vein, the modifications needed to transform a civilian space-launch vehicle into a long-range ballistic missile capable of carrying nuclear warheads are so minor that it is also probably useful to assume that a country that is building a civilian space-launch vehicle is also engaged in backroom research and development to build long-range missiles. This line of reasoning is an important reason why the United States moved so fast to pressure South Africa, Brazil, and South Korea to close down their space-launch-vehicle research at an early stage. However, as the current demand now outstrips the supply of space-launch vehicles, there are increasingly important economic reasons for developing countries to pool their resources with the resources of other actors to develop or relaunch space-launch vehicles. The problems associated with controlling this type of missile proliferation threat promise to be harder to deal with in the future.

Before South Africa had missiles, the plan was to drop a nuclear bomb from a conventional air force bomber. This idea has been replicated several times in other countries, so it may be prudent to assume that countries who have a national airline, a sophisticated technological and scientific base, and a modern defense industry are likely to be engaged in covert research into missiles capable of carrying weapons of mass destruction bombs.

> Policy Lesson 21: Future nonproliferation efforts are likely to require additional cooperative programs among agencies in several countries to contain the spread of knowledge of nuclear, chemical and biological weapons.

One of the most striking aspects about proliferation trends in South Africa after the benefit of nearly a decade of experience with dismantlement is the absence of a Cooperative Threat Reduction program (often called the Nunn-Lugar program)[3] in South Africa. This absence contrasts sharply with the programs initiated with Russia and several other former Soviet Republics to ensure that scientists and engineers are kept working and do not represent a proliferation threat. As early as 1994, a group of desperate unemployed South African nuclear scientists and engineers threatened to sell their expertise to the highest bidder. The unsuccessful efforts by Dr. Goosen and his associates in 2003 to generate employment opportunities and financial support—in effect, their own ad hoc Nunn-Lugar work program—in the United States illustrate that the problem of unemployed nuclear and biowarfare weapon scientists is not likely to go away.

As we enter the twenty-first century, which many call the biological age, it is apparent that new types of biological weapons may be developed under the guise of civilian biotechnology research. In an era when much of the proliferation seems to be occurring through black-market channels, expanding programs to keep foreign former scientists working may prove to be an efficient way for the U.S. government not only to prevent future proliferation threats but also to learn more about how best to monitor potential dual-use threats in civilian sectors of the economy.

> Policy Lesson 22: New methods and approaches will be needed to monitor and control future weapons of mass destruction programs.

One reason few analysts were alarmed when Nigeria and South Africa recently expressed their intention to develop national space-launch capabilities is that both efforts are cooperative undertakings involving a number of different countries and private companies. In a world increasingly characterized by globalism, a private-sector consortium approach where all parties share the same desire for profit may become the most effective and efficient way to monitor and control future weapons of mass destruction and missile threats.

> Policy Lesson 23: South Africa, along with several other African states, will continue to attract terrorists affiliated with al-Qaeda and other groups with extreme political views that are trying to obtain weapons of mass destruction, missiles, or sanctuary in a remote area of the world.

As a former nuclear- and biochemical-weapons state, South Africa will likely be a target of efforts by al-Qaeda and its affiliates who are looking for weapons of mass destruction materials and expertise. The country's modern financial and transportation network and the relative lack of concern about international terrorism by radical Islamic fundamentalists in South Africa make the country a perfect one to live in while waiting for the next operation.

A recent tightening of security at South African nuclear facilities, a review of policies regarding arms exports, and increased cooperation with agencies in other countries will not entirely address the problem. South Africa will continue to be an attractive target for Islamic terrorists, both as a source of weapons of mass destruction materials and a source of potential recruits. Young Africans will be attracted to groups such as al-Qaeda as long as social, political, and economic inequalities fuel alienation. Moreover, as the recent resurgence in white right-wing supremacist groups illustrates, al-Qaeda is not the only radical ideological group that is willing to use and is looking to acquire weapons of mass destruction.

Notes

ONE. INTRODUCTION

1. The term "weapons of mass destruction" has been used as a shorthand reference for nuclear, biological, and chemical weapons and their means of delivery. Many analysts also consider radiological weapons to be weapons of mass destruction. Most of the research and development on vehicles that deliver weapons of mass destruction focused on ballistic missiles and bombers until the late 1990s, when Russia and the United States officially acknowledged the existence of miniaturized nuclear warheads that could be delivered by other means. Today there is greater recognition that a variety of means may be used to deliver nuclear, radiological, biological, and chemical weapons.

2. Neorealist theory emerged with Kenneth Waltz's book *Theory of International Politics* (1979). Waltz believed that "classical realism" had defects that could be cured by applying a more scientific approach. He defined the international system as a precise three-dimensional structure. First, anarchy is the ordering principle of the "self-help" international system, where the quest for survival requires all states to seek security through the accretion of military power. Second, in this anarchic system, each state is a separate, autonomous, and formally equal unit and each must count only on its own resources, not on those of other states. Third, states cannot be differentiated by their functions, but they differ in their capabilities. The distribution of capabilities, unequal and shifting, defines the relative power of states and predicts variations in "balance of power" behavior. Thus, international orders vary according to the number of great powers. Waltz argued that states in anarchy choose between "balancing power" and "bandwagoning" and prefer balancing because the power of other states is always a threat. Waltz's book influenced a generation of international relations scholars.

3. Organizational theory is a body of generalizations about the patterned regularities in the behavior found in large modern organizations. Bureaucratic politics is a related set of propositions that explains decision making in large organizations as political games based upon struggles between contending factions with different positions, and hypothesizes that "where you stand depends on where you sit." See Graham Allison and Philip Seiko, *Essence of Decision: Explaining the Cuban Missile Crisis,* 2nd ed. (New York: Longman, 1999).

4. Throughout the book we draw upon several different bodies of theoretical and empirical research. Relevant explanations using neorealist theory include Bruce Buenos de Mesquita, *Principles of International Politics: People's Power, Preferences, and Perceptions* (Washington, D.C.: CQ Press, 2000); Michael P. Sullivan, *Theories of International Relations: Transition vs. Persistence* (New York: Palgrave, 2001); and Kenneth N. Waltz, *Theory of International Politics* (New York: Random House, 1979).

We also found comparative foreign-policy theory and research useful for emphasizing the importance of such concepts as culture, historical linkages, and the impact of changes in the external environment, including the foreign policies of other countries. See, for example, C. F. Hermann, C. W. Kelley, Jr., and James N. Rosenau, *New Directions in the Study of Foreign Policy* (Boston, Mass.: Allen & Unwin, 1987); James N. Rosenau, *The Scientific Study of Foreign Policy* (New York: The Free Press, 1980).

At the microlevel, several lines of research were helpful in this study, including organizational and bureaucratic politics approaches and political psychological research on determinants of recurring foreign-policy decisions. We also looked at approaches that focused on perceptual, cognitive, and other individual characteristics of political leaders; the role of shared national images; small-group interactions; and shared representations of problems developed by political actors viewed as processors of limited information attempting to reach agreement on ill-defined problems and group-interaction processes. See D. Sylvan and J. F. Voss, eds., *Problem Representation in International Relations* (Cambridge: Cambridge University Press, 1998).

For relevant research on organizational and bureaucratic politics, see Graham Allison and Philip Seiko, *Essence of Decision: Explaining the Cuban Missile Crisis,* 2nd ed. (New York: Longman, 1999); John Steinbruner, *The Cybernetic Theory of Decision* (Princeton, N.J.: Princeton University Press, 1974); and Sagan's analysis in Scott D. Sagan and Kenneth N. Waltz, *The Spread of Nuclear Weapons: A Debate* (New York: Norton, 1995).

For recent works on the determinants of sequential foreign-policy decision making relating to recurring political problems, see Helen E. Purkitt and Stephen Burgess, "Changing Course and Responding to Negative Feedback: A Case of Sequential Decision-Making in South Africa, 1989–1994," paper presented at the symposium Responding to Negative Feedback in Foreign Policy Decision-Making, George Bush Center for Presidential Studies, Bush School of Government and Public Service, College Station, Texas, May 18–20, 2001. See also Charles F. Herman, "Changing Course: When Governments Choose to Redirect Foreign Policy," *International Studies Quarterly* 34 (1990): 3–21; M. G. Hermann and C. F. Hermann, "Who Makes Foreign Policy Decisions and How?" *International Studies Quarterly* 33 (1989): 361–388; and Helen E. Purkitt, "A Problem-Centered Approach for Understanding Foreign Policy," in *Global International Policy: Among and Within Nations,* ed. Stuart Nagel (New York: Marcel-Dekker, 2000), 79–101. For research on individual and small-group variables, see Robert Jervis, "Political Psychology: Some Challenges and Opportunities," *Political Psychology* 10, no. 3 (1989); Eric Singer and Valerie Hudson, eds., *Political Psychology and Foreign Policy* (Boulder, Colo.: Westview Press, 1992); Sylvan and Voss, eds., *Problem Representation in International Relations*; and Thomas J. Scheff, *Bloody Revenge: Emotions, Nationalism, and War* (Boulder, Colo.: Westview Press, 1994).

5. See Sylvan and Voss, eds., *Problem Representation in International Relations.*

6. Several of the recent rumors are similar to those reported and discussed in depth in Peter Hounam and Steve McQuillen, *The Mini-Nuke Conspiracy: Mandela's Nuclear Nightmare* (New York: Viking, 1995). For a more recent book that discusses aspects of past programs not covered in the initial official account, see Hilton Hamann, *Days of the Generals* (Cape Town: Zebra Press, 2001).

7. See, for example, "South Africa: Seven Right-Wingers Facing Charges of 'Treason, Terrorism,'" *Financial Times* (London), April 8, 2002; Martin Schonteich, "The Power to Disrupt," *Mail & Guardian* (Johannesburg), September 19, 2002; Mariette Le Roux, "Boeremag Treason Trial Starts," *The Herald* (Port Elizabeth), May 16, 2003, 8. South African officials are confident that they will defeat the current right-wing wave of terrorist violence. However, opposition to the political status quo by former members of the apartheid regime remains a serious security threat for South African officials. Senior political and military officials of South Africa, interviews by Helen Purkitt, South African Embassy, Washington, D.C., 2003.

8. In April 2002, Basson was acquitted on forty-five charges that ranged from murder and drug-trafficking to fraud and theft. See Chapter 7 for more details.

9. In the aftermath of the anthrax-letter murders, many civilian agencies, including the new Department of Homeland Security, several organizations within the U.S. Department of Defense, and the National Institutes of Health, received large increases in their budgets for new initiatives to improve defensive and preventive measures for coping with biological attacks. For more information about specific budgetary amounts and programs see the web sites of federal agencies involved in U.S. homeland security such as the Department of Homeland Security at http://www.dhs.gov. For information on the biodefense initiatives and programs of the National Institutes of Health, see http://biodefense.niaid.nih.gov.

10. Edward Humes, "The Medicine Man," *Los Angeles Magazine,* July 2001. Thomas Byron and Victor Ray, interviews by Helen Purkitt, Irvine, California, 2001 and 2002.

11. "'Dr. Death': South Africa's Biological Weapons Program," episode of *60 Minutes,* CBS, aired November 3, 2002; summary available online at http://www.cbsnews.com/stories/2002/10/30/60minutes/main527530.shtml; Jo Thomas, "California Doctor's Suicide Leaves Many Troubling Mysteries Unsolved," *New York Times,* November 3, 2002.

12. Joby Warrick and John Mintz, "Lethal Legacy: Bioweapons for Sale; U.S. Declined South African Scientist's Offer on Man-Made Pathogens," *Washington Post,* April 20, 2003, A1. Other reports surfaced during the latter half of 2002 alleging that a deal involving the attempt of an apartheid-era general, Major-General Tai Minaar, to sell Project Coast pathogens to al-Qaeda had been foiled when he died under suspicious circumstances.

13. Daan Goosen, interview by Helen Purkitt, Pretoria, June 24, 2003.

14. For a summary of research on the nature of emerging biological warfare threats, see Guy B. Roberts, "Arms Control without Arms Control: The Failure of the Biological Weapons Convention Protocol and a New Paradigm for Fighting the Threat of Biological Weapons," Occasional Paper no. 49, USAF Institute for National Security Studies, March 2003.

TWO. SOUTH AFRICA IN A WORLD OF PROLIFERATING WEAPONS

1. Ralph E. Lapp, "The Einstein Letter That Started It All," *The New York Times Magazine,* August 23, 1964. Quoted in George Athens, "Rethinking Nuclear Proliferation," *Washington Quarterly* 18, no. 1 (Winter 1995): 181.

2. The other countries are Israel, India, and Pakistan.

3. There were over 100,000 immediate casualties in each Japanese city, and thousands more died in succeeding years from the delayed effects of radiation from bombs.

4. For a recent useful survey of tactical weapons, see John T. Coppell, Gwendolyn M. Hall, and Stephen P. Lambert, *Tactical Nuclear Weapons: Debunking the Mythology* (Colorado Springs: USAF Institute for National Security Studies, 2002).

5. The deaths of many of the 140 people killed in the raid were attributed to the chemicals used by the Russian government. At the time, Russian officials refused to disclose the type of gas used in the raid. Several commentators alleged that the gas was a BZ-type gas outlawed by the Chemical Weapons Convention that Russia had signed in 1997. See "Russia Seizes Theater as Crisis Ends," *New York Times,* October 26, 2002. Later the Russian government acknowledged using a liquid synthetic narcotic agent but denied using other agents.

6. For discussions of the possible use of chemical and biological agents in guerrilla and counterinsurgency warfare in Southern Africa, see John Marcum, *The Angolan Revolution: Exile Politics and Guerrilla Warfare, 1962–1976* (Cambridge, Mass.: MIT Press, 1978); Ron Reid as told to Peter Stiff, *Selous Scouts: Top Secret War* (Alberton, South Africa: Galago, 1982); and Peter Stiff, *The Silent War: South African Recce Operations: 1969–1994* (Alberton, South Africa: Galago, 1999). See also Chapter 5 of this book.

7. In 1984, during a bid to win a local election, a religious cult, the Rajneeshees, used salmonella bacteria in an effort to poison citizens opposed to their political agenda and to keep political opponents from the polls in a small town in Oregon. See Judith Miller, Stephen Engelberg, and William Broad, *GERMS: Biological Weapons and America's Secret War* (New York: Simon and Schuster, 2001).

8. Kenneth N. Waltz, *Theory of International Politics* (New York: Random House, 1979).

9. Classical realism dates back more than 2,000 years to Thucydides and starts with a pessimistic view that self-interested, competitive, and power-hungry behavior among statesmen means that each state must act selfishly in order to preserve itself, which normally leads to conflict. International politics is characterized by the struggle for national power between states and the belief that the balance of power among states is the best way to maintain peace. See Hans J. Morgenthau, *Politics among Nations* (New York, Alfred A. Knopf, 1948).

10. There have been efforts to use biowarfare since ancient times. This early history is beyond the scope of our study, but a chronology of the history of biological warfare, "History of Biowarfare," is available at the *Nova Online* web site: http://www.pbs.org/wgbh/nova/bioterror/hist_nf.html.

11. L. F. Haber, *The Poisonous Cloud: Chemical Warfare in the First World War* (Oxford: Oxford University Press, 1986).

12. Erhard Geissler and John Ellis van Courtland Moon, eds., *Biological and Toxin Weapons: Research, Development and Use from the Middle Ages to 1945* (New York: Oxford University Press, 1999); Ken Alibek with Stephen Handelman, *Biohazard* (New York: Random House, 1999); Tom Mangold and Jeff Goldberg, *Plague Wars: A True Story of Biological Warfare* (New York: St. Martin's Press, 1999).

13. Edward Regis, *The Biology of Doom: The History of America's Secret Germ Warfare Project* (New York: Henry Holt, 1999); Alibek, *Biohazard*.

14. Sheldon H. Harris, *Factories of Death: Japanese Biological Warfare, 1932–1945, and the American Cover-Up* (London: Routledge, 1994).

15. Geissler and van Courtland Moon, eds., *Biological and Toxin Weapons*.

16. Bruce D. Larkin, *Nuclear Designs: Great Britain, France, and China in the Global Governance of Nuclear Arms* (New Brunswick, N.J.: Transaction Publishers, 1996); John C. Hopkins and Weixing Hu, *Strategic Views from the Second Tier: The Nuclear Weapons Policies of France, Britain, and China* (New Brunswick, N.J.: Transaction Publishers, 1995).

17. Nina Tannenwald, *The Nuclear Taboo: The United States and the Non-Use of Nuclear Weapons Since 1945* (Cambridge: Cambridge University Press, 2003).

18. Regis, *The Biology of Doom*; Alibek, *Biohazard*; Mangold and Goldberg, *Plague Wars*.

19. In December 1953, U.S. President Eisenhower gave a famous speech at the United Nations called the Atoms for Peace speech. In the speech, Eisenhower emphasized the importance of international cooperation between the United States and the former Soviet Union in order to ensure that weapons-grade fissile materials were used only for peaceful energy purposes. In subsequent years, the term

"Atoms for Peace" was used as the umbrella label for a collection of agreements on bilateral technical cooperation and information exchange between the United States and other countries that were designed to promote the peaceful use of nuclear energy.

20. Ralph Sanders, *Project Plowshare: The Development of the Peaceful Uses of Nuclear Explosions* (Washington, D.C.: Public Affairs Press, 1962). See also A. R. Newby-Fraser, *Chain Reaction* (Pretoria, South Africa: Atomic Energy Board, 1979).

21. Larkin, *Nuclear Designs;* Hopkins and Hu, *Strategic Views from the Second Tier.*

22. Avery Goldstein, *Deterrence and Security in the 21st Century: China, Britain, France, and the Enduring Legacy of the Nuclear Revolution* (Stanford, Calif.: Stanford University Press, 2000); T. V. Paul, *Power versus Prudence: Why Nations Forgo Nuclear Weapons* (Montreal: McGill-Queen's University Press, 2000).

23. Larkin, *Nuclear Designs;* Hopkins and Hu, *Strategic Views from the Second Tier.*

24. Mitchell Reiss reports that J. W. de Villiers claims that the South Africans were encouraged to believe that testing a nuclear device "would not lead to excessive international reaction" after watching the tepid international reaction to India's test of a nuclear explosive. See Mitchell Reiss, *Bridled Ambition: Why Countries Constrain Their Nuclear Capabilities* (Baltimore: Johns Hopkins University Press, 1995), 9–10. See Chapter 3 of this book for more details.

25. Larkin, *Nuclear Designs;* Hopkins and Hu, *Strategic Views from the Second Tier.*

26. Brad Roberts, "Strategies of Denial," in *Countering the Proliferation and Use of Weapons of Mass Destruction,* ed. Peter L. Hays, Vincent J. Jodoin, and Alan R. Van Tassel (New York: McGraw-Hill, 1998), 63–88. In contrast to the 1972 Bacteriological and Toxin Weapons Convention, the 1993 Chemical Weapons Convention had stronger monitoring procedures. While the Bacteriological and Toxin Weapons Convention was devised during the Cold War, negotiations for a chemical-weapons convention were assisted by the U.S.-Soviet collaboration of the early 1990s. It was signed in 1993 and came into effect in 1997. However, problems remain with efforts to monitor dual-use facilities.

27. Alibek, *Biohazard;* Mangold and Goldberg, *Plague Wars.*

28. Roberts, "Strategies of Denial," 64. In 1968–1970, the strength of the Nuclear Non-Proliferation Treaty was questionable, but a number of measures, both multilateral (e.g., the Zangger Committee and the Nuclear Suppliers Group) and unilateral (by the United States), strengthened the Nuclear Non-Proliferation Treaty regime during the 1970s.

29. Albert J. Mauroni, *America's Struggle with Chemical-Biological Warfare* (Westport, Conn.: Praeger, 2000).

30. Marie I. Chevrier, "Strengthening the International Arms Control Regime," in *Biological Weapons and Warfare,* ed. Raymond A. Zilinskas (Boulder, Colo.: Lynne Rienner, 2000), 153. Other states that have been accused of having biological-weapons programs include India, Pakistan, Ukraine, Belarus, Kazakhstan, Jordan, Algeria, and Cuba.

31. Mauroni, *America's Struggle with Chemical-Biological Warfare.*

32. Avner Cohen, *Israel and the Bomb* (New York: Columbia University Press, 1998).

33. Anthony H. Cordesman, "Weapons of Mass Destruction in the Middle East: National Efforts, War Fighting Capabilities, Weapons Lethality, Terrorism, and Arms Control Implications," Center for Strategic and International Studies, Washington, D.C., February 1998, 16–17.

34. "President Delivers State of the Union Address," January 29, 2002, http://www.whitehouse.gov/news/releases/2002/01/20020129-11.html. Bush named North Korea, Iraq, and Iran as part of an "axis of evil" that supports terrorism and seeks to develop weapons of mass destruction.

35. Jonathan Tucker, "Motivations for and against Proliferation," in *Biological Weapons and Warfare,* ed. Raymond A. Zilinskas (Boulder, Colo.: Lynne Rienner, 2000), 49.

36. George Perkovich, *India's Nuclear Bomb* (Berkeley: University of California Press, 1999); Cohen, *Israel and the Bomb.*

37. F. W. de Klerk, *The Last Trek: A New Beginning* (London: Macmillan, 1998); David Ottaway, *Chained Together: Mandela, de Klerk, and the Struggle to Remake South Africa* (New York: Random House, 1993); Allister Sparks, *The Mind of South Africa: The Story of the Rise and Fall of Apartheid* (London: Mandarin, 1990).

38. Former senior South African politicians and generals, interviews by the authors, 1994 to 2003.

39. See Hannes Steyn, Richardt van der Walt, and Jan van Loggerenberg, *Armament and Disarmament: South Africa's Nuclear Weapons Experience* (Pretoria: Network Publishers, 2003) for a recent insiders' account that confirms this view.

40. According to several accounts, the United States supplied Saddam Hussein's regime with several biological agents. See, for example, Philip Shenon, "Iraq Links Germs for Weapons to U.S. and France," *New York Times,* March 16, 2003. Several other Western states supplied crucial knowledge and materials to former colonial states and key trade partners. For a discussion of the role of Western countries in supplying chemical weapons, see recent statements in Walter Pincus, "Chemicals Use Considered Less Likely," *Washington Post,* March 20, 2003, A19. As the current state of North Korea's nuclear program illustrates, a similar pattern of diffusion of knowledge and material occurred from the major powers of the Eastern bloc (the former Soviet Union and China) to their allies in the developing world.

41. In 2002, the FBI acknowledged in a public statement that the anthrax used in the letter attacks had been traced back to a strain developed at the U.S. Army Research Institute of Infectious Diseases at Fort Detrick in 1980. However, samples of the strain were sent to several laboratories in the United States and abroad. Consequently, the U.S. government does not know today who manufactured or mailed the anthrax spores sent in 2001.

42. Jonathan Tucker examines the effect of a number of "predisposing domestic factors" as well as short-term "precipitating factors" and existing threats in his analysis of the proliferation of biological weapons in the Middle East. Tucker, "Motivations for and against Proliferation," 49.

43. In complex organizations facing uncertain situations, stringent rules for decision making are relaxed and a decision is made that seems "reasonable." "Satisficing" is the term used to describe the characteristic decision-making logic used in complex organizations because decision makers typically make "good enough" judgments and decisions. The concept was first developed by Herbert A. Simon in *Administrative Behavior: A Study of Decision-Making Processes in Administrative Organizations* (New York: Free Press, 1997). For a discussion of the important role of standard operating procedures and organizational culture in making decisions by groups of professionals in public organizations see Scott D. Sagan, *The Limits of Safety: Organizations, Accidents, and Nuclear Weapons* (Princeton, N.J.: Princeton University Press, 1995); and Diane Vaughan, *The Challenger*

Launch Decision: Risky Technology, Culture and Deviance at NASA (Chicago: University of Chicago Press, 1995).

44. Cohen, *Israel and the Bomb,* 76–77; and Perkovich, *India's Nuclear Bomb,* 39–40.

45. Ibid.

46. Waldo Stumpf, "South Africa's Nuclear Weapons Program: From Deterrence to Dismantlement," *Arms Control Today* 25, no. 10 (December 1995/January 1996): 4–7. Domestic politics helps explain the 1974 Indian nuclear test. A domestic crisis had driven Prime Minister Gandhi's approval ratings down, and the test boosted her popularity by more than 30 percent. See Scott D. Sagan, "Why Do States Build Nuclear Weapons? Three Models in Search of a Bomb," *International Security* 21, no. 3 (Winter 1996/97): 67–69.

47. See, for example, the studies included in D. Sylvan and J. Voss, eds., *Problem Representation and Political Decision Making* (Cambridge: Cambridge University Press, 1998); and Yaacov Y. I. Vertzberger, *The World in Their Minds: Information Processing, Cognition, and Perceptions in Foreign Policy Decision-making* (Stanford, Calif.: Stanford University Press, 1990). Several studies have documented the convergence between changes in the official foreign-policy "script" evident in foreign-policy rhetoric and subsequent foreign policy. For South Africa, see especially H. Purkitt, "A Problem-Centered Approach for Understanding Foreign Policy: Some Examples from U.S. Foreign Policy toward Southern Africa," in *Global International Policy among and within Nations,* ed. S. Nagel (New York: Marcel-Dekker, 2000), 79–101; and H. Purkitt and James W. Dyson, "U.S. Foreign Policy towards Southern Africa during the Carter and Reagan Administrations: An Information Processing Perspective," *Political Psychology* 7, no. 3 (September 1986): 507–532.

48. R. P. Abelson, "The Psychological Status of the Script Concept," *American Psychologist* 33 (1981): 273–309.

49. For an in-depth analysis of the forces cementing the former South African–Israeli secret relationship, see Deon Geldenhuys, *Isolated States* (Cambridge: Cambridge University Press, 1991). See also Benjamin Beit-Hallahmi, *The Israeli Connection: Who Israel Arms and Why* (New York: Phantom Books, 1987). For a further description of the laager complex in Afrikaner culture, see Ivor Wilkins and Hans Strydom, *The Super-Afrikaners* (Johannesburg: Jonathan Ball Publishers, 1978). See also Thomas J. Scheff, *Bloody Revenge: Emotions, Nationalism, and Warfare* (Boulder, Colo.: Westview Press, 1994).

50. C. F. Hermann, "Changing Course: When Governments Choose to Redirect Foreign Policy," *International Studies Quarterly* 34 (1990): 3–21; and Helen E. Purkitt and Stephen Burgess, "Changing Course and Responding to Negative Feedback," paper presented at the symposium Responding to Negative Feedback in Foreign Policy Decision-Making, George Bush Center for Presidential Studies, Bush School of Government and Public Service, College Station, Texas, May 18–20, 2001. For relevant comparative foreign-policy research, see Charles W. Kegley, Jr., Charles F. Hermann, and James N. Rosenau, eds., *New Directions in the Study of Foreign Policy* (New York: Routledge, 1987).

51. Robert Jervis, "Political Psychology: Some Challenges and Opportunities." *Political Psychology* 10, no. 3 (1989): 481–516; Scheff, *Bloody Revenge;* Tucker, "Motivations for and against Proliferation," 49; Jacques E. C. Hymans, "Taking the Plunge: Emotion and Identity in the Decision to Build Nuclear Weapons," paper presented at the American Political Science Association Annual Meeting, Washington, D.C., August 31–September 3, 2000, 58–59.

52. Hymans, "Taking the Plunge," 58–59.

53. Ibid., 28–29.

54. Tucker, "Motivations for and against Proliferation," 49.

55. "Securocrats" was a term used to describe top officials in the government of P. W. Botha in the late 1970s and throughout the 1980s. These officials came from the security forces (military, police, and intelligence) and played an important role in decision making, advocating hard-line repression. See Kenneth Grundy, *The Militarization of South African Politics* (London: Tauris, 1986).

56. For example, Dr. Renfrew Christie served seven years in prison for stealing classified documents about South Africa's nuclear-weapons program. After gaining his freedom, he was among the first academics to document the evolution of the apartheid regime's secret nuclear-weapons program. See Renfrew Christie, "South Africa's Nuclear History," paper presented at the Nuclear History Program Fourth International Conference, Nice, France, June 23–27, 1993.

57. For example, South Africans for the Abolition of Vivisection (SAAV) continues to monitor the research activities of companies that were founded by Project Coast scientists. For more details, see the SAAV web site: http://www.saav.org.za/home.php.

58. William J. Long and Suzette R. Grillot, "Ideas, Beliefs, and Nuclear Policies," *Nonproliferation Review* 7, no. 1 (Spring 2000): 24–40. In addition, the difficulty of ending the Russian biological-weapons program well after any threat from the United States had diminished demonstrates the limitations of neorealist theory and is explained mainly by bureaucratic factors and economic costs.

59. Sagan, "Why Do States Build Nuclear Weapons?" 81.

60. Ibid., 69–71; Waldo Stumpf, "South Africa's Nuclear Weapons Program: From Deterrence to Dismantlement," *Arms Control Today* 25, no. 10 (December 1995/January 1996): 4–7; David E. Albright, "South Africa and the Affordable Bomb," *Bulletin of Atomic Scientists* (July/August 1994): 37–47. See also Deon Geldenhuys, *Isolated States: A Comparative Analysis* (Johannesburg: Jonathan Ball Publishers, 1990); and Neta C. Crawford and Audie Klotz, eds., *How Sanctions Work: Lessons from South Africa* (New York: St. Martin's Press, 1999).

THREE. ORIGINS AND EVOLUTION OF NUCLEAR-WEAPONS RESEARCH AND DEVELOPMENT

1. Kenneth Waltz, *The Spread of Nuclear Weapons: More May Be Better* (London: International Institute for Strategic Studies, 1981).

2. The National Party shared power with coalition partners from 1924 to 1934. The "reunited National Party" that swept the 1948 elections was more right wing than the old National Party and dominated South African government and politics until 1994.

3. Several other analysts have emphasized variables related to threat perceptions and technical capabilities in discussions of why South Africa decided to go nuclear. These themes were stressed in Hannes Steyn, Richardt van der Walt, and Jan van Loggerenberg, *Armament and Disarmament: South Africa's Nuclear Weapons Experience* (Pretoria: Network Publishers, 2003), v–xii. Several other authors have stressed the importance of one or both of these variable clusters in their analyses of South Africa's decision to build the bomb. See, for example, David Albright, "South Africa and the Affordable Bomb," *The Bulletin of Atomic Scientists* (July/August 1994): 37–47; Deon Geldenhuys, *Isolated States: A Comparative Analysis* (Johannesburg: Jonathan Ball Publishers, 1990); Roy E. Horton, III, *Out of (South) Africa: Pretoria's Nuclear Weapons Experience* (Colorado Springs: USAF Institute for National Security Studies, 1999); Peter Liberman, "The Rise

and Fall of the South African Bomb," *International Security* 26, no. 2 (Fall 2001): 45–86; Scott D. Sagan, "Why Do States Build Nuclear Weapons? Three Models in Search of a Bomb," *International Security* 21, no. 3 (Winter 1996/97): 69–71; William J. Long and Suzette R. Grillot, "Ideas, Beliefs, and Nuclear Policies: The Cases of South Africa and Ukraine," *Nonproliferation Review* 7, no. 1 (Spring 2000): 24–40; Mitchell Reiss, *Bridled Ambition: Why Countries Constrain Their Nuclear Capabilities* (Washington, D.C.: Woodrow Wilson Center Press, 1995); Leonard S. Spector with Jacqueline R. Smith, *Nuclear Ambitions: The Spread of Nuclear Weapons 1989–1990* (Boulder, Colo.: Westview Press, 1990); Waldo Stumpf, "South Africa's Nuclear Weapons Program: From Deterrence to Dismantlement," *Arms Control Today* 25, no. 10 (December 1995/January 1996): 4–7.

4. Michael Schmidt, "Proof of SA Nuclear Plan," *Sunday Times* (Johannesburg), October 12, 2003, 5.

5. Earlier versions of this chapter were presented in a series of conference papers, including Helen E. Purkitt, "The Politics of Denuclearization: The Case of South Africa," final report to the Institute for National Strategic Studies, U.S. Air Force Academy, November 9, 1994. See also Helen E. Purkitt and Stephen F. Burgess, "Correspondence: South Africa's Nuclear Decisions," *International Security* 27, no. 1 (Summer 2002): 186–194.

6. Geldenhuys, *Isolated States,* 116; Alistair Sparks, *The Mind of South Africa: The Story of the Rise and Fall of South Africa* (London: Mandarin, 1990).

7. The male-only Broederbond continued to influence government long after the 1948 election. By the late 1970s, an estimated 12,000 members were active participants in every town, city council, school board, and agricultural union in the country. Broederbond members managed the state-controlled radio and television network and were key representatives in industry, commercial banks, and building societies. For more details, see J. H. P. Serfontein, *Brotherhood of Power: An Exposé of the Secret Afrikaner Broederbond* (Bloomington: Indiana University Press, 1978).

8. Renfrew Christie, "South Africa's Nuclear History," paper presented at the Nuclear History Program Fourth International Conference, Nice, France, June 23–27, 1993, 7–9. See also Geldenhuys, *Isolated States,* 111.

9. Donald B. Sole, "The South African Nuclear Case in the Light of Recent Revelations," paper presented at the conference New Horizons in Arms Control and Verification, John G. Tower Center for Policy Studies, Southern Methodist University, Dallas, Tex., October 1993, 1–6.

10. Christie, "South Africa's Nuclear History"; Sole, "The South African Nuclear Case"; A. R. Newby-Fraser, *Chain Reaction* (Pretoria: Atomic Energy Board, 1979), 5.

11. Newby-Fraser, *Chain Reaction,* 17; Steyn, van der Walt, and van Loggerenberg, *Armament and Disarmament,* 31.

12. Apartheid means "separateness" in the Afrikaans language.

13. Sparks, *The Mind of South Africa.*

14. Steyn, van der Walt, and van Loggerenberg, *Armament and Disarmament,* v–vii.

15. Christie, "South Africa's Nuclear History," 7.

16. Ibid., 12; Sole, "The South African Nuclear Case," 1.

17. Steyn, van der Walt, and van Loggerenberg, *Armament and Disarmament,* 31.

18. Newby-Fraser, *Chain Reaction, 5.*

19. Christie, "South Africa's Nuclear History," 10.

20. Newby-Fraser, *Chain Reaction, 17.*

21. J. W. de Villiers, Roger Jardine, and Mitchell Reiss, "Why South Africa Gave Up the Bomb," *Foreign Affairs* 72, no. 5 (November/December 1993): 99.

22. J. de St. Jorre, *A House Divided: South Africa's Uncertain Future* (New York: Carnegie Endowment for International Peace, 1977).

23. For additional discussions of the foreign-policy script used by U.S. government officials and the wider U.S. foreign-policy elite to frame and justify U.S. policy toward South Africa, see Helen E. Purkitt, "A Problem Centered Approach for Understanding Foreign Policy," in *Global International Policy among and within Nations,* ed. S. Nagel (New York: Marcel-Dekker, 2000), 79–101. See also T. Borstelmann, *Apartheid's Reluctant Uncle: The United States and South Africa in the Early Cold War* (New York: Oxford University Press, 1993).

24. G. J. B. Mills, "South Africa: The Total National Strategy and Regional Policy During the Botha Years, 1978–1989" (Ph.D. dissertation, University of Lancaster, United Kingdom, 1990).

25. Peter Hounam and Steve McQuillen, *The Mini-Nuke Conspiracy: Mandela's Nuclear Nightmare* (New York: Viking, 1995), 145. The South Atlantic Anomaly is the geographical area where the ionized layer comes relatively close to the earth and results in a high level of background radiation.

26. Geldenhuys, *Isolated States,* 111.

27. Several past studies have analyzed when and why South Africa decided to pursue a nuclear-weapons program. See, for example, Sagan, "Why Do States Build Nuclear Weapons?" 69–71; Stumpf, "South Africa's Nuclear Weapons Program," 4–7; Albright, "South Africa and the Affordable Bomb," 37–47; Horton, *Out of (South) Africa;* Liberman, "The Rise and Fall of the South African Bomb," 45–86. Most past analyses share the view that South Africa's Atomic Energy Board was authorized to develop a gun-type explosive device for peaceful nuclear explosions in the 1970s.

28. Steyn, van der Walt, and van Loggerenberg, *Armament and Disarmament,* 31–32.

29. Sole, "The South African Nuclear Case," 1–6.

30. These exchanges led to a proposal that the German firm Steag and South African authorities cooperate on a comparative study of German enrichment technology developed at Karlsruhe. According to Ambassador Sole, nothing came of these proposals because of adverse publicity. Sole, "The South African Nuclear Case," 3.

31. Ibid., 4.

32. Ibid.

33. Waldo Stumpf, "The Accession of a 'Threshold State' to the NPT: The South African Experience," presentation given at the Conference on Nuclear Non-Proliferation: The Challenges of a New Era, The Carnegie Endowment for International Peace, Washington, D.C., November 17–18, 1993, 1; see also Waldo Stumpf, "South Africa's Limited Nuclear Deterrent Programme and the Dismantling Thereof Prior to South Africa's Accession to the Nuclear Non-Proliferation Treaty," address at the South African Embassy, Washington, D.C., July 23, 1993.

34. Christie, "South Africa's Nuclear History," 16; S. M. Naude, *A Nuclear Energy Research Program* (Pretoria: Council for Scientific and Industrial Research, 1958).

35. Newby-Fraser, *Chain Reaction,* 50. Highly enriched uranium fuel, such as that supplied by the United States to the Safari-1 experimental reactor, is considered to be weapons grade, since it consists of 90 percent or more U-235 and can be used in nuclear weapons.

36. N. B. Badenhorst, "The Bomb, the Missile, and the Future," *Armed Forces of Southern Africa* (November 1993): 27–34. Newby-Fraser intimates that the

design of the Council for Scientific and Industrial Research for the cyclotron was aided by information obtained from Sweden through work completed by a South African, Dr. Dreyfus, one of the world's foremost authorities on magnet design.

37. Senior South African research scientists, interviews by Helen Purkitt, 1994 and 2002.

38. Christie, "South Africa's Nuclear History," 16.

39. Ibid.

40. Dissenting views among AEB board members over a phrase in the Atomic Energy Act reportedly delayed Cabinet approval for more than a year. The cause of the disagreements may never be known, since the notes from the AEB meetings were destroyed. For more details about these decisions, see Newby-Fraser, *Chain Reaction,* 42; and Hounam and McQuillen, *The Mini-Nuke Conspiracy,* 70–71.

41. Steyn, van der Walt, and van Loggerenberg, *Armament and Disarmament,* 35.

42. Newby-Fraser, *Chain Reaction,* 50.

43. Steyn, van der Walt, and van Loggerenberg, *Armament and Disarmament,* 34.

44. Albright, "South Africa and the Affordable Bomb," 37–47; Stumpf, "South Africa's Nuclear Weapons Program," 4–7.

45. Ibid.

46. Steyn, van der Walt, and van Loggerenberg, *Armament and Disarmament,* 32–33; Newby-Fraser, *Chain Reaction,* 17.

47. Newby-Fraser, *Chain Reaction,* 95.

48. International Atomic Energy Agency, *Report by the Director General: The Agency's Verification Activities in South Africa* (Vienna, Austria: International Atomic Energy Agency, 1993); International Atomic Energy Agency, *International Nuclear Safeguards 1994: Vision for the Future,* 2 vols. (Vienna: International Atomic Energy Agency, 1995); Waldo Stumpf, interview by Helen Purkitt, Pelindaba, 1994; ARMSCOR and Denel officials, interviews by Helen Purkitt, Gauteng Province, 1994. The charges were fueled by the fact that South African nuclear scientists had access to Professor Becker's work by the early 1960s and continued to enjoy close collaboration with several German firms that were producing uranium-enrichment technology at least through the mid-1970s. See also Darryl Howlett and John Simpson, "Nuclearization and Denuclearization in South Africa," *Survival* 35, no. 3 (Autumn 1993): 160; and Christie, "South Africa's Nuclear History," 39.

49. Albright, "South Africa and the Affordable Bomb," 37–47; Stumpf, "South Africa's Nuclear Weapons Program," 4.

50. The early work on the South African process for producing enriched uranium was conducted in a small warehouse in downtown Pretoria. Later the work was moved to a downtown office building. The researchers had to appeal directly to Prime Minister Vorster when they needed laboratory facilities to conduct further experiments using uranium hexaflouride. Verwoerd's support resulted in a dedicated lab built at Pelindaba in 1965. A. R. Newby-Fraser, *Chain Reaction,* 100; David Albright, *South Africa's Secret Nuclear Weapons* (Washington, D.C.: Institute for Science and International Security Report, May 1994), 4.

51. According to A. R. Newby-Fraser, "Pelindaba" is a conjunction of two indigenous African words: "pelile" meaning "finished" and "indaba" meaning "council" (or "the council is finished"); *Chain Reaction* (Pretoria: Pretoria Atomic Energy Board, 1979), 50. In the same idiom as "Pelindaba," "Valindaba" was a conjunction of two words which are common to as many as 70-odd indigenous Southern African languages: "vala" (to close) and again "indaba" (thus "the coun-

cil is closed"); *Chain Reaction,* 104. See also Steyn, van der Walt, and van Log-gerenberg, *Armament and Disarmament,* 35.

52. Sole, "The South African Nuclear Case," 5–6. Ambassador Sole notes that the only public expression of foreign interest in Vorster's offer to share South Africa's highly enriched uranium process with others came from Count Lambs-dorff, the economic expert of the German Free Democratic Party. The superpowers were not happy with South Africa's announcement after having just finalized ne-gotiations on the Nuclear Non-Proliferation Treaty. Some unofficial observers at the time questioned the need to produce highly enriched uranium to power nu-clear-energy stations since power plants typically use low-enriched uranium.

53. Hounam and McQuillen, *The Mini-Nuke Conspiracy,* 174.

54. Zdenek Cervenka and Barbara Rogers, *The Nuclear Axis: Secret Collabo-ration between West Germany and South Africa* (London: Julian Friedmann, 1978), 212.

55. Newby-Fraser, *Chain Reaction,* 118; see also Albright, "South Africa and the Affordable Bomb," 37–47; Stumpf, "South Africa's Nuclear Weapons Pro-gram," 4.

56. Stumpf, "South Africa's Nuclear Weapons Program," 4.

57. Steyn, van der Walt, and van Loggerenberg, *Armament and Disarmament,* 37.

58. According to one longtime analyst of South Africa's nuclear-weapons pro-grams, the South African government designed or planned at least four nuclear reactors; the well-known Pelinduna/04 critical assembly that used low-enriched uranium, and the 30-megawatt thermal prototype reactor based on the same tech-nology. South Africa intended and may have actually built a 300-megawatt ther-mal power reactor. The fourth, a 150-megawatt thermal pressurized water reactor, was planned for research and development near Mossel Bay, but it was never built. Pressurized water reactors are light-water reactors and use low-enriched uranium as fuel. "Excavations at the site of the planned 150-megawatt pressur-ized water reactor might have indicated that the South Africans planned to con-struct a subterraneous reprocessing plant—in effect copying what the Israelis did at their Dimona nuclear complex"; N. Badenhorst, personal communication, July 2003.

59. Steyn, van der Walt, and van Loggerenberg, *Armament and Disarmament,* 37–38.

60. At the secret Swords into Plowshares conference at Lawrence Radiation Laboratory in February 1957, scientists discussed the peaceful applications of nu-clear devices and highlighted numerous concerns. In June 1957, the U.S. Atomic Energy Commission approved the Plowshare Program, and in June 1957, Law-rence Radiation Laboratory formally established the Plowshare Project. Under this program, twenty-seven nuclear tests consisting of thirty-five individual detonations were conducted from 1962 to 1971. The program was terminated in 1975. See Christie, "South Africa's Nuclear History"; Mark Hibbs, "South Africa's Secret Nuclear Program: From a PNE to a Deterrent," *Nuclear Fuel,* May 10, 1993, 3; Stumpf, "The Accession of a 'Threshold State' to the NPT." At least one South Afri-can scientist studied the application of peaceful nuclear explosions in the United States. Former South African official, interview by Helen Purkitt, Pretoria, July 1994.

61. Hibbs, "South Africa's Secret Nuclear Program," 3–6; Christie, "South Africa's Nuclear History," 30.

62. Albright, "South Africa and the Affordable Bomb," 37–47.

63. Horton, *Out of (South) Africa,* 2.

64. In a footnote to a published paper, Peter Liberman notes that a 1970 AEB proposal recommended the development of gun-type, implosion, boosted fission, and thermonuclear peaceful nuclear explosion designs. According to his sources, the conceptual studies on the thermonuclear peaceful nuclear explosion designs were approved at a later date. Liberman, "The Rise and Fall of the South African Bomb," 50 n12.

65. Steyn, van der Walt, and van Loggerenberg, *Armament and Disarmament,* 37–38.

66. Steyn, van der Walt, and van Loggerenberg, ibid., describe the names and research activities of the nine working groups. Liberman reports the recommendations of the 1970s AEB study in "The Rise and Fall of the South African Bomb," 50 n20.

67. Frank V. Pabian, "South Africa's Nuclear Weapon Program: Lessons for Nonproliferation Policy," *The Nonproliferation Review* 3, no. 1 (Fall 1995): 11.

68. See J. V. Retief, *Seismiese Beskadiging Tydens Die Kostruktiewe Gebruik Van Kernplofstowwe* [*Seismic Damage During the Constructive Use of Nuclear Explosives, Atomic Energy Board*] (Pretoria: Raad Op Atoomkrag, Pelindaba, July 1972).

69. Hounam and McQuillen, *The Mini-Nuke Conspiracy,* 139.

70. Albright, "South Africa and the Affordable Bomb," 37–47; Stumpf, "South Africa's Nuclear Weapons Program," 4–7. See also Waldo Stumpf's comments in "South Africa's Limited Nuclear Deterrent Programme and the Dismantling Thereof Prior to South Africa's Accession to the Nuclear Non-proliferation Treaty," address at the South African Embassy, Washington, D.C., July 23, 1993; Howlett and Simpson, "Nuclearization and Denuclearization in South Africa," 154–173; Waldo Stumpf, interview by Helen Purkitt, July 1994. After 1979, the Somchem facility was part of ARMSCOR.

71. Senior SADF military officers and senior officials at ARMSCOR, interviews by Helen Purkitt, 1994. Similar views were reported to other interviewers. See de Villiers, Jardine, and Reiss, "Why South Africa Gave Up the Bomb," 102. There are inconsistencies in the public record about when senior South African government officials approved the shift from a peaceful nuclear explosion program to a program to develop nuclear weapons. Many participants who are willing to go on record have stressed the importance of the 1974 test. However, a previously classified CIA report states that "the thermonuclear device" was originally tested in 1973; Central Intelligence Agency, Directorate of Intelligence, "New Information on South Africa's Nuclear Program and South African–Israeli Nuclear and Military Cooperation, 30 March 1983," 1, approved for release May 7, 1996. ARMSCOR official documents claim the program did not go military until 1978. This difference may be semantic or may indicate that many aspects of the nuclear program have not yet been disclosed.

72. De Villiers, Jardine, and Reiss, "Why South Africa Gave Up the Bomb," 99.

73. International Atomic Energy Agency, *Report by the Director General: The Agency's Verification Activities in South Africa.*

74. Steyn, van der Walt, and van Loggerenberg, *Armament and Disarmament,* 14–15.

75. Several recent analyses of South African nuclear decision making published in the United States have emphasized the importance of organizational politics and the role of nuclear scientists. See Liberman, "The Rise and Fall of the South African Bomb," 45–86; and Sagan, "Why Do States Build Nuclear Weapons?" 67–69. Sagan concluded that the domestic-politics model, especially the role played by nuclear scientists, explains the decision to develop nuclear weapons.

This conclusion is remarkably similar to one reached years earlier by a former U.S. diplomat in Sole, "The South African Nuclear Case," 7.

76. Ibid., 49. The most authoritative account of the evolution of the Armaments Corporation of South Africa (ARMSCOR) is Helmoed-Romer Heitman, *South Africa War Machine* (Johannesburg: Central News Agency, 1985).

77. Steyn, van der Walt, and van Loggerenberg, *Armament and Disarmament,* xvii.

78. Christie, "South Africa's Nuclear History," 46. Although the first nuclear device was produced at the Pelindaba weapons facilities, the actual nuclear bombs were built at another site, Building 5000 complex.

79. One of the test shafts was completed in 1976 and the other in 1977. These shafts were 385 and 216 meters deep and 1 meter in diameter. In *Out of (South) Africa,* Horton notes that the AEC device was described as a "monster." A third shaft was sunk but was abandoned due to geological problems. Hilton Hamann, *Days of the Generals* (Cape Town: Zebra, 2001), 166; South African nuclear scientists, engineers, and journalists, interviews conducted by H. Purkitt, Gauteng Province, June and July 1994.

80. Steyn, van der Walt, and van Loggerenberg, *Armament and Disarmament,* 41.

81. Ibid., 40–42.

82. The Council for Scientific and Industrial Research formed the National Institute for Defence Research in 1964. The NIDR had a broad research agenda, but its main focus was rocket and missile research.

83. Steyn, van der Walt, and van Loggerenberg, *Armament and Disarmament,* 40. The National Institute for Defence Research was part of the state-owned Council for Scientific and Industrial Research.

84. Hamann, *Days of the Generals,* 166.

85. Steyn, van der Walt, and van Loggerenberg, *Armament and Disarmament,* 41–42.

86. Former senior ARMSCOR officials, interviews by Helen Purkitt, June 1994. The site was not dismantled until June 1978. See Mitchell Reiss, *Bridled Ambition: Why Countries Constrain Their Nuclear Capabilities* (Washington, D.C.: Woodrow Wilson Center Press, 1995), 201.

87. Steyn, van der Walt, and van Loggerenberg, *Armament and Disarmament,* 42–43.

88. Ibid.

89. Albright, "South Africa and the Affordable Bomb," 37–47; Badenhorst, "The Bomb, the Missile, and the Future," 27–34. A criticality test, also known as "tickling the tail of a sleeping dragon," involves bringing together fissile material to create the conditions for a nuclear explosion. During the test, the energy production in watts, the temperature increase, and the neutrons produced are measured. These measurements provide direct evidence of an explosive chain reaction. The chain reaction ceases as the materials move away from each other after the "drop."

90. Senior managers of the nuclear-bomb program, interviews by Helen Purkitt, July 1994.

91. Seymour M. Hersh, *The Samson Option* (New York: Random House, 1991), 217, 266–268, 277–281. This contention is consistent with Hersh's reports that there was widespread concern throughout the U.S. national-security community in the early 1970s about the ambitious Israeli artillery program. The general supposition was that the Israelis had developed a miniaturized nuclear shell, wanted to test it, and found a willing partner in South Africa.

92. Hounam and McQuillen claim that Taiwanese officials were on a South African navy ship in the area at the time of the 1979 test; *The Mini-Nuke Conspiracy*, 145. There have been reports that South Africa, Taiwan, and Israel were cooperating covertly on nuclear weapons at the time. In September 1976, the *Financial Mail* reported that South Africa was supplying Taiwan with uranium for its nuclear-weapons program. See also Cervenka and Rogers, *The Nuclear Axis*, 153; and William E. Burrows and Robert Windrem, *Critical Mass: The Dangerous Race for Superweapons in a Fragmenting World* (New York: Simon and Schuster, 1994), 452. According to a CIA report, "African scientists had expected a yield of 20kt"; Central Intelligence Agency, "New Information on South Africa's Nuclear Program and South African–Israeli Nuclear and Military Cooperation," 1.

The term "primary" refers to the first stage of a nuclear weapon. It consists of a central core, called the pit, which contains plutonium-239 and/or highly enriched uranium.

93. Burrows and Windrem, *Critical Mass;* Abdul Minty, "The Apartheid Bomb," *Africa*, February 1985, 60.

94. Schmidt, "Proof of SA Nuclear Plan," 5.

95. Hersh, *The Samson Option*, 297. See Badenhorst, "The Bomb, the Missile, and the Future," 27–34, for more details about the "flash" event.

96. Tom Lodge, *Black Politics in South Africa Since 1945* (London: Longman, 1983), 210.

97. Geldenhuys, *Isolated States*, 503.

98. In the 1970s, South Africa's neighbors established the Southern African Development and Co-ordinating Conference (SADCC) in an effort to reduce historic dependence on South Africa's trade and transportation routes and to coordinate their efforts to oppose South Africa. The SADCC evolved into the Southern African Development Community (SADC) and later the Southern African Development Organization (SADO). Since majority rule was instituted in South Africa in 1994, the SADC, which is modeled along the lines of the European Union, has worked to increase the free movement of goods, services, and people and to maintain regional peace.

99. William H. Vatcher, *White Laager: The Rise of Afrikaner Nationalism* (New York: Praeger, 1965).

100. Jacques Hymans, "Taking the Plunge: Emotion and Identity in the Decision to Build Nuclear Weapons," paper presented to the Annual Meeting of the American Political Science Association, Washington, D.C., August 31–September 3, 2000, 58–59.

101. Geldenhuys, *Isolated States*, 181.

102. South Africa considered South West Africa/Namibia to be its territory in the 1960s. This was contested, and the World Court ruled that South West Africa/Namibia was a UN trust territory in 1971.

103. The South African Defence Force was the armed force of South Africa before 1994. It controlled four components—the South African Army, the South African Navy, the South African Air Force, and the South African Medical Service (SAMS).

104. Kenneth Grundy, *The Militarization of South African Politics* (London: Tauris, 1986); Robert S. Jaster, *The Defence of White Power: South African Foreign Policy Under Pressure* (London: Macmillan, 1988); Robert S. Jaster, "Pretoria's Nuclear Diplomacy," *CSIS Africa Notes* 81, no. 22 (January 1988); G. J. B. Mills, "South Africa: The Total National Strategy and Regional Policy During the Botha Years, 1978–1989" (doctoral dissertation, University of Lancaster, United Kingdom, 1990).

105. At least one person with access to highly classified information, the spy Dieter Gerhardt, told South African reporters in 1993 that South African senior leaders had decided to develop nuclear weapons by the mid-1960s. Stephen Laufer and Arthur Gavshon, "The Real Reasons for South Africa's Nukes," *Weekly Mail & Guardian* (Johannesburg), March 26–April 1, 1993, 3.

106. ARMSCOR and Denel officials, interviews by Helen Purkitt, South Africa, June and July 1994.

107. For additional details about how various units of different government entities worked together to develop and test nuclear weapons, see Steyn, van der Walt, and van Loggerenberg, *Armament and Disarmament*, 43.

108. Leonard S. Spector with Jacqueline R. Smith, *Nuclear Ambitions: The Spread of Nuclear Weapons 1989–1990* (Boulder, Colo.: Westview Press, 1990), 271. See Nick Badenhorst, "South Africa's Nuclear Program," unpublished manuscript, May 2000, 30–31, for a more technical discussion of the new nuclear device and facilities at Pelindaba.

109. In 1975, the United States Congress abrogated a contract to supply 93 percent enriched uranium for the Safari-1 research reactor. In 1978, Congress passed the Nuclear Nonproliferation Act, which precluded the transfer of nuclear technology to countries lacking IAEA safeguards and thereby canceled the highly enriched uranium slated for the Koeberg nuclear power station, leaving South Africa with no source of highly enriched uranium.

110. "S. Africa Says Reagan Helped It Get Nuclear Fuel," Reuters World Service, January 10, 1995.

111. "South Africa Confirms Nuclear Deal with France," Reuters World Service, January 9, 1995.

112. "S. Africa Says Reagan Helped It Get Nuclear Fuel."

113. Willem Steenkamp, interview by Helen Purkitt, Cape Town, 1994. See also Willem Steenkamp, *South Africa's Border War 1966–1989* (Gibraltar: Asanti Publishing, 1989), 69.

114. The debate over whether or not U.S. sanctions were effective is beyond the scope of this analysis. For a useful introduction to the sanctions literature, see Neta C. Crawford and Audie Klotz, *How Sanctions Work: Lessons from South Africa* (New York: St. Martin's, 1999), especially David Fig, "Sanctions and the Nuclear Industry," 75–102; and David Fig, "Apartheid's Nuclear Arsenal: Deviation From Development," in *From Defence to Development: Redirecting Military Resources in South Africa,* ed. Jacklyn Cock and Penny Mckenzie (Cape Town: David Philip, 1998), 163–180.

115. U.S. unilateral sanctions did not prevent South Africa from obtaining some technical advice and equipment from a few U.S.-based companies. South Africa was able to obtain even more technical advice and equipment for covert weapons programs related to the nuclear-weapons program from European companies in France, Germany, and Switzerland throughout the 1970s. See Fig, "Sanctions and the Nuclear Industry," 75–102, and "Apartheid's Nuclear Arsenal," 163–180, for more details.

116. General Pierre Steyn, interview by Helen Purkitt, Midrand, June 1994.

117. Before the Simonstown Agreement ended in the mid-1970s, the South African defense establishment, especially the South African Navy, relied heavily on the methods, procedures, and standards of the military of the United Kingdom. Steyn, van der Walt, and van Loggerenberg, *Armament and Disarmament*, 47.

118. Albright, *South Africa's Secret Nuclear Weapons*, 5; Benjamin Beit-Hallahmi, *The Israeli Connection: Who Israel Arms and Why* (New York: Phantom Books, 1987); Geldenhuys, *Isolated States*, 525; Benjamin M. Joseph, *Besieged Bedfellows: Israel and the Land of Apartheid* (New York: Greenwood Press,

1998); former senior South African military officials, interviews by Helen Purkitt, 1994.

119. Beit-Hallahmi, *The Israeli Connection,* 122.

120. Hounam and McQuillen, *The Mini-Nuke Conspiracy,* 174; Badenhorst, "The Bomb, the Missile, and the Future," 27–34. Badenhorst reports that Israel may have been able to produce Israeli bombs by 1963 using fissile material acquired abroad.

121. Geldenhuys, *Isolated States.* See also Beit-Hallahmi, *The Israeli Connection.*

122. Hersh, *The Samson Option,* reports that South Africa and Israel concluded secret nuclear agreements in 1972. Badenhorst, "The Bomb, the Missile, and the Future," 33, describes a declassified CIA report that claimed that South Africa supplied the Israelis with natural uranium rods and depleted uranium for anti-tank rounds throughout the early 1970s.

123. Hounam and McQuillen, *The Mini-Nuke Conspiracy,* 202–204.

124. Horton, *Out of (South) Africa.*

125. Cervenka, *The Nuclear Axis,* 209.

126. For a further discussion, see Hounam and McQuillen, *The Mini-Nuke Conspiracy,* 150; and Hersh, *The Samson Option,* 276. Although Hounam and McQuillen cite an unnamed source who claimed that the South African military had "neutron shells" in 1982, they do not cite other sources or explain whether these shells were built in South Africa or obtained from Israel; *The Mini-Nuke Conspiracy,* 184.

127. Steyn, van der Walt, and van Loggerenberg, *Armament and Disarmament,* 76.

128. Israeli sources cited by Hersh put the number of secret military and nuclear understandings between Israel and South Africa at "six or seven" by the end of the Vorster visit. According to Hersh, the Begin government agreed to honor past commitments made to South Africa, including "promises to give these guys nuclear warheads"; *The Samson Option,* 265, 276. In *Critical Mass,* Burrows and Windrem claim that Israel made similar and parallel missile and nuclear-weapons deals with Taiwan and Iran in early 1977 before the Labor Party lost to Menachem Begin's Likud Party.

129. D. Blow, "Nuke Bombshell," *City Press* (Johannesburg), March 28, 1993, 1; D. Blow, "Nuke Bombshell: Government to Get Rhoodie Awakening," *City Press* (Johannesburg), April 18, 1993, 1; Burrows, *Critical Mass,* 451.

130. Blow, "Nuke Bombshell," March 28, 1993; David Beresford, "Pretoria 'Lied' about Nuclear Swap," *Mail & Guardian* (Johannesburg), February 11, 1994, 3; Albright, "South Africa and the Affordable Bomb," 37–47; Burrows and Windrem, *Critical Mass,* 452.

131. F. W. de Klerk, Speech in Parliament, Republic of South Africa, *Debates of Parliament (Hansard), 5th Session–9th Parliament,* vol. 8, cols. 3574–3576 (Cape Town, 1993); Tielman de Waal, Presentation to the Foreign Correspondents' Association, Pretoria, July 13, 1994; Stumpf, "South Africa's Nuclear Weapons Program," 4–7. For additional analyses of these statements, see Hibbs, "South Africa's Secret Nuclear Program"; Albright, "South Africa and the Affordable Bomb," 37–47; Howlett, "Nuclearization"; Reiss, *Bridled Ambition;* Sagan, "Why Do States Build Nuclear Weapons?"; and de Villiers, Jardine, and Reiss, "Why South Africa Gave Up the Bomb," 98–109.

132. Former South African government officials, interviews by Helen Purkitt, 1994, 1997, and 2000; former South African government officials, interviews by Stephen Burgess, 2000.

133. Badenhorst, *South Africa,* 27–34.

134. Our interpretation, which was formulated in the mid-1990s, is remarkably congruent with the most detailed insiders' accounts available to date. See preface in Steyn, van der Walt, and van Loggerenberg, *Armament and Disarmament,* xiii–xvii.

135. Former defense minister Magnus Malan, interview by Stephen Burgess, Pretoria, June 23, 2000.

136. Steenkamp, *South Africa's Border War,* 54.

137. Former SADF generals and apartheid South African officials, interviews by Helen Purkitt, 1994 and 1998; former SADF generals and apartheid South African officials, interviews by Stephen Burgess, 2000.

138. Robert S. Jaster, "South Africa's Narrowing Security Options," Adelphi Paper no. 159, International Institute for Strategic Studies, London, 1980, 28.

139. John Harker, ed., *Collaborative Security in South Africa* (Ottawa: Canadian Council for International Peace and Security, 1996), 216, 108; Lodge, *Black Politics in South Africa Since 1945.*

140. Harker, *Collaborative Security,* 108; Lodge, *Black Politics in South Africa Since 1945.*

141. The impact of the arms embargo can be seen in this simple statistic: in 1977, 57 percent of South Africa's defense budget went to foreign nations for weapons; by 1982, a mere 15 percent was spent abroad for weapons. For more details, see Geldenhuys, *Isolated States,* 508; Paul H. Wingeart, "Nuclear Proliferation: Factors, Reasons, and Remedies" (B.S. honors thesis, Department of Political Science, United States Naval Academy, May 1995).

142. Eschel Rhoodie, *The Real Information Scandal* (Pretoria: Orbis SA, 1983), 110–111. See also Blow, "Nuke Bombshell: Government to Get Rhoodie Awakening."

143. Geldenhuys, *Isolated States,* 209. Several other American analysts have emphasized the importance of the perceptions and beliefs of senior South African decision makers for understanding South Africa's nuclear policies. For example, the importance of South Africa's belief that it was part of the West and its subsequent isolation are discussed by William J. Long and Suzette R. Grillot, "Ideas, Beliefs, and Nuclear Policies: The Cases of South Africa and Ukraine," *The Nonproliferation Review* (Spring 2000): 24–40. Long and Grillot downplay the impact of neorealist theory and domestic-politics theory, highlighting instead the use of psychological (ideational) models to explain key shifts in South African nuclear policies. See also T. V. Paul, *Power versus Prudence: Why Nations Forgo Nuclear Weapons* (Montreal: McGill-Queen's University Press, 2000), 113–117. However, many American analysts adhere to neorealist models for an analysis of decisions to adopt nuclear weapons. See, for example, Bradley A. Thayer, "The Causes of Nuclear Nonproliferation and the Utility of the Nuclear Nonproliferation Regime," *Security Studies* 4, no. 3 (Spring 1995): 494–495.

144. David Albright and Kevin O'Neill, "Jury Rigged, but Working," *Bulletin of the Atomic Scientists* (January/February 1995): 20.

FOUR. WARHEADS, MISSILES, AND NUCLEAR-DETERRENCE STRATEGY

1. Quote from 1975 top-secret South African memo entitled "The Jericho Weapons Missile System," which was declassified in 2003. See Michael Schmidt, "Proof of SA Nuclear Plan," *Sunday Times* (Johannesburg), October 12, 2003, 5.

2. Ibid.

3. Ibid.

4. The targeting maps attached to "The Jericho Weapons Missile System" were made available to N. Badenhorst by librarians working for the South African History Archives project at the University of the Witwatersrand; Badenhorst secured the classified documents under the Access to Information Act in 2003.

5. Annette Seegers, *The Military in the Making of Modern South Africa* (New York: St. Martin's Press, 1996).

6. See Hannes Steyn, Richardt van der Walt, and Jan van Loggerenberg, *Armament and Disarmament: South Africa's Nuclear Weapons Experience* (Pretoria, South Africa: Networks Publishers, 2003), especially vii–x.

7. See David Albright, "South Africa and the Affordable Bomb," *The Bulletin of Atomic Scientists* (July/August 1994): 37–47; David Albright, *South Africa's Secret Nuclear Weapons* (Washington, D.C.: Institute for Science and International Security Report, 1994), 1–12; Peter Liberman, "The Rise and Fall of the South African Bomb," *International Security* 26, no. 2 (Fall 2001): 45–86; William J. Long and Suzette R. Grillot, "Ideas, Beliefs, and Nuclear Policies: The Cases of South Africa and Ukraine," *Nonproliferation Review* 7, no. 1 (Spring 2000): 24–40; Leonard S. Spector with Jacqueline R. Smith, *Nuclear Ambitions: The Spread of Nuclear Weapons 1989–1990* (Boulder, Colo.: Westview Press, 1990); and Waldo Stumpf, "South Africa's Nuclear Weapons Program: From Deterrence to Dismantlement," *Arms Control Today* 25, no. 10 (December 1995/January 1996): 4–7.

8. See Steyn, van der Walt, and van Loggerenberg, *Armament and Disarmament,* 47–60.

9. Ibid., x–xi.

10. Senior manager of South Africa's nuclear-bomb program, interview by Helen Purkitt, July 1994.

11. Lieutenant General Pierre Steyn and Brigadier General Bill Sass, interview by Helen Purkitt, Halfway House, South Africa, July 1994.

12. Members of the committee included the prime minister; the ministers of mineral and energy affairs, defense, foreign affairs, finance; and the chairmen of ARMSCOR and the AEB. Peter Hounam and Steve McQuillen, *The Mini-Nuke Conspiracy: Mandela's Nuclear Nightmare* (New York: Viking, 1995), 148. Steyn, van der Walt, and van Loggerenberg discuss the military oversight role of this committee in *Armament and Disarmament,* 43.

13. Steyn, van der Walt, and van Loggerenberg, *Armament and Disarmament,* 43.

14. Liberman, "The Rise and Fall of the South African Bomb," 53.

15. Hounam and McQuillen, *The Mini-Nuke Conspiracy,* 175.

16. Newby-Fraser, *Chain Reaction,* 100.

17. Ibid.

18. Liberman, "The Rise and Fall of the South African Bomb," 53. According to David Albright, ARMSCOR officials took the position that credibility required deliverability. South Africa needed ways to deliver its nuclear devices if it wanted to demonstrate to Western powers that it was a nuclear power. If the devices had been only test devices, Western powers might not have taken South Africa's threat seriously enough to intervene on its behalf. *South Africa's Secret Nuclear Weapons,* 8.

19. Liberman, "The Rise and Fall of the South African Bomb," 45–86. ARMSCOR officials, interview by Helen Purkitt, July 1994.

20. Steyn, van der Walt, and van Loggerenberg, *Armament and Disarmament,* 73–75.

21. Ibid., 43–44.

22. Stumpf, "South Africa's Nuclear Weapons Program," 4–7; Albright, "South Africa and the Affordable Bomb," 37–47; former South African officials, interview by Helen Purkitt, June and July 1994.

23. Albright, *South Africa's Secret Nuclear Weapons,* 10.

24. Mark Hibbs, "South Africa's Secret Nuclear Program: From a PNE to a Deterrent," *Nuclear Fuel,* May 10, 1993, 3–6; Darryl Howlett and John Simpson, "Nuclearization and Denuclearization in South Africa," *Survival* (Autumn 1993): 161. South African officials, interviews by Helen Purkitt, June and July 1994. Official accounts also cite problems in maintaining an adequate output of enriched uranium to meet production schedules.

25. Stumpf, "South Africa's Nuclear Weapons Program," 4–7.

26. Albright, *South Africa's Secret Nuclear Weapons,* 10.

27. Officials at the AEC and ARMSCOR, interviews by Helen Purkitt, June 1994.

28. Steyn, van der Walt, and van Loggerenberg, *Armament and Disarmament,* vii.

29. Based on a verbal report of an anonymous observer who claims to have viewed the reactor at the facility. Interview by Helen Purkitt, South Africa, July 1997.

30. Hibbs, "South Africa's Secret Nuclear Program," 3–6.

31. Albright, *South Africa's Secret Nuclear Weapons,* 11; ARMSCOR officials, interviews by Helen Purkitt, June 1994. According to ARMSCOR officials, these bombs were nearly identical in design. The total mass of a completed device was about 1 metric ton; its diameter was about 65 centimeters and it was about 1.8 meters long. Each device contained an estimated 55 kilograms of highly enriched uranium. The cores of the second through the seventh bombs contained weapons-grade uranium. The reflector was made of tungsten. The calculated yield of each device was about 10 to 18 kilotons when the core had weapons-grade uranium. Using 80 percent enriched material halved the expected yield. See Albright, *South Africa's Secret Nuclear Weapons,* 12.

32. Steyn, van der Walt, and van Loggerenberg, *Armament and Disarmament,* 74–75.

33. Stumpf, "South Africa's Nuclear Weapons Program," 4–7. South African scientists, nuclear engineers, military and political officials, and generals, interviews by Helen Purkitt, South Africa, June and July 1994. The details of when and where all the components for the bombs were built once the program shifted to ARMSCOR management are still not clear. However, there is general agreement that the first to be produced at the Kentron Circle was finished in 1982. Nick Badenhorst, "South Africa's Nuclear Program," unpublished manuscript, May 2000, 45–46; Albright, *South Africa's Secret Nuclear Weapons,* 10.

34. Stumpf, "South Africa's Nuclear Weapons Program," 6; Liberman, "The Rise and Fall of the South African Bomb," 73.

35. Hounam and McQuillen, *The Mini-Nuke Conspiracy,* 82–83. Hounam and McQuillen claim that the bomb was stored in an abandoned coal mine. A more recent account based on extensive interviews with large numbers of former SADF officers, including several generals, said the bombs were stored in an ammunition depot; see Hilton Hamann, *Days of the Generals* (Cape Town: Zebra, 2001), 167.

36. Stumpf, "South Africa's Nuclear Weapons Program," 12.

37. Steyn, van der Walt, and van Loggerenberg, *Armament and Disarmament,* 82–87.

38. David Albright and Corey Hindertein, *South Africa's Nuclear Weapons Storage Vault* (Washington, D.C.: Institute for Science and International Security,

2001), quoted in Steyn, van der Walt, and van Loggerenberg, *Armament and Disarmament*, 88.

39. Steyn, van der Walt, and van Loggerenberg, *Armament and Disarmament*, 75.

40. Ibid., 87–88.

41. Ibid., 49.

42. David Fig, "Apartheid's Nuclear Arsenal: Deviation from Development," in *From Defence to Development: Redirecting Military Resources in South Africa,* ed. Jacklyn Cock and Penny Mckenzie (Cape Town: David Philip, 1998), 163–180; David Fig, "Sanctions and the Nuclear Industry," in *How Sanctions Work: Lessons from South Africa*, ed. Neta C. Crawford and Audie Klotz (New York: St. Martin's Press, 1999), 75–102.

43. By the end of the sanctions era, an estimated 600 people worked informally for ARMSCOR as procurement agents who scoured the world for needed materials and spare parts. Some of this foreign technology was for the nuclear program and other covert weapons programs. Senior ARMSCOR officials, interviews by Helen Purkitt, July 1994.

44. For example, Houwteq, the development and manufacturing facility that built the system used to integrate a reconnaissance satellite or a warhead with the rocket, established a partnership with the engineering faculty at the Technopark at Stellenbosch University. Steyn, van der Walt, and van Loggerenberg, *Armament and Disarmament,* 76.

45. Ibid., 48–49.

46. South African scientists and engineers involved with the program in Gauteng Province, interviews by Helen Purkitt, Pretoria and Johannesburg, 1994. See Helen E. Purkitt, "The Politics of Denuclearization: The Case of South Africa," final report to the Institute for National Strategic Studies (INSS), U.S. Air Force Academy, November 9, 1994.

47. Steyn, van der Walt, and van Loggerenberg, *Armament and Disarmament,* 50–54.

48. Ibid., 54–55.

49. Deon Geldenhuys, *Isolated States: A Comparative Analysis* (Johannesburg: Jonathan Ball Publishers, 1990), 209.

50. Stumpf, "South Africa's Nuclear Weapons Program," 5.

51. According to Hamann, *Days of the Generals,* 167, storage facilities built under the Gerotek vehicle-testing facility at Kentron Circle were designed for nuclear devices that "had a mass of about one metric ton, and used tungsten as a neutron reflector." The South Africans reportedly obtained the tungsten, a designated controlled mineral by the Nuclear Suppliers Group, from neighboring countries, including Zimbabwe, Zambia, and Zaire. See Badenhorst, "South Africa's Nuclear Program" for a more technical description of advanced research and development activities at Advena.

52. Renfrew Christie, "South Africa's Nuclear History," paper presented at the Nuclear History Program Fourth International Conference, Nice, France, June 23–27, 1993, 59.

53. ARMSCOR officials, interviews by Helen Purkitt, Gauteng Province, 1994. See also Liberman, "The Rise and Fall of the South African Bomb," 45–86.

54. "Boosting" increases the explosive yield of a fission device. In such a device, the thermonuclear reaction of tritium and deuterium produces significantly more plutonium or highly enriched uranium.

55. International Atomic Energy Agency, *Report by the Director General: The Agency's Verification Activities in South Africa* (Vienna: International Atomic Energy Agency, 1993). South African officials told IAEA investigators that no tritium

was used in the research. The AEC acknowledged that it had received some tritium in 1977 and that it withdrew a small sample to verify the quality. It said that the material remained in storage until 1987, when it was used to commercially produce radio-luminescent light sources. The AEC also established facilities and techniques to handle trans-uranium elements based on development work using americium and neptunium. These facilities and techniques were used to recover the plutonium from a damaged plutonium/beryllium neutron source.

56. Hounam and McQuillen, *The Mini-Nuke Conspiracy,* 179–180.

57. See Steyn, van der Walt, and van Loggerenberg, *Armament and Disarmament,* Chapters 4 and 6.

58. Badenhorst, "South Africa's Nuclear Program"; and Hamann, *Days of the Generals.* Both of these accounts are consistent with descriptions of similar facilities that Hounam and McQuillen provided in *The Mini-Nuke Conspiracy.*

Locations, capabilities, and activities supported at certain facilities, particularly underground locations, have been described only obliquely by knowledgeable insiders or analysts because this information is still classified under South African secrecy laws. Those who intentionally disclose information to the public about facilities and underground bunkers where weapon systems were located face criminal penalties. South African government officials continue to deny the existence of any other facilities that supported more-advanced nuclear-weapons systems. However, a few details about the location of specific facilities or weapons systems have leaked into the public record. See for example, Badenhorst, "South Africa's Nuclear Program," and Hounam and McQuillen, *The Mini-Nuke Conspiracy.* The insider account of the network of facilities developed in conjunction with the former nuclear and space programs by Steyn, van der Wald, and van Loggerenberg in *Armament and Disarmament* is also highly instructive. A few details about underground facilities and additional weapons systems were also disclosed during interviews of former South African officials with H. Purkitt in 1994, 1997, and 2000, and 2002 and with Stephen Burgess in 2000. See also Hamann, *Days of the Generals.*

59. See Steyn, van der Walt, and van Loggerenberg, *Armament and Disarmament,* 74.

60. Several former senior military officials of the South African Air Force and Army used the expression "PW's toys" to describe the most sophisticated weapons systems South Africa was developing in the 1980s. Interviews by Helen Purkitt, Halfway House, Midrand, 1994. Stephen Burgess heard similar descriptions in interviews conducted in 2000.

61. Steyn, van der Walt, and van Loggerenberg, *Armament and Disarmament,* 55–56.

62. Lieutenant General Pierre Steyn and Brigadier General Bill Sass, interviews by Helen Purkitt, Midrand, July 1994, and by Stephen Burgess, Pretoria, June 2000.

63. Neta C. Crawford, "How Arms Embargoes Work," in Crawford and Klotz, eds., *How Sanctions Work,* 60.

64. Steyn, van der Walt, and van Loggerenberg, *Armament and Disarmament,* 59–60.

65. Ibid.; South African senior rocket scientists, interviews by Helen Purkitt, Gauteng Province, 1994, and Pretoria, 2002.

66. Steyn, van der Walt, and van Loggerenberg, *Armament and Disarmament,* viii–ix.

67. See Badenhorst, "South Africa's Nuclear Program"; Hounam and McQuillen, *The Mini-Nuke Conspiracy;* and Frank V. Pabian, "South Africa's Nuclear Weapon Program: Lessons for Nonproliferation Policy," *The Nonprolifera-*

tion Review 3, no. 1 (Fall 1995): 11. Helen Purkitt received confirmation in July 2002 of the existence of a project to build a five-story missile during an interview with a chief weapons researcher who was involved in rocket research from the beginning of South Africa's programs.

68. Hibbs, "South Africa's Secret Nuclear Program," 3–6; Hounam and Mc-Quillen, *The Mini-Nuke Conspiracy.*

69. Senior rocket scientists, interviews by Helen Purkitt, Gauteng Province, 1994, and Pretoria, 2002.

70. Steyn, van der Walt, and van Loggerenberg, *Armament and Disarmament,* 56–57.

71. See, for example, Badenhorst, "South Africa's Nuclear Program"; Hamann, *Night of the Generals;* and Hounam and McQuillen, *The Mini-Nuke Conspiracy.*

72. Steyn, van der Walt, and van Loggerenberg, *Armament and Disarmament,* 75.

73. This summary of multiple-use facilities is taken from ibid., 73–80 and 92. Somchem was one of many parastatals under the control of ARMSCOR until the early 1990s. Somchem had several facilities, among which were the development and manufacturing facilities for large rocket motors at Somerset West. This was the same location where ARMSCOR's facility for developing explosives and rocket systems was located. Somchem also established a facility to test huge motors in the nearby Hangklip Mountains. For more details, see Steyn, van der Walt, and van Loggerenberg, *Armament and Disarmament,* 76–77.

74. The Joint Air Reconnaissance and Interpretation Center (JARIC) was an air force unit that had air reconnaissance and satellite photography experts and facilities. JARIC became involved in the space program because of its experience with reconnaissance satellites.

75. Steyn, van der Walt, and van Loggerenberg, *Armament and Disarmament,* 76–77.

76. Marie Muller, "South Africa Crosses the Nuclear Threshold," in *South Africa's Defence and Security into the 21st Century,* ed. William Gutteridge (Aldershot: Dartmouth, 1996), 29–48.

77. Liberman states that the actual costs are many times greater than the official estimates; "The Rise and Fall of the South African Bomb," 45–86.

78. Roy E. Horton, III, *Out of (South) Africa: Pretoria's Nuclear Weapons Experience* (Colorado Springs: USAF Institute for National Security Studies, 1999).

79. Our official estimates are based on interviews by Helen Purkitt in 1994 through 2002. See also Badenhorst, "South Africa's Nuclear Program"; and Horton, *Out of (South) Africa.*

80. The most widely cited source that details secret agreements between South Africa and Israel is still Seymour M. Hersh, *The Samson Option* (New York: Random House, 1991). Hersh reported that South Africa and Israel negotiated the secret nuclear agreements in 1972. Liberman also discusses the content of these secret agreements, including the possibility of building an intercontinental missile; "The Rise and Fall of the South African Bomb," 63.

81. Benjamin M. Joseph, *Besieged Bedfellows: Israel and the Land of Apartheid* (New York: Greenwood Press, 1998), 51; Geldenhuys, *Isolated States,* 522.

82. The exact date when South Africa started building the RSA-3 is not known. This project, widely assumed to have been a collaborative project with Israel, is thought to have started during the 1974–1976 time frame. Three dates are important for understanding the growing cooperation between South Africa and Israel in the area of long-range missiles. In November 1974, during a secret meeting between Vorster, P. W. Botha, and Israeli Prime Minister Shimon Peres at Geneva, a

mutual defense pact known as ISSA was reached. In the pact, the parties agreed to store all types of weapons on each others' soil. A clause in ISSA known as "Chalet" specifically committed the Israelis to arm eight Jericho-2 missiles with "special" warheads. During a visit by Vorster to Israel in April 1976, a second agreement was reached that reportedly gave South Africa access to Israeli missile technology. The third key date is November 4, 1977. This is when the UN Security Council agreed to impose a mandatory arms embargo (Resolution 418) against South Africa. Growing collaboration between Israel and South Africa on the space-launch-vehicle project, better known as the RSA-3 in South Africa, was probably already under way by the time the Security Council imposed its mandatory embargo. However, growing international isolation is widely cited as an important factor that fueled increased collaboration between the two isolated states. Hersh, *The Samson Option;* William E. Burrows and Robert Windrem, *Critical Mass: The Dangerous Race for Superweapons in a Fragmenting World* (New York: Simon and Schuster, 1994); and Geldenhuys, *Isolated States.*

83. Burrows, *Critical Mass.*

84. See Hersh, *The Samson Option,* 220–221, for a detailed description of Israel's nuclear-deterrence strategy. South African military officials made similar statements about the importance of maintaining enough nuclear capabilities to deter would-be aggressors in the region and worldwide during the 1970s. For a discussion of South Africa's nuclear strategy, see Steyn, van der Walt, and van Loggerenberg, *Armament and Disarmament.* See also Burrows and Windrem, *Critical Mass* for a discussion of South African efforts to develop the capabilities needed to implement this strategy.

85. Benjamin Beit-Hallahmi, *The Israeli Connection: Who Israel Arms and Why* (New York: Phantom Books, 1987).

86. Former senior military personnel, interviews by Helen Purkitt, Midrand and Pretoria, July 1994.

87. Beit-Hallahmi, *The Israeli Connection,* 42, 68; Geldenhuys, *Isolated States,* 522.

88. Burrows, *Critical Mass,* 454–466.

89. Ibid.; Bill Gertz, "S. Africa to Test Ballistic Missile," *Washington Times,* May 3, 1991, A3.

90. N. B. Badenhorst, "The Bomb, the Missile, and the Future," *Armed Forces of Southern Africa,* November 1993, 27–34; former South African officials, interviews by Helen Purkitt, Gauteng and Cape Provinces, June and July 1994.

91. Dirty bombs spread radioactive materials because of their specific burst altitude or the materials used in the bombs themselves. A ground burst sucks up tons of radiated soil and deposits the soil according to the prevailing winds. An air burst produces less airborne radiated soil because the fireball does not touch the ground. The bomb itself also produces radioactivity. The South African "museum piece" bombs did not use U-238 as a tamper. Instead, they were pure fission devices fueled by highly enriched uranium.

92. De Ionno, "Nuclear Scientists," 1–2.

93. Steyn, van der Walt, and van Loggerenberg, *Armament and Disarmament,* 92. The authors mention Clyde Ivy, an American engineer alleged to have close ties with employees in ARMSCOR and Kentron until about 1980. They note that "Ivy, and his American employer, [were] later indicted by the US government on sanctions-busting charges" (p. 92).

94. Burrows, *Critical Mass.*

95. *United States v. Jasin,* U.S. Court of the Appeals for the Third Circuit, 280 F.3d 355; 2002 U.S. app. LEXIS 1733, December 7, 2001, submitted under Third

Circuit LAR 34.1(a), February 5, 2002. See also *In re Assets of Parent Indus., Inc.,* Misc. No. 90-0210, United States District Court for the Eastern District of Pennsylvania, 739 F. Supp. 248; 1990 U.S. Dist. LEXIS 6920, June 1, 1990.

96. Ibid.

97. ARMSCOR official, interview by Helen Purkitt, Gauteng Province, July 1994.

98. Stefaans Brummer, "SA's Arms-Dealing Underworld," *Weekly Mail & Guardian* (Johannesburg), June 2–8, 1995, 9; Peter de Ionno, "Armscor Tries to Hush up Saddam Deals," *Sunday Times* (Johannesburg), July 10, 1994; former South African and U.S. officials, interviews by Helen Purkitt, Pretoria, South Africa, June and July 1994.

99. The most widely circulated story at the time of the explosion and for several years afterward was that the *Helderberg* was carrying a kilogram of a chemical substance used to manufacture bombs for miniaturized pocket nukes. (The discussion of pocket nukes was hampered throughout the 1990s by the fact that the United States and Russia governments denied their existence. The Russian government did not acknowledge that they had miniaturized nukes in their arsenal until 1997, when a senior Russian military officer claimed that one had been stolen from the Russian arsenal.) The rumor that the *Helderberg* was carrying chemicals for a pocket nuke was widely discounted by South African officials both before and after the 1994 political transition. Instead, officials often claim that red mercury was an explosive trigger or booster for conventional bombs. This explanation continues to be provided by South African officials. For example, in 2003, Andre Kudlinski, acting director of the Chemical and Allied Division of the South African Ministry of Trade and Industry, said that his understanding was that red mercury was used in detonators; interview with Helen Purkitt, Pretoria, June 25, 2003. However, many observers continue to believe that red mercury is used to fuel pocket nukes. The most frequently cited explanation for the spate of murders of alleged arms traffickers for the old South African regime using red mercury was that they were illicit arms deals gone bad. For more details, see "Key Helderberg Evidence Uncovered," *Mail & Guardian* (Johannesburg), March 10, 2001.

100. The most detailed coverage of the red mercury murders in South Africa is found in a series of articles published in the South African *Mail & Guardian* in the mid-1990s. See, for example, Stefaans Brummer, "SADF Linked to Red Mercury," *Mail & Guardian* (Johannesburg), December 20, 1995. There were also reports that red mercury may have been a substance produced by Project Coast front companies, such as Delta G Scientific, for use in nerve gas and other chemical products. See, for example, Stefaans Brummer, "Red Mercury Secret Chemical War Remains Secret," *Mail & Guardian* (Johannesburg), August 23, 1996.

101. Mr. Patti Prior, advocate, and Legal Department of Truth and Reconciliation Commission, interview by Helen Purkitt, Cape Town, July 2000.

102. "Key Helderberg Evidence Uncovered," *Mail & Guardian* (Johannesburg), March 10, 2001; and "The TRC's Helderberg Tragedy," *Mail & Guardian* (Johannesburg), November 21, 2000. See also the transcript of the hearing on the *Helderberg* crash during the Truth and Reconciliation Commission hearings at www.doj.gov.za/trc.

103. Albright, *South Africa's Secret Nuclear Weapons,* 1; Dr. Waldo Stumpf, AEC, interview by Helen Purkitt, Pelindaba, July 1994; Dr. Dean Smith, Denel and ARMSCOR managers, and military officers, interviews by Helen Purkitt, Pretoria and other locations in Gauteng Province, July 1994.

104. Former South African military and ARMSCOR officials, interviews by Helen Purkitt, Pretoria and other locations in Gauteng Province, 1994.

105. J. W. de Villiers, Roger Jardine, and Mitchell Reiss, "Why South Africa Gave Up the Bomb," *Foreign Affairs* 72, no. 5 (November/December 1993): 101; Stumpf, "South Africa's Nuclear Weapons Program," 4–7.

106. Helen Purkitt and Stephen Burgess heard remarkably similar descriptions of South Africa's three-stage nuclear-deterrence strategy in separate interviews with senior South African military, ARMSCOR, AEC, and political officials in 1994, 2000, and 2001.

107. Hersh, *The Samson Option.*

108. Former South African senior military officers, interviews by Helen Purkitt, Midrand and Pretoria, July 1994.

109. Peter de Ionno, "SA Military's Amazing Underground Bomb-Proof Laager," *Sunday Times* (Johannesburg), May 22, 1994. Albright, *South Africa's Secret Nuclear Weapons,* 2.

110. The maps attached to the secret memo indicate the maximum reach of a missile with a range of 500 kilometers. In the new weapons system, missiles deployed along the northern border of South Africa or other territories controlled by South Africa (i.e., South West Africa) could reach Lusaka, Zambia, and the capital cities of several other African countries that hosted ANC rebel camps.

111. For another analysis that emphasizes the importance of understanding the political leadership's shared beliefs, see William J. Long and Suzette R. Grillot, "Ideas, Beliefs, and Nuclear Policies: The Cases of South Africa and Ukraine," *The Nonproliferation Review* (Spring 2000): 24–40.

112. Albright, *South Africa's Secret Nuclear Weapons,* 8.

113. Senior military officials, Helmoed-Romer Heitman of *Jane's Defense Weekly,* Willem Steenkamp, and other experts on South African defense matters, interviews by Helen Purkitt, Cape Town, July 1994 and July 1997. See also Willem Steenkamp, *South Africa's Border War 1966–1989* (Gibraltar: Asanti Publishing, 1989).

114. Stumpf, "South Africa's Nuclear Weapons Program," 4–7; ARMSCOR officials, interviews by Helen Purkitt, July 1994.

115. Ibid.

116. Chester A. Crocker, *High Noon in Southern Africa: Making Peace in a Rough Neighborhood* (New York: W.W. Norton, 1992); Steenkamp, *South Africa's Border War 1966–1989;* South African political officials, interviews by Helen Purkitt, Pretoria, June 1994; Willem Steinkamp and Helmoed-Romer Heitman, interviews by Helen Purkitt, Cape Town, July 1994.

117. Steyn, van der Walt, and van Loggerenberg, *Armament and Disarmament,* 94.

FIVE. PROJECT COAST
AND ITS ORIGINS

Much of the material in this chapter was published in Helen E. Purkitt and Stephen F. Burgess, "South Africa's Chemical and Biological Warfare Programme: A Historical and International Perspective," *Journal of Southern African Studies* 28, no. 2 (June 2002): 229–253.

1. Dr. Wouter Basson's quote is given on page 234 of Tom Mangold and Jeff Goldberg, *Plague Wars* (New York: St. Martin's Press, 1999). Dr. Jerry Nilsson was Dr. Larry Ford's medical partner; he allegedly worked for years as a Selous Scout in Rhodesia (now Zimbabwe). He made this comment to several close friends and associates and to journalists investigating Larry Ford's death. Detective Victor Ray confirmed this fact in an interview with Helen Purkitt in September 2001. Thomas Byron met Larry Ford, Jerry Nilsson, and Pat Riley in the 1980s

in Los Angeles and he accompanied Larry Ford on several trips to South Africa and claims to have worked for U.S. government agencies on the activities of Ford and his associates. Byron remains in touch with right-wing supremacists associated with the former South African government who remain in South Africa. He made this claim about the program objectives of Project Coast in a phone interview with Helen Purkitt on March 30, 2002. More details about Byron's experiences with Dr. Ford and U.S. and former South African officials are contained in his book *Elimination Theory* (Baltimore, Md.: PublishAmerica, 2004).

2. Dr. Renfrew Christie, interview by Stephen Burgess at University of the Western Cape, Belleville, June 26, 2000.

3. Mangold and Goldberg, *Plague Wars*, 219.

4. Dr. Renfrew Christie, interview by Stephen Burgess, Belleville, June 26, 2000.

5. General Jannie Geldenhuys (Ret.), interview by Stephen Burgess, Pretoria, June 13, 2000.

6. Dr. Vernon Joynt, Mechem and the Council for Scientific and Industrial Research, interview by Stephen Burgess, Pretoria, June 14, 2000.

7. CX powder is known by the scientific name of phosgene oxime. Since CX's effects are immediate and painful, it is unclear exactly how Dr. Joynt and the South Africans used it for "tracking."

8. Dr. Torie Pretorius, prosecutor in the Basson trial, interview by Stephen Burgess, Pretoria, June 21, 2000.

9. Helmoed-Romer Heitman of *Jane's Defense Weekly,* interview by Stephen Burgess, Cape Town, June 26, 2000.

10. Mark Malan, former SADF officer and senior researcher at the Institute for Strategic Studies, interview by Stephen Burgess, June 23, 2000 and interview by Helen Purkitt, July 3, 2000.

11. For a further discussion of the role of former Selous Scouts and other foreigners in South Africa during the 1980s, see Mangold and Goldberg, *Plague Wars*, 218–223. See also Henrik Ellert, *The Rhodesian Front War: Counter-Insurgency and Guerrilla War in Rhodesia, 1962–1980* (Gweru, Zimbabwe: Mambo Press, 1989).

12. *Analysis of the TRC Report by the SADF Contact Bureau, 28 May, 1998, Pretoria, South Africa* and *The Military in a Political Arena: The South African Defence Force (SADF) and the Truth and Reconciliation Commission (TRC)*, Pretoria, June 2000. Unpublished reports.

13. There was a general awareness during the 1960s of the potency of anthrax and other biological agents as counterinsurgency weapons. In the 1960s, comic books featured the character of "Captain Devil," who poured anthrax into the Orange River and killed communist guerrillas; Dr. Ian Phillips, ANC defense expert, interview by Stephen Burgess, Pretoria, June 13, 2000.

14. South African military planners were impressed with the ability of the Portuguese to regain the offensive in the late 1960s by using helicopters, poison, land mines, and other techniques to counter guerrilla gains. See John Marcum, *The Angolan Revolution: Exile Politics and Guerrilla Warfare, 1962–1976* (Cambridge, Mass.: MIT Press, 1978), 116–118. Even though they viewed a guerrilla threat at home to be highly unlikely at the time, South African military and political planners during the late 1960s and early 1970s carefully studied the effectiveness of Portuguese "protected villages" in preventing guerrillas from gaining control of large sections of Angola; Rocklyn Williams, interview by Helen Purkitt, Pretoria, July 5, 2000. In planning for the possibility of long-term guerrilla activity, the South African government moved to expand the Bantu homeland policy to Lebowa and Venda and instituted policies to depopulate northern areas of South

Africa. They saw this as a more effective way to handle future problems and deflected external critics with a promise of eventual independence for the ten designated homelands.

15. Dr. Ian Phillips, interview by Stephen Burgess, Pretoria, June 13, 2000.

16. The SAP started helping the Rhodesians counter their growing insurgency problem in the mid-1960s. The number of SAP (and SADF) personnel grew until there were about 1,200 members of the SAP stationed in Rhodesia in 1974. While Rhodesia initially welcomed South African help, tensions quickly developed as a result of reports that SAP personnel were illegally shooting rhinoceroses for their horns in a Chiwore game reserve and that they were ill-disciplined, bored, and poorly trained. The first SAP contingents were relieved after three months. South Africa attempted to solve the problem by screening members of the SAP they sent to Rhodesia; they tried to send better-trained personnel who spoke English. Tensions developed again as Rhodesians began to rely more and more on South African manpower and military hardware in the early 1970s. Many Rhodesian troops resented South African efforts to tell them how to conduct their counterinsurgency campaigns. These tensions were one reason why the South African police presence in Rhodesia was reduced during the 1970s. Defense Intelligence Agency officials, interviews by Helen Purkitt, Washington, D.C., September 13, 2000. See also Ellert, *The Rhodesian Front War;* and Ron Reid-Daly with Peter Stiff, *Selous Scouts: Top Secret War* (Alberton, South Africa: Galago, 1983).

17. Mangold and Goldberg, *Plague Wars,* 214–218.

18. Jakkie Cilliers, director of the Institute for Security Studies, Pretoria, interview by Stephen Burgess, June 12, 2000 and by Helen Purkitt, July 5, 2000. In the Basson trial, the South African state planned to use information gathered by journalists to support charges against Basson related to the use of chemical and biological warfare in Rhodesia. However, the prosecution was unable to discuss this evidence while the trial was ongoing.

19. After 1978, South African intelligence services stepped up their efforts to recruit former Rhodesian Special Forces personnel. For more details, see Ellert, *The Rhodesian Front War,* 90–93; Peter Stiff, interview by Helen Purkitt, Johannesburg, July 12, 2000.

20. Jacques Pauw, *Into the Heart of Darkness* (Johannesburg: Jonathan Ball, 1997); South Africa Truth and Reconciliation Commission, *Truth and Reconciliation Commission of South Africa Report* (Cape Town: The Truth and Reconciliation Commission, 1998). Another version of this report was published by Macmillan Reference in 1999. The Civil Cooperation Bureau (CCB) was formed in the early 1980s by the South African Defence Force with the approval of Defence Minister Magnus Malan to collect intelligence, evade sanctions, and assassinate "enemies" of the apartheid regime. Operating with a global reach, the CCB set up front companies in Western Europe to beat sanctions and import sensitive weapons materials. Wouter Basson used his connections with the CCB to test and market his chemical and biological warfare products. CCB operatives used Project Coast toxins to poison prisoners and "disloyal" black CCB colleagues; they also mailed anthrax letters to enemies. The CCB was disbanded in August 1990. Pauw, *Into the Heart of Darkness,* 224.

21. Former defense minister Magnus Malan, interview by Stephen Burgess, Pretoria, June 23, 2000.

22. According to Brigadier General Phillip Schalwyk (Ret.), who was interviewed by Helen Purkitt in Pretoria in July 2000, South African forces in Angola received an urgent cable from UNITA commanders during Operation Savannah asking for help because they had been attacked by Cuban troops who wore "pig face masks."

23. General Georg Meiring (Ret.), interview by Stephen Burgess, Pretoria, July 3, 2000.

24. The Cassinga raid highlights the difficulties involved in verifying chemical and biological warfare incidents. The Truth and Reconciliation Commission concluded that this alleged use was developed under auspices of Project B. A report on the Cassinga attack was prepared by a joint UNHCR/WHO mission on May 30, 1978 and reproduced as Annex V in UN document 13473 of July 27, 1979. However, military observers from Western countries who arrived thirty minutes after the attack found no evidence of the use of chemical weapons. Former SADF Special Forces officers and U.S. military officers, interviews by Helen Purkitt, Pretoria, July 2000.

25. Former SADF Special Forces officers, interviews by Helen Purkitt, Cape Town, Durban, and Port Elizabeth, July 2000.

26. Dr. G. Scharf, former director of Medical Hospital One, Pretoria, interview by Helen Purkitt, July 2000. Like most former South African defense forces, Dr. Scharf knew about the large number of UNITA forces injured in Angola but had no knowledge about the cause of the injuries.

27. South African military officers and political officials, interviews with Stephen Burgess and Helen Purkitt in the United States and South Africa during 2000. See also Helmoed-Romer Heitman, *War in Angola: The Final South African Phase* (Gibraltar: Ashanti Publishing, 1990).

28. One indirect indication that government-sponsored covert research started several years before the official declaration of Project Coast is the fact that many scientists who worked for Project Coast routinely talk about their secret research conducted in the 1970s when talking about their biowarfare research. Former Project Coast scientists, interviews by Helen Purkitt, 2002 and 2003.

29. Annette Seegers, *The Military in the Making of Modern South Africa* (New York: St. Martin's Press, 1996).

30. Magnus Malan, interview by Stephen Burgess, June 23, 2000.

31. Chandré Gould, Truth and Reconciliation Commission, interviewed by Stephen Burgess, Johannesburg, June 29, 2000. See also Marléne Burger and Chandré Gould, *Secrets and Lies: Wouter Basson and South Africa's Chemical and Biological Warfare Programme* (Cape Town: Zebra, 2002), 14–16.

32. Dr. Vernon Joynt, interview by Helen Purkitt, Pretoria, July 5, 2002.

33. Dr. Vernon Joynt, interview by Stephen Burgess, Pretoria, June 14, 2000. Dr. Joynt claims that although he declined the directorship of a chemical weapons program, many scientists and specialists accepted research projects offered by Nieuwoudt and Basson and many did not tell their superiors that they had done so.

34. Seegers, *The Military*. See also S. A. Watt, "The Anglo-Boer War: The Medical Arrangements and Implications Thereof During the British Occupation of Bloemfontein: March–August, 1900," *Military History Review* 9, no. 2 (December 1992), available online at http://rapidttp.com/milhist/vol092sw.html.

35. Dr. G. Scharf, former director of Military Medical Hospital One, interview by Helen Purkitt, Pretoria, July 5, 2000. Although 7th Medical Battalion Group is still in existence and is tasked with the mission of supporting the 44th Parachute Brigade and the Special Forces Brigade, the military medical service has undergone a dramatic reorganization since 1994. The minister of defense authorized a reorganization of the service in March 1999, when it was renamed the SANDF Medical Service (SAMS). It has a much broader mandate today that includes providing assistance to the health services of South Africa and comprehensive military health service to the SANDF and the South African Police Service.

36. In an interview in Pretoria on June 13, 2000, General Chris Thirion (Ret.) told Stephen Burgess that he first met Basson when Basson was chosen in the late

1970s to become the doctor for SADF Special Forces. Thirion claims that Basson was arrogant, that he was Defence Minister Magnus Malan's "blue-eyed boy," and that he had the ear of General Kat Liebenberg of Special Forces. Thirion complained when Basson was given access to military intelligence and short-circuited the command structure. Thirion said that in the 1980s, Malan became a Member of Parliament and began the custom of demonstrating to people in his constituency that the SADF was winning the war in Namibia and Angola. Malan would bring SADF generals to constituency meetings, where they would make presentations regarding the war in Angola and Namibia. Basson was not a general, but he made the presentations at the constituency meetings rather than the surgeon-general.

37. His Master of Science thesis was entitled "Aspects of Human Immune Response to Invasion by Trypanosoma Species." Basson wrote this thesis while working at the government laboratory now called the National Institute for Communicable Diseases. Dr. Barry D. Schoub, executive director, National Institute for Communicable Diseases, Johannesburg, interview by Helen Purkitt, Johannesburg, June 24, 2003.

38. ANC defense expert Dr. Ian Phillips, interview by Stephen Burgess, Pretoria, June 13, 2000.

39. Magnus Malan, interview by Stephen Burgess, Pretoria, June 23, 2000.

40. See Surgeon General D. P. (Niels) Knobel's testimony to the Truth and Reconciliation Commission, July 1998. *Truth and Reconciliation Commission of South Africa Report* (Cape Town: Truth and Reconciliation Commission, 1998).

41. Mangold and Goldberg, *Plague Wars,* 236. Mangold and Goldberg estimated that the budget was £4 to 5 million.

42. Dr. Ian Phillips, interview by Stephen Burgess, Pretoria, June 13, 2000.

43. Rocklyn Williams, interview by Helen Purkitt, Pretoria, July 5, 2000.

44. Helmoed-Romer Heitman (*Jane's Defense Weekly* correspondent for South Africa), interviewed by Stephen Burgess, Cape Town, June 26, 2000 and by Helen Purkitt in July 1994 and 1997; the evidence was not conclusive. Heitman was among the first journalists to raise questions about South African allegations that the Cubans had used chemical weapons in Angola and to highlight the difficulty of verifying the source of alleged chemical and biological warfare attacks. See also H. R. Heitman, *South African War Machine* (Johannesburg: Central News Agency, 1985); Heitman, *War in Angola;* and Willem Steenkamp, *South Africa's Border War: 1966–1989* (Gibraltar: Ashanti Publishing Ltd., 1989).

45. General Magnus Malan (Ret.), interview by Stephen Burgess, Pretoria, June 23, 2000; and Mark Malan, former SADF officer and senior researcher at the Institute for Strategic Studies, interview by Stephen Burgess, June 23, 2000, and by Helen Purkitt, Pretoria, July 3, 2000. Despite concerns by senior military leaders that Cubans might use chemical and biological warfare in Angola, little time was spent on defensive training against this kind of warfare during the 1970s. From the mid-1970s through the late 1970s, only a few hours during one day of SADF infantry personnel training was devoted to chemical and biological warfare. Most of these sessions focused on the use of CS gas. Many more hours of training were devoted to ways to counter urban violence.

46. Dr. Hans Jager, director of research and development, Avimune Pty Ltd. (and former director of research and development at Ondestepoort), interview by Helen Purkitt, Durban, July 1, 2003.

47. Dr. Vernon Joynt, interview by Helen Purkitt, Pretoria, July 4, 2002; and Dr. Hans Jager, interview by Helen Purkitt, Durban, July 1, 2003. Another Project Coast scientist, Dr. André Immelman, was formally disciplined by the South Afri-

can Veterinary Council for his treatment of animals in tests for Project Coast research projects.

48. General Georg Meiring (Ret.), interview by Stephen Burgess, Pretoria, July 3, 2000.

49. Mangold and Goldberg, *Plague Wars,* 243.

50. U.S. officials, interviews by Stephen Burgess and Helen Purkitt, Washington, D.C., 2001. While U.S. officials involved with the dismantlement of Project Coast maintain that the South Africans developed some unique processes and procedures for producing biological warfare agents, other U.S. officials have maintained that Project Coast scientists did not produce anything new. At least this was the official rationale the U.S. government gave for declining Dr. Goosen's offer in 2003 to sell it agents that had been genetically modified at Project Coast and for refusing to employ former Project Coast scientists. For a further discussion of the question of what was developed by the South Africans, see Joby Warrick, "Biotoxins Fall into Private Hands; Global Risk Seen in S. African Poisons," *Washington Post,* April 21, 2003, A1; and Joby Warwick and John Mintz, "Lethal Legacy: Bioweapons for Sale; U.S. Declined South African Scientist's Offer on Man-Made Pathogens," *Washington Post,* April 20, 2003, A1.

51. Mangold and Goldberg, *Plague Wars,* 241.

52. Burger, *Secrets and Lies,* 116–117. Fort Detrick was the site of the U.S. offensive biological warfare program, begun in 1942, under the direction of a civilian agency, the War Reserve Service. The Army Chemical Warfare Service was given responsibility and oversight for the effort. Fort Detrick was chosen for the site because of its reasonably remote location north of Frederick, Maryland, and relative proximity to Washington, D.C. In 1969, the offensive program ceased, and in 1971, the U.S. Biological Defense Research Laboratory was organized.

53. Magnus Malan indicated as much to Stephen Burgess in a June 23, 2000 interview.

54. For a more detailed summary of Dr. Odendaal and other witnesses at the Basson trial, see Chandré Gould and Marléne Burger, weekly reports on the trial of Wouter Basson and on the South African chemical and biological warfare program for the Centre for Conflict Resolution; available online at http://ccrweb.ccr. uct.ac.za/cbw/cbw_index.html.

55. Dr. Rocklyn Williams says he debriefed an SADF sergeant in 1983, who talked about the development of a "black bomb." Interview by Stephen Burgess, Pretoria, June 15, 2000.

56. See Burger, *Secrets and Lies;* and Gould and Burger, weekly reports on the trial of Wouter Basson and on the South African chemical and biological warfare program.

57. Dr. Daan Goosen, former Project Coast scientist, interview by Helen Purkitt, June 24, 2003. For a discussion of recent trends in genetic research in South Africa, see Helen E. Purkitt, with scientific support by Dr. Virgen R. Wells, "What's Over the Biotechnological Horizon? R&D Trends in South African Civilian Biotechnology & Implications for Monitoring Future Dual Use Biotechnology Trends in the Developing World," report prepared for the Defense Threat Reduction Agency and the U.S. Naval Academy, November 2003.

58. Mangold and Goldberg, *Plague Wars,* 244.

59. Ibid. In an interview for the television documentary, Dr. Daan Goosen acknowledged again that the black population was the target of Project Coast's work on drugs to induce infertility. He said, "[T]he most serious problem as told to us [was] the birth rate of the black population, and that it would outgrow the resources of the country and it was very important that this be brought under con-

trol. There was no doubt about that. This was given to us by Basson, by the surgeon general. . . . [I]t was very clear that this was the most important project we had to work on." Interview in *Frontline* episode entitled "Plague War: What Happened in South Africa," available online at http://www.pbs.org/wgbh/pages/frontline/shows/ plague/sa.

60. South African journalist, interview by Helen Purkitt, Cape Town, July 20, 2000.

61. Dr. Goosen admitted that one vial of the HIV virus existed but adamantly denied that Project Coast researchers under his supervision worked on HIV/AIDS as a biological weapon in interviews with several interviewees, including an interview with Tom Mangold both on and off camera in 2001. He maintained this position in face-to-face interviews with Joby Warwick, Pretoria, April 2003 and with Helen Purkitt, Pretoria, July 2003.

62. South African government officials, interviews by Helen Purkitt, Pretoria, July 2002.

63. According to Chandré Gould, Centre for Conflict Resolution, in a presentation attended by Stephen Burgess, June 29, 2000.

64. Burger, *Secrets and Lies,* 56–57.

65. Ibid., 202. See also the 1999 prosecution charge sheet against Basson.

66. General Chris Thirion (Ret.) and General Jannie Geldenhuys (Ret.), interviews by Stephen Burgess, Pretoria, June 13, 2000.

67. General Georg Meiring (Ret.), interview by Stephen Burgess, Pretoria, July 3, 2000. As a subscriber to the Geneva Protocol, South Africa could not legally develop lethal agents of chemical warfare.

68. On June 13, 2000, General Thirion claimed that he had proposed a gendarmerie, or carabinieri, to serve as the third force. Instead, P. W. Botha, Magnus Malan, and Adriaan Vlok devised the Civil Cooperation Bureau and other agencies that were more covert and far more lethal. Interview by Stephen Burgess, Pretoria, June 13, 2000.

69. General Chris Thirion (Ret.) and General Jannie Geldenhuys (Ret.), interviews by Stephen Burgess, Pretoria, June 13, 2000.

70. David Steward, executive director, De Klerk Foundation and President de Klerk's chief of staff (1989–1994), interview by Stephen Burgess, Cape Town, June 26, 2000, and interview by Helen Purkitt, Cape Town, July 17, 2000.

71. "TRC Urges Malan to Seek Amnesty," South African Press Association, May 9, 1997, available online at http://www.anc.org.za/anc/newsbrief/1997/news 0510. Also, Magnus Malan, interview with Stephen Burgess, Pretoria, June 23, 2000.

72. South Africa Truth and Reconciliation Commission, "Special Investigation into Project Coast: South Africa's Chemical and Biological Warfare Programme," *Truth and Reconciliation Commission of South Africa Report,* vol. 2, Chapter 6, available online at http://www.fas.org/nuke/guide/rsa/cbw/2chap6c.htm.

73. Testimony by Dr. Mike Odendaal in the Basson trial, May 24, 2000. See "HIV Blood Sample Frozen for Chemical Warfare, Basson Trial Hears," South African Press Association, May 25, 2000, available online at http://www.geocities. com/project_coast/deadly.htm. From the mid-1980s to the mid-1990s, the rand-dollar rate was two rand to the dollar.

74. A biosafety laboratory-4 (BSL-4) is the most secure of all biological research facilities. BSL-4 laboratory facilities have equipment that allows researchers to handle extremely hazardous pathogen. BSL-4 labs are used for sophisticated civilian biotechnology and state-of-the-art biowarfare research. The only other BSL-4 laboratory in South Africa at the time of Project Coast was at the government-run National Institute for Communicable Diseases (NICD) in Johannesburg.

Since the mid-1970s, this institute has operated the only laboratory on the African continent that is capable of identifying and diagnosing infectious diseases. NICD scientists were not involved with Project Coast projects and continue to enjoy credibility and support from the South African government and public. For more details, see Purkitt and Wells, "What's Over the Biotechnological Horizon?"

75. Mangold and Goldberg, *Plague Wars,* 243.

76. Testimony by Dr. Mike Odendaal in the Basson trial, May 24, 2000. See "HIV Blood Sample Frozen for Chemical Warfare, Basson Trial Hears," South African Press Association, May 24, 2000, available online at http://www.geocities.com/project_coast/deadly.htm.

77. Interviews by Stephen Burgess in the United States and South Africa, 2000 through 2001, including officials in the Office of the Secretary of Defense.

78. The program manager of South Africa's former nuclear-weapons program confirmed in 1994 that several of the weapon systems ARMSCOR developed were capable of carrying chemical and biological warheads but refused to elaborate on the division of labor between ARMSCOR and other organizations involved in covert biochemical activities such as Project Coast. Helen E. Purkitt, "The Politics of Denuclearization: The Case of South Africa," final report to the Institute for National Strategic Studies, U.S. Air Force Academy, November 9, 1994.

79. Ambassador Princeton Lyman, e-mail correspondence with Stephen Burgess, September 18, 2000. In an August 31, 2000 interview with Stephen Burgess, Ambassador Lyman did not confirm his earlier statement that weaponization took place. Ambassador Donald Mahley of the U.S. State Department, who was part of the delegation to South Africa after the démarche of April 11, 1994, also downplayed evidence of weaponization in a August 30, 2000 interview. At least two former senior officials report that South African government officials were surprised and puzzled by the U.S. 1994 démarche, since they claim U.S. officials at lower levels of the U.S. government had a full picture of what they had developed in this area. Two former senior South African officials, interviews by Helen Purkitt, Pretoria, July 2002.

80. See Thomas Byron, *Elimination Theory.*

81. Burger, *Secrets and Lies,* 189–219.

82. Mangold and Goldberg, *Plague Wars,* 242. Skepticism still surrounds Basson and Knobel's claims about Basson's international activities. According to several interviews, it is doubtful if Basson ever penetrated Porton Down or U.S. and Soviet facilities. U.S. government officials, interviews by the authors in Washington, D.C., and Pretoria, 2000–2003.

83. Mangold and Goldberg, *Plague Wars,* 242.

84. Ibid., note 443. Dr. Basson told Tom Mangold in 1998 that the reason a detailed investigation by Britain's MI6 security service failed to substantiate the allegations that he had visited Porton Down is because he used false names and passports for his frequent visits. Another possibility is that Basson met with former Porton Down employees. Several former employees of Porton Down reported that British authorities asked them to pose as current employees after they reported that Wouter Basson had contacted them. See Michael Evans, "South Africa May Have Ordered British Deaths," *The Times* (London), July 14, 1998, 7.

85. Dr. Niels Knobel, interview by Helen Purkitt, Pretoria, July 3, 2002. Dr. Barry D. Schoub, executive director of the National Institute for Communicable Diseases in Johannesburg, confirmed in an interview with Helen Purkitt, Johannesburg, June 24, 2003, that the U.S. and South African governments worked closely to contain suspected outbreaks of Ebola during the 1980s.

86. It is not known whether any of the Centers for Disease Control specimens shipped to South Africa provided researchers with specimens they did not already

have. Many infectious diseases, including Ebola, foot-and-mouth disease, and an-thrax, are indigenous to the region. The National Institute for Communicable Dis-eases in Johannesburg has been collecting specimens from neighboring coun-tries as far away as Pakistan since 1976. Dr. Barry D. Schoub, interview by Helen Purkitt, Johannesburg, June 24, 2003.

87. General Bill Sass (Ret.), telephone interview by Stephen Burgess, Pretoria, June 12, 2000, and interviews with other former senior South African officials de-tailed in Helen E. Purkitt, "The Politics of Denuclearization."

88. General Bill Sass (Ret.), telephone interview by Stephen Burgess, Pretoria, June 12, 2000, and by Helen Purkitt, Pretoria, July 5, 1994, and June 24, 2000; and officials in U.S. Department of State and U.S. Department of Defense and ex-perts in think tanks, interviews by Stephen Burgess and Helen Purkitt in Washing-ton, D.C. during 2000 and 2001.

89. Uzi Manheim and Marie Colvin, "Genetic Warfare Nearing Reality," *Times* (London), November 1998, available online at http://www.peace.ca/geneticwarfare. htm.

90. As Daan Goosen noted, "Biological weapons was a new field, and it was done all over by all countries, even England at Porton Down and the Americans at Fort Detrick. We know they were doing it, and we had contacts with all that work and the weapons that were developed." Interview in *Frontline* episode entitled "Plague War: What Happened in South Africa," available online at http://www. pbs.org/wgbh/pages/frontline/shows/plague/sa.

91. These claims were made at several different times and venues during the Truth and Reconciliation Commission investigation and during Basson's trial. See Basson trial transcripts and Burger, *Secrets and Lies* for more details.

92. Jo Thomas, "California Doctor's Suicide Leaves Many Troubling Myster-ies Unsolved," *New York Times,* November 3, 2002. Edward Humes, "The Medi-cine Man," *Los Angeles Magazine,* July 2001, 95–99. Jack Leonard and his asso-ciates at the *Los Angles Times* conducted the best and most detailed coverage of the unfolding case. See Scott Martelle, Jeff Gottlieb, and Jack Leonard, "A Doctor, a Deal Maker and a Mystery," *Los Angeles Times,* March 20, 2000. See also http://www.geocities.com/project_coast/docdeal.htm.

93. Jeff Collins, "Suspects All Visited the Home of a South African Trade Offi-cial, Police Say," *Orange Country Register,* July 18, 2000. Dr. Ford, Dino D'Saachs and Dr. Jerry Nilsson were all suspects initially in the police investigation of who conspired to kill Biofem Inc. chief executive James Patrick Riley. Riley and several other of Ford's associates had also visited the South Africa trade attaché, Gideon Bouwer, in Los Angeles in the 1980s.

94. Arthur Allen, "Vaginal Detergent," *Salon.com,* June 26, 2000, available on-line at http://dir.salon.com/health/feature/2000/06/26/microbicide/index.html?sid= 860634.

95. Ibid. In July 2000, microbicide researchers from UNAIDS discovered to their horror that the spermicide nonoxynol-9, a chemical found in many contra-ceptives, lubricants, and gels worldwide, was not only ineffective against HIV, it ac-tually appears to increase the chance of infection in high-risk women. Of 999 pros-titutes in Africa and Thailand, 59 women using a nonoxynol-9 contraceptive gel called Advantage-S became infected with HIV, compared with 41 women using a placebo. Claudia Kalb, "We Have to Save Our People," *Newsweek,* July 24, 2000.

96. Prof. Frank Otto Muller, managing director and director of scientific and regulatory affairs, QdotPharma, interview by Helen Purkitt, George, South Africa, July 3, 2003.

97. Jeff Collins, "Suspects All Visited the Home of a South African Trade Offi-cial, Police Say." This article cites an interview with Knobel in which he confirmed

that he relied on Ford's expertise whenever he had questions about chemical or biological weapons, and said that he helped Ford and Riley gain approval for the use of products produced by Biofem. Knobel also confirmed that he introduced Dr. Ford to Wouter Basson. Basson then arranged a briefing for Ford with Project Coast scientists at Fort Klapperkop outside Pretoria in June or July 1987, where Ford demonstrated how to lace teabags, doilies, and even a *Playboy* magazine with deadly bacteria. Reportedly, a new project, code-named Project Larry, was started around the time of Ford's visit but was closed within a few months. While Dr. Knobel reports no knowledge of a Project Larry, Adrian Botha, a Project Coast scientist who attended this briefing, reported that Ford sent them five bags of biological material they hoped to cultivate into organisms that could be used to kill the enemies of apartheid. Jeff Collins, "Ford Advised South Africa on Warfare Devices," *Orange County Register,* March 15, 2000.

98. Civilian biotechnology entrepreneur, interview by Helen Purkitt, outside George, South Africa, July 2003.

99. For more details, see transcripts of Helen Purkitt interviews and other interviews conducted by Mike Wallace for an episode of the television program *60 Minutes,* "'Dr. Death' and His Accomplice," aired November 3, 2002, summary available online at http://www.cbsnews.com/stories/2002/10/30/60minutes/main 527530.shtml; and Burger, *Secrets and Lies.*

100. Detective Victor Ray, Irvine Police, interviews by Helen Purkitt, September 2001. See also Humes, "The Medicine Man."

101. Jo Thomas, "California Doctor's Suicide"; Detective Victor Ray, interview by Helen Purkitt, Irving, California, 2001; and Tom Byron, phone interviews with Helen Purkitt, 2001 and 2002.

102. Dr. G. Scharf, former director of Medical Hospital One (Pretoria) and SADF Special Forces physician, interview by Helen Purkitt, Pretoria, July 6, 2000.

103. Detective Victor Ray, interview by Helen Purkitt, Irvine, California, September 2001.

104. Spring clinics are annual clinics that South African military doctors and other personnel hold in the spring for local residents. Dr. Ford wanted to extract amniotic fluid from the placentas of pregnant women. Because this proposed procedure was likely to cause spontaneous abortions, Dr. Scarf was extremely offended by Ford's proposal.

105. A brief account of this project appeared in Jo Thomas, "California Doctor's Suicide Leaves Many Troubling Mysteries Unsolved." Statements made by Detective Victory Ray in several press conferences in Irvine, California, in 2000 and 2001 corroborate our narrative. See also comments by Helen Purkitt in an interview with Mike Wallace on "'Dr. Death" and His Accomplice," episode of the television program *60 Minutes,* aired November 3, 2002.

106. Dr. Niels Knobel, interview by Helen Purkitt, Pretoria, July 3, 2002.

107. Jo Thomas, "California Doctor's Suicide Leaves Many Troubling Mysteries Unsolved."

108. Arthur Allen, "Mad Scientist."

109. Detective Victor Ray, interviews by Helen Purkitt, Irving, California, September 2001. See also Jack Leonard and Jeff Gottlieb, "Meetings with S. Africa Attaché Under Scrutiny," *Los Angeles Times,* July 17, 2000.

110. See Humes, "The Medicine Man," 95–99, 166–168; Andrew Bluth and Tony Saavedra, "The Materials Are Collected at the Home of Jerry Nilsson, Who Was Questioned and Released," *Orange County Register,* April 2, 2000; and Tony Saavedra, "Surgeon Says He Doesn't Know Why He Was Subjected to a Search," *Orange County Register,* April 5, 2000.

111. There were also allegations that Ford tested his birth-control product on prostitutes in South Africa. Julian Rademeyer, "Illegal Tests on SA Prostitutes?" *Pretoria News,* July 22, 2000, http://www.geocities.com/project_coast/ptabio.htm; and Arthur Allen, "Mad Scientist." See also articles about Project Coast in *Los Angeles Times.*

112. Dr. Torie Pretorius (South African prosecutor in the Basson case), interview by Helen Purkitt, Pretoria, July 4, 2000, and July 5, 2002.

113. Burger, *Secrets and Lies,* 158.

114. Dr. Villa-Vicencia, former senior investigator for the Truth and Reconciliation Commission and current head of the Institute for Justice and Reconciliation, interview by Helen Purkitt, Cape Town, July 20, 2000.

115. Mangold and Goldberg, *Plague Wars,* 277–278.

116. In 1988, Jerry D. Nilsson organized a group of doctors, including Dr. Larry Ford, to buy a defunct Los Angeles hospital and turn it into a state-of-the-art infectious-disease research center. Nilsson told potential investors that the new clinic had links with researchers doing sophisticated medical research worldwide, including researchers in South Africa. Nilsson was quoted as telling the *Los Angeles Times* that the Lake View Terrace Institute would be "one cog in a complex, far-reaching project" with related facilities in Africa, Germany, Italy, and Britain. The scheme failed when research groups denied Nilsson's claims that they were backing the venture.

117. Dr. Daan Goosen, former managing director of Roodeplaat Research Laboratories, claimed that Project Coast never conducted research on HIV as a weapon. However, he acknowledged that Project Coast scientists were planning to do some work that he termed "legitimate work" for a European pharmaceutical company. Interview in *Frontline* episode entitled "Plague War: What Happened in South Africa," available online at http://www.pbs.org/wgbh/pages/frontline/shows/plague/sa.

118. For a good recent summary of President Mbeki's position before South Africa's 2003 decision to change the policy and support public funding for an antiretroviral program to combat HIV/AIDS, see Samantha Power, "The AIDS Rebel," http://www.pbs.org/pov/pov2003/stateofdenial/special_rebel.html. The article was originally published in *The New Yorker,* May 2003.

119. Thomas Byron, telephone interview by Helen Purkitt, March 30, 2002. For more details about this and other covert projects undertaken in the United States and South Africa, see the 2004 book by Byron entitled *Elimination Theory.*

120. South African reporters who covered the Truth and Reconciliation Commission hearings, interviews by Helen Purkitt, Cape Town, July 2000.

121. Truth and Reconciliation Commission investigators, interviews by Helen Purkitt, Cape Town, July 2000.

122. See Burger, *Secrets and Lies.*

123. Prosecutor in the Basson trial, interview by Helen Purkitt, Pretoria, July 2000.

124. Ibid.

125. Laura Polleciett, executive director, Freedom of Expression Institute, interview by Helen Purkitt, Johannesburg, July 2000; and affidavits and memorandums on file at the Freedom of Expression Institute, Johannesburg. Prosecutors at Basson's trial introduced documents found in Webster's possession that indicated that the WPW Investments group was started in the early 1980s by a group of South African doctors. According to these documents, they were tasked by Southern African health authorities to set up clinics in various African countries. The state alleges that Basson set up the companies to create a cover for himself as a successful businessman. "Audit Reveals Basson Fraud," *Business Day,* June 14, 2000.

126. Jacques Pauw, interview by Stephen Burgess, Johannesburg, June 29, 2000. Pauw had interviewed Project Coast scientists, including Andre Immelman, Schalk van Rensburg, Mike Odendaal, Daan Goosen, and Peter Lourens.

127. Truth and Reconciliation Commission, "Special Investigation into Project Coast."

128. Colonel Johann Smith (Ret.), interview by Stephen Burgess, Pretoria, June 30, 2000. Negotiations with Mandela and the end of the Angolan war led Basson and others to take advantage of a window of opportunity to get rich. He was able to deceive top generals and salt away millions. Smith was certain that Basson turned to selling Ecstasy and other drugs because his money was in Swiss banks and he still needed to raise cash in South Africa.

129. South Africa Truth and Reconciliation Commission, *Truth and Reconciliation Commission of South Africa Report* (Cape Town: Truth and Reconciliation Commission, 1998), 514.

130. South Africa Truth and Reconciliation Commission, "Special Investigation into Project Coast."

131. Dr. Niels Knobel, interview by Stephen Burgess, Pretoria, June 15, 2000.

132. General Jannie Geldenhuys (Ret.), interview by Stephen Burgess, Pretoria, June 13, 2000.

SIX. DISMANTLING THE NUCLEAR-WEAPONS PROGRAM

1. Statement attributed to John F. Kennedy by Henry Sokolski in his essay entitled "Ending South Africa's Rocket Program: A Nonproliferation Success," Nonproliferation Policy Education Center, Washington, D.C., August 27, 1996, available online at http://www.npec-web.org/essay/southafrica.htm.

2. South Africa Profile: Missile Facilities, available online at http://nti.org/e_research/profiles/Safrica/Missile/1601.html.

3. Hannes Steyn, Richardt van der Walt, and Jan van Loggerenberg, *Armament and Disarmament: South Africa's Nuclear Weapons Experience* (Pretoria: Networks Publishers, 2003), 98–99

4. Ibid.; Waldo Stumpf, "South Africa's Nuclear Weapons Program: From Deterrence to Dismantlement," *Arms Control Today* 25, no. 10 (December 1995/January 1996): 4–7; Waldo Stumpf, "South Africa's Limited Nuclear Deterrent Programme and the Dismantling Thereof Prior to South Africa's Accession to the Nuclear Non-Proliferation Treaty," address at the South African Embassy, Washington, D.C., July 23, 1993.

5. The term "full-scope safeguards agreement" refers to an International Atomic Energy Agency Safeguards Agreement that covers all materials, facilities, and activities required to be declared by the Nuclear Non-Proliferation Treaty.

6. Henry Sokolski, "Ending South Africa's Rocket Program: A Nonproliferation Success," available online at http://www.npec-web.org/essay/southafrica.htm. Waldo Stumpf, head of the AEC, detailed some of the difficulties South African officials encountered in dismantling their nuclear-weapons program in a way that would meet the requirements of the International Atomic Agency and the Non-Proliferation Treaty. Their experience may still be relevant today. For example, in an interview in 1994 with H. Purkitt at Pelindaba, Stumpf outlined some of the difficulties involved in meeting the requirements for a full-scope safeguard agreement that involves dismantling all nuclear facilities, applying safeguards, and opening up all facilities involved in producing nuclear weapons for periodic international inspections. However, Stumpf noted that the AEC was unable to use ex-

isting INFCIRC-153-type Safeguard Agreements in its efforts to join the Nuclear Non-Proliferation Treaty. South African officials felt hampered by the fact that there was no legal way to join the treaty until all nuclear weapons had been dismantled and safeguards had been applied to all nuclear activities. Waldo Stumpf, interview by Helen Purkitt, Pelindaba, July 1994. In the early 1990s, Stumpf and his advisors felt that certain procedures might not actually be permitted under the treaty and that South Africa's only viable option was to design a "do-it-yourself" set of procedures in preparation for joining the Nuclear Non-Proliferation Treaty regime. Although Stumpf's observations may have been intended to provide a rationale for South Africa's unilateral disarmament process, they underscored some of the difficulties covert nuclear nations may face if they decide they want to place their nuclear facilities under IAEA safeguard agreements. Waldo Stumpf, "South Africa's Nuclear Weapons Program," 4–7.

7. See ibid. Also see David Albright, *South Africa's Secret Nuclear Weapons* (Washington, D.C.: Institute for Science and International Security, 1994); David Albright, "South Africa and the Affordable Bomb," *The Bulletin of Atomic Scientists* (July/August 1994): 37–47; and Peter Liberman, "The Rise and Fall of the South African Bomb," *International Security* 26, no. 2 (Fall 2001): 45–86.

8. Sokolski, "Ending South Africa's Rocket Program."

9. Ibid., 244.

10. Ibid. In April 1987, Canada, France, Germany, Italy, Japan, the United Kingdom, and the United States established the Missile Technology Control Regime (MTCR). It is now a voluntary arrangement among twenty-seven countries that consists of common export policies applied to a list of controlled items. The MTCR restricted the export of delivery systems and related technology for systems capable of carrying a 500-kilogram payload at least 300 kilometers and systems capable of carrying weapons of mass destruction. In September 1991, the United States invoked the MTCR when it applied sanctions against ARMSCOR.

For the official announcement of the agreement between South Africa and the United States, see "U.S. and South Africa Sign Missile Nonproliferation Agreement," U.S. Department of State Press Release, October 4, 1994.

11. The Non-Aligned Movement originated at a meeting in 1955 of twenty-nine Asian and African countries in Indonesia at which heads of state discussed common concerns, including colonialism and the influence of the West. The first summit of NAM heads of state took place in Belgrade, Yugoslavia, and set up the criteria for NAM membership. It ruled that member countries could not be involved in alliances or defense pacts with the main world powers. The NAM sought to prevent its members from becoming pawns in Cold War power games and distanced itself from the Western and Soviet power blocs. Since the collapse of the Soviet Union, the NAM has become concerned with globalization, trade and investment, debt, HIV/AIDS, and international crime. The NAM's February 2003 summit in Malaysia was dominated by issues of weapons of mass destruction in Iraq and North Korea. It also urged the United States not to invade Iraq.

12. The Mandela government supported AEC-sponsored research and development of uranium-enrichment technology with the French nuclear firm Cogema to explore the feasibility of a method called molecular laser isotope separation (MLIS). Cogema and the AEC built a demonstration MLIS facility at Pelindaba East and the AEC had plans to build a new pilot facility inside the abandoned Z-Plant to avoid the cost of a new building. The MLIS project was canceled at the end of 1997 due to funding and technical problems. "Atomic Corporation Abandons French Technology Project," *Sunday Independent* (Johannesburg), December 14, 1977.

13. Marina Ottaway, *South Africa: The Struggle for a New Order* (Washington, D.C.: Brookings Institution, 1993); see also Willem de Klerk, *F. W. de Klerk: The Man in His Time* (Johannesburg: J. Ball, 1991).

14. Stumpf, "South Africa's Nuclear Weapons Program."

15. F. W. de Klerk, *F. W. de Klerk: The Autobiography* (New York: St. Martin's Press, 1999).

16. For more-thorough discussions of this period of South African history, see Chris Alden, *Apartheid's Last Stand: The Rise and Fall of the South African Security State* (New York: St. Martin's Press, 1996); Dan O'Meara, *Forty Lost Years: The Apartheid State and the Politics of the National Party, 1948–1994* (Athens: Ohio University Press, 1996); and Tim D. Sisk, *Democratization in South Africa: The Elusive Social Contract* (Princeton, N.J.: Princeton University Press, 1995).

17. Throughout the tumultuous years leading up to the 1994 election, National Party leaders and the leaders of the ANC operated under the assumption that the other side was trying to be the dominant actor in the first government formed after the elections. All members of the ANC Steering Committee worked on the assumption that de Klerk felt that his party could retain its dominant position. Interviews conducted by Helen Purkitt during June and July 1994 with senior ANC officials in Johannesburg, Pretoria, and Cape Town.

18. J. W. de Villiers, Roger Jardine, and Mitchell Reiss, "Why South Africa Gave Up the Bomb," *Foreign Affairs* 72, no. 5 (November/December 1993): 98–109; and Stumpf, "South Africa's Nuclear Weapons Program," 4–7.

19. Steyn, van der Walt, and van Loggerenberg, *Armament and Disarmament,* 98–99.

20. For more details about the dismantlement process, see Albright, "South Africa and the Affordable Bomb"; Liberman, "The Rise and Fall of the South African Bomb"; Sokolski, "Ending South Africa's Rocket Program," 243–246; Helen E. Purkitt, "The Politics of Denuclearization: The Case of South Africa," final report to the Institute for National Strategic Studies, U.S. Air Force Academy, November 9, 1994.

21. De Villiers, Jardine, and Reiss say that the agencies involved were ARMSCOR and the AEC; "Why South Africa Gave Up the Bomb," 10. However, a more recent account by three insiders notes that the dismantlement process was an interagency joint effort involving the SADF, ARMSCOR, and the AEC; Steyn, van der Walt, and van Loggerenberg, *Armament and Disarmament,* 98–100.

22. Stumpf, "South Africa's Nuclear Weapons Program," 4–7.

23. Albright, "South Africa and the Affordable Bomb," 37–47; and Stumpf, "South Africa's Nuclear Weapons Program," 4–7.

24. International Atomic Energy Agency, *Report by the Director General: The Agency's Verification Activities in South Africa* (Vienna: International Atomic Energy Agency, September 1993).

25. Albright, "South Africa and the Affordable Bomb," 37–47; Stumpf, "South Africa's Nuclear Weapons Program," 4–7; Purkitt, "The Politics of Denuclearization."

26. David Albright, Frans Berkhout, and William Walker, *Plutonium and Highly Enriched Uranium 1996: World Inventories, Capabilities and Policies* (New York: Oxford University Press for Stockholm International Peace Research Institute, 1997), 391; Rodney W. Jones and Mark G. McDonough with Toby F. Dalton and Gregory D. Koblentz, *Tracking Nuclear Proliferation: A Guide in Maps and Charts, 1998* (Washington, D.C.: The Brookings Institution Press, 1998), 250.

27. Jones and McDonough with Dalton and Koblentz, *Tracking Nuclear Proliferation,* 250. For a more detailed discussion of this topic, see articles under

"South Africa" on the Institute for Science and International Security web site: http://www.isis-online.org/publications/southafrica/index.html. David Albright and Kevin O'Neill provide estimates of South Africa's uranium production as of 1999 as being "about 450 kilograms of HEU [highly enriched uranium] enriched over 80 percent to its nuclear-weapons program. Roughly 20–25 percent was HEU enriched to about 80 percent; the rest was enriched to 90–95 percent. Since the early 1990s, when it dismantled its nuclear weapons, South Africa has used an estimated 50–70 kilograms of its HEU enriched to over 90 percent to fuel the Safari research reactor. Ignoring the HEU remaining in the spent fuel from the Safari reactor, we arrive at the above estimate." Albright and O'Neill, eds., *The Challenges of Fissile Material Control* (Washington, D.C.: Institute for Science and International Security, 1999), available online at http://www.isis-online.org/publications/fmct/book/index.html.

28. Albright and O'Neill, *The Challenges of Fissile Material Control.*

29. "A Bungled Nuclear Deal," *Newsweek,* July 1994, 3. South African government officials and members of ANC Steering Committee, interviews conducted by Helen Purkitt, Pretoria and Cape Town, 1994; U.S. current and former State Department officials, interviews by Helen Purkitt, Washington, D.C., 1995.

30. Albright, *South Africa's Secret Nuclear Weapons,* 33; and Mark Hibbs, "South Africa's Secret Nuclear Program: From a PNE to a Deterrent," *Nuclear Fuel,* May 10, 1993, 3–6.

31. South Africa's first experimental nuclear reactor, the Safari-1, and the highly enriched uranium fuel needed to run the reactor were supplied by the United States under the Atoms for Peace program. The facility was commissioned in 1965 at Pelindaba. When the South Africans started building a second nuclear reactor at Pelindaba, they called it Safari-2.

32. Stumpf, "South Africa's Nuclear Weapons Program," 4–7.

33. Dr. Kader Asmal and other members of the ANC Executive Committee, interviews by Helen Purkitt, June–July 1994; ANC government officials, interviews by Helen Purkitt, July 2002.

34. Rodney and McDonough with Dalton and Koblentz, *Tracking Nuclear Proliferation,* 244, based on both public accounts and interviews with U.S. officials.

35. Former South African officials, interviews by Helen Purkitt, Pretoria and Cape Town, June–July 1994.

36. Ibid.

37. Ambassador Princeton Lyman, interview by Stephen Burgess, Washington, D.C., May 25, 2000; David Steward, interview by Stephen Burgess, Cape Town, June 26, 2000 and interview by Helen Purkitt, July 17, 2000. For an authoritative description of U.S. diplomatic moves during this period, see Princeton N. Lyman, *Partner to History: The U.S. Role in South Africa's Transition to Democracy* (Washington, D.C.: U.S. Institute of Peace Press, 2002).

38. See Donald B. Sole, "The South African Nuclear Case in the Light of Recent Revelations," paper presented at the conference New Horizons in Arms Control and Verification, John G. Tower Center for Policy Studies, Southern Methodist University, Dallas, Tex., October 1993; Willem Steenkamp, *South Africa's Border War 1966–1989* (Gibraltar: Asanti Publishing, 1989); South African officials, interviews by Helen Purkitt, Pretoria and Cape Town, June–July 1994.

39. Sole, "The South African Nuclear Case," 10.

40. See Agence France-Presse, January 25, 1995, for Botha's statement. Pik Botha's announcement regarding dismantlement by the end of March 1999 was taken from Jones and McDonough with Dalton and Koblentz, *Tracking Nuclear Proliferation,* 244, and was based on an announcement that was covered in the *Mail & Guardian* (Johannesburg), July 11, 1997.

41. Albright, "South Africa and the Affordable Bomb," 37–47.

42. Senior SADF senior officers, interviews by Helen Purkitt, Pretoria and Cape Town, June–July 1994. South African air force and navy officials, interviews by Stephen Burgess, Pretoria and Simonstown, March 2003.

43. General Pierre Steyn, interviews by Helen Purkitt, Pretoria, June 1994. The South African Air Force did not become involved in the nuclear-weapons program or become involved in plans to deliver nuclear weapons until the 1980s. See James Adams, *The Unnatural Alliance: Israel and South Africa* (New York: Quartet Books, 1984); and Steyn, van der Walt, and van Loggerenberg, *Armament and Disarmament,* Chapters 2 and 8.

44. Steyn, van der Walt, and van Loggerenberg, *Armament and Disarmament,* 98.

45. U.S. officials, interviews by Helen Purkitt, 1994 and by Stephen Burgess, Washington, D.C., May, June, August, and November 2000.

46. Sokolski, "Ending South Africa's Rocket Program."

47. O'Meara, *Forty Lost Years;* Sisk, *Democratization in South Africa.*

48. Albright, "South Africa and the Affordable Bomb," 37–47; Ottaway, *South Africa: The Struggle for a New Order;* Helen Purkitt, "The Cognitive Basis of Foreign Policy Expertise: Evidence from Intuitive Analyses of Political Novices and 'Experts' in South Africa," in *Problem Representation and Political Decision Making,* ed. D. Sylvan and J. Voss (Cambridge: Cambridge University Press, 1998), 147–186.

49. Jones and McDonough with Dalton and Koblentz, *Tracking Nuclear Proliferation,* 244. See footnote 10. See also Fred Bridgland, "South Africa Scraps Missile Plan After US Pressure," *The Daily Telegraph* (London), July 1, 1993, 2.

50. Jones and McDonough with Dalton and Koblentz, *Tracking Nuclear Proliferation,* 244. The agreement was announced in a U.S. Department of State press release on October 4, 1994, entitled "U.S. and South Africa Sign Missile Nonproliferation Agreement."

51. Very few analyses have been published about the decision-making process leading to the termination of the space-launch vehicle in South Africa. Henry Sokolski, a former Clinton official involved in the negotiations, has written an account about the negotiations. See Sokolski, "Ending South Africa's Rocket Program: A Nonproliferation Success," Nonproliferation Policy Education Center, Washington, D.C., August 27, 1996, available online at: http://www.npec-web.org/essay/southafrica.htm. For accounts from the South African perspective, see Steyn, van der Walt, and van Loggerenberg, *Armament and Disarmament,* Chapter 9; Fred de Lange, "Denel Drops Plans for Rocket, Missiles," *The Citizen* (Pretoria), July 1, 1993, 5; and "SA staak vuurply-projek" [South Africa Ceases Rocket-Project"], *Die Burger* (Cape Town), July 1, 1993, 1.

52. Former South African military officials, ARMSCOR managers, and politicians, interviews by Helen Purkitt, Pretoria, Gauteng, and Cape Town, June–July 1994.

53. Benjamin Beit-Hallahmi, *The Israeli Connection: Who Israel Arms and Why* (New York: Phantom Books 1987); Benjamin M. Joseph, *Besieged Bedfellows: Israel and the Land of Apartheid* (New York: Greenwood Press, 1998), 42, 68; Deon Geldenhuys, *Isolated States: A Comparative Analysis* (Johannesburg: Jonathan Ball Publishers, 1990).

54. Interviews conducted by Helen Purkitt, Pretoria, 1994.

55. Interviews conducted by Helen Purkitt, Pretoria, 1994; William E. Burrows and Robert Windrem, *Critical Mass: The Dangerous Race for Superweapons in a Fragmenting World* (New York: Simon and Schuster, 1994).

56. Burrows and Windrem, *Critical Mass*, 455; *United States v. Jasin*, U.S. Court of the Appeals for the Third Circuit, 280 F.3d 355; 2002 U.S. app. LEXIS 1733, December 7, 2001, submitted under Third Circuit LAR 34.1(a), February 5, 2002. See also *In re Assets of Parent Indus., Inc.*, Misc. No. 90-0210, United States District Court for the Eastern District of Pennsylvania, 739 F. Supp. 248; 1990 U.S. Dist. LEXIS 6920, June 1, 1990.; SADF officers, senior ARMSCOR personnel, and private military analysts, interviews by H. Purkitt, Pretoria, Gauteng, and Cape Town, June–July 1994.

57. ARMSCOR officials, interviews by Helen Purkitt, Gauteng, June 1994.

58. Senior weapons-system manager at ARMSCOR, interview by Helen Purkitt, Gauteng, June 1994.

59. Burrows, *Critical Mass*, 455.

60. Unless otherwise noted, this account of U.S. decision making is based on the case study in Henry Sokolski, "Ending South Africa's Rocket Program."

61. Ibid.

62. Ibid.

63. Ibid. See also Burrows, *Critical Mass*.

64. Sokolski, "Ending South Africa's Rocket Program"; see also Burrows, *Critical Mass*.

65. Former South African government officials, Dr. Kader Asmal, and other members of the ANC Executive Committee, interviews with Helen Purkitt, Pretoria and Cape Town, June–July 1994.

66. Members of the Mandela and Mbeki governments, interviews by Helen Purkitt, Pretoria and Cape Town, June–July 1997 and July 2002.

67. Burrows, *Critical Mass*, 455.

68. Allegations about U.S. pressure at the International Monetary Fund were made by several former South African government officials during interviews with Helen Purkitt in June and July 1994. The IMF position statement is taken from Sokolski, "Ending South Africa's Rocket Program."

69. Sokolski, "Ending South Africa's Rocket Program."

70. Lynn E. Davis, Testimony before the U.S. House of Representatives Committee on Appropriations, Foreign Operations Appropriations, Export Financing and Related Programs FY96, Federal Document Clearing House, Congressional Testimony, April 4, 1995.

71. "U.S. and South Africa Missile Nonproliferation Agreement," U.S. Department of State Fact Sheet, October 1994.

72. Ibid.

73. Sokolski, "Ending South Africa's Rocket Program."

74. Former South African government officials, interviews by Helen Purkitt, June–July 1994.

75. Steyn, van der Walt, and van Loggerenberg, *Armament and Disarmament*, 102.

76. Peter de Ionno, "Nuclear Scientists Threaten to Tell All," *Sunday Times* (Johannesburg), March 27, 1994.

77. Sokolski, "Ending South Africa's Rocket Program."

78. Krish Naidoo, "SA's Arms Industry: The Way Forward," *Weekly Mail & Guardian* (Johannesburg), May 5, 1995, 27.

79. Naidoo, "SA's Arms Industry," 27; Steyn, van der Walt, and van Loggerenberg, *Armament and Disarmament*, 101.

80. Steyn, van der Walt, and van Loggerenberg, *Armament and Disarmament*, 101.

81. ARMSCOR officials, interviews by Helen Purkitt, Gauteng, June–July 1994.

82. Based on briefings and conversations with representatives of South African defense companies in Gauteng and Cape Provinces during site visits by Helen Purkitt, June and July 2002.

83. Jones and McDonough with Dalton and Koblentz, *Tracking Nuclear Proliferation*, 244. See also Humphrey Crum Ewing, Robin Ranger, David Bosdet, and David Wiencek, *Cruise Missiles: Precision and Countermeasures*, Bailrigg Memorandum no. 10, Center for Defense and International Security Studies, 1995.

84. "SA in Satellite Race?" *Mail & Guardian* (Johannesburg), March 12, 1999.

85. Gerjo Hoffman, "SA Struggles into Space," *Die Burger* (Cape Town), June 11, 2003, 1.

86. Former South African senior military and government officials, interviews by Helen Purkitt, Gauteng and Pretoria, June–July 1994.

87. Non-Proliferation of Weapons of Mass Destruction Law, Act no. 87 of 1993.

88. Recent insider accounts by Steyn, van der Walt, and van Loggerenberg support the proposition that by the end of the 1980s, comprehensive international sanctions played a critical role in convincing the political, military, and business elite that the time to negotiate reform had arrived; *Armament and Disarmament*. For other analyses of the importance of international sanctions, see Neta C. Crawford and Audie Klotz, *How Sanctions Work: Lessons from South Africa* (New York: St. Martin's, 1999); F. W. de Klerk, *The Last Trek: A New Beginning* (London: Macmillan, 1998); Geldenhuys, *Isolated States;* Ottaway, *South Africa: The Struggle for a New Order;* Sagan, "Why Do States Build Nuclear Weapons?" 69–71; Stumpf, "South Africa's Nuclear Weapons Program," 4–7; and Albright, "South Africa and the Affordable Bomb," 37–47.

SEVEN. THE ROLLBACK
OF PROJECT COAST

1. Interview in *Frontline* episode entitled "Plague War: What Happened in South Africa," available online at http://www.pbs.org/wgbh/pages/frontline/shows/plague/sa.

2. Brigadier General Bill Sass (Ret.), interview by Helen Purkitt, Pretoria, July 1994. For further details of changes made at the end of P. W. Botha's rule, see Helen E. Purkitt, "The Politics of Denuclearization: The Case of South Africa," final report to the Institute for National Strategic Studies (INSS), U.S. Air Force Academy, November 9, 1994.

3. For evidence of how widespread this fear was in 1992 after negotiations had broken down, see H. Purkitt, "The Cognitive Basis of Foreign Policy Expertise: Evidence from Intuitive Analyses of Political Novices and 'Experts' in South Africa," in *Problem Representation and Political Decision Making,* ed. D. Sylvan and J. Voss (Cambridge: Cambridge University Press, 1998).

4. Dr. Ian Phillips, ANC defense expert, interview by Stephen Burgess, Pretoria, June 13, 2000

5. David Steward, interview by Stephen Burgess, Cape Town, June 6, 2000, and by Helen Purkitt, Cape Town, July 17, 2000. It should be noted that several former South African military officials dispute the claim that de Klerk did not initially know about the full scope of Project Coast. For example, one former South African official who was involved in de Klerk's initial briefs after assuming office claims that de Klerk spent two days with Wouter Basson and was fully briefed

about all aspects of Project Coast shortly after he took office. Claim made during interview with Helen Purkitt, Pretoria, July 2002.

6. General Georg Meiring (Ret.), interview by Stephen Burgess, Pretoria, July 3, 2000; senior official of the South Africa Office of the Secretary of Defence, interview by Helen Purkitt, Pretoria, July 1997.

7. Hannes Steyn, Richardt van der Walt, and Jan van Loggerenberg, *Armament and Disarmament: South Africa's Nuclear Weapons Experience* (Pretoria: Network Publishers, 2003), Chapter 9.

8. De Wet Potgieter, journalist and reporter for several South African newspapers, interview by Stephen Burgess, Pretoria, June 13, 2000.

9. Roelof "Pik" Botha, telephone interview by Helen Purkitt, Pretoria, July 13, 2000. Botha stressed in this interview that he did not receive detailed knowledge of South Africa's chemical and biological warfare program until he had to obtain assurances that the program was closed down before South Africa signed the Nuclear Non-Proliferation Treaty.

10. William Webster, "Nuclear and Missile Proliferation," hearing before the Committee on Governmental Affairs, U.S. Senate, May 18, 1989, *Congressional Record* (Washington, D.C.: Government Printing Office, 1990), 12.

11. Colonel Mike Ferguson, former defense attaché to South Africa, interview by Stephen Burgess, Washington, D.C., May 23, 2000.

12. General Chris Thirion (Ret.), interview by Stephen Burgess, Pretoria, June 13, 2000.

13. Colonel Mike Ferguson, interview by Stephen Burgess, Washington, D.C., May 23, 2000.

14. Colonel Joep Joubert (Ret.), interview by Stephen Burgess, Pretoria, June 23, 2000. Joubert worked with the Civil Cooperation Bureau and SADF Special Forces; he retired from the SADF.

The Reverend Frank Chikane was a leading member of the anti-apartheid movement inside South Africa in the 1980s. In the 1970s, he was a member of the South African Students Organization (SASO). After SASO was banned in 1977, he participated in the development of grassroots community-based organizations. In 1983, he was both a founding member and vice president of the United Democratic Front (UDF). During the latter part of the 1980s, Chikane became a founding member of the Soweto People's Delegation (SPD), which engaged in the first local government negotiations to create a just local government system, worked to create a common tax base between black and white areas, and strove to secure the free transfer of rented stock in the townships to those who had lived in them for more than twenty years. The SPD process gave birth to the Central Witwatersrand Metropolitan Chamber, which has been used as a model for the current nonracial local authorities. Chikane was detained without trial on several occasions in the late 1970s and early 1980s. In February 1985, he was arrested and charged with high treason along with other leaders of the UDF and the trade union movement. In December 1985, he was released because the state had failed to establish its case.

In testimony before the Harms Commission, Joubert said he believed that Chikane had to be eliminated as an "enemy." Joubert thought that the operation was well planned and that authority was given from the top, probably by P. W. Botha, Pik Botha, Adrian Vlok, and Magnus Malan. Joubert testified that he had full responsibility for the Civil Cooperation Bureau and Special Forces missions and the budgeting of secret funds. He believed that a chemical and biological warfare program was essential and that a good offensive program was a necessary component of a good defensive program.

15. Testimony of Roodeplaat Research Laboratories scientist Schalk van Rensburg to the Truth and Reconciliation Commission on June 9, 1998.

16. See W. Seth Carus, *Bioterrorism and Biocrimes: The Illicit Use of Biological Agents in the 20th Century,* 3rd ed. (Washington, D.C.: Center for Counterproliferation Research, National Defense University, 1998), 88. Bumbled assassination attempts using biological-weapons devices seem to have been pretty common. This fits with what experts on biological-weapons terrorism have found in other cases. Carus classifies this incident as probable or possible use with no authoritative confirmation. In some cases, a biological agent was used but there was no information to indicate whether the perpetrator knowingly caused the infection (90).

17. Jacques Pauw, *Into the Heart of Darkness: Confessions of Apartheid's Assassins* (Johannesburg: Jonathan Ball, 1997).

18. Ibid., 226.

19. Vlakplaas is the name of a farm and former special South African Police base about twenty kilometers (twelve miles) west of the capital, Pretoria. Eugene de Kock commanded Vlakplaas (the base and the unit that operated from the base) from June 1985 to 1993.

20. Dr. Vernon Joynt, interview by Stephen Burgess, Pretoria, June 14, 2000.

21. David Steward, interview by Stephen Burgess, Cape Town, June 26, 2000 and by Helen Purkitt, Cape Town, July 17, 2000.

22. "Seniors Should Take Rap for Killings, Assassin Tells Basson Trial," South African Press Association, May 11, 2000; Tom Mangold and Jeff Goldberg, *Plague Wars: A True Story of Biological Warfare* (New York: St. Martin's Press, 1999), 263.

23. Chris Oppermann, "How the Taxpayer Footed the Bill for Project Coast," *Weekly Mail & Guardian* (Johannesburg), June 27, 1997.

24. According to journalist De Wet Potgieter, interview by Stephen Burgess, June 13, 2000, Uwe Paschke, who married P. W. Botha's daughter, and Philip Mijburgh, Magnus Malan's nephew, both had connections to Basson and the chemical- and biological-weapons program. Mijburgh especially profited from the privatization of the front companies for Project Coast.

25. "Audit Reveals Basson Fraud," *Business Day* (Johannesburg), June 14, 2000. Many important documents were seized from Sam Bosch's house shortly after Basson was arrested in 1997. In 2000, the state called a number of witnesses in an attempt to prove that Basson had lived a life of luxury while defrauding the apartheid government of millions of rand, and Bosch agreed to be a witness for the state. The court presented evidence that Libya had shown an interest in Basson's luxurious Merton House in Pretoria for use as an embassy. The house became an embarrassment to both Basson and the South African government after extensive media coverage. It was eventually sold to the Zimbabwean government at a loss. Other witnesses at Basson's trial testified that he took business associates and employees on luxury overseas holiday trips and entertained lavishly while earning a public servant's salary. Angolan rebel leader Jonas Savimbi once hired a private aircraft belonging to a group of companies owned by Basson. According to Defence Advocate Jakkie Cilliers, the aircraft often landed at U.S. military bases and was familiar to customs officials. He said it was seldom searched, which made it easier for Basson to transport equipment earmarked for Project Coast and the SADF during the 1980s. See Marléne Burger and Chandré Gould, *Secrets and Lies: Wouter Basson and South Africa's Chemical and Biological Warfare Programme* (Cape Town: Zebra, 2002); and Basson trial transcript summaries accessible through South African Chemical and Biological Warfare Programme web page, available online at http://www.geocities.com/project_coast/cbw_index.html.

26. South Africa Truth and Reconciliation Commission, *Report of the Truth and Reconciliation Commission of South Africa* (Cape Town: The Truth and Reconciliation Commission, 1998), 515.

27. A bearer bond is one which does not record its owner's name anywhere (as opposed to a registered bond). The interest and principal goes to holder of the bearer bond. Companies never know who holds their bearer bond certificates, so communication is limited to notices in newspapers. The entire responsibility for keeping bearer bonds safe, demanding interest payments, and requesting loan principal is the bondholder's. Criminals can negotiate bearer bond certificates as easily as rightful owners. The Banco di Napoli issued Vatican bearer bonds.

28. Stefaans Brummer, "SADF Linked to Red Mercury," *Weekly Mail & Guardian* (Johannesburg), December 20, 1995. See also Peter Hounam and Steve McQuillen, *The Mini-Nuke Conspiracy: Mandela's Nuclear Nightmare* (London: Faber & Faber, 1995); former South African military officers and journalists, interviews by Helen Purkitt, Gauteng and Pretoria, July 1994; South African journalists, interviews by Helen Purkitt, Johannesburg, Cape Town, and Durban, June–July 1997; former South African military intelligence informant, interview by Helen Purkitt, Port Elizabeth, July 1997; South African government officials and journalists, interviews by Helen Purkitt, Pretoria and Gauteng, June 2000, and Cape Town, July 2000.

29. Several aspects of these unsolved murders remain unexplained. The bodies of some of the victims thought to be murdered with red mercury were smeared with a substance that contained trace amounts of mercury; this is one reason why investigators believed these execution-style killings were linked. Remarkably similar explanations of why these individuals were murdered have been offered by several former and current South African government officials and reporters. The lead investigator in the case, Colonel Charles Landman, who conducted a vigorous investigation, was taken off the case after being charged with fraud and other violations inconsistent with discharging the duties of his public office. Reporters in South Africa no longer publish articles on the murders because there is no new information available about them. South African reporters in Pretoria, Gauteng, Cape Town, Durban, and Port Elizabeth, interviews by Helen Purkitt, June–July of 1994, 1997, 2000, 2002, and 2003.

30. Chris Oppermann, "Basson's Army Buddy Blows the Whistle," *Mail & Guardian* (Johannesburg), June 27, 1997.

31. The Truth and Reconciliation Commission cites Lieutenant General Pierre Steyn's report to President de Klerk on December 20, 1992, as the source for this incident.

32. See Purkitt, "The Politics of Denuclearization." Truth and Reconciliation Commission researchers could not arrange a meeting with the British investigator. Investigators met with a leading South African infectious-diseases specialist, Dr. Barry Staub, who was a member of both the Swiss and the UN investigating teams. Dr. Staub told them that he believed that the troops had suffered dehydration and were not the victims of a chemical attack. This explanation struck the commission's investigation unit as unlikely but is consistent with the assessment of foreign military personnel who investigated this and other alleged incidents of chemical and biological warfare in Mozambique during the early 1990s. Two foreign military officers who had investigated this incident found that it was impossible to determine the cause of these deaths. As one of these officials explained, "It's very difficult to isolate cause of death when people are so malnourished and dehydrated when they die." U.S. military officer, interview by Helen Purkitt, Pretoria, July 3, 1994.

33. Ambassador Princeton Lyman, interview by Stephen Burgess, Washington, D.C., May 25 and August 31, 2000.

34. Dr. Vernon Joynt, interview by Stephen Burgess, Pretoria, June 14, 2000.

35. Dr. Ian Phillips, interview by Stephen Burgess, Pretoria, June 13, 2000.

36. Dr. Torie Pretorius, prosecutor in the Basson case, interview by Stephen Burgess, Pretoria, June 20, 2000.

37. General Georg Meiring (Ret.), interview by Stephen Burgess, Pretoria, July 3, 2000.

38. Ibid. During the interview, Meiring asserted that ANC/MK troops were trained in chemical and biological warfare and that SADF intelligence concluded that there could have been chemical and biological agents in Mozambique provided to the ANC/MK by the Soviet Union and/or its allies.

39. David Steward, interview by Stephen Burgess, Cape Town, June 26, 2000.

40. General Georg Meiring (Ret.), interview by Stephen Burgess, Pretoria, July 3, 2000.

41. Burger, *Secrets and Lies,* 3.

42. *Weekly Mail & Guardian* (Johannesburg), November 14, 1997.

43. Former South African officials, interviews by Stephen Burgess, June and July 2000, particularly the interview with Lieutenant General Pierre Steyn, Pretoria, July 4, 2000.

44. General Georg Meiring (Ret.), interview by Stephen Burgess, Pretoria, July 3, 2000. Basson's soft retirement meant that he was no longer an active member of the SADF although he continued as a reserve officer.

45. David Steward, interview by Stephen Burgess, Cape Town, June 26, 2000.

46. Ibid.

47. General Georg Meiring (Ret.), interview by Stephen Burgess, Pretoria, July 3, 2000.

48. Burger, *Secrets and Lies,* 26. American officials were aware of and informally monitored the dismantlement process the de Klerk regime used. U.S. military and political officials, interviews conducted by Helen Purkitt, U.S. Embassy, Pretoria, June–July 1994, and with military and political officials, U.S. consulate, Cape Town, July 1994.

49. The prosecutors in the Basson trial were convinced that there was a link between the drugs manufactured under the auspices of Project Coast and the flood of drugs that appeared very suddenly in the townships in the early 1990s. However, they did not have the evidence to bring formal charges in the trial. Dr. Torie Pretorius, prosecutor in Basson case, interview by Helen Purkitt, Pretoria, July 4, 2000.

50. General Georg Meiring (Ret.), interview by Stephen Burgess, Pretoria, July 3, 2000.

51. Testimony of Dr. Niels Knobel, former surgeon general, to the Truth and Reconciliation Commission, July 1998.

52. General Georg Meiring (Ret.), interview by Stephen Burgess, Pretoria, July 3, 2000.

53. Ibid.

54. Ambassador Princeton Lyman, interviewed by Stephen Burgess, Washington, D.C., May 25 and August 31, 2000.

55. Peter Goosen, proliferation expert, Ministry of Foreign Affairs, interview by Stephen Burgess, Pretoria, June 15, 2000.

56. Dr. Ian Phillips, interview by Stephen Burgess, Pretoria, June 13, 2000. According to Phillips, during 1989–1994, the British were upset with the Americans for their efforts to promote their own "solution for South Africa." Phillips also felt that British and American cooperation on South Africa's nuclear, biological, and chemical programs was not as smooth as it may have seemed.

57. David Steward, interview by Stephen Burgess, Cape Town, June 26, 2000.

58. Ambassador Princeton Lyman, interview by Stephen Burgess, Washington, D.C., August 31, 2000.

59. Dr. Niels Knobel, interview by Stephen Burgess, Pretoria, June 15, 2000.

60. William Finnegan, "The Poison Keeper: Is an Afrikaner Doctor a Biowar Criminal?" *The New Yorker,* January 15, 2001, 58–75, and *Frontline* episode entitled "Plague War: What Happened in South Africa," available online at http://www.pbs.org/wgbh/pages/frontline/shows/plague/sa.

61. General Georg Meiring (Ret.), interview by Stephen Burgess, Pretoria, July 3, 2000.

62. U.S. officials, interviews by Stephen Burgess and Helen Purkitt, Washington, D.C., May, June, and August 2000.

63. U.S. officials, especially in the Office of the Secretary of Defense of the U.S. Department of Defense, interviews by Stephen Burgess, Washington, D.C., May 26 and August 31, 2000.

64. Many details about secret South African efforts to develop launch vehicles and warheads capable of carrying nuclear, biological, and chemical weapons remain classified. Some details about South Africa's launch vehicles are available in Hilton Hamann, *Days of the Generals* (Cape Town: Zebra, 2001). A more detailed but controversial account is that of Hounam and McQuillen in *The Mini-Nuke Conspiracy.*

65. Dr. Ian Phillips, interview by Stephen Burgess, Pretoria, June 13, 2000.

66. Senior South African officials in the Office of the Secretary of Defence, interviews by Helen Purkitt, Johannesburg and Pretoria, June 1997.

67. South African military officials, interviews by Helen Purkitt, Pretoria, July 2002.

68. Eddie Koch and Derek Fleming, "Bizarre Experiments at SADF Research Firms," *Weekly Mail & Guardian* (Johannesburg), December 15, 1994.

69. Ibid.

70. *Sunday Tribune,* December 1994.

71. Koch and Fleming, "Bizarre Experiments at SADF Research Firms."

72. Ibid. For a description of current activities of Protechnik Laboratories (Pty) Ltd., which is now a private company, see its web site at http://www.sadid.co.za/SADID_7/edition7/protechnik/protechnik.html.

73. Koch and Fleming, "Bizarre Experiments at SADF Research Firms."

74. Tom Mangold and Jeff Goldberg, *Plague Wars: A True Story of Biological Warfare* (New York: St. Martin's Press, 1999), 270.

75. Finnegan, "The Poison Keeper," 58–75; Ambassador Princeton Lyman, interviews by Stephen Burgess, Washington, D.C., May 25 and August 31, 2000.

76. General Georg Meiring (Ret.), interview by Stephen Burgess, Pretoria, July 3, 2000; former South African officials and analysts, interviews by Helen Purkitt, Pretoria, June 2000. According to Rocky Williams, Basson technically never left the SADF payroll since he remained on reserve status after his retirement. The SAMS reactivated Basson to active-duty status due to repeated requests from the Americans. Williams was an ANC intelligence officer who is now at the Institute for Security Studies. Interview by Helen Purkitt, Pretoria, July 5, 2002.

77. Finnegan, "The Poison Keeper," 58–75. Although the number of Basson's trips to Libya decreased after he was "rehired," the South African government at one point placed Basson under an undeclared house arrest.

78. Colonel Bern McConnell, former deputy assistant secretary for African affairs in the Office of the Secretary of Defense at the Pentagon, and several other senior U.S. defense and intelligence officials, interviews by Helen Purkitt, Washington, D.C., May and June 1997 and September 1998.

79. Oppermann, "How the Taxpayer Footed the Bill"; Dr. Ian Phillips, interviewed by Stephen Burgess, Pretoria, June 13, 2000.

80. Stefaans Brummer, "Secret Chemical War Remains Secret," *Mail & Guardian* (Johannesburg), August 23, 1996.

81. This view was expressed to Helen Purkitt in confidential interviews with both South African and U.S. officials in July 2000.

82. Wendy Orr, *From Biko to Basson* (Saxonwold, South Africa: Contra Press, 2000), 326.

83. Dr. Charles Villa-Vicencia, interview by Helen Purkitt, Cape Town, July 21, 2000.

84. The *verkope lys* was a shopping list of items, including anthrax, infected cigarettes, shampoo poisoned with an insecticide, and poisoned chocolates, that Dr. Basson allegedly ordered and gave to Civil Cooperation Bureau operatives. Orr, *From Biko to Basson*, 328–329.

85. Truth and Reconciliation Commission officials, interviews by Helen Purkitt, Cape Town, July 2000.

86. Dr. Charles Villa-Vicencio, interview by Helen Purkitt, Cape Town, July 21, 2000.

87. Mangold and Goldberg, *Plague Wars*, 257–265. For example, during his Truth and Reconciliation Commission testimony, Dr. Jan Lourens, a bioengineer at Delta G who later headed Protechnik, produced James Bond–type weapons designed to deliver fatal doses of poison (including umbrellas, screwdrivers, and signet rings with spring-loaded poison powder) that had been made to order for Wouter Basson. Lourens testified that SADF chief Gen. Kat Liebenberg told him to "forget about the whole thing . . . and that . . . those are my toys. . . . I want them back." Instead, Lourens buried the "toys" at his farm and resigned from the military. Another Truth and Reconciliation Commission witness, a former senior procurement official for Delta G, provided details from eight years of diary entries about all the products and raw materials that entered Delta G. He also described the structure of Delta G as a series of five "state-of-the-art" research laboratories, each with a cell structure that ensured that nobody knew what others were doing.

88. "HIV Blood Sample Frozen for Chemical Warfare, Basson Trial Hears," *South African Press Association*, May 24, 2000, available online at http://www.geocities.com/project_coast/deadly.htm.

89. Mangold and Goldberg, *Plague Wars*, 243.

90. Ibid., 260.

91. M. Evans, "South Africa May Have Ordered British Deaths," *The Times* (London), July 14, 1998, 7.

92. Chandré Gould and Peter I. Folb, "The South African Chemical and Biological Warfare Program: An Overview," *The Nonproliferation Review* 7, no. 3 (Fall–Winter 2000): 11–23.

93. Comments made by Dr. Villa-Vicencia, senior investigator for the Truth and Reconciliation Commission, during an interview with Helen Purkitt in July 2000.

94. These off-the-record remarks were made by several officials involved in the Truth and Reconciliation Commission to Helen Purkitt during interviews in July 2000.

95. Interview with Dr. Daan Goosen in *Frontline* episode entitled "Plague War: What Happened in South Africa," available online at http://www.pbs.org/wgbh/pages/frontline/shows/plague/sa.

96. The Basson trial was conducted in Afrikaans and no English-language record of the proceedings was available to the public in South Africa or elsewhere. The principal source of information about the trial is weekly summaries prepared by Chandré Gould and South African freelance journalist Marléne Burger that were financed by the nongovernmental organization Centre for Conflict Resolution (South Africa). The summaries are posted on the centre's web site, http://ccr-web.ccr.uct.ac.za/cbw/cbw_index.html. Burger and Gould also published a book

based on their experiences as regular observers in the courtroom for more than two years. See Burger and Gould, *Secrets and Lies.*

97. Based on trial summaries posted at the Centre for Conflict Resolution and South African press coverage of the trial. See Burger and Gould, *Secrets and Lies.*

98. The 1988 deal that the United States brokered on Namibia and Angola included amnesty for all those who had committed war crimes; that is why the murder charges against Basson and other South African officials were thrown out. Even so, the prosecution maintained that the judge had exhibited bias from the outset by refusing the help of a technical advisor. Although many legal experts felt this ruling was sound, some of Judge Hartzenberg's comments and rulings during the trial were widely viewed as being unprofessional.

99. FBI agent, interview by Helen Purkitt, Pretoria, July 2000.

100. The material in this paragraph and the two preceding paragraphs is drawn from Andrew Donaldson, "'Dr Death' Tells His Macabre Secrets," *Sunday Times* (Johannesburg), July 29, 2001; Burger, *Secrets and Lies,* 204–206.

101. Jeremy Lawrence, "Marathon Trial That Went Nowhere," *Sunday Times* (Johannesburg), April 14, 2002, available online at http://www.sundaytimes.co.za/2002/04/14/insight/in02.asp; Burger, *Secrets and Lies,* 187–192, 194–203.

102. Lawrence, "Marathon Trial That Went Nowhere"; Burger, *Secrets and Lies,* 193.

103. Nashira Davids, "Basson Fights Interrogation by Swiss Officials," *Sunday Times* (Johannesburg), January 26, 2003, available online at http://www.sundaytimes.co.za/2003/01/26/news/news21.asp.

104. "Retrial of Wouter Basson Denied," *iafrica.com,* June 4, 2003, available online at http://iafrica.com/news/sa/241910.htm.

105. "SANDF Post Sought by Warfare Expert, 'General' Basson Wants His Job Back," *The Herald* (Port Elizabeth), June 6, 2003, 1.

106. See Joby Warrick and John Mintz, "Lethal Legacy: Bioweapons for Sale; U.S. Declined South African Scientist's Offer on Man-Made Pathogens," *Washington Post,* April 20, 2003, A1; and Joby Warrick, "Biotoxins Fall into Private Hands; Global Risk Seen in S. African Poisons," *Washington Post,* April 21, 2003, A1. For additional information about recent problems Project Coast scientists encountered in finding professional employment, see Robert Block, "Biohazard: Bitter Researchers Are Big Question in Germ Warfare: Closing of South African Lab in '90s Isolated Scientists Ripe for Recruitment Now Ankle-Deep in Chicken Guts," *Wall Street Journal,* May 20, 2002; and Robert Block, "A Cautionary Disarmament: South Africa's Surrender of Nuclear Arms Was Only Half the Battle," *Wall Street Journal,* January 31, 2003. Dr. Goosen felt that these press accounts, while generally correct, misreported certain details of these confidential negotiations. Dr. Daan Goosen, interview by Helen Purkitt, Pretoria, June 24, 2003.

EIGHT. DISARMAMENT TRENDSETTER

1. The first comment was made by the South African foreign minister in 1995 prior to a radio interview on National Public Radio, Washington, D.C. President Thabo Mbeki made the second comment in 2002. "Mbeki History Lesson," *Mail & Guardian* (Johannesburg), November 1, 2002.

2. Technically, South Africa was not dominated by a single party, since the ANC lacked the votes (by slightly less than one seat) needed to have the two-thirds majority to change the constitution on its own in 1999. However, the ANC was the dominant party for all intents and purposes in a government that includes only three members of the Inkatha Freedom Party. See "Southern Africa—Risk Point-

ers," *Jane's Sentinel Security Assessment,* October 17, 2003. In the 2004 national election, the African National Congress party won the majority of votes throughout South Africa. This election victory meant that for the first time the ANC had enough votes to unilaterally amend the constitution.

3. William J. Long and Suzette R. Grillot, "Ideas, Beliefs, and Nuclear Policies: The Cases of South Africa and Ukraine," *The Nonproliferation Review* (Spring 2000): 24–40.

4. Bruce M. Russett and Harvey Starr, "From Democratic Peace to Kantian Peace: Democracy and Conflict in the International System," in *Handbook of War Studies II,* ed. Manus I. Midlarsky (Ann Arbor: University of Michigan Press, 2000); Tarak Barkawi and Mark Laffey, eds., *Democracy, Liberalism, and War: Rethinking the Democratic Peace Debate* (Boulder, Colo.: Lynne Rienner Publishers, 2001); Joanne S. Gowa, *Ballots and Bullets: The Elusive Democratic Peace* (Princeton, N.J.: Princeton University Press, 1999).

5. Albert J. Mauroni, *America's Struggle with Chemical-Biological Warfare* (Westport, Conn.: Praeger, 2000).

6. Brad Roberts, "Strategies of Denial," in *Countering the Proliferation and Use of Weapons of Mass Destruction,* ed. Peter L. Hays, Vincent J. Jodoin, and Alan R. Van Tassel (New York: McGraw-Hill, 1998), 63–88.

7. Greg Mills and Martin Edmonds, *South Africa's Defence Industry: A Template for Middle Powers?* (Canberra: Strategic and Defence Studies Centre, Australian National University, 2001); Geoffrey Hayes, *Middle Powers in the New World Order* (Toronto: Canadian Institute of International Affairs, 1994).

8. Glenn D. Hook, *Militarization and Demilitarization in Contemporary Japan* (London: Routledge, 1996).

9. Russett and Starr, "From Democratic Peace to Kantian Peace"; Barkawi and Laffey, *Democracy, Liberalism, and War;* Gowa, *Ballots and Bullets.* Democratic peace theory arose from observations that democracies rarely, if ever, fight each other. The hypothesis is that the more democracy spreads, the more peace will spread.

10. Scott Thomas, *The Diplomacy of Liberation: Foreign Relations of the ANC Since 1960* (London: I. B. Tauris, 1996), 4–5.

11. Ibid., 181–182.

12. Thomas, *The Diplomacy of Liberation,* 164.

13. For example, Kader Asmal, who led the Weapons of Mass Destruction Committee in the first years of the Mandela-led government, was a strong advocate of the Nuclear Non-Proliferation Treaty. In 1995, he was appointed head of the National Conventional Arms Control Committee, a new body designed to limit conventional arms proliferation. Abdul Minty has held a number of senior posts in the Mandela and Mbeki governments and is currently the acting director general of foreign affairs.

14. The Black Sash was a (mainly white) anti-apartheid women's movement that helped black victims of apartheid from the 1960s to the 1990s.

15. According to Dr. Ian Phillips, the ANC wanted to know where the information about the chemical- and biological-weapons program was. It believed that people who were living in the Middle East as well as in the United States and the U.K. sold many of Project Coast's secrets to foreign agents and governments. Dr. Ian Phillips, interviewed by Stephen Burgess, Pretoria, June 13, 2000.

16. David Albright, "South Africa and the Affordable Bomb," *The Bulletin of Atomic Scientists* (July/August 1994): 37–47; Waldo Stumpf, "South Africa's Nuclear Weapons Program: From Deterrence to Dismantlement," *Arms Control Today* 25, no. 10 (December 1995/January 1996): 4–7.

17. See Dr. Niels Knobel's testimony to the Truth and Reconciliation Commission, July 1998.

18. African National Congress, *The Reconstruction and Development Programme: A Policy Framework* (Johannesburg: Umanyano Publications, 1994).

19. South African Department of Defence, *Defence in a Democracy: White Paper on National Defence* (Pretoria, Government Printer, 1996). Available online at http://www.gov.za/whitepaper/1996defencwp.htm.

20. See for example, Hannes Steyn, Richardt van der Walt, and Jan van Loggerenberg, *Armament and Disarmament: South Africa's Nuclear Weapons Experience* (Pretoria: Network Publishers, 2003), Chapter 9.

21. Dr. Ian Phillips, interview by Stephen Burgess, Pretoria, June 13, 2000.

22. David Steward, interview by Stephen Burgess, Cape Town, June 26, 2000.

23. Dr. Niels Knobel, interview by Stephen Burgess, Pretoria, June 15, 2000.

24. Office of the Secretary of Defense and Defense Intelligence Agency officials, interviews in the Pentagon and State Department by the authors, Washington, D.C., May 22–25, 2000. Confirmed by interviews by the authors in South Africa, June–July 2000.

25. South African Department of Defence, *Defence in a Democracy.*

26. Laurie Nathan, "The 1996 Defence White Paper: An Agenda for State Demilitarization?" in *From Defence to Development: Redirecting Military Resources in South Africa,* ed. Jacklyn Cock and Penny Mckenzie (Cape Town: David Philip, 1998), 41–57.

27. South African Department of Defence, *Defence in a Democracy.*

28. The chair of the Non-Proliferation Council is acting director general of foreign affairs. Other members of the council represent relevant cabinet departments or serve as representatives of specific industrial sectors. Two representatives are nominated by the Department of Foreign Affairs, two by the Department of Defense, one by the Department of Trade and Industry, one by the Atomic Energy Council, and one by the Ministry of Minerals and Energy. Three appointees represent the chemical, biological, and aeronautical industries. For a further discussion of the Non-Proliferation Council, see Helen E. Purkitt with scientific support by Dr. Virgen R. Wells, "What's Over the Biotechnological Horizon? Biological R&D Trends in South Africa and Implications for Future Efforts for Monitoring Future Dual Use Biotechnology Trends in the Developing World," report prepared for the Defense Threat Reduction Agency and the U.S. Naval Academy, Annapolis, Md., December 2003.

29. David Albright, "South Africa: The ANC and the Atom Bomb," *Bulletin of the Atomic Scientists* 49 (April 1993): 32. In an interview in July 1994 conducted with Helen Purkitt, Kader Asmal, then the head of the Nuclear Non-Proliferation Council, started the meeting by underscoring the commitment of the South African government to maintaining and, if possible, strengthening the provisions of the Nuclear Non-Proliferation Treaty.

30. U.S. government official, interview by Stephen Burgess, Washington, D.C., May 25, 2000.

31. South African Department of Foreign Affairs, "The African Nuclear-Weapon-Free Zone Treaty (the Treaty of Pelindaba)," available online at www.nti.org/db/china/engdocs/afrinwfz.htm. For a summary of the treaty, see http://www.nti.org/db/china/pelindab.htm.

32. Ibid.

33. Ibid. For a recent analysis of why African states are taking so long to ratify the Pelindaba Treaty and some of the benefits associated with joining the treaty, see Sola Ogunbanwo, "Accelerate the Ratification of the Pelindaba Treaty," *The Nonproliferation Review* (Spring 2003): 132–136.

34. Captain Jeff Rosen, U.S. Navy, interview by Helen Purkitt, Annapolis, Md., May 1995. Captain Rosen was one of several U.S. officials who studied the legal implications of the treaty for the U.S. military.

35. Human Rights Watch, *South Africa: A Question of Principle: Arms Trade and Human Rights* 12, no. 5A (October 2000), available online at http://www. hrw.org/reports/2000/safrica. South African arms industries employed as many as 160,000 workers in the 1980s.

36. Peter Batchelor and Susan Willet, *Disarmament and Defense Industrial Adjustment in South Africa* (Oxford: Oxford University Press, 1998), 148.

37. South African Department of Defence, *Defence in a Democracy.*

38. Human Rights Watch, *South Africa.*

39. Batchelor, *Disarmament and Defense Industrial Adjustment in South Africa,* 148–149.

40. Terry Crawford-Browne, Economists Allied for Arms Reduction, interview by Stephen Burgess, Cape Town, June 26, 2000. No evidence to support these accusations was ever made public.

41. Human Rights Watch, *South Africa.*

42. Batchelor, *Disarmament and Defense Industrial Adjustment in South Africa,* 148–149.

43. "South African Arms Trade: Defying the Arms Dealers," One World News Service, August 11, 1997, available online at http://www.oneworld.org/index_oc/ news/southafrica080897.html.

44. Human Rights Watch, *South Africa.*

45. "South Africa: An Irresponsible Arms Trader?" *Global Dialogue* 4, no. 2 (August 1999), available online at http://www.igd.org.za/pub/g-dialogue/Special_feature/trader.html.

46. Human Rights Watch, *South Africa.*

47. Former and current employees of the South African Office of the Secretary of Defence, interviews by Helen Purkitt, South Africa, June and July 2002.

48. Republic of South Africa, "Conventional Arms Control Bill," available online at http://www.info.gov.za/gazette/bills/2000/b50-00.pdf.

49. Terry Crawford-Browne, Economists Allied for Arms Reduction, interview by Stephen Burgess, Cape Town, June 26, 2000.

50. Ibid.

51. "Arms Deal Controversy Continues," *Africa Analysis,* May 24, 2002. In April 2002, the highest court in South Africa ordered President Mbeki's Cabinet to stop refusing to provide nevirapine to pregnant HIV-infected women. The drug prevents babies from contracting AIDS. The Mbeki government contended that the clinically proven drug was toxic and ineffective and appealed the ruling. In 2003, the Mbeki government changed its policy and agreed to initiate a program to provide generic antiviral drugs to pregnant HIV-infected women. Initially, lack of adequate funding delayed the program.

52. John Fraser, "SA Needs Good Military Force," *Business Day,* April 9, 2002.

53. South Africa has traditionally been a world leader in developing new artillery and propellants. It remains one of the premier suppliers of conventional ammunition and explosives because of certain unique properties developed during the sanctions era. Jim Stallard, General Dynamics, interviews by Helen Purkitt, Washington, D.C., January–March 2002. In recent years, South African defense corporations have been successful in identifying niche markets, developing components, and entering into co-production arrangements with American and European defense corporations.

54. "Tutu Gets 99th Degree Then Slams SA Government in Pretoria," *Mail & Guardian* (Johannesburg), September 6, 2002.

55. NTI, "Illicit Nuclear Trafficking in the NIS," available online at http://www. nit.org/e–research/e3_8a.html; Graham Allison and Andrei Kokoshin, "The New Containment: An Alliance against Nuclear Terrorism," *The National Interest,* Fall 2002, 35–43.

56. Based on summary located in NTI, "Illicit Nuclear Trafficking in the NIS." According to this summary prepared in 2002, there were 345 research reactors in fifty-eight states that together contained twenty metric tons of highly enriched uranium. Many individual locations had enough highly enriched uranium to produce a nuclear bomb.

57. Vernon Loeb, "Terrorism Trail Pulls Veil from Hard Cell," *Washington Post,* May 24, 2001, A16.

58. The quote is taken from a U.S. State Department report on terrorism published in 2002 and summarized in a South African newspaper account. See Adam Tanner, "Al-Qaeda Presence in SA—Expert," *Die Burger* (Cape Town), November 28, 2002.

59. Pierre Steyn, "Concern about al-Qaeda in SA," *Die Burger* (Cape Town), October 12, 2002.

60. Ibid.

61. This account of the arrest of the Vaids is taken from ibid. Some of the recent concerns about al-Qaeda's use of South Africa to move diamonds and money are listed in the U.S. State Department's 2002 terrorism report that Steyn discusses. Since 1994, South African businesses have expanded throughout Africa and are now the single largest source of foreign investment in many African states. Much like other large corporations throughout the developed world, South African multinationals are now consolidating and expanding their investments. One recent merger that may be relevant to future war-on-terrorism activities involves South African–based Anglo Gold and Ghana's Ashanti Goldfields. In 2003, the two companies announced their intention to create the world's largest gold producer with twenty-six mines on four continents. Ashanti has been burdened by high operating costs and had experienced problems raising cash to pay short-term debt. The company recently received the go-ahead from the Ghanaian government. This new corporation, much like de Beers in the diamond sector, promises to play an important role in future efforts to track gold flows. Based on a report in the *Mail & Guardian* (Johannesburg), March 25, 2003.

62. Two youth leaders of People Against Drugs and Violence (PADAV), interview by Helen Purkitt, Port Elizabeth, July 2000.

63. According to information contained in "Letter from South Africa," *Africa Defence Journal* 3 (2002), Harare, Zimbabwe.

64. A South African investigative journalist described to Helen Purkitt during July 2003 the threats of another group of weapons scientists. However, to date, the report of these alleged threats has not appeared in the press.

65. Dr. Vernon Joynt, Mechem and the Council for Scientific and Industrial Research, Pretoria, interview by Stephen Burgess, Pretoria, June 14, 2000.

66. According to a report by an independent military weapons specialist provided to Helen Purkitt during an interview conducted in 2002.

67. Former weapons researcher, interview by Helen Purkitt, Pretoria, July 2002.

68. Ibid. The South African weapons designers also developed 23mm military aircraft cannons that could be shot through minefields. The SADF used these weapons in attacks against SWAPO.

69. Former South African military intelligence informant, interview by Helen Purkitt, Eastern Cape Province, July 2003.

70. Most Afrikaners and English-speaking people who were opposed to a majority-rule government in South Africa emigrated or withdrew from politics in the mid-1990s. Although the Conservative Party was the official "white" opposition in the House of Assembly and received one in three white votes in the 1989 election, the party disappeared quickly from the political scene and was reorganized and renamed the New National Party. The party sought to represent the interests of both whites and Coloureds. New National Party leader Marthinus van Schalkwyk, who is the Western Cape premier, took his party into a pact with the ANC at the end of 2001. The two parties governed the Western Cape together during 2002. While more-liberal whites joined the Democratic Party, the traditional English-speaking opposition party, the electoral strength of the Democratic Party has also declined dramatically in recent years as the ANC continues to consolidate power as the dominant political party in the country, especially since entering into an agreement with the New National Party in 2002 to cooperate during elections. See Martin Schonteich, "The Power to Disrupt," *Mail & Guardian* (Johannesburg), September 19, 2003.

71. This account is based on an interview conducted with a South African military intelligence undercover agent by Helen Purkitt in July 2003 and on press accounts. See especially "Two Groups of Rightwingers Are Refused Bail," South African Press Association, April 19, 2002; "Amazing Coup Plot Unfolds in SA Court," *Cape Argus,* April 18, 2002; "Safrica: Two Jailed Right-Wingers Deny Knowledge of Alleged Jailbreak Plot," *BBC Worldwide Monitoring,* April 9, 2002; "South Africa: Seven Right-Wingers Facing Charges of 'Treason, Terrorism,'" Financial Times/BBC Monitoring Service, April 8, 2002; and "Three Whites Accused of Plotting to Topple S. Africa's Mbeki," Agence France-Presse, April 8, 2002.

72. Three of the accused individuals were also implicated in a plot to topple the government and help some high-profile prisoners escape, including Vlakplaas commander Eugene de Kock, Clive Derby-Lewis, Janusz Walus, and former Pretoria Boer Commando leader Willem Ratte. Mariette Le Roux, "'PW Advised Right-Wingers," *The Herald* (Port Elizabeth), August 22, 2002.

73. Quote taken from ibid.

74. Truth and Reconciliation Commission investigators, interview by Helen Purkitt, Cape Town, July 20, 2000. See also the account of events presented by Windy Orr in *From Biko to Basson* (Saxonwold, South Africa: Contra Press, 2000).

75. Erika de Beer, "State 'Undecided' on Basson Retrial," *The Herald* (Port Elizabeth), November 5, 2003, 7.

76. This prediction was made to Stephen Burgess by nearly all of the former senior military officers he interviewed during June 2000. Several members of the former government offered similar predictions to Helen Purkitt during July 2000.

77. For a comprehensive list of many of these unanswered questions stemming from Project Coast, see Marléne Burger and Chandré Gould, *Secrets and Lies: Wouter Basson and South Africa's Chemical and Biological Warfare Programme* (Cape Town: Zebra, 2002).

78. For a published account of the trial of Marike de Klerk's murder, see "Dancing Teacher Fingered in Marike Murder Trial," South Africa Press Association, September 10, 2002. Tai Minaar, who allegedly had worked in the past with both U.S. and South African military intelligence, was recruited to help Dr. Goosen and his associates in their efforts to approach the Americans with a proposed deal in 2002. When the proposed deal stalled, he allegedly tried to sell the exotic materials to other parties. In the midst of these dealings, he died suddenly in a death that was ruled a heart attack. Immediately before his death he was vomiting, and

his corpse swelled rapidly after his death. These symptoms led many to believe that he may have been poisoned. See Joby Warrick and John Mintz, "Lethal Legacy: Bioweapons for Sale; U.S. Declined South African Scientist's Offer on Man-Made Pathogens," *Washington Post,* April 20, 2003; and Joby Warrick, "Biotoxins Fall into Private Hands; Global Risk Seen in S. African Poisons," *Washington Post,* April 21, 2001.

79. Mangold and Goldberg, *Plague Wars.* Similar accounts were conveyed to Helen Purkitt in phone interviews conducted with a former FBI informant and a South African who worked for the former government and who requested anonymity in 2003 because he is still afraid for his life if certain people find out he has been talking. Additional details about interactions among white supremacists living in the United States, Europe, and South Africa since the 1970s is found in Byron's *Elimination Theory.*

80. Mangold and Goldberg, *Plague Wars.* Several points in this section about the alternative story of how South Africa closed down her weapons of mass destruction were based on Helen Purkitt and Stephen Burgess, "Changing Course and Responding to Negative Feedback: A Case of Sequential Decision-Making in South Africa, 1989–94," paper presented at the symposium Responding to Negative Feedback in Foreign Policy Decision-Making, Center for Presidential Studies, Bush School of Government and Public Service, College Station, Texas, May 18–20, 2001.

81. Condoleezza Rice, "Why We Know Iraq Is Lying," *New York Times,* January 23, 2003, op-ed page.

NINE. EMERGING ISSUES
AND RESIDUAL CONCERNS

1. Gavin Cameron, "Nuclear Terrorism Reconsidered," *Current History* (April 2000): 154–157.

2. Henry Sokolski, "Ending South Africa's Rocket Program: A Nonproliferation Success," unpublished paper, Washington, D.C.: Nonproliferation Policy Education Center, August 27, 1996, available online at http://www.npec-web.org/essay/southafrica.htm.

3. Helen E. Purkitt and Stephen F. Burgess, "Correspondence: South Africa's Nuclear Decision," *International Security* 27, no. 1 (Summer 2002): 186–194.

4. Scott D. Sagan, "Why Do States Build Nuclear Weapons? Three Models in Search of a Bomb," *International Security* 21, no. 3 (Winter 1996/1997): 69–71; Waldo Stumpf, "South Africa's Nuclear Weapons Program: From Deterrence to Dismantlement," *Arms Control Today* 25, no. 10 (December 1995/January 1996): 4–7. David E. Albright, "South Africa and the Affordable Bomb," *Bulletin of Atomic Scientists* (July/August 1994): 37–47.

5. Barton Gellman, "Al Qaeda Near Biological, Chemical Arms Production," *Washington Post,* March 23, 2003, A10.

6. For further discussions of recent biochemical developments that are likely to be translated into new weapons of mass destruction in the future, see Mark Wheelis, "Biotechnology and Biochemical Weapons," *Non-Proliferation Review* 9, no. 1 (Spring 2002): 48–53; and Helen E. Purkitt with scientific support by Dr. Virgen R. Wells, "What's Over the Biotechnological Horizon? Biological R&D Trends in South Africa and Implications for Future Efforts for Monitoring Future Dual Use Biotechnology Trends in the Developing World," report prepared for the Defense Threat Reduction Agency and the U.S. Naval Academy, Annapolis, Md., December 2003.

APPENDIX

1. Hannes Steyn, Richardt van der Walt, and Jan van Loggerenberg, *Armament and Disarmament: South Africa's Nuclear Weapons Experience* (Pretoria: Network Publishers, 2003), xvii.

2. Retired South African general, interview by Stephen Burgess, Pretoria, July 2000.

3. The Nunn-Lugar program is a cooperative threat reduction program that allocates money from the U.S. defense budget every year to help the states of the former Soviet Union eliminate and safeguard nuclear weapons and other weapons of mass destruction. Since the early 1990s, it has funded many large engineering projects throughout Russia, as well as in Kazakhstan, Ukraine, Belarus, and elsewhere. These projects have helped safeguard weapons storage sites; given new research opportunities to scientists who used to work on chemical, biological, or nuclear weapons; dug up missile silos; chopped up missiles and old bombers; and helped remove fissile material.

Bibliography

PRIMARY SOURCES

DOCUMENTS AND PAPERS

Analysis of the TRC Report by the SADF Contact Bureau. Pretoria, South Africa, May 28, 1993.

Badenhorst, Nick. "South Africa's Nuclear Program." Unpublished manuscript, May 2000.

Barletta, Michael, Christina Ellington, and Zondi Masiza. "South Africa's Nuclear History: An Annotated Chronology, 1944–1999." Unpublished manuscript, Center for Nonproliferation Studies, Monterey Institute of International Studies, Monterey, Calif., March 1999.

Burgess, Stephen F., and Helen E. Purkitt. "The Rollback of the South African Chemical and Biological Warfare Program." Maxwell Air Force Base, Alabama: USAF Counterproliferation Center, 2001.

Central Intelligence Agency, Directorate of Intelligence. New Information on South Africa's Nuclear Program and South African-Nuclear and Military Cooperation. March 1983, approved for release May 7, 1996.

Christie, Renfrew. "South Africa's Nuclear History." Paper presented at Nuclear History Program Fourth International Conference, Nice, France, June 23–27, 1993.

Davis, Lynn E. Testimony before the U.S. House of Representatives Committee on Appropriations, Foreign Operations Appropriations, Export Financing and Related Programs FY96, Federal Document Clearing House, Congressional Testimony, April 4, 1995.

De Klerk, F. W. Speech in Parliament, Republic of South Africa. Debates of Parliament (Hansard), 5th Session–9th Parliament (Cape Town, 1993), vol. 8, cols. 3576–3574.

de Waal, Tielman. Presentation to the Foreign Correspondent's Association, Pretoria, South Africa, July 13, 1994.

Gould, C., and M. Burger. *Weekly Trial Reports of the South African Chemical and Biological Warfare Programme.* Centre for Conflict Resolution, University of Cape Town. Available online at http://ccrweb.ccr.uct.ac.za/cbw/cbw_index.html.

Hymans, Jacques. "Taking the Plunge: Emotion and Identity in the Decision to Build Nuclear Weapons." Paper presented to the Annual Meeting of the American Political Science Association, Washington, D.C., September 2000.

Marais, Major General Dirk (Ret.). *The Military in a Political Arena: The South African Defence Force (SADF) and the Truth and Reconciliation Commission (TRC).* Pretoria, June 2000.

The Military in a Political Arena: The South African Defence Force (SADF) and the Truth and Reconciliation Commission (TRC), Pretoria, South Africa, June 2000.

Mills, G. "South Africa: The Total National Strategy and Region Policy During the Botha Years, 1978–1989." Doctoral dissertation, University of Lancaster, United Kingdom, 1990.

Purkitt, Helen E. "The Politics of Denuclearization: The Case of South Africa." Final report to the Institute for National Strategic Studies, U.S. Air Force Academy, November 9, 1994.

———. "The Politics of Denuclearization: The Case of South Africa." Paper presented at the Defense Nuclear Agency's Fourth Annual International Conference on Controlling Arms, Philadelphia, Pa., June 21, 1995.

Purkitt, Helen E., and Stephen Burgess. "Changing Course and Responding to Negative Feedback: A Case of Sequential Decision-Making in South Africa, 1989–94." Paper presented at the symposium Responding to Negative Feedback in Foreign Policy Decision-Making, Center for Presidential Studies, Bush School of Government and Public Service, College Station, Tex., May 18–20, 2001.

Purkitt, Helen E., with scientific support by Dr. Virgen R. Wells. "What's Over the Biotechnological Horizon? Biological R&D Trends in South Africa and Implications for Future Efforts for Monitoring Future Dual Use Biotechnology Trends in the Developing World." Report prepared for the Defense Threat Reduction Agency and the U.S. Naval Academy, Annapolis, Md., December 2003.

Roberts, Guy B. "Arms Control Without Arms Control: The Failure of the Biological Weapons Convention Protocol and a New Paradigm for Fighting the Threat of Biological Weapons." Institute for National Security Studies Occasional Paper 49, U.S. Air Force Academy, March 2003.

Sokolski, Henry. "Ending South Africa's Rocket Program: A Nonproliferation Success." Unpublished paper. Washington, D.C.: Nonproliferation Policy Education Center, August 27, 1996. Available online at http://www.npec-web.org/essay/southafrica.htm.

Sole, Donald B. "The South African Nuclear Case in the Light of Recent Revelations." Paper presented at the conference New Horizons in Arms Control and Verification. John G. Tower Center for Policy Studies, Southern Methodist University, Dallas, Tex., October 1993.

South Africa: A Question of Principle: Arms Trade and Human Rights. Human Rights Watch 12, no. 5A (October 2000). Available online at http://www.hrw.org/reports/2000/safrica.

South Africa. Department of Defence. *Defence in a Democracy: White Paper on National Defence.* Pretoria: Government Printer, 1996. Available online at http://www.gov.za/whitepaper/1996/defencwp.htm.

South Africa. Truth and Reconciliation Commission. *Hearings of the Truth and Reconciliation Commission.* Available online at www.doj.gov.za/trc.

The State v *Wouter Basson.* Vol. II: *Drugs, Murder, Conspiracy and Related Charges.* High Court of South Africa, n.d.

Stumpf, Waldo. "The Accession of a 'Threshold State' to the NPT: The South African Experience," presentation given at the Conference on Nuclear Non-Proliferation: The Challenge of a New Era, The Carnegie Endowment for International Peace, Washington, D.C., November 17–18, 1993.

———. "South Africa's Limited Nuclear Deterrent Programme and the Dismantling Thereof Prior to South Africa's Accession to the Nuclear Non-Proliferation Treaty." Address at the South African Embassy, Washington, D.C., July 23, 1993.

U.S. Department of State. "U.S. and South Africa Missile Nonproliferation Agreement." U.S. Department of State Fact Sheet, October 1994.

Wingeart, Paul H. "Nuclear Proliferation: Factors, Reasons, and Remedies." B.S. Honors Thesis, Department of Political Science, United States Naval Academy, 1995.

INTERVIEWS

Interviews by Helen Purkitt and Stephen Burgess

Ackermann, Anton. Chief prosecutor, Basson trial. Interview by Stephen Burgess. Pretoria, June 13, 2000.

Asmal, Dr. Kader and other members of the ANC Executive Committee. Interview by Helen Purkitt. Cape Town, July 1994.

Badenhorst, Nick. Independent defense analyst. Interview by Helen Purkitt. Port Elizabeth, July 1994 and 2000.

Bolick, Daniel C. Supervisory special agent on assignment in South Africa. Interview by Helen Purkitt, Pretoria, July 2000.

Botha, Roelof "Pik." Former South African foreign minister. Telephone interview by Helen Purkitt, Pretoria, July 13, 2000.

Boulden, Laurie. RPI Consulting Company. Interview by Stephen Burgess. Washington, D.C., May 21, 2000.

Brand, Robert. Reporter, *The Star* (Johannesburg). Interview by Helen Purkitt, Cape Town, July 2000. Brand covered the Project Coast hearings at the Truth and Reconciliation Commission.

Byron, Thomas. Former pilot and associate of Dr. Larry Ford. Telephone interviews by Helen Purkitt. October 2001 through November 2002.

Brummer, Stefaans. Reporter. Telephone interview by Stephen Burgess. July 4, 2000.

Burger, Marléne. Journalist, Centre for Conflict Resolution. Interview by Stephen Burgess. Pretoria, June 13, 2000.

———. Telephone interviews with Helen Purkitt. July 2002 and May 2003.

Buys, Professor Andre. Director of Institute for Technical Innovation, University of Pretoria. Telephone interview by Stephen Burgess. June 14, 2000.

Campher, Gabriel. Joint Committee on Defense, Parliamentary Monitoring Group. Interview by Helen Purkitt. Cape Town, July 17, 2000.

Carus, Dr. Seth. National Defense University, Interview by Stephen Burgess. Washington, D.C., May 26, 2000.

———. Interview by Helen Purkitt. Washington, D.C., June 2002.

Cawthra, Dr. Gavin. Center for Defense Management, University of the Witwatersrand. Interview by Helen Purkitt. Johannesburg, July 4, 2000.

Christie, Dr. Renfrew. Director of Research, University of Western Cape, Belleville. Interview by Stephen Burgess. Belleville, June 26, 2000.

———. Interviews by Helen Purkitt, Belleville, July 1994; Cape Town, July 16, 2002 and July 8, 2003.

Cilliers, Dr. Jakkie. Director, Institute of Security Studies. Interview by Stephen Burgess. Pretoria, June 12, 2000.

———. Interviews by Helen Purkitt, Halfway House, July 3, 1994; and Pretoria, July 4, 2000.

Cohen, Dr. Henry. Assistant secretary of state for Africa, 1989–1993 and Cohen and Woods International. Telephone interview by Stephen Burgess. May 15, 2000.

Cornwall, Dr. Richard. Institute of Security Studies, Interview by Helen Purkitt. Pretoria, July 3, 2000.

Courville, Dr. Cindy. Defense Intelligence Agency, Africa, Washington, D.C. Interview by Stephen Burgess. Washington, D.C., May 22, 2000.

Crawford-Browne, Terry. Economists Allied for Arms Reduction, Cape Town. Interview by Stephen Burgess. Cape Town, June 26, 2000.

Crocker, Dr. Chester. Former assistant secretary of state for Africa, 1981–1989, now at Institute for the Study of Diplomacy, Georgetown University. Telephone interview by Stephen Burgess. May 15, 2000.

De Beer, Hannelie. Former South African military intelligence officer, now at Institute of Security Strategic Studies. Interview by Helen Purkitt. Pretoria, July 3, 2000.

Ferguson, Colonel Mike. Defense Intelligence Agency. Interview by Stephen Burgess. Washington, D.C., May 23, 2000.

Fourie, Professor Deon. Military historian, University of Pretoria. Interview by Helen Purkitt. Pretoria, June 1994.

Geldenhuys, General Jannie (Ret.). Former SADF chief of staff. Interview by Stephen Burgess. Pretoria, June 13, 2000.

Goosen, Dr. Daan. Former Project Coast scientist. Interview by Helen Purkitt. Pretoria, June 24, 2003.

Goosen, Peter. Ministry of Foreign Affairs, Office of Non-Proliferation. Interview by Stephen Burgess. Pretoria, June 15, 2000.

Gould, Chandré. Researcher, Truth and Reconciliation Commission and Centre for Conflict Resolution. Interview by Stephen Burgess. Johannesburg, June 29, 2000.

Grissom, Adam, Don Hammond, and Chuck Ikins. Office of the Secretary of Defense, Africa. Interviews by Stephen Burgess. Washington, D.C., May 22 and August 31, 2000.

Heitman, Helmoed-Romer. Reporter and correspondent, *Jane's Defense Weekly* and expert on South African defense matters. Interview by Stephen Burgess. Cape Town, June 26, 2000.

———. Interviews by Helen Purkitt. Cape Town, July 1994; July 1997; July 17, 2000; June 30, 2002; and July 8, 2003.

Henningsen, Colonel Kim (Ret.). U.S. defense attaché in South Africa, 1993–1997, Pretoria. Interview by Helen Purkitt. Cape Town, June 1994.

———. E-mail correspondence with Stephen Burgess. May 2000.

Jager, Dr. Hans. Former director of research and development, Onderstepoort Veterinary Institute, now director of research and development, Avimune Pty Ltd. Interview by H. Purkitt. Durban, July 1, 2003.

Joubert, Brigadier Joep (Ret.). SADF Army Intelligence and Civil Cooperation Bureau. Interview by Stephen Burgess. Pretoria, June 23, 2000.

Joynt, Dr. Vernon. Mechem and the Council for Scientific Research. Interview by Stephen Burgess. Pretoria, June 14, 2000.

———. Interview by Helen Purkitt. Pretoria, July 2, 2002.

Knobel, Dr. Niels. Former surgeon general (1988–1995). Interview by Stephen Burgess. Pretoria, June 15, 2000.

———. Interview by Helen Purkitt. Pretoria, July 3, 2002.

Kudlinski, Mr. Andre. Acting director, Chemical and Allied Industries Division, Department of Science and Technology. Interview by Helen Purkitt. Pretoria, June 25, 2003.

Lyman, Princeton. Former ambassador to South Africa, 1992–1996, now at U.S. Institute of Peace, Washington, D.C. Interviews by Stephen Burgess. Washington, D.C., May 25, 2000 and August 31, 2000.

Machem, Major Walter. Army attaché, U.S. Embassy. Interview by H. Purkitt. Pretoria, June 2000.

Mahley, Ambassador Donald. U.S. State Department. Interviews by Stephen Burgess. Washington, D.C., May 25 and August 31, 2000.

Malan, General Magnus (Ret.). Army chief, South Africa, 1971–1976; SADF chief, 1976–1980; minister of defense, 1980–1991. Interview by Stephen Burgess. Pretoria. June 23, 2000.

Malan, Mark. Former SADF officer and senior researcher at the Institute for Strategic Studies, South Africa. Interview by Stephen Burgess. Pretoria, June 23, 2000.

———. Interview by Helen Purkitt. Pretoria, July 3, 2000.

Mangold, Tom. Senior author of *The Plague Wars*. Telephone interview by Helen Purkitt. June 2000.

Marais, General Dirk. Former SADF general and current head of SADF communications with SANDF. Interview by Helen Purkitt. Pretoria, July 13, 2000.

Marutle, Colonel Raymond, defense and military attaché, and other military and political officials at South African Embassy. Interview by Helen Purkitt. Washington, D.C., January 2003.

Maynier, David. Senior researcher, DP Parliamentarian. Interview by Helen Purkitt. Cape Town, July 2000.

McConnell, Colonel Bernd. Deputy assistant secretary of defense for Africa, Office of Secretary for Defense/African Affairs, the Pentagon. Interview by Stephen Burgess. Washington, D.C., August 30, 2000.

———. Interviews by Helen Purkitt, Annapolis, Md., 1995 and Washington, D.C., 2000.

Meiring, General Georg (Ret.). Former SADF chief of staff and SANDF chief of staff, 1993–1998. Interview by Stephen Burgess. Pretoria, July 3, 2000.

Mills, Dr. Greg. Director of South African Institute of International Affairs, University of the Witwatersrand. Interviews by Helen Purkitt. Johannesburg, July 1994 and July 1997.

Moorsman, Gaile. Parliamentary Monitoring Group. Interview by Helen Purkitt. Cape Town, July 2000.

Mortimer, Major General Deon (Ret.). Interview by Stephen Burgess. Pretoria, June 23, 2000.

Muller, Professor Frank Otto. Managing director, Scientific & Regulatory Affairs, QdotPharma. Interview by H. Purkitt. George, South Africa, July 3, 2003.

Orbann, Carl. Woods and Cohen Company. Interview by Stephen Burgess. Washington, D.C., May 23, 2000.

Ottaway, Dr. Marina. Carnegie Endowment for International Peace. Interview by Stephen Burgess. Washington, D.C., May 23, 2000.

Parrachini, Dr. John. Monterey Institute. Interview by Stephen Burgess. Washington, D.C., May 23, 2000.

Pauw, Jacques. Producer, SABC TV. Interview by Stephen Burgess. Johannesburg, June 29, 2000.

Phillips, Dr. Ian. INFOTECH and ANC defense expert, Pretoria. Interview by Stephen Burgess. Pretoria, June 13, 2000.

Polleciett, Laura. Executive director, Freedom of Expression Institute. Interview by Helen Purkitt. Johannesburg, July 7, 2000.

Potgieter, De Wet. Journalist, Pretoria. Interview by Stephen Burgess. Pretoria, June 13, 2000.

Powell, Ivor. Expert on arms sales. Telephone interview by Stephen Burgess. July 4, 2000.

Pretorius, Dr. Torie. Prosecutor in Basson case. Interview by Stephen Burgess. Pretoria, June 20, 2000.

———. Interviews by Helen Purkitt. Pretoria, July 4, 2000 and July 5, 2002.

Pringle, Robert. U.S. deputy ambassador to South Africa, 1996–1999. Interview by Helen Purkitt. Washington, D.C., June 2000.

Prior, Patti. Advocate, Legal Department, Truth and Reconciliation Committee. Interview by Helen Purkitt. Cape Town, July 2000.

Ray, Victor. Police detective on Larry Ford case, Irvine, California. Oral and telephone interviews by Helen E. Purkitt. September 2001 through December 2002.

Redman, Colonel (Ret.). South African military officer. Interview by Helen Purkitt. Windhoek, Namibia, July 1997.

Rosen, Captain Jeff. U.S. Navy. Interview by Helen Purkitt, Annapolis, Md., May, 1995.

Ryder, Colonel Dennis. Defense attaché, Pretoria. Interview by Helen Purkitt. Pretoria, June, 2000.

Sass, General Bill (Ret.). SADF, former member of State Security Council and Chief of Operations. Interviews by Helen Purkitt. Halfway House, South Africa, July 5, 1994, and Pretoria, June 24, 2000.

———. Telephone interview by Stephen Burgess. June 12, 2000.

Schalwyk, Brigadier General Phillip (Ret.). Democratic Party Member of Parliament and senior military adviser to the Democratic Party. Interview by Helen Purkitt. Pretoria, July 12, 2000.

Scharf, Dr. G. Former Director of Medical Hospital One (Pretoria) and former SADF Special Forces M.D. Interview by Helen Purkitt. Pretoria, July 6, 2000.

Schoub, Dr. Barry D. Executive director, National Institute for Communicable Diseases. Interview by Helen Purkitt. Johannesburg, June 24, 2003.

Seegers, Professor Annette. Department of Political Science, Cape Town University. Interview by Helen Purkitt. Cape Town, June 4, 2000.

Smith, Dr. Deon. Denel and former ARMSCOR manager. Interview by Helen Purkitt. July 1994.

Smith, Lieutenant Colonel Johann (Ret.). Former SADF liaison with UNITA in 1980s, now advisor to South African government on Angola and Democratic Republic of the Congo. Interview by Stephen Burgess. Pretoria, June 30, 2000.

Snyder, Charles. U.S. Department of State. Interview by Stephen Burgess. Washington, D.C., May 24, 2000.

Spivak, Matthew A. Second political secretary, U.S. Embassy, Pretoria. Interview by Helen Purkitt. Pretoria, June 2000.

Stallard, Jim. Vice president, General Dynamics. Interviews by Helen Purkitt. Washington, D.C., January–March 2002.

Steenkamp, Willem. Former SADF officer and military journalist, Cape Town. Interviews by Helen Purkitt. Cape Town, July 1994 and July 21, 2000.

Steward, David. Executive director, De Klerk Foundation and President de Klerk's chief of staff, 1989–1994. Interview by Stephen Burgess. Cape Town, June 26, 2000.

———. Interview by Helen Purkitt. Cape Town, July 17, 2000.

Steyn, Lieutenant General Pierre (Ret.). Former South African Air Force officer who headed the 1992 Steyn Commission investigation. Interview by Stephen Burgess. July 3, 2000.

————. Interview by Helen Purkitt, Pretoria, July 1994 and July 1997, and Cape Town, July 2000.

Stiff, Peter. Writer, Pretoria. Telephone interview by Stephen Burgess. June 28, 2000.

————. Telephone interview by Helen Purkitt. July 12, 2000.

Stumpf, Waldo. Interview by Helen Purkitt. Pelindaba, July 1994.

Sullivan, Linda, and Elizabeth Manak. CIA. Interview by Stephen Burgess. Langley, Va., August 31, 2000.

Thirion, General Chris (Ret.). Former chief of SADF Military Intelligence, 1987–1992. Interview by Stephen Burgess. Pretoria, June 13, 2000.

Thom, William. Defense Intelligence Agency and director, Africa Program. Interview by Stephen Burgess. Washington, D.C., May 22, 2000.

————. Interview by Helen Purkitt. May 2000.

Thomashausen, Prof. Andre. Law professor. Interview by Stephen Burgess. Johannesburg. June 19, 2000.

Thornycroft, Peta. Journalist. Telephone interview by Stephen Burgess. June 12, 2000.

Turton, Anthony R. Head, African Water Issues Research Unit, University of Pretoria and former SADF Special Forces Officer. Interview by Helen Purkitt. Pretoria. July 2000.

Venter, Zelda. Reporter, *Pretoria News*. Interview by Stephen Burgess. Pretoria. June 21, 2000.

Villa-Vicencia, Dr. Charles. Former senior investigator for the Truth and Reconciliation Commission and current head, Institute for Justice and Reconciliation. Interview by Helen Purkitt. Cape Town. July 2000.

Whelan, Theresa. Africa analyst, Office of the Secretary of Defense, Department of Defense. Interviews by Stephen Burgess. Washington, D.C. May 22 and August 31, 2000.

————. Interviews by Helen Purkitt. Midrand, 1995 and Pretoria, 2000.

Williams, Rocky. Institute for Strategic Studies and former ANC intelligence officer, 1979–1994. Interviews by Stephen Burgess. Pretoria, South Africa, June 15 and 30, 2002.

————. Interviews by Helen Purkitt. July 1994 and July 5, 2003.

Woods, James. Deputy Assistant secretary of defense for Africa, 1992–1994 and Cohen and Woods, International. Telephone interview by Stephen Burgess, May 15, 2000.

Z, Mr. Former intelligence officer for *Afrikaner Weerstandsbeweging*. Interview by Helen Purkitt. Port Elizabeth. July 2000.

SECONDARY SOURCES

BOOKS

Adams, James. *The Unnatural Alliance: Israel and South Africa*. New York: Quartet Books, 1984.

African National Congress. *The Reconstruction and Development Programme: A Policy Framework*. Johannesburg, South Africa: Umanyano Publications, 1994.

Albright, David. *South Africa's Secret Nuclear Weapons.* Washington, D.C.: Institute for Science and International Security Report, May 1994.

Albright, David, Frans Berkhout, and William Walker. *Plutonium and Highly Enriched Uranium 1996: World Inventories, Capabilities and Policies.* New York: Oxford University Press for Stockholm International Peace Research Institute, 1996.

Albright, David, and Kevin O'Neill, eds. *The Challenges of Fissile Material Control.* Washington, D.C.: Institute for Science and International Security, 1999. Available online at http://www.isis-online.org/publications/fmct/book/index.html.

Alden, Chris. *Apartheid's Last Stand: The Rise and Fall of the South African Security State.* New York: St. Martin's Press, 1996.

Alibek, Ken, with Stephen Handelman. *Biohazard.* New York: Random House. 1999.

Allison, Graham, and Philip Seiko. *Essence of Decision: Explaining the Cuban Missile Crisis.* 2nd ed. New York: Longman. 1999.

Baker, P. *The United States and South Africa: The Reagan Years.* New York: Ford Foundation and Foreign Policy Association, 1989.

Barkawi, Tarak, and Mark Laffey, eds. *Democracy, Liberalism, and War: Rethinking the Democratic Peace Debate.* Boulder, Colo.: Lynne Rienner Publishers, 2001.

Batchelor, Peter, and Susan Willet. *Disarmament and Defense Industrial Adjustment in South Africa.* Oxford: Oxford University Press, 1998.

Beit-Hallahmi, Benjamin. *The Israeli Connection: Who Israel Arms and Why.* New York: Phantom Books 1987.

Bissell, Richard E. *South Africa and the United States: The Erosion of an Influence Relationship.* New York: Praeger, 1982.

Borstelmann, T. *Apartheid's Reluctant Uncle: The United States and South Africa in the Early Cold War.* New York: Oxford University Press, 1993.

Bueno de Mesquita, Bruce. *Principles of International Politics: People's Power, Preferences, and Perceptions.* Washington, D.C.: CQ Press, 2000.

Burger, Marléne, and Chandré Gould. *Secrets and Lies: Wouter Basson and South Africa's Chemical and Biological Warfare Programme.* Cape Town, South Africa: Zebra, 2002.

Burrows, William E., and Robert Windrem. *Critical Mass: The Dangerous Race for Superweapons in a Fragmenting World.* New York: Simon and Schuster, 1994.

Byron, T. J. *Elimination Theory.* Frederick, Md.: PublishAmerica, 2004.

Carus, W. Seth. *Bioterrorism and Biocrimes: The Illicit Use of Biological Agents in the 20th Century.* 3rd revision. Washington, D.C.: Center for Counterproliferation Research, National Defense University, 1998.

———. *Working Paper Bioterrorism and Biocrimes: The Illicit Use of Biological Agents in the 20th Century.* 3rd revision. Washington, D.C.: Center for Counterproliferation Research, National Defense University, 1998.

Cervenka, Zdenek, and Barbara Rogers. *The Nuclear Axis: Secret Collaboration between West Germany and South Africa.* London: Julian Friedmann, 1978.

Cock, Jacklyn, and Penny Mckenzie. *From Defence to Development: Redirecting Military Resources in South Africa.* Cape Town, South Africa: David Philip, 1998.

Cohen, Avner. *Israel and the Bomb.* New York: Colombia University Press, 1999.

Crawford, Neta C., and Audie Klotz. *How Sanctions Work: Lessons from South Africa.* New York: St. Martin's, 1999.

Crocker, Chester A. *High Noon in Southern Africa: Making Peace in a Rough Neighborhood.* New York: W.W. Norton, 1992.

Croddy, Eric. *Chemical and Biological Warfare: An Annotated Bibliography.* Lanham, Md.: Scarecrow Press, 1997.

Daly, Ron R., with Peter Stiff. *Selous Scouts Top Secret War.* Alberton, South Africa: Galago, 1983.

de Klerk, F. W. *The Last Trek: A New Beginning.* London: Macmillan, 1998.

———. *F. W. de Klerk: The Autobiography.* New York: St. Martin's Press, 1999.

de Klerk, Willem. *F. W. de Klerk: The Man in His Time.* Johannesburg: Jonathan Ball Publishers, 1991.

de St. Jorre, J. *A House Divided: South Africa's Uncertain Future.* New York: Carnegie Endowment for International Peace, 1977.

Ellert, Henrik. *The Rhodesian Front War: Counter-Insurgency and Guerrilla War in Rhodesia, 1962–1980.* Gweru, Zimbabwe: Mambo Press, 1989.

Geissler, Erhard, and John Ellis van Courtland Moon, eds. *Biological and Toxin Weapons: Research, Development and Use from the Middle Ages to 1945.* New York: Oxford University Press, 1999.

Geldenhuys, Deon. *The Diplomacy of Isolation: South African Foreign Policy Making.* New York St. Martin's Press 1984.

———. *A General's Story: From an Era of War and Peace.* Johannesburg: Jonathan Ball Publishers, 1995.

———. *Isolated States: A Comparative Analysis.* Johannesburg, South Africa: Jonathan Ball Publishers, 1990.

Gowa, Joanne S. *Ballots and Bullets: The Elusive Democratic Peace.* Princeton, N.J.: Princeton University Press, 1999.

Grundy, Kenneth. *The Militarization of South African Politics.* London, UK: Tauris, 1986.

Hamann, Hilton. *Days of the Generals.* Cape Town, South Africa: Zebra, 2001.

Harker, John, ed. *Collaborative Security in South Africa.* Ottawa: Canadian Council for International Peace and Security, 1996.

Hayes, Geoffrey. *Middle Powers in the New World Order.* Toronto: Canadian Institute of International Affairs, 1994.

Heitman, Helmoed-Romer. *South Africa War Machine.* Central News Agency, 1985.

———. *War in Angola: The Final South African Phase.* Gibraltar: Ashanti Publishing, 1990.

Hermann, C. F., C. W. Kelley, Jr., and James N. Rosenau. *New Directions in the Study of Foreign Policy.* Boston: Allen & Unwin, 1987.

Hersh, Seymour M. *The Samson Option.* New York: Random House, 1991.

Hook, Glenn D. *Militarization and Demilitarization in Contemporary Japan.* London: Routledge, 1996.

Hough, M., and A. du Plessis, eds. *Selected Official Strategic and Security Perceptions.* University of Pretoria, Institute for Strategic Studies, November 2000.

Hounam, Peter, and Steve McQuillen. *The Mini-Nuke Conspiracy: Mandela's Nuclear Nightmare.* London: Faber & Faber, 1995.

International Atomic Energy Agency. *The Agency's Verification Activities in South Africa.* Vienna, Austria: International Atomic Energy Agency, September 1993.

———. *International Nuclear Safeguards 1994: Vision for the Future.* 2 vols. Vienna, Austria: International Atomic Energy Agency, 1995.

Jaster, Robert S. *The Defence of White Power: South African Foreign Policy Under Pressure*. London: Macmillan, 1988.

———. *South Africa's Narrowing Security Options*. Adelphi Paper no. 159. London: International Institute for Strategic Studies, 1980.

Johnson, Dana J., Scott Pace, and C. Bryan Gabbard. *Space: Emerging Options for National Power*. Santa Monica, Calif.: RAND 1998.

Jones, Rodney W., and Mark G. McDonough, with Toby F. Dalton and Gregory D. Koblentz. *Tracking Nuclear Proliferation: A Guide in Maps and Charts, 1998*. Washington, D.C.: The Brookings Institution Press, 1998.

Joseph, Benjamin M. *Besieged Bedfellows: Israel and the Land of Apartheid*. New York: Greenwood Press, 1998.

Lodge, Tom. *Black Politics in South Africa Since 1945*. London: Longman, 1983.

Lyman, Princeton N. *Partner to History: The U.S. Role in South Africa's Transition to Democracy*. Washington, D.C.: U.S. Institute of Peace Press, 2002.

Mangold, Tom, and Jeff Goldberg. *Plague Wars: A True Story of Biological Warfare*. New York: St. Martin's Press, 1999.

Marcum, John. *The Angolan Revolution*. Vol. II, *Exile Politics and Guerrilla Warfare (1962–1976)*. Cambridge, Mass.: MIT Press, 1978.

Mauroni, Albert J. *America's Struggle with Chemical-Biological Warfare*. Westport, Conn.: Praeger, 2000.

Miller, Stephen Engelberg, and William Broad. *GERMS: Biological Weapons and America's Secret War*. New York: Simon and Schuster, 2001.

Mills, Greg, and Martin Edmonds. *South Africa's Defence Industry: A Template for Middle Powers?* Canberra, Australia: Strategic and Defence Studies Centre, Australian National University, 2001.

Mutimer, David. *The Weapons State: Proliferation and the Framing of Security*. Boulder, Colo.: Lynne Rienner Publishers, 2000.

Newby-Fraser, A. R. *Chain Reaction*. Pretoria: Pretoria Atomic Energy Board, 1979.

Nolan, Janne E. *An Elusive Consensus: Nuclear Weapons and American Security after the Cold War*. Washington, D.C.: Brookings Institution, 1999.

O'Meara, Dan. *Forty Lost Years: The Apartheid State and the Politics of the National Party, 1948–1994*. Athens: Ohio State Press, 1996.

Orr, Wendy. *From Biko to Basson*. Saxonwold, South Africa: Contra Press, 2000.

Ottaway, Marina. *South Africa: The Struggle for a New Order*. Washington, D.C.: Brookings Institution, 1993.

Paul, T. V. *Power versus Prudence: Why Nations Forgo Nuclear Weapons*. Montreal: McGill-Queen's University Press, 2000.

Pauw, Jacques. *Into the Heart of Darkness*. Johannesburg: Jonathan Ball, 1997.

Regis, Edward. *The Biology of Doom: The History of American's Secret's Germ Warfare Project*. New York: Henry Holt, 1999.

Reid, Ron, as told to Peter Stiff. *Selous Scouts: Top Secret War*. Alberton, South Africa: Galago, 1983.

Reiss, Mitchell. *Bridled Ambition: Why Countries Constrain Their Nuclear Capabilities*. Washington, D.C.: Woodrow Wilson Center Press, 1995.

Retief, J. V. *Seismiese Beskadiging Tydens Die Kostuktiewe Gebruik Van Kernplofstowwe Raad Op Atoomkrag [Seismic Damage During the Constructive Use of Nuclear Explosives, Atomic Energy Board]*. Pelindaba, Pretoria, 1972.

Rhoodie, Eschel. *The Real Information Scandal*. Pretoria, South Africa: Orbis, 1983.

Rosati, J. *The Carter Administration's Quest for Global Community: Beliefs and Their Impact on Behavior.* Columbia: University of South Carolina Press, 1987.

Rosenau, James N. *The Scientific Study of Foreign Policy.* New York: The Free Press, 1980.

Sagan, Scott D., and Kenneth N. Waltz. *The Spread of Nuclear Weapons: A Debate.* New York: Norton, 1995.

Scheff, Thomas J. *Bloody Revenge: Emotions, Nationalism, and War.* Boulder, Colo.: Westview Press, 1994.

Seegers, Annette. *The Military in the Making of Modern South Africa.* New York: St. Martin's Press, 1996.

Serfontein. J. H. P. *Brotherhood of Power: An Exposé of the Secret Afrikaner Broederbond.* Bloomington: Indiana University Press, 1978.

Singer, Eric, and Valerie Hudson, eds. *Political Psychology and Foreign Policy.* Boulder, Colo.: Westview Press, 1992.

Sisk, Tim D. *Democratization in South Africa: The Elusive Social Contract.* Princeton, N.J.: Princeton University, 1995.

Sokolski, Henry D. *Best of Intensions: America's Campaign against Strategic Weapons Proliferation.* Westport, Conn.: Praeger, 2001.

Solomon, Brian, ed. *Chemical and Biological Warfare.* New York: H. W. Wilson Co., 1999.

South Africa. Truth and Reconciliation Commission. *Truth and Reconciliation Commission of South Africa Report.* Cape Town: The Truth and Reconciliation Commission, 1998. Also published by New York: Macmillan Reference, 1999.

Sparks, Alistair. *The Mind of South Africa: The Story of the Rise and Fall of South Africa.* London: Mandarin, 1990.

———. *Tomorrow Is Another Country: The Inside Story of South Africa's Road to Change.* New York: Hill and Wang, 1995.

Spector, Leonard S., with Jacqueline R. Smith. *Nuclear Ambitions: The Spread of Nuclear Weapons 1989–1990.* Boulder, Colo.: Westview Press, 1990.

Steenkamp, Willem. *South Africa's Border War, 1966–1989.* Gibraltar: Asanti Publishing, 1989.

Steinbruner, John. *The Cybernetic Theory of Decision.* Princeton, N.J.: Princeton University Press, 1974.

Steyn, Hannes, Richardt van der Walt, and Jan van Loggerenberg. *Armament and Disarmament: South Africa's Nuclear Weapons Experience.* Pretoria, South Africa: Networks Publishers, 2003.

Stiff, Peter. *The Silent War: South African Recce Operations, 1969–1994.* Alberton, South Africa: Galago, 1999.

———. *See You in November.* Alberton, South Africa: Galago, 1985.

Sullivan, Michael P. *Theories of International Relations: Transition vs. Persistence.* New York: Palgrave, 2001.

Sylvan, D., and J. F. Voss, eds. *Problem Representation in International Relations.* Cambridge: Cambridge University Press, 1998.

Thomas, Scott. *The Diplomacy of Liberation: Foreign Relations of the ANC Since 1960.* London: I. B. Tauris, 1996.

Vatcher, William H. *White Laager: The Rise of Afrikaner Nationalism.* New York: Praeger, 1965.

Waldmeir, Patti. *Anatomy of a Miracle: The End of Apartheid and the Birth of the New South Africa* New York: W.W. Norton, 1997.

Waller, Robert. *Chemical and Biological Weapons and Deterrence.* Case Study 2: *Libya.* Alexandria, Va.: Chemical and Biological Arms Control Institute, 1998.

Walters, Ronald W. *South Africa and the Bomb: Responsibility and Deterrence.* Washington, D.C.: Lexington Books, 1987.

Waltz, Kenneth. *The Spread of Nuclear Weapons: More May Be Better.* Adelphi Papers no. 171. London: International Institute for Strategic Studies, 1981.

———. *Theory of International Politics.* New York: Random House, 1979.

Zilinskas, Raymond A., ed. *Biological Warfare: Modern Offense and Defense.* Boulder, Colo.: Lynne Rienner Publishers, 2000.

ARTICLES AND ONLINE SOURCES

"A Bungled Nuclear Deal." *Newsweek,* July 1994, 3.

Abelson, R. P. "The Psychological Status of the Script Concept." *American Psychologist* 33 (1981): 273–309.

Africa Defence Journal's Letter from South Africa. Issue no. 3, 2002, Harare, Zimbabwe.

Agence France-Presse. "Armscor Used 130 Companies to Get Around Arms Embargo." June 30, 1995.

Albright, David. "South Africa and the Affordable Bomb." *The Bulletin of Atomic Scientists* (July/August 1994): 37–47.

———. "South Africa's Secret Nuclear Weapons." Washington, D.C.: Institute for Science and International Security Report, May 1994, 1–12.

Albright, David, and Corey Gay. "A Flash from the Past." *The Bulletin of Atomic Scientists* 53, no. 6 (November 21, 1997): 15ff.

Albright, David, and Kevin O'Neill. 1995. "Jury Rigged, but Working." *Bulletin of the Atomic Scientists* 15, no. 1, January/February, 20.

Allen, A. 2000. "Mad Scientist." *Salon.com,* June 26, 2000, available online at http://salonmag.com/health/feature/2000/06/26/biofem.

———. 2000. "Vaginal Detergent." *Salon.com,* August 9, 2000, available online at http://dir.salon.com/health/feature/2000/06/26/microbicide/index.html?sid=860634.

Allison, Graham, and Andrei Kokoshin. "The New Containment: An Alliance against Nuclear Terrorism." *The National Interest Journal* (Fall 2002): 35–43.

"Amazing Coup Plot Unfolds in SA Court." *Cape Argus,* April 18, 2002.

"Arms Deal Controversy Continues." *Africa Analysis,* May 24, 2002.

"Atomic Corporation Abandons French Technology Project." *Sunday Independent* (Johannesburg), December 14, 1997.

"Audit Reveals Basson Fraud." *Business Day* (Johannesburg), June 14, 2000.

Badenhorst, N. P. "The Bomb, the Missile, and the Future." *Armed Forces of Southern Africa,* November 1993, 27–34.

Beinart, Peter. "Out of Africa." *The New Republic,* December 26, 1994, 16, 18–20.

Bender, G. "Kissinger in Angola: Anatomy of Failure." In *American Policy in Southern Africa: The Stakes and the Stance,* 2nd ed., ed. R. Lemarchand, 65–143. Washington, D.C.: University Press of America, 1981.

Block, Robert. "Biohazard: Bitter Researchers Are Big Question in Germ Warfare: Closing of South African Lab in '90s Isolated Scientists Ripe for Recruitment Now Ankle-Deep in Chicken Guts." *Wall Street Journal,* May 20, 2002.

———. "A Cautionary Disarmament: South Africa's Surrender of Nuclear Arms Was Only Half the Battle." *Wall Street Journal,* January 31, 2003.

Blow, D. "Nuke Bombshell." *City Press* (Johannesburg), March 28, 1993.

———. "Nuke Bombshell: Government to Get Rhoodie Awakening." *City Press* (Johannesburg), April 18, 1993.

Bluth, Andrew and Tony Saavedra. "The Materials Are Collected at the Home of Jerry Nilsson, Who Was Questioned and Released." *Orange County Register,* April 2, 2000.

Bridgland, Fred. "South Africa Scraps Missile Plan After US Pressure." *The Daily Telegraph,* July 1, 1993.

Brummer, Stefaans. "SA's Arms-Dealing Underworld." *Weekly Mail & Guardian* (Johannesburg), June 2–8, 1995, 9.

———. "SADF Linked to Red Mercury." *Mail & Guardian* (Johannesburg), December 20, 1995.

Cameron, Gavin. "Nuclear Terrorism Reconsidered." *Current History* (April 2000): 154–157.

Collins, Jeff. "Ford Advised South Africa on Warfare Devices." *Orange County Register,* March 15, 2000.

———. "Suspects All Visited the Home of a South African Trade Official, Police Say." *Orange Country Register,* July 18, 2000.

Crawford, Neta C. "How Arms Embargoes Work." In *How Sanctions Work: Lessons from South Africa,* ed. Neta C. Crawford and Audie Klotz. New York: St. Martin's Press, 1999.

Crocker, C. A. "South Africa: Strategy for Change." *Foreign Affairs* 59, no. 2 (Winter 1980/81): 323–351.

"Dancing Teacher Fingered in Marike Murder Trial." South Africa Press Association, September 10, 2002.

Davids, Nashira. "Basson Fights Interrogation by Swiss Officials." January 26, 2003. Available online at http://www.sundaytimes.co.za/2003/01/26/news/news21.asp.

de Beer, Erika. "State 'Undecided' on Basson Retrial." *The Herald* (South Africa), November 5, 2003, 7.

de Ionno, Peter. "Armscor Tries to Hush Up Saddam Deals." *Sunday Times* (Johannesburg), July 10, 1994.

———. "Nuclear Scientists Threaten to Tell All." *Sunday Times* (Johannesburg), March 27, 1994.

———. "SA Military's Amazing Underground Bomb-Proof Laager." *Sunday Times* (Johannesburg), May 22, 1994.

de Lange, Fred. "Denel Drops Plans for Rocket, Missiles." *The Citizen* (Pretoria), July 1, 1993, 5.

de Villiers, J. W., Roger Jardine, and Mitchell Reiss. "Why South Africa Gave Up the Bomb." *Foreign Affairs* 72, no. 5 (November/December 1993): 98–109.

"Defying the Arms Dealers." One World News Service, August 11, 1997. Available online at http://www.oneworld.org/index_oc/news/southafrica080897.html.

Donaldson, Andrew. "'Dr Death' Tells His Macabre Secrets." *Sunday Times* (Johannesburg), July 29, 2001.

"'Dr. Death': South Africa's Biological Weapons Program." Summary of *60 Minutes* episode, CBS. Aired November 3, 2002. Available online at http://www.cbsnews.com/stories/2002/10/30/60minutes/main527530.shtml.

Evans, M. "South Africa May Have Ordered British Deaths." *The Times* (London), July 14, 1998, 7.

Fig, David. "Apartheid's Nuclear Arsenal: Deviation from Development." In *From Defence to Development: Redirecting Military Resources in South Africa*, Jacklyn Cock and Penny Mckenzie, eds., 163–180. Cape Town, South Africa: David Philip, 1998.

———. "Sanctions and the Nuclear Industry." In *How Sanctions Work: Lessons from South Africa*, ed. Neta C. Crawford and Audie Klotz, 75–102. New York: St. Martin's Press, 1999.

Finnegan, W. "The Poison Keeper: Is an Afrikaner Doctor a Biowar Criminal?" *The New Yorker,* January 15, 2001, 58–75.

Fischer, David. "South Africa." In *Nuclear Proliferation After the Cold War,* ed. Robert Litwak and Mitchell Reiss, 207–230. Washington, D.C.: The Woodrow Wilson Center Press, 1994.

Fraser, John. "SA Needs Good Military Force." *Business Day,* April 9, 2002.

Gellman, Barton. "Al Qaeda Near Biological, Chemical Arms Production." *Washington Post,* March 23, 2003, A10.

Gertz, Bill. "S. Africa to Test Ballistic Missile." *The Washington Times,* May 3, 1991, A3.

Gould, Chandré. "More Questions Than Answers: The Ongoing Trial of Dr Wouter Basson." *Disarmament Diplomacy,* no. 52 (November 2000). Available online at http://www.acronym.org.uk/dd/dd52/52trial.htm.

Gould, Chandré, and Peter I. Folb. "The South African Chemical and Biological Warfare Program: An Overview." *The Nonproliferation Review* 7, no. 3 (Fall–Winter 2000): 10–23.

Hermann, Charles F. "Changing Course: When Governments Choose to Redirect Foreign Policy." *International Studies Quarterly* 34 (1990): 3–21.

Hermann, M. G., and C. F. Hermann. "Who Makes Foreign Policy Decisions and How?" *International Studies Quarterly* 33 (1989): 361–388.

Hibbs, Mark. "South Africa's Secret Nuclear Program: From a PNE to a Deterrent." *Nuclear Fuel,* May 10, 1993, 3–6.

"HIV Blood Sample Frozen for Chemical Warfare, Basson Trial Hears." South African Press Association, May 25, 2000. Available online at http://www.geocities.com/project_coast/deadly.htm.

"History of Biowarfare." *Nova Online.* Available online at http://www.pbs.org/wgbh/nova/bioterror/hist_nf.html.

Hoffman, Gerjo. "SA Struggles into Space." *Die Burger* (Cape Town), June 11, 2003, 1.

Horton, Roy E., III. *Out of (South) Africa: Pretoria's Nuclear Weapons Experience.* Institute for National Security Studies Occasional Paper no. 27. Colorado Springs, USAF Institute for National Security Studies, USAF Academy, 1999.

Howlett, Darryl, and John Simpson. "Nuclearization and Denuclearization in South Africa." *Survival Journal* 35, no. 3 (Autumn 1993): 157.

Humes, Edward. "The Medicine Man." *Los Angeles Magazine,* July 2001, 95–99, 166–68.

Jaster, Robert S. "Pretoria's Nuclear Diplomacy." *CSIS Africa Notes,* no. 81 (January 22, 1988).

Jervis, Robert. "Political Psychology: Some Challenges and Opportunities." *Political Psychology* 10, no. 3 (1989): 481–516.

Kalb, Claudia. "We Have to Save Our People." *Newsweek,* July 24, 2000.

"Key Helderberg Evidence Uncovered." *Mail & Guardian* (Johannesburg), March 10, 2001.

Koch, Eddie, and Derek Fleming. "Bizarre Experiments at SADF Research Firms." *Mail & Guardian* (Johannesburg), December 15, 1994.

Laufer, Stephen, and Arthur Gavshon. "The Real Reasons for South Africa's Nukes." *Weekly Mail & Guardian* (Johannesburg), March 26–April 1, 1993, 3.

Lawrence, Jeremy. "Marathon Trial That Went Nowhere." *Sunday Times* (Johannesburg), April 14, 2002. Available online at http://www.sundaytimes.co.za/ 2002/04/14/insight/in02.asp.

Le Roux, Mariette. "Boeremag Treason Trial Starts." *The Herald* (Port Elizabeth), May 16, 2003.

———. "PW Advised Rightwingers." *The Herald* (Port Elizabeth), August 22, 2002.

"Letter from South Africa." *Africa Defence Journal,* no. 3 (2002).

Liberman, Peter. "The Rise and Fall of the South African Bomb." *International Security* 26, no. 2 (Fall 2001): 45–86.

Liebenberg, General Kat. "The Excellence of the South African Defence Force with Special Reference to My Tours of Duty as Head of The South African Defence Force, Head of The South African Army and Officer Commanding Special Forces." Address to the South African Military Historical Society. Available online on 32 Battalion Home Page, http://www.netcentral.co.uk/~cobus/ 32BAT. Accessed in 2000.

Loeb, Vernon. "Terrorism Trail Pulls Veil from Hard Cell." *Washington Post,* May 24, 2001, A3, A16.

Long, William J., and Suzette R. Grillot. "Ideas, Beliefs, and Nuclear Policies: The Cases of South Africa and Ukraine." *The Nonproliferation Review* (Spring 2000): 24–40.

Manheim, Uzi, and Marie Colvin. "Genetic Warfare Nearing Reality." *The Times* (London), November 1998. Available online at http://www.peace.ca/ geneticwarfare.htm.

Martelle, Scott, Jeff Gottlieb, and Jack Leonard. "A Doctor, a Deal Maker and a Mystery." *Los Angeles Times,* March 20, 2000. Available online at http:// www.geocities.com/project_coast/docdeal.htm.

"Mbeki's History Lesson." *Mail & Guardian* (Johannesburg), November 1, 2002.

McDowell, Patrick. "South Africa's Nuclear Deterrent Aimed at Western Help: An Interview with de Waal." AP Worldstream, April 7, 1995.

Minty, Francois. "The Apartheid Bomb." *Africa,* February 1985, 60.

Misser, Francois. "Ebola: The Military Connection." *New African* 339 (March 1996): 12–14.

Muldoon, Timothy J. "South Africa: A Case Study in Nuclear Proliferation and Nuclear Rollback." *National Security Studies Quarterly* 5, no. 2 (Spring 1999): 83–106.

Muller, Marie. "South Africa Crisscrosses the Nuclear Threshold." In *South Africa's Defence and Security into the 21st Century,* ed. William Gutteridge. Aldershot, UK: Dartmouth, 1996.

Murphy, Dean E. "Dr. Wouter Basson's Connections to U.S. Intelligence." *Los Angeles Times,* August 1, 1998.

Naidoo, Krish. "SA's Arms Industry: The Way Forward." *Weekly Mail & Guardian* (Johannesburg) May 5, 1995.

Nass, Meryl. "Anthrax Epizootic in Zimbabwe, 1978–1980: Due to Deliberate Spread?" *The PSR Quarterly* 2, no. 4 (December 1992).

Nathan, Laurie. "The 1996 Defence White Paper: An Agenda for State Demilitarization?" In *From Defence to Development: Redirecting Military Resources in South Africa,* ed. Jacklyn Cock and Penny Mckenzie, 41–57. Cape Town, South Africa: David Philip, 1998.

Nuclear Threat Initiative. "South Africa Profile." Available online at http://www. nti.org/e_research/profiles/SAfrica/index.html.

Ogunbanwo, Sola. "Accelerate the Ratification of the Pelindaba Treaty." *The Nonproliferation Review* (Spring 2003): 132–136.

Oppermann, Chris. "Basson's Army Buddy Blows the Whistle." *Mail & Guardian* (Johannesburg), June 27, 1997.

———. "How the Taxpayer Footed the Bill for Project Coast." *Weekly Mail & Guardian* (Johannesburg), June 27, 1997.

Pabian, Frank V. "South Africa's Nuclear Weapon Program: Lessons for Nonproliferation Policy." *The Nonproliferation Review* 3, no. 1 (Fall 1995): 11.

"Plague War: What Happened in South Africa?" Transcript of *Frontline* episode. Available online at http://www.pbs.org/wgbh/pages/frontline/shows/plague/sa.

Power, Samantha. "The Aids Rebel." *The New Yorker,* May 2003.

Prados, John. "All Weapons Great and Small." *Washington Post Book World,* January 16, 2000, 7.

Purkitt, H. E. "The Cognitive Basis of Foreign Policy Expertise: Evidence from Intuitive Analyses of Political Novices and 'Experts' in South Africa." In *Problem Representation and Political Decision Making,* ed. D. Sylvan and J. Voss, 147–186. Cambridge: Cambridge University Press, 1998.

———. "A Problem Centered Approach for Understanding Foreign Policy." In *Global International Policy among and within Nations,* ed. S. Nagel, 79–101. New York: Marcel-Dekker, 2000.

Purkitt, Helen E., and Stephen F. Burgess. "Correspondence: South Africa's Nuclear Decisions." *International Security* 27, no. 1 (Summer 2002): 186–194.

Purkitt, H., and James W. Dyson. "U.S. Foreign Policy towards Southern Africa during the Carter and Reagan Administrations: An Information Processing Perspective." *Political Psychology* 7, no. 3 (1986): 507–532.

Rademeyer Julian. "Illegal Tests on SA Prostitutes?" *Pretoria News,* July 22, 2000. Available online at http://www.geocities.com/project_coast/ptabio.htm.

"Retrial of Wouter Basson Denied." *iafrica.com,* June 4, 2003. Available online at http://iafrica.com/news/sa/241910.htm.

Rice, Condoleezza. "Why We Know Iraq Is Lying." *New York Times,* January 23, 2003.

Roberts, Brad. "Strategies of Denial." In *Countering the Proliferation and Use of Weapons of Mass Destruction,* ed. Peter L. Hays, Vincent J. Jodoin, and Alan R. Van Tassel, 63–88. New York: McGraw-Hill, 1998.

Russett, Bruce M., and Harvey Starr. "From Democratic Peace to Kantian Peace: Democracy and Conflict in the International System." In *Handbook of War Studies II,* ed. Manus I. Midlarsky. Ann Arbor: University of Michigan Press, 2000.

"S. Africa Says Reagan Helped It Get Nuclear Fuel." Reuters World Service, January 10, 1995.

"SA in Satellite Race?" *Mail & Guardian* (Johannesburg), March 12, 1999.

"SA staak vuurply-projek" ["South Africa Ceases Rocket-Project"]. *Die Burger* (Cape Town), July 1, 1993, 1.

Saavedra, Tony. "Surgeon Says He Doesn't Know Why He Was Subjected to a Search." *Orange County Register,* April 5, 2000.

"Safrica: Two Jailed Right-Wingers Deny Knowledge of Alleged Jailbreak 'Plot.'" BBC Worldwide Monitoring, April 9, 2002.

Sagan, Scott D. "Why Do States Build Nuclear Weapons? Three Models in Search of a Bomb." *International Security* 21, no. 3 (Winter 1996/97): 69–71.

"SANDF Post Sought by Warfare Expert, 'General' Basson Wants His Job Back." *The Herald* (Port Elizabeth), June 6, 2003, 1.

Schmidt, Michael. "Proof of SA Nuclear Plan. " *Sunday Times* (Johannesburg), October 12, 2003, 5.

Schonteich, Martin. "The Power to Disrupt." *Mail & Guardian* (Johannesburg), September, 19, 2002.

"Seniors Should Take Rap for Killings, Assassin Tells Basson Trial." South African Press Association, May 11, 2000.

Sokolski, Henry. "Ending South Africa's Rocket Program: A Nonproliferation Success." Nonproliferation Policy Education Center, Washington, D.C., Fall 1993. Available online at http://www.npec-web.org/essay/southafrica.htm.

Solingen, Etel. "The Political Economy of Nuclear Restraint." *International Security* 19, no. 2 (Fall 1994): 126–169.

"South Africa: An Irresponsible Arms Trader?" *Global Dialogue* 4 (August 2, 1999). Available online at http://www.igd.org.za/pub/g-dialogue/Special_feature/trader.html.

"South Africa Confirms Nuclear Deal with France." Reuters World Service, January 9, 1995.

South Africa. Department of Foreign Affairs. "The African Nuclear-Weapon-Free Zone (Treaty of Pelindaba)." Available online at http://www.opanal.org/NWFZ/Pelindaba/pelindaba.htm.

———. "Treaty on the Non-Proliferation of Nuclear Weapons (NPT)." Available online at http://www.un.org/Depts/dda/WMD/treaty.

South Africa. Military Health Service. "History of the South African Military Health Service." Available online at http://www.mil.za/CSANDF/SurgeonGeneral/SAMHS/SAMHS%20HQ/main_samhs_hq.htm.

"South Africa: Seven Right-Wingers Facing Charges of 'Treason,' Terrorism.'" *Financial Times* (London), April 8, 2002.

"South African Official Offers Post Mortem of Atomic Bomb." *The Risk Report* 2, no. 4 (July–August 1996).

"South Africa's Nuclear Weapons Program: An Annotated Chronology: 1969–1994." Available online at http://cns.miis.edu/research/safrica/chron.htm.

"Southern Africa—Risk Pointers." *Jane's Sentinel Security Assessment.* October 17, 2003.

Steyn, Pierre. "Concern about al-Qaeda in SA." *Die Burger* (Cape Town), October 12, 2002.

———. "SA Expert Investigated over Anthrax." *Die Burger* (Cape Town), August 2, 2000, 7.

Stumpf, Waldo. "South Africa's Nuclear Weapons Program: From Deterrence to Dismantlement." *Arms Control Today* 25, no. 10 (December 1995/January 1996): 4–7.

Tanner, Adam. "Al-Qaeda Presence in SA—Expert." *Die Burger* (Cape Town), November, 28, 2002.

Thayer, Bradley A. "The Causes of Nuclear Nonproliferation and the Utility of the Nuclear Nonproliferation Regime." *Security Studies* 4, no. 3 (Spring 1995): 449–494.

Thomas, Jo. "California Doctor's Suicide Leaves Many Troubling Mysteries Unsolved." *New York Times*, November 3, 2002.

Thornycroft, Petra. "SA's Poison Gas Secrets Sold to Libya." *Mail & Guardian* (Johannesburg), January 7, 1997.

"Three Whites Accused of Plotting to Topple S. Africa's Mbeki." Agence France-Presse, April 8, 2002.

"The TRC's Helderberg Tragedy." *Mail & Guardian* (Johannesburg), November 21, 2000.

"Tutu Gets 99th Degree Then Slams SA Govt Pretoria. " *Mail & Guardian* (Johannesburg), September 6, 2002.

"Two Groups of Rightwingers Are Refused Bail." South African Press Association, April 19, 2002.

"Vaccine Theory on AIDS Upset." *Washington Post,* May 20, 2002, A9.

Warrick, Joby. "Biotoxins Fall into Private Hands; Global Risk Seen in S. African Poisons." *Washington Post,* April 21, 2001.

Warrick, Joby, and John Mintz. "Lethal Legacy: Bioweapons for Sale; U.S. Declined South African Scientist's Offer on Man-Made Pathogens." *Washington Post,* April 20, 2003.

Watt, S. A. "The Anglo-Boer War: The Medical Arrangements and Implications Thereof During the British Occupation of Bloemfontein, March–August 1900." *Military History Review* 9, no. 2 (December 1992). Available online at http://rapidttp.com/milhist/vol092sw.html.

Weiss, Rick. "Made-from-Scratch Pathogen Prompts Concerns about Bioethics, Terrorism." *Washington Post,* July 12, 2002, A1.

Wheelis, Mark. "Biotechnology and Biochemical Weapons." *Non-Proliferation Review* 9, no. 1 (Spring 2002): 48–53.

INTERNET SOURCES

Business Day (South Africa), http://www.bd.co.za.

Federation of American Scientists, http://www.fas.org.

Freedom of Expression Institute (South Africa), http://fxi.org.za.

Mail & Guardian (Johannesburg), http://www.mg.co.za.

Southern Africa Environment Project, http://www.saep.org.

South African Military History Society web site, http://rapidttp.com/milhist.

South Africans for the Abolition of Vivisection, http://www.saav.org.za/home.php.

32nd Battalion Home Page, http://www.netcentral.co.uk/~cobus/32BAT/32BAT.htm.

Truth and Reconciliation Commission Web site, http://www.truth.org.za.

Index

Helen E. Purkitt is Professor of Political Science at the U.S. Naval Academy.

Stephen F. Burgess is Associate Professor in the Department of Strategy and International Security at the U.S. Air War College and Assistant Director, Regional Studies, of the U.S. Air Force Counterproliferation Center.